THE COMMODIFICATION OF IDENTITY IN VICTORIAN NARRATIVE

In the first half of the nineteenth century, autobiography became, for the first time, an explicitly commercial genre. Drawing together quantitative data on the Victorian book markets, insights from the business ledgers of Victorian publishers and close readings of mid-century novels, Sean Grass demonstrates the close links between these genres and broader Victorian textual and material cultures. This book offers fresh perspectives on major works by Charles Dickens, George Eliot, Mary Elizabeth Braddon, Wilkie Collins, and Charles Reade, while also featuring archival research that reveals the volume, diversity, and marketability of Victorian autobiographical texts for the first time. Grass presents life writing not as a stand-alone genre, but as an integral part of a broader movement of literary, cultural, legal, and economic practices through which the Victorians transformed identity into a textual object of capitalist exchange.

SEAN GRASS is Professor of English at the Rochester Institute of Technology and is the author of *The Self in the Cell: Narrating the Victorian Prisoner* (2003), *Charles Dickens's* Our Mutual Friend: *A Publishing History* (2014), and several essays on Victorian literature and culture. He received two awards from the National Endowment for the Humanities in support of the current work.

CAMBRIDGE STUDIES IN NINETEENTH-CENTURY
LITERATURE AND CULTURE

General editor
Gillian Beer, *University of Cambridge*

Editorial board
Isobel Armstrong, Birkbeck, *University of London*
Kate Flint, *University of Southern California*
Catherine Gallagher, *University of California, Berkeley*
D. A. Miller, *University of California, Berkeley*
J. Hillis Miller, *University of California, Irvine*
Daniel Pick, Birkbeck, *University of London*
Mary Poovey, *New York University*
Sally Shuttleworth, *University of Oxford*
Herbert Tucker, *University of Virginia*

Nineteenth-century British literature and culture have been rich fields for interdisciplinary studies. Since the turn of the twentieth century, scholars and critics have tracked the intersections and tensions between Victorian literature and the visual arts, politics, social organization, economic life, technical innovations, scientific thought – in short, culture in its broadest sense. In recent years, theoretical challenges and historiographical shifts have unsettled the assumptions of previous scholarly synthesis and called into question the terms of older debates. Whereas the tendency in much past literary critical interpretation was to use the metaphor of culture as 'background', feminist, Foucauldian, and other analyses have employed more dynamic models that raise questions of power and of circulation. Such developments have reanimated the field. This series aims to accommodate and promote the most interesting work being undertaken on the frontiers of the field of nineteenth-century literary studies: work which intersects fruitfully with other fields of study such as history, or literary theory, or the history of science. Comparative as well as interdisciplinary approaches are welcomed.

A complete list of titles published will be found at the end of the book.

THE COMMODIFICATION OF IDENTITY IN VICTORIAN NARRATIVE

Autobiography, Sensation, and the Literary Marketplace

SEAN GRASS

Rochester Institute of Technology, New York

CAMBRIDGE
UNIVERSITY PRESS

University Printing House, Cambridge CB2 8BS, United Kingdom

One Liberty Plaza, 20th Floor, New York, NY 10006, USA

477 Williamstown Road, Port Melbourne, VIC 3207, Australia

314-321, 3rd Floor, Plot 3, Splendor Forum, Jasola District Centre, New Delhi - 110025, India

103 Penang Road, #05-06/07, Visioncrest Commercial, Singapore 238467

Cambridge University Press is part of the University of Cambridge.

It furthers the University's mission by disseminating knowledge in the pursuit of education, learning and research at the highest international levels of excellence.

www.cambridge.org
Information on this title: www.cambridge.org/9781108706209
DOI: 10.1017/9781108613347

© Sean Grass 2019

This publication is in copyright. Subject to statutory exception and to the provisions of relevant collective licensing agreements, no reproduction of any part may take place without the written permission of Cambridge University Press.

First published 2019
First paperback edition 2021

A catalogue record for this publication is available from the British Library

ISBN 978-1-108-48445-9 Hardback
ISBN 978-1-108-70620-9 Paperback

Cambridge University Press has no responsibility for the persistence or accuracy of URLs for external or third-party internet websites referred to in this publication, and does not guarantee that any content on such websites is, or will remain, accurate or appropriate.

*For Iris, my parents, and my brother
and in memory of
Lucero, Tennessee, and Nimbus
(the world's least effective but most entertaining research assistants)*

Contents

List of Figures	*page* viii	
Acknowledgments	ix	
	Introduction. Life Upon the Exchange: Commodifying the Victorian Subject	1
1	"A Vile Symptom": Autobiography and the Commodification of Identity	17
	1.1 Autobiography in the Literary Market 1820–1860	21
	1.2 Autobiography and the Cultural Field	39
	1.3 Autobiography and Anxiety	57
2	"Portable Property": Commodity and Identity in *Great Expectations*	78
3	Lady Audley's Portrait: Textuality, Gender, and Power	105
4	Amnesia, Madness, and Financial Fraud: Ontologies of Loss in *Silas Marner* and *Hard Cash*	126
5	"What Money Can Make of Life": Willing Subjects and Commodity Culture in *Our Mutual Friend*	161
6	*The Moonstone*, Sacred Identity, and the Material Self	189
	Conclusion. Money Made of Life: The Tichborne Claimant	211
Appendix	222	
Notes	227	
Works Cited	257	
Index	271	

Figures

1.1	Increase in titles with the word "autobiography" 1841–1860	*page* 24
1.2	Autobiographical titles published each year 1841–1869	26
1.3	Rate of increase in titles published by decade 1800–1860	27
4.1	Dodd's receipt, from *Very Hard Cash*	148
4.2	The "recovered" receipt, from *Very Hard Cash*	149
5.1	Monthly wrapper from *Our Mutual Friend*	167

Acknowledgments

This project unfolded over so many years, and with the assistance of so many people, that it is hard even to know where to begin. Most of the early work involved cobbling together the grant support to conduct archival research at libraries across the United States and in the United Kingdom. On this front, I am deeply grateful first and foremost to the National Endowment for the Humanities, who supported this work twice: first, tangentially, by awarding me a slot in John Bowen's Summer Seminar, "The Remaking of Charles Dickens: Crisis and Transformation," at the Dickens Project at the University of California, Santa Cruz in 2004; and second, directly, by granting me a Summer Stipend in 2006 that allowed me several weeks of sustained research at the British Library and the National Archives. These were the proving grounds and launch pad for the work contained here. I am also grateful to the Department of English, the College of Arts & Sciences, and the Gloria Lyerla Memorial Travel Fund at Texas Tech University, and to the Department of English and the College of Liberal Arts & Sciences at Iowa State University, who supported me in the form of small research grants and periods of sabbatical that allowed me to complete the research and move on to the daunting task of explaining what I'd found. I am also grateful to the indefatigable staff at the British Library; the National Archives; the National Library of Scotland; the Rare Collections at the University of Illinois at Urbana-Champaign; the Harry Ransom Center at the University of Texas at Austin; and the Rare Books Library at the University of North Carolina-Chapel Hill. Wonderful people at all of these places aided me in ransacking their collections, often when I couldn't even be sure what I was looking for. And I am endlessly indebted to the interlibrary loan staffs at the Texas Tech University Library, the Parks Library at Iowa State University, and the Wallace Library at Rochester Institute of Technology (especially Morna Hilderbrand). I am in awe of their ability to locate and procure obscure odds and ends, and generally to make tireless efforts on my behalf when I was myself tired of the work.

Scholarship, like a scholarly institution, depends on the unbounded generosity of individuals who go above and beyond the call, for no reasons other than sheer intellectual curiosity and the satisfaction of a job well done.

But I do want to count and thank certain individuals specifically, even though I will surely forget many I ought to mention. Chief among these are scholars and friends who read and offered suggestions for the manuscript in its various stages: Patrick Leary, who read a (quite lame) early draft of the introduction; Trev Lynn Broughton, who read a (much better) later one; and Anne Helmreich, who read the long first chapter and offered invaluable advice about much more than the discussion of art history. I must also thank John Drew, whom I have only met recently, but who had already given kind assistance with the illustrations from *All the Year Round* that appear in Chapter 4. I also owe a debt of gratitude to the irrepressible Sara Malton, who entered the fray at a late date and gave sensible, thoughtful advice on revisions. Thank you as well to the Birkbeck Centre for Nineteenth-Century Studies and David McAllister, who invited me to speak twice about different parts of this project, and who thereby afforded me crucial chances to air my work and get advice from other scholars. And I want to thank, too, the unknown readers at Cambridge University Press (and the perfectly well-known series editor Dame Gillian Beer), who instilled confidence by approving the unconventional aspects of this project and provided advice that led to improvements throughout. The book is stronger for their interventions. It is stronger, too, for many conversations and correspondences that have helped to shape it: with Simon Eliot, Lisa Surridge, Robert Patten, Chris Keep, and Linda Hughes, among others. Then there is the practical assistance. Thank you to Kit and Rob Hume and Judith Milhous for giving guidance during my first research trip to London; to Paul Deslandes and Greg Colon-Semenza for their camaraderie during the same; to friends Ann Hawkins, Miles Kimball, Michael Borshuk, and Brian and Sue McFadden, who supported me through much of the writing; and to Jonathan Wendel and Kathleen Foster-Wendel, who hosted me for one last visit to the British Library as I revised. Too – though they both have moved on to their real life's work – I must thank my two undergraduate research assistants, Shannah Head and Cassandra Gearheart, who at different stages of the project did legwork that spurred it on when I was struggling to get to it on my own.

This book was a long time coming – so long, that I published a different one in the middle of writing it – which of course means that I could never have finished it without the patience and loving indulgence of my wife Iris, our parents, and other family. All of them, at various times, have tolerated my grumpiness and need for solitude, broken plans and invitations declined, early mornings and late nights, as I worked on this book. I appreciate that indulgence more than I can say. Without it I would have to aim lower, and fall short even of that. And without Iris my world would be innumerable shades of gray rather than the carnival of color she makes it. Finally, thank you to Lucero, Isabella, Nimbus, Monty, Phoenix, and the inimitable Tennessee. They have slept on my books, hogged my chair, disordered my desk, stomped on my keyboard, assailed my typing fingers, and sat between my eyes and my monitor – often all at once. Any typos in what follows are certainly theirs. I only regret that I could not finish the book faster, since a few of them will never get the chance to loll and doze across its pages. They have all, I hope, found sunny places where they can rest.

I have made the shoes.

INTRODUCTION

Life Upon the Exchange: Commodifying the Victorian Subject

In 1859 at the venerable age of eighty-four, Lord Thomas Cochrane, tenth Earl of Dundonald and Rear-Admiral of the United Kingdom, contracted George Butler Earp to write his *Autobiography of a Seaman* (1860) recounting his early life and experiences as a naval commander during the Napoleonic Wars. There was much to tell. Having begun in 1793 as a midshipman aboard his uncle's ship the *Hind*, Cochrane quickly earned a reputation for daring, and received his first command, the *Speedy*, in 1800. By mixing unconventional tactics with clever deceptions – he once had the *Speedy* painted like a Danish brig and hired a Danish quartermaster to complete the masquerade – Cochrane captured fifty ships and more than 500 prisoners in fifteen months while developing a penchant for brutally effective coastal assaults.[1] His crowning achievement came in 1809 at Basque Roads when he led a night foray that drove much of the French fleet aground. Only the hesitation of his fleet commander Admiral James Gambier in following up the advantage prevented the decimation of the French ships, a failure that ended in Cochrane complaining publicly of Gambier and irritating Gambier's many supporters in the Admiralty. Driven to request a court-martial to consider his conduct, Gambier won acquittal. Cochrane resigned his command and retreated to Parliament where he spent the next several years advocating radical reform and attacking "maladministration" and cronyism in the Royal Navy.[2] Still, his military service was remarkable enough that in 1887 the *Dictionary of National Biography* called him "one of the greatest of our admirals, whose name must be ranked with those of Nelson, Hawke, Rodney, or Blake," and his adventures have served as a basis for C.S. Forester's Horatio Hornblower and Patrick O'Brian's Captain Jack Aubrey.[3] Appearing at the end of a decade in which the Duke of Wellington died, a new Napoleon rose, and England's military suffered serious embarrassment in the Crimea, Cochrane's thrilling accounts of naval victories over the French and his diatribes against entrenched interests suited his autobiography perfectly to the mid-century Victorian temper.

But *Autobiography of a Seaman* had also another story to tell, or at least one to deny – a story of false identity, conspiracy, and financial intrigue that belonged more to the sensational 1860s than to the decade that came before. In the morning hours of February 21, 1814, a man dressed in military attire and claiming to be Lord Cathcart's aide-de-camp turned up at the Ship Inn at Dover and demanded a post-chaise to London where he had urgent news to deliver.[4] He could not, he said, proclaim that news publicly until his dispatches had been received in London, but he confided it nonetheless to innkeepers and postboys along the way: Napoleon had been overtaken and cut down by the Cossacks. The war was over. The man's loose tongue meant that his news preceded him to London, to the jubilation of those on the Stock Exchange. By late morning, Omnium, the primary government trading stock, had risen from 26½ to 30¼; by late afternoon it was at 32½, though nervous investors were still awaiting official confirmation of Napoleon's death.[5] None came. By the next morning it was clear that the news had been a hoax, and Omnium fell again to 26½. The ensuing investigation determined that the six primary beneficiaries – all of whom sold Omnium shares on February 21, at a profit of £4,800 – included Cochrane, his uncle, and their stockbroker, and it found also that a military man, whom several witnesses identified as the aide-de-camp, had arrived at Cochrane's home at around the time that the news reached London. In what the *Autobiography* later described as a politically motivated trial, Cochrane and his five co-defendants were convicted of conspiracy and fraud, and Cochrane was sentenced to twelve months' imprisonment, a £1,000 fine, and an hour in the pillory across the street from the Exchange.[6] He was also dismissed from the Royal Navy and the Order of the Bath, expelled from the House of Commons, and humiliated by having his banner and coat of arms torn down from Henry VII's chapel and kicked down the stairs and into the street.[7] The Westminster electors defiantly reelected Cochrane in the special election to fill his seat. But for practical purposes, though he was not yet forty, his naval and political careers were over.

Cochrane's biographers usually assert that he wrote *Autobiography of a Seaman* mainly to exonerate himself in the eyes of the Victorian public. "What mattered to Cochrane," Richard Dale writes, "was to have the slate wiped clean, which meant nothing less than restoration to the position he would have been in had the case against him never been brought."[8] David Cordingly agrees, arguing that although we can read the autobiography as the protestations "of an arrogant man . . . it seems more likely to have been driven by the natural desire of an innocent man to clear the stain on his character and on the Dundonald family name."[9] To be sure, Cochrane was near the end of his life – he died just two weeks after the publication of *Autobiography of a Seaman*'s second volume – and may well have been concerned about posterity. Yet while he likely hoped that his autobiography would set the record straight, he almost certainly wrote it, too, with another aim in mind: reaping a financial windfall by turning his life into a commodity for the literary market. Cochrane had always been avaricious, having been raised in aristocratic penury and instilled with a fierce desire to restore the fortune his father had squandered by abandoning his own naval career and becoming a professional inventor. An Englishman who knew Cochrane in South America in 1820 remarked that "[a]varice and selfishness do certainly appear to form the groundwork of his character," and Lord St. Vincent, First Lord of the Admiralty, once called Cochrane "mad, romantic, money-getting and not truth-telling," further remarking that one could not trust him "out of sight."[10] Cochrane's earliest disagreements with the Admiralty stemmed not from the Basque Roads affair, in fact, but from an 1808 revision to rules regarding prize money, which slashed the share that captains and fleet admirals could claim while nearly doubling payments to the crew.[11] After he resigned his command in 1809, Cochrane's financial position deteriorated markedly, at least according to his accounts with his banker.[12] Meanwhile, his reputation for greed, irascibility, and deception made it easy for many to believe him guilty when he was tried for conspiracy and fraud.

In the decades after his imprisonment, Cochrane earned enormous sums but never arrived at a position of financial ease. He softened the loss of his naval pension by spending 1818–1828 in the service of Chile, Peru, Brazil, and Greece, commanding their navies in their wars for independence and, in after years, quarreling with them about how much they owed him in prize money and other claims. Each paid him a handsome salary: £1,200 per year from Chile and Peru, £2,400 per year from Brazil, and a huge £37,000 advance from Greece.[13] But his retirement in England after 1828 found him spending money at astonishing rates, mainly on the kinds of illadvised inventions that had ruined his father. Late in her life, Cochrane's wife Kitty recalled bitterly the enormous sums that he had wasted in speculative projects, including £20,000 experimenting with lamp designs and copper-rolling machinery, £16,000 on his failed steamship the *Janus*, and £70,000 on Parliamentary elections.[14] Public opinion during these years had turned steadily in his favor, owing to the more liberal political climate and his unremitting campaign of petitions and appeals. In 1832 Cochrane received a free pardon and was restored to the Royal Navy, and in 1847 he was readmitted to the Order of the Bath. Yet he never ceased to press financial claims on the Crown, including the remittance of his fine and back pension amounting to £4,000.[15] Just a month before he was remade a Knight Grand Cross, he went so far as to publish a detailed account of the financial losses he had suffered from his conviction – an account, Cordingly points out, that prepared the ground for his autobiography – and was delighted to find that "the pamphlet has made, and is making, a great impression."[16] He also continued to expand his claims against Chile and Brazil, demanding more than £150,000.[17] Though his public rehabilitation was complete, and despite a lifetime of remarkable earnings, he remained beset by financial worries. Replying just before his death to a letter from his son, Cochrane wrote, "I can not supply you with money, there not being *above* ground wherewith to put me below it."[18]

Cochrane's decision to publish *Autobiography of a Seaman* must therefore be understood as partly – perhaps principally – a financial endeavor that he hoped to profit from in two distinct ways. First, by using *Autobiography* to highlight his heroic naval service and deny one last time his involvement in the Stock Exchange scandal, Cochrane likely hoped to strike one final blow in his quest for financial restitution from the Crown. Just a year earlier he had done the same thing to press his claims against Chile and Brazil, working with Earp to publish the autobiographical *Narrative of Services in the Liberation of Chili, Peru, and Brazil from Spanish and Portuguese Domination* (1859), which pressed publicly the case that the governments of these places still owed him immense sums for helping to free them from colonial rule.[19] He was hard at work on the *Narrative*, in fact, when he received word in June 1858 that the Chilean prize tribunal had denied him further payments. Incensed, he wrote to his secretary William Jackson, "It is lucky my Memorial is in hand shewing what they really do owe me," and in another letter he declared his intention of making "[t]he Memorials ... irresistible."[20] The plan appears to have worked, in the cases of both *Narrative* and *Autobiography*. Though Cochrane received £6,000 from Chile and £34,000 from Brazil in the years just before *Narrative* was published, subsequent settlements with Brazil eventually netted his estate another £50,000.[21] In 1878 the Crown, too, made reparation, granting £5,000 to Cochrane's grandson in lieu of "the arrears of half-pay without interest."[22]

Second – and more important for the purposes of this study – Cochrane expected to profit from *Autobiography of a Seaman* simply by selling books, for he understood what scholars have mostly forgotten: by 1859, autobiography was big business, capable of generating huge profits in the Victorian literary market. Whether this was true of *Narrative* may be impossible to know. It was published by the radical bookseller James Ridgway, whose business records appear to have been swallowed up by history. *Autobiography* is another matter, for the information that survives about its publication suggests that Cochrane probably earned a tidy sum by making his life into a literary commodity. Published by Richard Bentley in November 1859, *Autobiography*'s first volume generated subscriptions for a modest 317 copies.[23] But this must only have whetted readers' appetites. Publication of the second volume the following October generated 2,700 subscriptions for the two-volume set, 1,000 of them for the circulating library giant Charles Mudie, and in April 1861 the *Autobiography* passed into a second edition that sold another 1,400 copies. The records do not include the original publication agreement between Cochrane and Bentley, but in November 1861, a year after Cochrane's death, Bentley paid Earp £750 for his "share" in the copyright.[24] In the absence of the original agreement it is hard to know what this means – whether £750 represents payment for full copyright, half copyright, or another fraction, or how Earp's share compared with Cochrane's. But it is striking that several months after the remarkable sales of the first two editions, when the market for the book might well have been exhausted, Bentley was willing to pay £750 to acquire *any* share in the copyright. The sum was his second-highest payout for copyright between 1840 and 1865.[25] Considering the potential profits from selling more than 5,000 copies of *Autobiography of a Seaman*'s first two editions, it is not unreasonable to think that Cochrane and his estate profited handsomely. As Ian Grimble puts it, of all Cochrane's inventions and speculations, his autobiographical works "proved to have been among [his] most profitable enterprises."[26] Had he lived to see it, the "money-getting" Lord Thomas Cochrane would certainly have laughed all the way to the bank.

Viewed as a literary commodity, Cochrane's mostly forgotten autobiography illustrates the proposition that drives this project: that Victorian autobiographies were economic as well as discursive transactions, and that they belonged – like *The Pickwick Papers*, gift books, illustrated newspapers, and sensation novels – to the wondrous complexity of the Victorian literary market. Despite the account of the Stock Exchange scandal that frames this introduction, the following pages have little to do with Threadneedle Street, financial frauds, stockjobbers, speculators, or notorious fictional financiers such as Charles Dickens's Mr. Merdle and

Anthony Trollope's Augustus Melmotte. Rather, this project explores the imaginative and ideological consequences of making "life" into a textual commodity, a material object of exchange like the countless others that were bought, sold, owned, and consumed in Victorian England's growing, teeming capitalist market. In the forms of thousands of published autobiographies, life really was "upon the exchange" for the first time in England, and in ways that reshaped not only the legal, economic, and discursive practices associated with identity but also the narrative representation and ontological status of subjectivity, which ceased to exist as a thing apart from property and economic exchange. Victorian autobiography was not quite the genre that we have tended to make it, notable mainly for the momentous self-narratives written by such eminent Victorians as John Stuart Mill, Charles Darwin, and Harriet Martineau. It was a commercial force and engine of cultural transformation, pressing identity into the shape required by modern capitalism and driving novelists to represent the implications of subjecting identity to the forces of the emerging capitalist age. *The Commodification of Identity in Victorian Narrative: Autobiography, Sensation and the Literary Marketplace* thus analyzes the rise of autobiography as a commercial genre during the first decades of the Victorian period and traces the implications of that rise in several mid-century novels – especially, though not exclusively, sensational ones – that center upon the textualization and commodification of identity, by which I mean the literary, cultural, legal, and economic practices by which Victorians transformed identity into a text and thus an object of capitalist exchange. Beginning with an account of the expansion of English autobiographical production 1820–1860, I argue that the proliferation and commercialization of the genre during these years provoked intense anxiety regarding the tendency to transform identity into a text for the literary market, and that novelists responded by representing identity's thorough pervasion by economic concerns, expressed in recurrent tropes such as multiplied identities, fragmented subjectivities, temporal disruptions, fetishized texts, and transfigured sexual desire. During these years, autobiographies became popular and profitable things for the first time, designed for industrial production and a mass market rather than for private reading by family and friends, or the spiritual edification of religious believers. They became commodities, reifications of the self-alienation that Karl Marx was simultaneously identifying as endemic to the capitalist age. In his account of the rise of Victorian commodity culture, Thomas Richards writes that "fundamental imperatives of the capitalist system became tangled up with certain kinds of cultural forms, which after a time became indistinguishable from economic forms."[27] Early in the period, autobiography became a cultural and an economic form, eroding the conceptual boundary between property and identity by making identity a material thing. Novels came to reflect the cultural and imaginative refiguration of subjectivity that this nexus of textual self-production and commodity exchange provoked.

By writing of subjectivity in this way, I mean for the most part to use the term in its postmodern critical sense: to indicate an intentional and self-reflective individual consciousness, however much that consciousness must be understood as decentered, mediated, alienated, and contested. But throughout this work I will use "subjectivity" and "identity" interchangeably, which may make some readers cringe. Presently, the term "identity" belongs commonly to discussions of the biological, legal, and financial proofs of who one is; it is the sum of an enormous and expanding array of intersecting texts, from DNA profiles to birth certificates to government identification cards to credit histories. Victorians certainly used the word "identity" in this context, but they used it also to cover the aspects of conscious selfhood for which "subjectivity" seems now to be the more appropriate term. It was during the Victorian period that rising literacy rates, cheap paper, finance capitalism, and bureaucratic expansion first converged and created the sense of identity as a thing constituted in and through texts rather than as an essential, insubstantial interiority. And it was this transformation of identity into a material thing that first interlaced it with economic meanings, forming new relations between identity and the law, finance, and other forms of literary and cultural production. We have cultivated the term subjectivity partly in response to this interlacing, to recoup a sense of the conscious, intentional, psychological self that stands apart from the legal, financial, and medical records that constitute our postmodern lives. Using "subjectivity" and "identity" interchangeably restores a purposeful slippage that helps to demystify the commodified status of subjectivity during the middle of the Victorian period.

So, too, does my implicit assertion that subjectivity and autobiography are equivalents – that the former inheres in the latter, such that the Victorian traffic in autobiographies meant, necessarily and unproblematically, traffic in the subjectivities themselves. More typically, we think of self-narrative as constructing identity, and of initiation into language, and mediation by it, as preconditions for the emergence of a conscious self. In this context autobiography is at best, in Avrom Fleishman's words, "a literary form for the creation of selfhood" rather than a means of exposing or describing it; at worst it is pure performance, a means of constructing and displaying publicly a self that never was.[28] Yet as autobiography rose to prominence early in the nineteenth century, many of its earliest reviewers regarded it as intimate revelation, with the autobiographical text standing for and granting unmediated access to the subjectivity that had produced it. As James Treadwell notes in his excellent account of Romantic autobiography, some early responders celebrated autobiography's power to create "intimacy between author and reader," while others saw in it a dangerous "circulation of privacy itself . . . a prominent and unsettling overlap of public and private spheres, or a reconfigured relationship between them, in the literary field."[29] Both kinds of response agree on the fundamental point that, to a degree, the author's subjectivity inheres in the autobiographical text, so that an equivalency or identity exists between them. The commercialization of autobiography during the first half of the century eroded this sense of equivalency, made readers and reviewers more aware of its function as discursive performance, but not without leaving behind a sense of violation and disruption, of subjectivity transformed and pervaded by economic concerns. To the extent that Victorians saw autobiography as textualizing real subjectivity, they found in it a dangerous means of exposing identity to the market and rendering it vulnerable to the demands of production, consumption, and exchange. To the extent that they regarded it as a mercenary construction or performance – a form designed to appeal to publishers and readers rather than to reveal the self – they saw it textualizing a subjectivity that had already been adapted to the terms of its commodification. If, as Linda Peterson suggests, Victorians read autobiographies hermeneutically, with the aim of divining patterns and meanings for their own lives, they found in the ones published at mid-century the impetus for basing their identities upon the formal, symbolic, and ideological structures of commodity culture.[30]

This focus on subjectivity's instantiation as a material text subject to capitalist dynamics of ownership and exchange explains why, despite my interest in commodified identities, this project does not take up an obvious subject: the vast, complicated, contemporary problem of slavery in the United States or in colonies such as Jamaica, Barbados, and Antigua. And it does not do so even though abolition efforts in the United States especially relied upon the preparation and dissemination of autobiographies by escaped and emancipated slaves. In *The Self in the Cell: Narrating the Victorian Prisoner* (2003), I drew heavily upon William Andrews's account of slave narratives in *To Tell a Free Story* (1986) in order to describe the ideological complexities that shaped the production of prisoner autobiographies in mid-century English prisons, since these often emerged from the interplay of disempowered (even illiterate) subjects, privileged amanuenses, and specific political imperatives. But for reasons both practical and conceptual, slavery lays beyond the scope of the present study. Despite extensive archival research involving the business records of Victorian publishers, I did not discover – or at least did not identify – a single instance in which those records included an entry for a slave autobiography. This may only reflect the lack of an international copyright agreement during the first half of the century, which meant that British publishers of such works did not need to provide contracts, keep records of profits and losses to satisfy authors writing for half-profits, or otherwise maintain specific financial records related to such titles, though many would probably have done so in order to track the sizes of print runs, printings costs, charges for illustrations, subscription lists, and other details. While slave autobiographies served crucial and obvious political purposes in both the United States and England, then, and while they might have been profitable and widely disseminated, I found no particular evidence that they were part of the broad commercialization of life writing that this project takes as its foundation.

In the absence of such evidence, slavery seems qualitatively different from the matter at hand. This book is concerned with the ways in which, between 1820 and 1860, autobiographical production, the rise of paper money, copyright law, census-taking, and the broad cultural conditions produced by finance capitalism collaborated to transform identity from an internal, immaterial thing into a textual, material one. But slavery worked differently, transforming racial difference and violent conquest into the explicit ownership of physical bodies, typically while asserting that nonwhite bodies contained no relevant subjectivity at all. Moreover, we might understand the Confederacy's determination to preserve slavery before and during the US Civil War as not only an indication and effect of racial prejudice but also, structurally, a mode of resistance to industrialization and the larger forces of economic modernity. The commodification of black bodies in the American south was, in other words, a linchpin in the rejection of – not an effect of the transition to – the finance capitalism that figures so heavily in my analysis here. Financial evidence related to the publication of slave autobiographies might eventually be found in the archives of British publishers, or this book's discussion of practices such as census-taking or cartes-de-visite might suggest fruitful avenues by which other scholars might imagine analogs to or components of the explicit forms of commodification that occurred under American and colonial slavery. But this study focuses elsewhere: on the circumstances by which identity became, early in the nineteenth century, a textual and commodified thing, which transformed it profoundly and perhaps permanently in both the cultural and the literary imagination.

In its attentiveness to the rise of Victorian autobiography as a commercial genre and its use of this development as a basis for assessing the Victorian novel, this book departs markedly from earlier studies of autobiography and from accounts of the relationship between the novel and the financial sphere. It does so first by considering autobiography's proliferation during the early part of the nineteenth century as a matter of book history, using quantitative data to situate the genre within the broader patterns of the Victorian book trade. The study of Victorian autobiography has produced important books from scholars such as Peterson, Sidonie Smith, Regenia Gagnier, Martin Danahay, and Trev Lynn Broughton, to name only a few. Most of this work has been of two kinds: the historical review of autobiographical forms, conventions, and traditions, often with the aim of providing a bibliographic or structuralist sense of the genre; and the critical/cultural analysis of specific autobiographies for what they reveal of Victorian self-fashioning along the lines of gender, sexuality, race, class, and other aspects of identity. Earlier studies in particular tended to read autobiography as emanating from cultural conditions that provoked a deeply felt need to express the self. In his introduction to *Approaches to Victorian Autobiography* (1979), George Landow wrote of the genre's interest in "the question of how the individual relates to what is outside himself" and argued that the Victorian determination to write autobiography stemmed from the period's momentous "disturbances and dislocations, the break-up of [its] culture."[31] Peterson, conversely, intellectualized the rise of autobiography, arguing that Victorians "chose to write autobiography in part because ... they sensed the disjunction between the inherited literary forms of self-interpretation and contemporary hermeneutic theory."[32] Jonathan Loesberg agrees, writing that autobiography "offered [Victorians] a mediating position between philosophies claiming that all knowledge is experiential and others that tended to insist on the possibility and indeed central importance of an intuitional knowledge of a priori truths about the world."[33]

Common to these early studies is a sense of autobiography as a measured, introspective, and comprehensive account of the author's life – a sense that this project does not share. Instead, I use the term autobiography as Eugene Stelzig does when he calls it "a convenient umbrella term for a type of writing proliferating in a variety of forms and modes ... in the later eighteenth and early nineteenth century ... To try to rigorously define the meaning," he continues, "or delimit the range of reference and denotation of autobiography during the Romantic era would be futile, for it is everywhere."[34] In writing of autobiography's stunning proliferation, then, I mean to include not just comprehensive and carefully composed "lives" but also memoirs, diaries, and volumes of letters, many of which were not meant to be published, as well as books of travel and exploration that were designed for publication, though perhaps with little intention of describing the intimate life of the narrating I. All of these forms meet Danahay's persuasive definition of autobiography as a work that gives "forceful expression" to the "absolute identification between author and text," or what we might regard as a direct relation between the lived experience of the author, of whatever nature and duration, and the account of that experience that s/he gives in discursive form.[35] Most recent scholarship on autobiography has proceeded from this messier sense of the genre, which posits less generic coherence or sense of tradition but gives – precisely because of its diversity – a richer idea of both the subjectivities that comprised the Victorian age and the diverse forms in which they found expression. In the introduction to his indispensable *Life Writing and Victorian Culture* (2006), David Amigoni articulated nicely the new direction for such work. "Victorian identity," he writes, "is now regularly acknowledged to be a complex compound derived from multiple sources: sexuality and gender, class and status, colonial, ethnic and familial. The challenge for nineteenth-century life writing research is to use its rich textual resources to map the relations between these sources of identity."[36]

Missing from these discussions, though, is sustained consideration of autobiography as an object of exchange: of who printed, published, sold, bought, and profited from these exposures of Victorian identity, of autobiography's complicated position within a literary market undergoing massive reorganization and expansion, or of the genre's mobilization of and adaptation to the first mass-reading public in England's history. As Treadwell notes, the "raw bibliographic facts" hint at the robust appetite for life writing early in the nineteenth century, but "the consumption of autobiography remains largely invisible."[37] I aim here to bring the production and consumption of autobiography into view, not only by describing the proliferation of autobiographical titles but also by examining how publishers and authors attempted to cash in on such works. Broughton points out that autobiographical production changed radically during the nineteenth century, when it passed from being "part of the fabric of social obligation" – composed by loving husbands or wives, sons or daughters, or intellectual or spiritual protégés – and became instead "a means of regulating and profiting from what Richard Sennett has called the 'market exchange in intimate relations'."[38] Under such circumstances, she warns, "the complex role of life writing as a 'technology of identity' should not lead us to overlook the plain fact that many, if not most, lives were published to make money," so that "the relationship between financial gain and identity was necessarily convoluted."[39] Or, to put it as Samuel Johnson did, "No man but a blockhead ever wrote, except for money."[40] But we have not yet taken seriously the need to account for this relationship between life writing and economic exchange, or at least we have not yet done so by examining carefully the position that autobiography held in the Victorian literary market. This means that we have not yet come to grips, either, with the theoretical, cultural, or literary implications of textualizing and commodifying the Victorian subject.

This project works at the intersection of book history and close reading to uncover both the wide economic significance of Victorian autobiography and the emergence of certain modes for representing subjectivity during the 1860s, a decade I have chosen because it follows the century's last powerful surge in autobiographical titles. In digging for information on publishing and sales rather than "reading" individual autobiographies, I draw mainly from the methodological models provided by such scholars as Simon Eliot, John Sutherland, Alexis Weedon, and Richard St. Clair, all of whom have done crucial work on the nineteenth-century book trade. But I also depart from them by moving on to situate autobiography's commercial rise alongside contemporary developments in finance, copyright law, the visual arts, and bureaucratic expansion, all of which reified and reinforced the tendency to textualize identity and formalized its relation to the capitalist sphere. As the book moves from its account of autobiographical production to these wider cultural matters, it attempts to follow in the scholarly wake of Mary Poovey's *Genres of the Credit Economy* (2008) and, more distantly, Richards's *The Commodity Culture of Victorian England* (1990), both of which are centrally concerned with the cultural formations that emerged from Victorian capitalism. Both books have been significant to my thinking about autobiography and the literary market, but Poovey's particular interest in financial documents as "genres" – the primacy that she grants to material texts in her analysis of Victorian finance – makes her work the more important touchstone for my own. I draw heavily from her work in the part of my first chapter that considers the place of autobiography amid the complex textual culture of Victorian finance capitalism.

The subsequent close readings of novels from the 1860s and the attempt to articulate how they conveyed this sense of commodified subjectivity also bring this work into contact with two other recent books: Aeron Hunt's *Personal Business: Character and Commerce in Victorian Literature and Culture* (2014) and Anna Kornbluh's *Realizing Capital: Financial and Psychic Economies in Victorian Form* (2014). Both explore the relation between Victorian economics and matters of character and psychology in the mid-century novel, but neither covers the terrain that I handle here. Rather than trace the significance of character in records from the Victorian financial sphere, as *Personal Business* does, my work here treats such documents as evidence of a larger cultural moment, exploring how Victorians came in the first place to locate identity in texts designed to formalize subjectivity's entanglement in commodity culture. Kornbluh's argument resembles mine more closely, but she focuses principally on similarities between the discursive fields of finance journalism and psychology. These become less surprising, though, when we consider that by mid-century autobiography had for decades been making subjectivity into a commodity, refiguring its imaginative and discursive status, and eroding its position as a thing apart from economic exchange. By the 1860s, novelists as different as Dickens, Mary Elizabeth Braddon, George Eliot, Charles Reade, and Wilkie Collins were finding in the textualization and commodification of identity a powerful trope for imagining the psychic, social, and ideological disruptions engendered by Victorian capitalism. Not all of them wrote sensation fiction. But the timing of that genre's emergence makes it possible to conjecture that sensation's characteristic preoccupations – endangered fortunes, proliferating texts, multiple identities, distemporal plots, and aberrant sexualities – derive partly from the anxieties engendered by autobiography's commercial rise. To the extent that it speculates in this way about the relation between commodity, identity, and the development of the novel, this book claims one final scholarly affinity: with the critical line mapped by Winifred Hughes, Patrick Brantlinger, Nicholas Daly, Pamela Gilbert, and others who have explored sensation fiction's origins and linked the genre to other contemporary literary and cultural forms.

My argument begins with an extended, multipart chapter describing autobiography's commercialization during the first half of the century, the simultaneous emergence of other cultural practices for textualizing and commodifying identity, and the anxieties that reviewers expressed regarding the tendency to transform identity into an object of exchange. Part one, "Autobiography in the Literary Market 1820–1860," uses both quantitative and anecdotal evidence to argue that autobiographical titles not only proliferated rapidly during these years but also began increasingly to appear from major commercial publishing houses that aimed at mass-readership and financial gain. An Appendix describes in detail the methods I employed to arrive at my quantitative arguments and the archive I have developed identifying nearly 2,500 autobiographical works published in England during these decades. Part two, "Autobiography and the Cultural Field," situates autobiography's rise as a commercial genre alongside developments in copyright law and finance capitalism to expose the ways in which autobiography depended upon legal and economic formations that had already begun to render subjectivity vulnerable to capitalist exchange. This section also argues that autobiography rose alongside other practices – in portraiture, photography, census-taking, and other bureaucratic expansions – for textualizing and commodifying the Victorian subject. The final part, "Autobiography and Anxiety," explores the contemporary critical response to autobiography to show that a general frustration with mercenary (and unseemly) autobiographical disclosure in the 1820s had evolved by the 1850s into more nuanced critiques of the tendency of autobiography, in the age of its mechanical reproduction, to multiply, abridge, distend, and displace identity in the act of adapting it to the demands of the literary market. In the end, I argue, the anxieties engendered by autobiography pushed mid-century novelists toward representations of identity that stressed its thorough pervasion by economic concerns.

Subsequent chapters read individual novels from the 1860s closely with the aim of tracing these representations in the period's fiction. Though I want partly to show parallels between the sensation novel and the anxieties provoked by autobiography, my chapters of close reading begin not with the obvious choice, Collins's *The Woman in White* (1859–1860), but rather with its successor in *All the Year Round*, Dickens's *Great Expectations* (1861). Chapter 2 argues that *Great Expectations*' autobiographical form and complex relation to Dickens's publishing practices and personal history provide a multilayered illustration of autobiography's implications for the textual, imaginative, and ontological status of the subject. Obsessing simultaneously about capital accumulation, identity, and authorship, *Great Expectations* underscores both the insufficiency of texts for representing subjectivity and the inevitable commodification of subjectivity once it has been pressed into textual form. The novel unmasks the autobiographical text, in other words, as simultaneously an inadequate and thoroughly commercial thing. Chapter 3 extends this argument by taking up Braddon's *Lady Audley's Secret* (1862), which permits a more robust discussion of gender and commodification while also shifting the textual grounds of my analysis. By foregrounding the remarkable portrait of Lady Audley but also reminding us that it belongs to specific sets of economic relations, Braddon's novel goes beyond treating Lady Audley as a commodified, sexualized feminine object. Instead, I argue, it suggests a problem that exceeds gender by linking her portrait to both commodity exchange and other texts – gift books, luggage labels, half-burnt telegrams – that collaborate to expose her identity to the disruptive dynamics of the capitalist market.

Chapter 4, treating both Eliot's *Silas Marner* (1861) and Reade's *Hard Cash* (1863), marks a turning point in the project by taking up novels that deal less with specific instances of textualized subjectivity than with the abstract implications of identity's material status at mid-century. Dealing with these novels in terms of what I call "ontologies of loss," I illustrate how both books treat the loss of property – Silas's bag of gold, Captain Dodd's £14,000 – as equivalent to loss of memory and of self, suggesting a crucial homology between property and identity. Each novel engages seriously with problems of economics and abnormal psychology, and each treats financial loss as a sudden annihilation of both the linguistic ability to express subjectivity and the intrinsic desires that ought to sustain it. My last two chapters press this point by turning to novels that show how the commodification of identity finally collapses the boundary between property and identity, such that the failure to distinguish between the two appears as a broad cultural condition rather than an isolated or idiosyncratic response. Chapter 5, on *Our Mutual Friend* (1864–1865), argues that Dickens's novel describes a culture that naturalizes the commodification of subjectivity, making it part of a grotesque artificial ecology in which subjectivity has no safe haven from the capitalist sphere. Chapter 6, on Collins's *The Moonstone* (1868), brings the problem of identity and textuality into full view, arguing that the novel's multivalent colonial backdrop stages a contest between the sense of identity as immaterial, essential, and "sacred" and the sense of it as the material thing that capitalism had made it. The result of this contest, I suggest, is a novel that attempts – however paradoxically – to hold identity sacrosanct against textualization and commodification while exploiting the commercial power of first-person form. In this sense, *The Moonstone* epitomizes the ideological tensions and oppositions that pervaded identity during the 1860s.

I conclude with a brief study of the famous case of the Tichborne Claimant, Arthur Orton, who culminated in real life the decades during which autobiography had worked alongside finance capitalism, the law, and the literary market to create a sense of identity as permeated thoroughly by economics and defined entirely by its existence in and as text. Orton arrived in England in 1866 claiming to be the long, lost Sir Roger Tichborne, heir to a baronetcy and an immense fortune. In an attempt to perpetrate this elaborate and potentially lucrative fraud, he devised a series of textual and other measures for becoming Tichborne, his identity assuming gradually the character of a Dickensian contest between affidavits, letters, diaries, pictures, and wills, each one proclaiming a different relation between the impostor and the property he hoped to claim. In a twist that even the ingenious Cochrane never imagined in his wildest dreams of the Stock Exchange, Orton even cashed in on his identity in the form of "Tichborne Bonds," which he sold to a gullible public to raise the money to pay his legal expenses, allowing investors to buy him up as a form of currency, trading and speculating in his contested identity. This book closes, in other words, by addressing the cultural significations of a man who pressed the ideological implications of autobiography and finance capitalism to their logical conclusion by transforming himself into the very thing – money – that Karl Marx calls in *Capital* (1867) the "absolutely alienable commodity" of the modern economic age.[41]

CHAPTER 1

"*A Vile Symptom*": Autobiography and the Commodification of Identity

The rise of autobiography as a commercial genre during the first half of the nineteenth century was, in its way, one of the decisive developments of the Victorian period in England. Amid a growing culture of celebrity, a maturing literary market, and the broad social concussions caused by England's transformation into a modern industrial state, autobiography's commercial rise embodied the emerging relations between the Victorian subject and the capitalist market and made the commodification of identity an explicit and unsettling feature of the age. John Gibson Lockhart's essay in the January 1827 *Quarterly Review* illustrates just how unsettling, turning a review of ten recent autobiographies into a fierce attack on this new and unaccountable tendency to textualize and commodify the self. Beginning with the complaint that "[t]he classics of the *papier maché* age of our drama have taken up the salutary belief that England expects every driveller to do his Memorabilia" – leaving England miserably awash in the memoirs of "primer-makers," "mob-orators," "[c]abin-boys and drummers," "pickpockets," and the various "John Gilpins of 'the nineteenth century'" – Lockhart works himself gradually toward this crescendo of literary and cultural discontent:

> The mania for this garbage of Confessions, and Recollections, and Reminiscences, and Aniliana, "is indeed a vile symptom." It seems as if the ear of that grand impersonation "the Reading Public," had become as filthily prurient as that of an eaves-dropping lackey.
>
> If this voluntary degradation be persisted in, the effects of it will, ere long, be visible elsewhere than in literature. An universal spirit of suspicion will overspread the intercourse of society, and no class of persons will suffer more, than those who found easy access in former days to circles much above their station, in virtue of the general belief, that their garrulity was not at least the veil of a calculating curiosity, and that, however poor their wit might be, they were capable of receiving kindness and condescension, without any notions of turning a penny by the systematic record of privacies too generously exposed.[1]

Lockhart's sneering in a conservative review like the *Quarterly* makes sense, for the autobiographical proliferation of the 1820s signaled, among other things, the democratization of the genre in the hands of minor literary men, Peninsular War veterans, notorious criminals, and other representatives of the increasingly literate but still unwashed masses. Even just twenty years earlier, the genre had remained mostly divided between the two narrative modes that had characterized it since the 1600s, neither of which aimed for wide readership or commercial gain. The more public of these was the spiritual autobiography, typically written, published, and read by Dissenters or other religious enthusiasts and meant to yield a profit of an altogether different kind; the less public was the memoir or diary of an aristocratic sire, most often printed and published at the family's expense and disseminated only to relatives or some other sliver of the ruling class. To be sure, eighteenth-century novelists such as Daniel Defoe, Samuel Richardson, Laurence Sterne, and Tobias Smollett had all exploited the possibilities of the genre, as had biographers and diarists such as James Boswell and Samuel Pepys. Yet James Olney still describes the nineteenth century as a time "when secular autobiography was slowly developing out of spiritual autobiography and when autobiography as a literary mode was emerging out of autobiography as a confessional act."[2] During the late 1700s it had developed nearly to the point of literary legitimacy, owing largely to the first English translation of Jean-Jacques Rousseau's *Confessions* in 1783 and the publication of Edward Gibbon's *Memoirs* in 1796. But by 1827, the authors, readers, and conventions of autobiography had changed. To Lockhart and others, the genre already appeared as a literary and economic excrescence, a mercenary violation of English subjects who should be preserved against transformation into commodified texts.[3] It was one thing that there should be so many autobiographies, that they should be written by cabin-boys and thieves, and that the vulgarity of authors and readers should, in Lockhart's words, embolden "beings who, at any period, would have been mean and base in all their objects and desires."[4] It was quite another, and a more troubling, that autobiographers might expose their social betters to a "filthily prurient" reading public for the sake of "turning a penny."

The elegant vitriol of Lockhart's review contextualizes the two arguments that shape this chapter: first, as a matter of book history, that English autobiographical production rose sharply 1820–1860, outstripping the growth of the book market as a whole and making autobiography, for the first time, into an explicitly commodified genre; and second, as a matter of critical and theoretical inquiry, that autobiography's commercial rise –

which coincided with the emergence of several other cultural practices for textualizing and commodifying the self – engendered powerful anxiety about the ontological status of subjectivity, and that this anxiety found expression in not only contemporary reviews but also several novels publishing during the 1860s, just after the century's last great surge in autobiographical titles. Scholars have often written of the Victorian period as a golden age of autobiography, though principally for the notable instances of life writing published at and after mid-century rather than for the remarkable developments that came before. In 1850, Leigh Hunt published his autobiography, and Robert Southey's *Recollections* appeared that same year in his posthumous *Life and Correspondence*. Thereafter, many other eminent Victorians – Charles Darwin, William Gladstone, Harriet Martineau, John Stuart Mill, John Henry Newman, Margaret Oliphant, John Ruskin, and Anthony Trollope, to name only a few – wrote and published accounts of their lives. Around mid-century the impulse to self-narration began to shape much imaginative literature, too, in novels such as *Jane Eyre* (1847), *Margaret Maitland* (1849), *David Copperfield* (1849–1850), and *Alton Locke* (1850), and in poetic memoirs such as *The Prelude* (1850), *In Memoriam, A.H.H.* (1850), and *Aurora Leigh* (1856), though the first two of these were largely written long before their publication. We might read this spectacular profusion of first-person works as a culmination of particular aesthetic concerns, for instance as evidence of the maturation of writers who had been raised on the Romantic ideals of introspection and artistic self-revelation. But it seems likely that something more mundane was at work – the something that prompted a consummate businessman like Dickens to write *Copperfield* and expect it to sell.

The outpouring of real and imagined lives that began at mid-century was enabled by the hundreds of autobiographies that had come before, and that had helped to make the genre into a popular and profitable part of the Romantic and early-Victorian literary market. For each famous autobiography that came later in the century, there was first a *Memoir of the Rev. Henry Martyn* (1819), a *Narrative of the Life and Travels of Serjeant B –* (1823), and a *Horrid Confession of John Kean* (1825). For each famous autobiography that remains a familiar object of scholarly study, scores of others have vanished into obscurity, though they helped early in the century to produce a reading culture hungry for autobiographical disclosures and willing to sanction new relations between identity, textuality, and economic exchange. These forgotten works need not become objects of close reading. But neither do they belong to a separate literary past. Assessing the cultural position of Victorian autobiography means remembering that what Stelzig calls "the *autobiographization* of literature" began with the Romantics, who were formalizing during the late 1700s the practice of writing one's own life.[5] The next century's innovation was to turn such narratives into popular, profitable, explicitly commodified texts, so that autobiography matured alongside baggy monsters into a characteristic form of Victorian prose. Between 1820 and 1860, autobiographies became more numerous and more commercial. They passed from being quiet works for niche audiences to being very big business, sought, published, and sold by the same leviathan houses that published Dickens, Eliot, Collins, Thackeray, and Trollope. This change occurred within a wider field of financial practices, copyright laws, portraiture, photography, census-taking, and civil service examinations that were insisting generally on textualizing Victorian identity and transforming it into an object of economic exchange.

The period of autobiography's commercial rise thus coincides with a complex cultural moment when Victorians were coming increasingly to understand and represent identity as a material thing, a potential commodity, to the dismay of observers who feared the erosion of the boundary between identity and property precisely because it metonymized the erosion of other boundaries: between private and public, individual and social, genteel and vulgar, England and empire. In this respect Lockhart's complaint tells us much about the anxieties that autobiography provoked. What price could be placed on the exposure of privacy, and who would pay for such a thing or take money to produce it? Who owns the experiences recorded by autobiography when they are intersubjective, and who may claim them once they have been made into a material thing, designed deliberately for textual production and commercial exchange? In the rapidly modernizing literary market of the 1820s and after, how might the interplay of self-narrative impulse and capitalist demand transform the social, economic, and ideological functions of autobiography, and how might such changes transform also the cultural, legal, and imaginative status of the subject, to say nothing of the representation of the subject in discursive form? Identity, textuality, commodity: during the middle of the nineteenth century, these converged in unprecedented ways. Lockhart suggests that the inevitable consequence of this "voluntary degradation" would be the reinstantiation of rigid class lines, a shoring up of especially upper-class identity in the face of mercenary encroachments on the privacy and integrity of the subject. Even as it brought identity into material existence, autobiography seems – ironically – to have destabilized rather than concretized the self, leaving observers searching for means of resisting and representing the new relation between identity and the commercial sphere.

Describing this new relation is the purpose of this chapter, and analyzing the means by which Victorian novelists tried to represent it is the aim of the chapters that follow. In the form of autobiography, Victorian identity was not just textualized, bought, and sold. It was copied, revised, disseminated, fragmented, and temporally ruptured, interlaced with the demands of economic desire. It also became both more and less than the sum of its textual parts, always exceeding imaginatively the limits of its material representation even as developments during the middle of the century gradually restricted "identity" to the economic and legal meanings inherent in textual form. The proliferation of autobiography during the first half of the nineteenth century was, in this sense, less "a vile symptom" than a first cause, a provocation to the development of new strategies of narrative representation as novelists sought ways to show subjectivity under economic duress, pervaded by economic demands and collapsed imaginatively into the realm of property. As I show in subsequent chapters, *Great Expectations, Lady Audley's Secret, Silas Marner, Hard Cash, Our Mutual Friend*, and *The Moonstone* all traverse this imaginative and ideological ground, transforming sensational plots about economic hardships, contested wills, and stolen wealth into explorations of self-division, madness, cognitive loss, and textual, physical, and psychological multiplicity. And they do so insistently enough that it is worth considering whether the sensation novel – which emerged as autobiography reached its final extraordinary peak around 1860 – might best be understood as a form catalyzed by the anxieties surrounding the growing tendency to commodify the self. I begin, though, with a simpler proposition: that the commercial rise of autobiography 1820–1860 transformed the genre, with momentous implications for the Victorian subject and the Victorian novel.

1.1 Autobiography in the Literary Market 1820–1860

Autobiography's commercial rise must be charted through the terrain of imperfect quantitative data on the book market, anecdotal evidence about particular titles, financial details mined from the surviving ledgers of Victorian publishers, and inferences that attempt to make sense of them all. Precision is impossible. But we can learn enough to arrive at two major conclusions about autobiography's position in the literary market between 1820 and 1860: first, that the period saw a continuous, often spectacular increase in autobiographical titles; and second, that publishers came increasingly to perceive the genre as an explicitly commercial one and to treat it as a commodity. The rise began just before 1820 amid the exuberant nationalism that followed the Napoleonic Wars. According to totals drawn from the *Nineteenth-century Short Title Catalog* (hereafter *NSTC*), nearly twice as many new autobiographical titles appeared during the 1820s as during the decade before, and in 1825 – the peak year of this initial surge – the number of new titles was nearly triple what it had been in 1815. Some of these, such as *Memoirs of the Life and Religious Experience of William Lewis* (1820), belonged to the familiar seventeenth- and eighteenth-century types. But many did not, and these new manifestations of the genre fueled its expansion. Renewed tourism on the continent in the years after Napoleon's defeat led to travel books about Holland, the Rhine, Italy, and Moscow, among other places, while exploration and colonial expansion yielded published journals from expeditions to Egypt, the Congo, Korea, New South Wales, South America, and the Arctic. These narratives were joined by a growing number of military memoirs written by men who had fought against France and hoped to capitalize on that experience by selling it to the reading public. John Edgecombe Daniel published his *Journal of an Officer* in 1820, Joseph Donaldson his *Recollections of an Eventful Life Chiefly Passed in the Army* in 1824, and James Hale his *Journal of . . . [a] Late Sergeant in the Ninth Regiment of the Foot* in 1825. Nor were these all. Having vanquished Napoleon, England flexed its military and political muscle in print, commemorating its victory and asserting implicitly its commitment to engagement in Europe and expansion abroad.

The rising autobiographical tide of the 1820s thus appears first as an expression of renewed cultural cohesion after a period of intense worry about matters on the continent and amid the turmoil engendered by industrialization at home. But travel narratives and military memoirs were not the only kinds of autobiographical works that began to flourish, nor were they the only kinds that Lockhart had in mind when he attacked autobiography so furiously in the *Quarterly*. In fact, Lockhart's targets included no travel narratives and just two military memoirs, one of which – *The Life and Correspondence of Major Cartwright* (1826) – was mainly a compilation about John Cartwright's decades as a radical reformer advocating universal suffrage and annual parliaments. The rest were the autobiographies and memoirs of a diverse group of men: minor authors Frederick Reynolds and Joseph Craddock, the Pennsylvania Quaker Lindley Murray, shipboy and sailor John Nicol, the London silversmith Joseph Brasbridge, and the notorious felons James Moffat and David "the

Switcher" Haggart. Such works hardly expressed nationalist exuberance or cultural cohesion. Rather, they signified the expansion of literacy, authorship, and readership; religious and political nonconformity; "vulgar" interest in seafaring and criminal lives; and, more generally, the rising prosperity and influence of the middle class. Nationalism, exploration, industrialization, and dislocation may have collaborated, as Landow asserts, in producing conditions favorable to the expansion of life writing. But by the 1820s writing and publishing one's life required also able purchasers and willing readers. To the extent that this is so, autobiography's initial proliferation did not serve the needs of authors anxious about personal identity and social upheaval so much as it served the interests of a widening class of readers finding their places within an evolving capitalist sphere.

Autobiographical titles continued to proliferate after 1825, but for the next two decades they did so less spectacularly and steadily than they had during these early years.[6] The number of new titles declined in 1826 before climbing for the rest of the decade, reaching another small peak during 1829–1830 and then resuming a gentle rise that lasted another fifteen years. By 1833, then, Thomas Carlyle's Editor could rightly remark "these Autobiographical times of ours" in *Sartor Resartus*, even if autobiography developed unevenly and in myriad forms.[7] Martin Hewitt has noted that the diary became popular as early as the 1810s and was a "widely consumed literary genre ... by the 1830s" – so widely consumed, he writes, that "[d]iaries became commodities, not merely in their own right, but as components of popular fiction" in novels ranging from Anne Brontë's *The Tenant of Wildfell Hall* (1848) to Collins's *The Moonstone*.[8] Peterson has likewise observed that the "domestic memoir ... flourished from the 1830s onward in privately printed and formally published works."[9] The *NSTC* confirms what Hewitt and Peterson imply: that different autobiographical forms came into vogue at slightly different times, perhaps in response to changing tastes. While travel narratives and military memoirs flourished during the 1820s, they diminished in number thereafter, fading during the 1830s and 1840s as volumes of letters peaked. Books calling themselves "diary" or "confession" also rose sharply during the 1820s, then surged again during the 1840s even though, in the latter case, the number of such works that the *NSTC* classes as real autobiographies scarcely rises at all. As Figure 1.1 shows, during the 1840s and 1850s, while the appetite for letters, diaries, and confessions remained robust, works bearing the word "autobiography" in their names especially experienced rapid growth, flourishing in both real life writing and fiction. This might suggest that mid-century

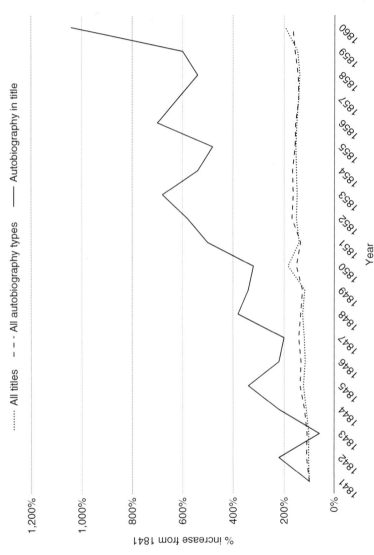

Figure 1.1 Increase in titles with the word "autobiography" 1841–1860, compared with the increase in all titles and the increase of autobiographical titles of all kinds, compiled from the *Nineteenth-century Short Title Catalog*.

readers wanted not undigested or piecemeal compilations but rather comprehensive narratives characterized by moral, ethical, and chronological arcs. They wanted to buy not scraps and relics but "lives," complete and coherent identities given in textual form.

Indeed, though the publication of certain forms of life writing had plateaued by the mid-1840s, the *NSTC* suggests that 1845–1861 witnessed the period's most sustained and significant rise in autobiographical production. The number of new autobiographical titles spiked 1845–1847, declined slightly over the next five years, then, as Figure 1.2 shows, jumped sharply in 1852 to a new level that held for a decade. In using annual *NSTC* data, one must discount peak years such as 1850 and 1860 since the database assigns titles of uncertain date to the first year of their presumed decade of publication. Figure 1.2 begins with 1841 rather than 1840 to eliminate this "noise," especially since the *NSTC* shows that a total of 561 autobiographical works were published in 1840 versus only 381 the following year – unlikely, given that no other year reaches that figure reliably until 1852. All told, autobiographical production was four times higher during the 1840s than it had been during the first decade of the century and nearly 2.5 times what it had been in the 1820s. Between 1841 and 1852, the number of new autobiographical titles appearing annually rose by nearly 70 percent, and it remained at this new level until early the next decade, when it receded briefly before beginning a gentle climb that lasted until 1869. The number of new autobiographical titles published that year was still markedly lower (−11 percent) than it had been in 1855, and in total the 1860s saw roughly 10 percent fewer autobiographies published than the 1850s, the first decade-to-decade decline of the century. By the 1860s, the rapid increase in autobiographical titles had ended. But it had been extraordinary while it lasted, and it altered permanently the place of the genre in the literary market.

The growth of autobiography 1820–1860 even outpaced the simultaneous expansion of the British book trade, which was itself remarkable (Figure 1.3). Fueled by rising literacy rates, technological innovations in printing and paper-making, and the removal of the taxes on knowledge, these decades saw rapid growth in periodical titles and readership, an industrial reorganization of the activities involved in producing and selling books, and the consolidation of major publishing houses within an increasingly nuanced literary market. Simon Eliot has shown that the 1810s and 1820s were characterized by rising book production, with occasional years of small decline but also stunning years like 1825, when the market for all books surged.[10] This surge was followed

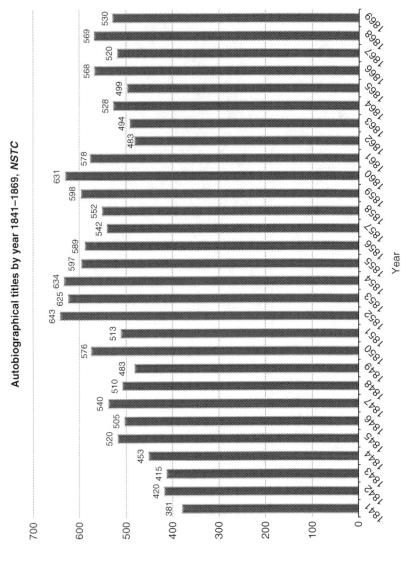

Figure 1.2 Autobiographical titles of all kinds published each year 1841–1869, compiled from the *Nineteenth-century Short Title Catalog*.

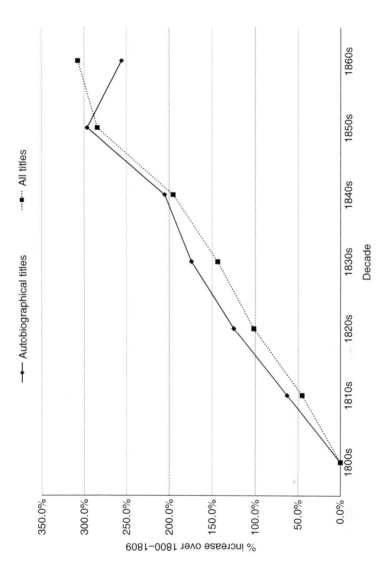

Figure 1.3 Rate of increase in all titles published and autobiographical titles of all kinds by decade 1800–1860, compiled from the *Nineteenth-century Short Title Catalog*.

immediately by an industry-wide downturn that Sutherland traces to the economic crash of 1826, sparked by shrinking cash supplies and a sudden drop in the stock market.[11] The crash "did not," Alexander Dick writes, "destroy the publishing industry ... [but it] did change its character."[12] Before the crash, publishers regularly paid their genteel authors handsomely in advance, often borrowing to do so. But the straitened cash supply crippled houses that had debt or needed further outlays to pay for new titles. The crisis ruined some publishers, including Scott and Ballantyne, Hurst and Robinson, Hunt and Clarke, and Thomas Constable and his prize author Sir Walter Scott; those that survived were forced to adopt new patterns for paying authors and producing books.[13] The effect of the 1826 crash was thus not collapse but transformation, as "[c]ultural commentators and literary writers began to conceive of the market economy not as something distinct from the self or its communities but rather as the condition in which all selves and communities exist and to which, paradoxically, they owed that existence."[14]

The book trade rebounded quickly – Sutherland notes that "1827 was a better year than 1825" – and the number of new titles ticked upward for the next two decades, with flurries of them appearing at moments of heated political debate, as in the case of the 1832 Reform Act.[15] Meanwhile, the character of the book market continued to change. While reputable publishers like Constable and John Murray had long embraced a model that favored authors with substantial reputations and expensive books in small editions, the troubles of 1826 had opened the door for entrepreneurs who paid little up front and believed that "financial reward came from mass sales."[16] Richard Bentley began exploiting this model during the early 1830s, and Chapman and Hall did so with spectacular results in 1836 when they began serial publication of *The Pickwick Papers*. During the 1840s this low-expenditure, high-volume approach became the hallmark of rising firms like Blackwood's, Macmillan, and Smith, Elder and paved the way to the 1849 launch of George Routledge's Railway Library, a monument to the power of mass-marketed editions of second-rate copyrights.[17] The late 1830s also saw the emergence of "a generalised textbook market ... led by Longmans" and including Macmillan, George Bell and Sons, and Oliver and Boyd, who capitalized on the expansion of an examination culture that, by 1860, drove "the annual order for readers ... [to] the region of 660 000 copies."[18] In all of these ways the mid-century book market was assuming the modern commercial character that Carlyle had sensed in it years earlier when he grumbled of "[t]hat waste chaos of Authorship by Trade."[19]

Like autobiography, the British publishing industry experienced its most robust growth during the period of national prosperity that began around 1846 and lasted until the outbreak of the US Civil War. Owing partly to the pamphleteering surrounding John Newman's conversion in 1845, the Great Exhibition in 1851, the Duke of Wellington's death in 1852, and the outbreak of the Crimean War in 1853, the number of new titles increased greatly during these years.[20] So did paper production, by more than 54 percent between 1850 and 1859, though not all of this new paper went to the pamphleteers.[21] This was the decade, Sutherland asserts, in which "the great Victorian reading public" was formed and the market came first to be dominated by the cheap book."[22] These developments – along with Mudie's circulating library, W.H. Smith's book-stalls, and Dickens's novels in parts, among other things – were the first "symptoms of industrial mass-production" in the British book market and early evidence of the book's rise as an exemplary form of "portable property."[23] And, as with autobiographies, this growth ended in 1861. By then, England's annual book exports earned half a million pounds, one-third of them from the United States.[24] The US Civil War thus cost British publishers more than £150,000 annually by closing off the American market, besides provoking a recession that left domestic readers, too, with less money to buy books. The result was a trough in both autobiographical production and the number of titles published generally after 1861, at least until the market began to rebound in 1865.[25] Autobiography did not just participate in the expansion of British publishing: it catalyzed and outstripped it, becoming a critical part of the industry's growth and modernization. Taking into account all forms of life writing, the *NSTC* shows that autobiographical titles proliferated more rapidly than all titles did during the 1810s and 1820s, with increases of 69 percent and 42 percent for autobiographical works during these decades versus 45 percent and 39 percent for the market as a whole. If we consider that diaries and letters peaked during the 1820s and 1830s and focus only on those works that claimed to be "autobiography," the picture becomes sharper. The number of works using the word "autobiography" in their title grew in every decade from 1820 to 1860, and in every decade but the 1830s it did so far more rapidly than titles did generally. Predictably, in the 1820s – the first decade in which the word "autobiography" entered common use – the number of titles bearing the word rose 575 percent from the prior decade while titles generally rose 45 percent. The following decade, though these figures were just 15 percent for "autobiography" and 21 percent for titles generally, the *Quarterly* complained of autobiography as a mass-market genre:

> The most remarkable feature, we think, in the literature of the present day is the great and increasing proportion which biography, and particularly *autobiography*, appears to bear to the general mass of publications ...
> ... In short, what with increasing the quantity of the article and deteriorating the quality, we fear it must be confessed that at this moment biography is perhaps the very lowest of all the classes of literature; it has become a mere *manufacture*, which seems in great measure to have superseded that of novels ...[26]

According to the *NSTC*, that "*manufacture*" continued to increase – by 42 percent during the 1840s compared against 21 percent for titles generally, and by 112 percent during the 1850s versus 30 percent for titles generally. During the 1860s, amid the general slowdown, and although other kinds of life writing had plateaued or declined, works called "autobiography" increased 43 percent compared with 6 percent for all titles. During the 1840s, 1850s, and 1860s, in other words, "autobiography" proliferated at two times, then four times, then seven times the rate of all titles, and it did so within a literary market that was, for much of this time, experiencing unprecedented growth.

These figures tell the story of autobiography's rise, but they do not tell the whole story, for the number of titles published tells us little about how many copies of books were printed, purchased, or read.[27] Throughout the Romantic period, an out-of-copyright work such as *Robinson Crusoe* might be published in a print run of 5,000 cheap copies that would eventually reach more like 50,000 readers, and in 1823 "one could buy a beautifully illustrated edition of *Robinson Crusoe* for one penny (0.08 shillings) a week."[28] During these same years, autobiographical works – if they were marketed at all instead of appearing as religious texts or privately printed family accounts – appear to have been published more commonly in smaller editions of 1,000 or so copies, often in quarto formats priced between £1 and £3 and thus far too large and valuable to lend or carry about.[29] Eventually publishers began to treat autobiography as they treated the novel, publishing it in one, two, or three octavo volumes, sometimes more, and printing it in cheap formats for mass sales. In 1852, Murray published Theodore Hook's *Life* in a large first edition of 5,000 priced at 8d., and Ward and Lock brought out P.T. Barnum's *Autobiography* at 1s. in 1855. Still others appeared serially, whether in a literary magazine, as *Life of an Architect* did in *Bentley's Miscellany* 1852–1854, or in monthly parts, as David George Goyder's *My Battle for Life; the Autobiography of a Phrenologist* did from Simpkin, Marshall and Co. in 1856–1857.

Authors and publishers were obviously treating autobiography as a profitable commercial genre by the 1850s and adapting it to the demands of an increasingly broad literary market. But considerable evidence suggests that this was happening much earlier: in the 1810s, for instance, when Henry Colburn paid Lady Morgan more for her account of her travels in *France* (1817) than for her novel *O'Donnel* (1814), and in the 1820s, when Hunt and Clarke launched the series *Autobiography: A Collection of the Most Instructive and Amusing Lives Ever Published, Written by the Parties Themselves*.[30] As its title implies, Hunt and Clarke's series mostly *republished* autobiographies by eighteenth-century men – David Hume, Voltaire, and others – who could enlighten civilized minds, which may explain why Lockhart spared it in the *Quarterly*. Still, as Treadwell writes, the mere existence of *Autobiography* indicates that "a consensus about the discrete status of self-writing was forming among readers."[31] Hunt and Clarke's business records have not survived, so it is hard to know whether their highbrow series succeeded commercially at a time when "vulgar" lives were attracting both readers and critical scorn. But it seems telling that, although "Hunt and Clarke apparently went bankrupt in 1829," the series continued until 1833 and eventually reached thirty-two volumes.[32] Even so, *Autobiography* accounted for only around 15 percent of all autobiographical titles published 1826–1833. By the mid-1820s, then, the sea change had begun. Autobiographies would appear increasingly, like works of other kinds, from major publishers with profitability in mind.

The first major publisher to understand the commercial possibilities for autobiography seems to have been John Murray, whose correspondence and business ledgers show him trying to profit from it in several ways beginning in the 1820s. In 1821 Murray gave Thomas Moore 2,000 guineas for Byron's manuscript memoirs, likely weighing the loan against the anticipated proceeds of publication.[33] But Byron was a celebrity, and anything he wrote was likely to sell. Six years later, Murray may have learned something about the public appetite for life writing, even by obscure persons, from dealing with John Knapp, who offered Murray his *Journal of a Naturalist* (1829) in July 1827. Perhaps thinking of his own review's hostility to autobiography earlier that year – Murray published the *Quarterly* – he offered just one hundred guineas for the copyright, which Knapp "decline[d] accepting without any hesitation."[34] Instead, Knapp chose a half-profits arrangement, with the delightful result that he made over £1,300, more of which might have gone to Murray had he offered more generously for the book.[35] When the actress Fanny Kemble wrote to Murray in 1834 offering her journal for publication, he replied enthusiastically almost before he had read a word of it, writing that he "felt every disposition to be her publisher" and "would immediately view what she had sent & make a specific offer for her work."[36] The offer was cautious, like the alternative he had given Knapp: half-profits on an edition of 2,000 priced at 12s. 10d. But Murray's outward enthusiasm in securing his author is suggestive, as is his later reassurance regarding the book's success. Just before publication in May 1835, Murray wrote to Kemble predicting that it would "command a very great sale" and encouraging her to "continue [her] Journal, in the same original style, through Life" – advice she seems to have taken, since she eventually published six more such volumes.[37] Even this first effort netted Kemble and Murray each £315 and nearly exhausted the edition.

Murray also devised other ways to capitalize on autobiography, most notably in the case of the poet George Crabbe, whose copyrights Murray had purchased for £3,000 in 1819, but whose works sold so anemically that a decade later he remained out of pocket for half the sum.[38] When Crabbe died in 1832, Murray used autobiography as a way of resurrecting interest in his works. He approached George Crabbe, Jr. about the prospect of bringing out a new edition of the poems prefaced by a volume describing Crabbe's life, composed from his own words and supplemented by family and friends.[39] Though he agreed to compile such a memoir, the younger Crabbe wrote to Murray expressing confusion about its intent. "I do not perceive," he admitted, "how a poem or tale could be inter-woven with a Memoir, tho' some small pieces could be inserted with great advantage."[40] But Murray perceived it. He intended to reissue the poems with the included memoir while also holding down the price, so directing the new edition at the same middle-class readers who were devouring autobiographies. He moved forward so aggressively with engravings for the edition that Crabbe protested, begging Murray to stop going to lavish expense when he was not yet sure what sort of memoir he could produce. By September 1833, Murray had the completed memoir in hand and turned it over to none other than Lockhart for thorough rewriting.[41] After circulating a prospectus for the new edition, to be issued monthly in eight volumes at 5s. each, Murray got the desired response: having initially planned print runs of 5,000 copies per volume, he wound up printing 7,090 copies of the first volume – the *Life* – in February 1834 and a total of nearly 9,400 copies by early 1840.[42] By March 1846, though every volume had required printing of at least 7,290 copies, sales of the *Life* outstripped the others by more than 2,000 copies.[43] In total, Crabbe's sons received more than £900 from the *Life and Works* and Murray cleared £2,125.[44]

After a quarter century, by relying on the marketing power of autobiography and a cheaper format, Murray had recouped his investment in the works of a long-unfashionable poet.

Though Murray is perhaps best known for publishing Byron and the *Quarterly Review*, and for marketing ventures such as the Family Library (1829–1834) and the Colonial and Home Library (1847–1849) aimed at middle-class readers, he actually owed much of his success during the period to his willing publication of autobiography. The fifty-one works in the Family Library included John Barrow's *A Family Tour through South Holland* (1831), Dixon Denham's *Travels and Discoveries in Northern and Central Africa* (1826), and Henry Coleridge's *Six Months in the West Indies* (1826), besides biographies of Napoleon, Lord Nelson, Peter the Great, Sir Isaac Newton, and several artists, physicians, and Scottish worthies.[45] The seventy-six titles of the Colonial and Home Library tilted, understandably, more heavily toward travel narratives, offering accounts of life in Canada, India, the Baltic, and Sierra Leone.[46] The house's growing emphasis on life writing at mid-century, noticeable especially in its ledgers, may owe to the reorganization of the business after the death of John Murray II in 1843, which resulted in the discontinuation of accounts for many titles that had long been on the books. The list of active titles shrank from 280 in 1845 to just 148 in 1851 before climbing again to 292 by 1855. Whatever prompted it, the purge seems to have worked. In the 1845 records, 51 percent of the 280 active accounts show as unprofitable, while in the 1855 records, only 42 percent do. The change in Murray's fortunes might reflect greater caution in acquiring titles during the economic downturn of the late 1840s or greater success during the financial exuberance of the 1850s. Perhaps it reflects both. Either way, this period of greater commercial success for Murray coincided with a 32 percent rise in autobiographical titles, which increased from 7.2 percent to 9.5 percent of their total list.[47]

Moreover, Murray was more likely to reap profits from autobiography than from books of other kinds. The house's business ledgers can be difficult to decipher because of chronological overlaps that appear to be the result of certain titles remaining active so long that their accounts carried over into multiple ledgers. Properly read, however, Copies Ledger D and Copies Ledger E, which together cover the period 1838–1880, appear to show that Murray acquired more than 650 new titles 1838–1859, that he purchased copyrights outright for 31 percent of them, and that nearly one-third of the purchased copyrights were for life writing. They also show that, of the copyrights he purchased, those most likely to turn out profitable were for autobiographies. Partly this is because, by the 1830s at least,

Murray was less likely to pay lavishly for autobiography than for another genre, making him less likely to come out a loser. He paid just £105 each for Barrow's *A Visit to Iceland* (1835), Lady Eastlake's *Letters from the Shores of the Baltic* (1842), and Robert Fortune's *Three Years' Wanderings in the Northern Provinces of China* (1847), and he profited handsomely from all three. When he spent lavishly on copyrights or illustrations, he tended to lose. Through much of the century, Murray's great money makers were Maria Rundell's *Domestic Cookery* (1807), Charles Lyell's *Principles of Geology* (1830), Charles Darwin's *Journal of the Beagle* (1845) and *On the Origin of Species* (1859), and Byron's works, all of which appeared in many editions. But the fact that Murray was more likely to turn profits on autobiographies than on other works suggests that the genre occupied much the same position that Sutherland describes for the triple-decker, when he writes that the reliable profits they generated, though often modest, stabilized the publishing industry by providing "a kind of built-in insurance against loss."[48] Like triple-deckers, autobiographies had become – in Murray's hands, at least – not just commodities but crucial cogs in the industrialization and expansion of British publishing.

By the 1840s, virtually all of the major houses were following Murray's lead by investing in autobiography and reaping significant returns. Chief among them was Bentley, whose list of autobiographical titles was nearly as extensive as Murray's. Bentley may be best remembered as a publisher of fiction, if only because he quarreled famously with Dickens over the editorship of *Bentley's Miscellany* and the contract for *Oliver Twist*.[49] But by the 1830s, Bentley was spending big on other kinds of works, including autobiographies, for the excellent reason that they were more likely than fiction to make money. As Sutherland writes, Bentley probably "financed innumerable unprofitable novels with his books of travels, memoirs, and cookery books," which he had begun publishing during his brief partnership with Colburn, who handled many autobiographies 1825–1829.[50] Over the next two years, Bentley and Colburn published fifteen autobiographical and biographical works, including John Bernard's *Retrospections of the Stage* (1830), George Thomas Keppel's *Narrative of a Journey across the Balcan* (1831), and *The Life and Adventures of Nathaniel Pierce* (1831). After they dissolved their partnership in 1832, Bentley continued to publish in the genre actively – so much so that he accounts for nearly 10 percent of the autobiographical titles I have collected, though this surely owes in part to the availability of Bentley's business records, and the disappearance of those from many other publishers. During the 1830s, eight of Bentley's ten highest payments for copyright went to biographers.[51] Thereafter, his list trended toward autobiographies, particularly correspondence.

Including all forms of life writing, Bentley published sixty-three such titles 1840–1863, or nearly four times as many autobiographical works as novels. He brought out the correspondence of the Earl of Malmesbury, Philip Stanhope, Queen Henrietta Marie, Horace Walpole, and Mary Granville Delany, among others, and he often paid notable sums for the copyright. During the 1840s and 1850s, Bentley purchased copyright outright for approximately 75 percent of the titles he published, with an average price of £140. But he paid £500 each for Malmesbury's letters, Walpole's, and Delany's, as well as for *Memoirs of George Selwyn and His Contemporaries* (1841). He also paid the French biographer Francois Guizot £800 for the right to translate his *Memoirs to Illustrate the History of My Time* (1857). Though Bentley remained a significant publisher of fiction and brought out early works by Collins and Trollope, he estimated in 1855 that his most valuable copyrights were for *The Letters and Works of Lady Mary Wortley Montagu* (1830) and the Malmesbury and Walpole letters; two years later, he estimated them to be Montagu again and the *Letters of Lord Chesterfield* (1846). In 1862, though Bentley shrewdly advertised a new edition of Collins's *Rambles Beyond Railways* (1851) as the work of the "author of *The Woman in White*," it was outsold two-to-one by the second series of the *Autobiography and Correspondence of Mary Granville Delany* (1860) and by Joseph Devey's *Life of Joseph Locke* (1862) – the latter though Devey had to pay Bentley to get it into print, defraying the costs and providing a commission of £50.[52] During the early 1860s, besides Ellen Wood's smash *East Lynne* (1861), Bentley's best-selling title was Cochrane's *Autobiography*, and he routinely paid autobiographers, not novelists, the highest sums for copyright. Between 1840 and 1863, just two of Bentley's ten biggest contracts went to novelists – to Collins for *Basil* (1852) and Wood for *The Channings* (1862). Only two other novels, Lady Blessington's *Memoirs of a Femme de Chambre* (1846) and *Marmaduke Herbert* (1847), even make the top twenty. The rest went to autobiographers, diarists, travel writers, and editors of letters. And while it could be coincidence, all of the exceptional novels but *The Channings* are written in the first person.

During the 1850s virtually all of the major commercial houses made autobiographies staples of their lists, a condition that would have been unthinkable forty years earlier. Simpkin and Marshall, Hurst and Blackett, Ward and Lock, and Thomas Cautley Newby all began publishing autobiographies in significant numbers around this time. So did Routledge, who resurrected old titles such as Selina Bunbury's *A Visit to My Birthplace* (1828) and Frederick Chamier's *Life of a Sailor* (1832) and revitalized recent autobiographical fictions including Frederick Marryat's *Valerie* (1849) and Charles Lever's *Confessions of Con Cregan* (1850), both of which sold thousands of copies.[53] With the exception of Simpkin and Marshall, whose list of autobiographies tended toward the religious, these houses seem generally to have favored first-person works at mid-century, and to have featured both real and fictional self-narratives. Hurst and Blackett published Mary Ann Lupton's novel *Ada Gresham: An Autobiography* (1853) and Frances Trollope's novel *The Life and Adventures of a Clever Woman* (1853) but also Oliphant's semiautobiographical *The Days of My Life: An Autobiography* (1857) and Edward Alexander's *Passages in the Life of a Soldier* (1857). Ward and Lock brought out George Whyte-Melville's *Kate Coventry: An Autobiography* (1850), Eliza Rowe's *My Life; or the Autobiography of a Village Curate* (1855), and two volumes of *Recollections* (of an Irish police magistrat, and a half-pay officer) by Henry Addison – all novels – but also *The Autobiography of P. T. Barnum* (1855). Meanwhile, Saunders and Otley, though they published almost no life writing before 1840, began at mid-century to dabble in travel writing and also anonymous, probably fictional "confessions" that hinted at salacious content: *Confessions of an Etonian* (1846), *Confessions of a Hypochondriac* (1849), and *Confessions of a Too-Generous Young Woman* (1859). But the king of fictional autobiographies was the barely reputable Newby, who published no fewer than eight novels called "An Autobiography" 1855–1869, besides publishing Anne Brontë's *Agnes Grey* (1847) and Emily Brontë's *Wuthering Heights* (1847), both of which rely upon first-person form.[54]

Of the other major publishers, Longman and Smith, Elder stand out as the most active participants in the mid-century mania for autobiographical works. Between 1818 and 1835, by my count, Longman published just a half dozen autobiographical titles: two travel books, three volumes of poetry with an included memoir, and the military *Journal of James Hale* (1826). But from 1846 to 1865, Longman published more than twenty such works, virtually all of them real autobiographies by figures such as Charles Babbage, Thomas Bewick, James Silk Buckingham, Benjamin Robert Haydon, and Hester Lynch Piozzi. Smith, Elder, on the other hand, did not even begin publishing until 1839, but they incorporated life writing into their list immediately. A March 1839 catalog describes eleven autobiographical works as "Preparing for Publication" with Smith, Elder, including W.G. Leigh's *Narrative of a Residence at Adelaide*, Andrew Smith's *Journal of an Expedition in the Interior of Southern Africa*, and the anonymous *Argentine, an Autobiography* and *The Life-book of a Labourer*.⁵⁵ Between 1853 and 1859, some thirty-six of Smith, Elder's 285 titles were autobiographies – 12.6 percent of their list – and the records suggest that Smith, Elder's forays into the genre were serious business. For instance, though they were more likely to purchase copyright up front for novels than for autobiographies, they were more likely to purchase autobiographies than other nonfiction. And when they did pay, on average they paid significantly more for the copyright of autobiographical works than of fictional ones – £67 14s. 0d. compared with £54 6s. 4d. – even though by the 1850s, Smith, Elder's stable of novelists included Charlotte Brontë, Thackeray, Oliphant, and Trollope. In another way, too, Smith, Elder's practice resembled Bentley's and Newby's: Brontë's *Shirley* (1849), *Villette* (1853), and *The Professor* (1855), Thackeray's *Henry Esmond* (1852), and Oliphant's *Margaret Maitland* all are autobiographical fictions.

The anecdotal evidence supplied by the records of these Victorian publishers thus reinforces the quantitative evidence yielded by the *NSTC*, for it confirms that autobiographical titles surged at mid-century, and so much so that publishers and novelists had begun to use autobiographical form as a way of adapting fiction to the literary market. In some measure, English fiction had always relied upon the intimacy and immediacy of first-person narration. *Robinson Crusoe* (1719), *Moll Flanders* (1722), *Pamela* (1740), and *Tristram Shandy* (1759–1767), among other early novels, had all imitated, satirized, and/or capitalized on life writing. But in the middle of the nineteenth century, the autobiographical novel flourished as never before. Instead of the twenty or so published each decade between 1815 and 1844, nearly 100 autobiographical novels appeared between 1845 and 1861. It is hard to know even now how much publishers and authors were responding to a contemporary appetite and how much they were provoking it, just as it is hard to know how much *David Copperfield* reflects Dickens's urgent psychological needs and how much it reflects his urgent desire to please readers. What is more certain is that mid-century readers devoured both real and imaginative autobiographical works, as if they craved a certain kind of narrative and imaginative contact with other lives. As Sutherland notes of Dickens's *All the Year Round*, founded in 1859, the magazine quickly "came to specialise in ... autobiographical narrative (four out of the first six full-length novels had 'I' narrators) and stories based on crime."⁵⁶ Dickens the businessman guaranteed the success of his self-funded magazine, that is, partly by paying writers who could satisfy readers' desire for complex, transgressive subjectivities narrated from the inside.

Reading autobiography had become perforce a mode of knowing the unfamiliar, of conceiving and arranging imaginatively the relations among people, between people and things, and between people, things, and emerging patterns of modern financial life. The period 1770–1800 saw the production of dozens of narratives nominally "written" by household commodities and animals, with narrators ranging from a corkscrew to a kite, a watch, a quire of paper, a black coat, and a lapdog, as well as explicitly monetary objects such as a half guinea, a halfpenny, a shilling, a silver penny, a sovereign, a twenty-pound banknote, and a Birmingham counterfeit coin.[57] Around 1850, writers began to reinvigorate this genre, publishing autobiographies of many impossible things, including a pencil case, a pot-rose, an arm-chair, and a doll.[58] In 1849 the anonymously written *Duodecimo: or, the Scribbler's Progress* offered an "insignificant little volume's" account of its own production, and an August 1851 issue of *Household Words* featured the catalogue to the Great Exhibition turning narrator in "The Catalogue's Account of Itself."[59] Still other works – most often children's books – offered educational self-narratives of animals, dogs most often but also a cat, a donkey, and a spider.[60] In 1857 Michael Westcott, who had published the "Autobiography of a White Cabbage Butterfly" a year earlier, began his *Autobiography of a Gossamer Spider* by having the spider observe:

> Autobiographies seem to be the order of the day; they are becoming as numerous as gnats in summer. But I do not despise them on account of their abundance; for I am of opinion – an opinion in which our whole tribe will concur – that a feast is preferable to a famine.[61]

The *British Quarterly Review* congratulated Westcott for capturing the mid-century mood. "Nothing," the reviewer wrote, "can be more likely to interest a reader in the habits of a creature than the exhibition of its daily life thrown into biographical form."[62] But the most striking such autobiographies were the highly stylized romances and exposés that "purported to take readers into the recesses of the Stock Exchange and the Bank of England and into the boardrooms of fraudulent companies" – that deployed autobiography as not just a commodified genre but also a vehicle for demystifying commodification as it emerged from the troubling complexities of finance capitalism and commodity culture.[63] Works such as William Forbes's *Memoirs of a Banking-house* (1859) and Edward Roswell's *Autobiography of a Joint-stock Company* (1861) show that autobiography had acquired a multilayered cultural function, bringing readers into contact with the alien or even abstract other and promising knowledge of that other by providing for the possibility of transaction and ownership, of treating the textual, self-narrating "I" as a commodity in the market.

If, as Peterson argues, Victorian autobiography attempted from the beginning to use established typologies of self-representation to understand the idiosyncrasies of individual lives amid the tumult of a rapidly changing culture, then the genre has always depended upon an act of imaginative and literal appropriation, an implicit desire to claim some other's life as the pattern for one's own. The genre is not just hermeneutic, then. It is acquisitive, rooted in a dynamic of narrative ownership that was not, until the nineteenth century, expressed in explicitly economic terms. Danahay writes in *A Community of One* that "[t]he creation of the word *autobiography* in the Romantic period signaled the birth of a new literary form" that "formalized the existence of the nineteenth-century subject … [in] the liminal space between the competing dualisms of the individual and the social."[64] The nineteenth-century subject was "formalized" between morocco boards in one or several volumes, as lavish quarto or demy octavo or in cheap monthly parts. Autobiography formalized the existence of the subject, that is, by inscribing it on the page and recalibrating its relation to the public sphere particularly, bringing subjectivity into explicit economic relations with a literary field shaped by the demands of modern publishing houses, circulating libraries, and a mass market. Moreover, it did so within a cultural field that was simultaneously developing other techniques – from copyright law to the painted portrait, and from the census schedule to the carte-de-visite – for giving identity textual form. In this respect, the proliferation of autobiography 1820–1860 is more than a critical feature of the Victorian literary market. It is an emblem of the growing porosity of the boundary between property and identity that developed during the first half of the century.

1.2 Autobiography and the Cultural Field

The emergent impulse to textualize and commodify the Victorian subject might best be understood as the effect of two overlapping sets of cultural pressures. One, rooted narrowly in the financial sphere, sought increasingly to cause material texts to function as embodiments of value; the other, rooted in the literary sphere but also in Victorian jurisprudence, the visual arts, and evolving governmental practices, tended increasingly to locate identity in material texts that codified its pervasion by economic concerns. In *Genres of the Credit Economy*, Poovey details the ways in which paper became central to British capitalism during the early nineteenth century.

She reminds us in particular that paper currency is a text, even a genre, whether or not we still choose to read it. Though banks and their predecessors, scriveners and goldsmiths, had long issued certain kinds of paper notes, and though "truly negotiable paper was first introduced" in 1694 with the creation of the Bank of England, paper money really proliferated after the 1797 Restriction Act removed the Bank's obligation to redeem notes with gold.[65] Provoked by fears that an impending French invasion might cause a run on the banks, the Act was meant to last just six weeks; instead, the Restriction remained until 1821, by which point "Britain was awash in paper money."[66] Radicals such as William Cobbett accused the Crown of passing off worthless rags to the gullible poor. But the system of paper currency grew and consolidated, culminating in the 1844 Bank Charter Act, which tied the volume of the Bank's note issue to its gold reserves and limited the right of other banks to issue notes, and in 1855 the Bank went one step further by standardizing the appearance of its printed notes.[67] These developments, Poovey argues, made the substitution of paper money for coins noncontroversial by driving Bank of England notes "beneath the horizon of cultural visibility" and permitting them to function as unambiguous embodiments of economic value.[68]

But currency was by no means the only kind of paper fueling the transition to finance capitalism. Even in the days of scriveners and goldsmiths, other written documents from receipts to conveyancing records had helped to indicate value and facilitate trade. By the early nineteenth century, England's was increasingly a credit economy, dependent upon paper instruments such as bills of exchange, accommodation bills, checks, and IOUs that allowed value to change hands even when gold did not.[69] According to one estimate, in 1840 alone "the leading London banks ... paid bills of exchange amounting to more than one billion pounds."[70] Among the larger London firms, book accounting began to replace cash transactions, "mak[ing] the economy work by substituting writing for material objects."[71] As the financial journalist William Jevons described matters in 1875:

> In a room of moderate dimensions, entered from a narrow passage running from the post-office in King William Street across to Lombard Street, debts to the average amount of nearly twenty millions sterling per day are liquidated without the use of a single coin or bank-note. In the classic financial neighbourhood of Lombard Street, and even in this very chamber, the system of paper commerce has been brought nearly to perfection.[72]

Through a series of new laws that culminated in the 1856 Joint Stock Companies Act, Parliament also expanded possibilities for incorporation and provided for limited liability for shareholders, ushering in modern forms of investment and finance.[73] Kornbluh writes that this new economy was characterized by deferral and metalepsis, in which abstractions appeared as concretes and effects as causes.[74] The truly crucial abstraction was paper money, which Marx described around this time as "all other commodities divested of their shape, the product of their universal alienation."[75] To put it as Mark Rose does, this was the period during which money "became fantasmic, a matter of the circulation of signs abstracted from their material basis."[76]

Yet as capitalism's paper instruments lost their presumptive relation to a material basis, they acquired a new kind of rootedness in Victorian identity. The mundane realities of checks and bills of exchange had always required at least a signature to make them negotiable, so that each bill "carried its own history on its back."[77] Early on this was also the case, in a way, for paper currency, since one's willingness to accept a bank's note depended upon one's familiarity with the note's giver, the bank that the note drew upon, and whether both had a good name in the community. In the secondary market, moreover, accommodation bills and checks could always be bought for less than their face value, and the amount that a broker would pay typically depended on both the state of the bill market at the time and the quality of the signatures endorsing the bill.[78] Nor did joint-stock incorporation or limited liability alter immediately the structure of Victorian companies or their economic transactions. Kornbluh's work emphasizes the erosion of personal responsibility and the gradual refiguration of the corporation as a "person," but Hunt notes that limited liability ventures multiplied slowly during the century and that family partnerships remained the dominant form of business organization.[79] Victorian businesses thus continued to invest in "character" in matters of hiring, credit, and new economic relationships, as evidenced in the "information books (also called character books), which recorded testimonials, hearsay, and observational notes about ... business clients and associates, especially potential ones."[80] Throughout the century, reports to investors typically bore the names of company officials, and in 1836 the *Edinburgh Review* suggested that joint-stock banks could encourage trust by publishing the names and addresses of directors.[81]

These considerations illustrate two key features of the finance capitalism that evolved during the middle of the nineteenth century. First, it relied on the proliferation of textual instruments that functioned as "values" and commodities irrespective of any particular relationship with gold, and that permitted the transfer of wealth through the intervention of numerical entries and signatures on a page. Second, it required – or at least encouraged – the textualization of identity, not just in the form of the signature but also in the implication that intangibilities such as reputation, aptitude, and integrity could be imparted to texts, and that such texts allowed subjectivity to circulate as a material object. A consequence, as Sara Malton has argued in her work on Victorian forgery, is that the paper tools that permitted the expansion of finance capitalism engaged "broader questions of epistemology and the constitution of authentic identity and origins."[82] If joint-stock ventures were often "made" by the directors, solicitors, and investors whose names appeared on prospectuses and reports, Victorian financiers were often "made" by the papers to which they put their names. During the 1840s George Hudson, the "Railway King," inspired confidence in innumerable railway schemes just by lending them his name and even attained – however fleetingly – a position as a leading capitalist, society man, and Member of Parliament. He did so mainly by appearing as the director of dozens of railways, including the Newcastle and Darlington, York and North Midland, Brandling, Whitby and Pickering, Leeds and Selby, and Leeds and Bradford lines. By 1848 he controlled nearly one-third of England's 5,000 miles of rail.[83] Yet he was more entirely a textual production than even prospectuses and reports could suggest, for his reputedly immense wealth turned out to be nothing but cooked books, fraudulent shareholding, and circular contracts in which some of his companies purchased overpriced services and materials from others. Really, Hudson had not a fortune but an estimated liability of £750,000.[84] Like Dickens's Mr. Merdle and Trollope's Augustus Melmotte, he was a paper man, a financial construct premised upon an unlimited number of texts.

The conjunction of textuality, subjectivity, and commodity that characterized England's financial sector at mid-century had its literary corollary in the gradual elaboration of copyright law that stimulated autobiography's rise. The watershed moment, according to Rose, came in the 1774 case of *Donaldson v. Becket*, which generally ended perpetual copyright in favor of a fourteen-year term from the date of publication.[85] Brought by Alexander Donaldson, a Scots bookseller who had expanded his reprint business to London, the suit aimed to end the London booksellers' monopolies on works by ancient writers as well as recent standards by authors such as Shakespeare, Milton, Swift, Pope, and Defoe. The case broke the stranglehold of the London booksellers and the Stationers' Company, triggering the collapse of both the old patronage model of literary production and the several acts that had censored and delimited the production and dissemination of texts. In the decades after the 1774 decision, the defeated booksellers worked tirelessly to extend the period of copyright: to twenty-eight years in 1808, to the life of the author in 1814, and to the author's life plus seven years or to forty-two years from publication (whichever was longer) in 1842.[86] Lost amid the booksellers' continual wrangling over the term of copyright is the fact that *Donaldson v. Becket* came about in part because of decades of agitation by authors, not booksellers, regarding their right of property in their works.

The key change implied by the revised copyright law had less to do with the term of copyright than with an evolving sense of what kind of "property" inhered in literary works. For centuries, copyright had depended upon physical possession of the manuscript which, once acquired, could be used indefinitely to produce and profit from copies of an author's work. But *Donaldson v. Becket* – chief among several cases treating copyright during the eighteenth century – asserted that the property guaranteed by copyright derived from the work's individuality of thought and expression and thus was a material and idiosyncratic manifestation of the author's genius.[87] Under this revised idea of copyright "[t]he basis of literary property ... was not just labor but 'personality'," such that the literary work appeared as "the objectification of a writer's self ... [and] the commodity that changed hands when a bookseller purchased a manuscript or when a reader purchased a book was as much personality as ink and paper."[88] For the first time, the relations between authors and readers appeared as "intimate mutual relationships between privatized individuals," for "the subjectivity that had become fit to print, had in fact become the literature appealing to a wide public of readers."[89] Moreover, this shift was neither divinely nor philosophically inspired. It was driven by the literary market: by wrangling over sales and editions, by changes in technology, by the gradual spread of literacy, by innovations in publishing format, and by the transformation of printing and bookselling.

Autobiography proliferated partly as a culmination of this new logic of copyright, which transformed not just the utterances of authors but also authors themselves into the consumable products of the rising capitalist age. Danahay likewise has written that "autobiography ... was created in tandem with the laws of individual ownership that underlie the law of copyright."[90] For Victorian identity, the implications of this correlation are profound. Rose argues that one effect of the increasingly close identification of authors with their written works during the nineteenth century appears to have been an emergent tendency to read those works in the context of their authors' biographies, and Clinton Machann notes that the protagonists of Victorian autobiographies, when they are literary figures, came over time "to be identified with the selfhood or personality of the author as expressed not only in the autobiography itself but in earlier published works."[91] Literary autobiographers came to be regarded, in other words, as accumulations of their written texts, and the texts came to be regarded as a cumulative body of life writing. Autobiography rose from the ideological and imaginative pressures engendered by copyright, giving material form to what we might call the conceptual collapse of identity into the realm of textuality. And it did so at an auspicious moment, when authors were for the first time writing their works for a modernizing market increasingly responsive to larger readerships and increasingly aware of the commodity status of the book. Paradoxically, after a century of legal tussles, Romantic and early-Victorian authors secured rights of property in their works at the cost of eroding the notion that subjectivity might exist apart from commodity culture and capitalist exchange.

Particularly during the Romantic period, when copyright terms were short, many authors gladly encouraged or deliberately created a close identification between themselves and their works for the sake of financial gain. After *Donaldson v. Becket*, revisions of old works could qualify as new intellectual property if they differed substantially enough from the originals.[92] Consequently, Romantic poets adopted "an additive strategy to publishing poems and volumes of poetry," renewing copyright by "letting their corpus grow and evolve through gradually enlarged editions of complete works."[93] During the first four decades of the nineteenth century, when the copyright term extended at most through the life of the author, writers from Wordsworth to Scott to Southey adopted this strategy. Yet revisions and minor additions, while enough to extend copyright, did not necessarily encourage sales. Poets and publishers thus turned – as Murray had with Crabbe – to memoirs, letters, and autobiographical forms to renew the appeal of worn out works. Between 1819 and 1833, Anna Letitia Barbauld, William Cowper, Robert Fergusson, and Elizabeth Inchbald all issued new editions of their works with passages of autobiography, and Scott, who needed money badly and was, according to one reviewer, "a poet with all the thrifty calculations of a merchant," wrote "a connected history of his literary career" for his *Poetical Works*.[94] In 1837 Southey began preparing a ten-volume edition of his works to help Longmans combat the sale of a pirated French edition.[95] Key among his additions: an autobiographical preface to each volume describing the conditions under which he had written selected poems.[96]

But perhaps the best example of this traffic in poetry and autobiography comes from Wordsworth, who resisted publishing *The Prelude* for more than forty years, mainly so that it could remain under copyright for as long as possible to benefit his heirs. He had completed *The Prelude* in thirteen books as early as 1805 and revealed as much a decade later in his preface to *The Excursion* (1814), where he explained that he would not publish his autobiographical poem until he had completed a companion prose work called *The Recluse*.[97] Although it became increasingly clear that Wordsworth would not finish *The Recluse* – and although he continued to revise his poems right up to the publication of his final authorized edition in 1849–1850 – he withheld publication of *The Prelude* until the end, when it was discovered in perfect order for posthumous publication.[98] In the case of a poet who had taken a keen interest in debates over copyright during the 1830s, this hardly seems accidental.[99] On the contrary, he was especially canny about financial arrangements for his works during the last decades of his life and routinely proposed to his equally shrewd publisher, Edward Moxon, new formats and possibilities for the publication of his works. Once, Wordsworth even asked Moxon to receive in his London shop "the names of 'such persons as it *might* suit' to purchase at a guinea the [Henry] Pickersgill portrait of himself" since a subscription list would allow him and Pickersgill to seek an engraver for a potentially lucrative print.[100] With the print – as with *The Prelude* – Wordsworth appears to have been more concerned with his financial than his literary legacy. And it is this dual sense of "legacy" that gets to the heart of things: Wordsworth meant his masterpiece autobiographical poem – his intimate textualization of his poetic subjectivity – as both an artistic and material bestowal, an exemplary expression of the logic of copyright.

The example of Wordsworth, Moxon, and Pickersgill reminds us that the impulse to textualize identity extended beyond autobiography – and beyond literary discourse – into other cultural spheres. By the 1830s, the engraving and reproduction of portraits was so common that almost every published book by a noted author featured a portrait on the frontispiece, and often an engraving of the author's autograph. But these practices originated in older textual forms that had long bridged the gap between subject, text, and exchange. In her work on British portraiture, Marcia Pointon traces the enthusiasm for painting "heads" to the centuries-old use of heads on coins and medals, which served in their own time to legitimate state power by disseminating images of the monarch, military heroes, and members of the ruling class. But by the mid-1700s, coins and medals served a purpose allied more closely to the cultural functions of copyright and autobiography. In 1747 Joseph Ames, a collector of portraits and coins and Fellow of the Society of Antiquaries, published *A Catalogue of British Heads* documenting 2,000 engraved portraits, and James Granger expanded this work in 1769 with his *Biographical History of England from Egbert the Great to the Revolution*, which combined biography and visual representation.[101] First published in two volumes, *Biographical History* expanded to four in 1775 and six in 1824, and during the 1790s it was supplemented by the popular offerings *The Biographical Magazine* (1794), *The Biographical Mirror* (1795), and *The British Cabinet* (1799), all of which combined biography and portraiture to construct notable subjects from England's past.[102]

Granger stimulated so great an interest in notable portraits that he helped to make the practice of clipping heads from books commonplace by the turn of the century, driving the price of books that contained engraved portraits to five times their original value and leaving few of them unmutilated.[103] During the Romantic period, it became common for owners of books to clip printed portraits of authors from a biographical compilation in order to insert them onto the title pages of their works, or to clip several related heads – the Lake poets, Tory leaders, or famous actresses – or even apparently unrelated ones and arrange them as the clipper saw fit, creating new associations through their proximity to one another or to clippings from newspapers or journals. Each "grangerized" volume bespoke a desire to acquire and arrange others' identities to suit the clipper's idiosyncratic notions of meaning. As late as 1828, the fencing master Henry Angelo was still bemoaning the frenzy for clippable heads, and in 1829 Charles John Smith reinvigorated the craze by publishing *Autographs of Royal, Noble, and Illustrious Persons*, in which he argued that autographs, too, could be used to read the subjectivities of the past, particularly in the cases of figures for whom portraits did not exist.[104] Thereafter, autographs became "an integral part of the nascent National Portrait Gallery" and took their place alongside portraits at the museum.[105] Thus autographs joined the growing number of texts that were understood to materialize subjectivity, reconstituting it as an object of exchange.

Painted portraits served this function, too, particularly between 1780 and 1840 when portraiture held a central position among England's visual arts. In 1780, 44 percent of the paintings displayed by the Royal Academy in the Great Room at Somerset House were portraits, and while this figure dropped slightly at the end of the century, it rose again to 46 percent in 1829 even though the total number of works displayed more than doubled during these years.[106] During the 1780s, engravers displayed prints in the lower rooms of the Academy for the first time, and these also came to be dominated by portraits by the 1830s.[107] This is not to say that critics or painters regarded the genre highly. On the contrary, the Royal Academy displayed portraits for the same reason that artists painted them: they were immensely popular, and more likely than other genres to bring patrons to the doors. Every president of the Royal Academy from Sir Joshua Reynolds to Martin Archer Shee made his living primarily from portrait painting, as did most other professional artists.[108] In this sense, as David Solkin observes, the Academy exhibitions "operat[ed] as both a highly profitable spectacle and a marketplace for expensive luxury goods" where "the pretensions of artists to disinterested liberality came into open conflict time and again with the fiercely competitive nature of their trade."[109] (There was no such conflict for the innumerable invisible portraitists who painted miniatures, etched in glass, or worked in other cheap popular forms.) In 1820 the interest in portraiture led the British Institution for Promoting the Fine Arts to arrange an exhibition of 183 privately owned portraits, and a similar exhibition took place in 1846; a decade later England founded its National Portrait Gallery – "a phenomenon," Pointon notes, "exclusive to the industrialized west ... and to the modern period commencing around the mid-nineteenth century."[110] The interest in portraiture crested, that is, alongside the proliferation of autobiographies, the rise of finance capitalism, and the emergence of other techniques for making identity a textual thing.

Autobiography and portraiture are not identical, nor do they textualize subjectivity in quite the same way. Most obviously, portraiture does not emanate from the *autos* of self-narrative and cannot claim autobiography's authority for representing the self intimately or directly. Yet Pointon argues that portraiture's popularity during this period depended less upon its reproduction of physical appearance than its ability "to bridge the chasm between material existence and the interiority of the individual," and between individual experience and social forms of knowledge.[111] While portraits functioned allegorically during the seventeenth and early eighteenth centuries by putting their subjects in classical dress or amid typological scenes, Romantic viewers judged them by whether they were "like" their sitter, in terms of both physical resemblance and intangible attributes of character. Pointon thus concludes that "[t]he portrait has no unproblematic referent; it cannot be explained as a correlative to the text of a subject's life."[112] This is also true of autobiography, since its performative function – as well as its collaborative production by author, editor, compositor, bookbinder, and the many others who transform the manuscript into a material, disseminable text – means that its apparent intimacy is always mitigated by the work's status as an object of mechanical reproduction. Once it left the domain of the family memoir and spiritual record, autobiography entered a complex social space as both a commodified object shaped discursively and materially by market demands and a textualized subjectivity that signifies only in the act of going public and entering the dynamics of economic exchange. Like a portrait painted for an individual patron but later launched upon the market, the commercialized autobiography traded familial, or at least private, affiliations for commodity status and public consumption. It became a material, alienable form of subjectivity. As Fredric Jameson says of portraits – in words worthy of *Great Expectations'* Mr. Wemmick – in a commodifying age the "concrete activity" of looking at a portrait is "comfortably replaced by the act of taking possession of it and converting it into a form of portable property."[113]

The proliferation of portraits thus signified in many of the same ways as the proliferation of autobiography – the more so because, of all the genres of painting, it was the most integrated into modern systems of production and exchange. This may seem paradoxical, since portraits were the most likely to be commissioned, so that they rarely circulated as commodities until long after they were produced. Most of the ones displayed at the Royal Academy, in fact, had already been paid for; their display was not a matter of selling them but rather of transforming painting and sitter into advertisements for the artist's work.[114] When portraits did reach the open market, they tended to be worth less than paintings of other kinds since, as David Mannings explains, "While pictures of Our Lady, or of boys playing violins, could be considered 'rare pieces of art', a likeness of someone else's great-aunt was in a sense too specific and personal."[115] Yet this does not mean that portraiture was divorced from marketplace demands. On the contrary, the second half of the eighteenth century saw portraitists abandon the traditional patronage model and enter a "competitive free-for-all fuelled by anonymous and impersonal commercial demands."[116] Portraits did not quite circulate, but artists did, for working as a portraitist "implicated the artist as producer in a dense web of commerce and ideology" that depended as much on business acumen as on skill at taking a likeness.[117] During the 1750s Allan Ramsey, Thomas Hudson, and Sir Joshua Reynolds competed with one another and with other artists for London clients, setting their prices against both the demand for portraits and the ready supply of artists to paint them; by the 1780s artists had more or less standardized prices according to the format and dimensions of their work.[118] The traffic in portraits also created burgeoning secondary markets for everything from brushes to frames to apprentices, so that the successful portraitist found himself "at the centre of a flourishing industry, backed by other crafts and businesses" and with the "Royal Academy as his chief publicity agent" – this last, even though many Academicians regarded portraits as a threat to their cultural hegemony because they had entered common usage in decorative and utilitarian objects.[119]

By the time autobiographical production peaked in the 1850s, the textualizing and commodifying functions of portraiture were also being assumed by the photograph, mainly in the form of the mass-produced carte-de-visite, which imposed upon Victorian visual representation many of the same industrial exigencies that characterized book publishing. Originating in a method patented by the Frenchman André Adolphe-Eugéne Disdéri in 1854, cartes-de-visite quickly became a global phenomenon that persisted into the early twentieth century. Disdéri's invention allowed twelve identical photographs to be produced as a single sheet. Owing to the popular appeal of the practice, the number of photographic firms in London quadrupled between 1855 and 1864, and similar proliferations occurred in Liverpool, Manchester, and Aberdeen.[120] In 1862 alone, as many as 105 million cartes were produced in England.[121] This "cartomania," as Geoffrey Batchen calls it, was "the first major eruption of mass reproduction within the practice of photography" and expanded the commodity trade in visual images to a mass market that even cheap engravings and prints had never reached.[122] Cartes did not, though, quite democratize photographic images: at twelve shillings per dozen, they remained well beyond the means of those in the working class.[123] But they did announce the arrival of middle-class Victorian subjects, on a large scale, to the problems of textuality, identity, and commodity that undergirded autobiographical production. Cartes-de-visite belonged unequivocally to England's rising capitalism, not only because they materialized class consciousness and aspiration but because photography became itself a massive industry, consuming resources, producing manufactures, provoking exchange, and employing legions of Britons in establishments that ranged from high-end studios to small workshops like those of other manufacturer-retailers such as tailors, butchers, and bakers.[124] By 1861, more than 2,500 photographers and photographic assistants were plying their trade in England, and the production of those tens of millions of cartes in 1862 consumed six million egg whites, fifteen tons of silver nitrate, 1/3 of a ton of terchloride of gold, and 14,000 reams of paper.[125]

Batchen points out that the depressing uniformity of cartes-de-visite has tempted most modern scholars to dismiss them as unworthy of attentive reading, though Disdéri did not regard his innovation as purely technical. In his 1853 *Manuel* for photography, Disdéri wrote of the need for the photographer "to deduce who the subject is . . . his character, his intimate life, his habits; the photographer must do more than photograph, he must 'biographe'."[126] Probably few mass-producers of cartes aspired to any such thing. But the cultural and imaginative implications of cartes-de-visite were nevertheless complex. As Batchen writes:

> What happens when a photograph of Queen Victoria is distributed in thousands of identical copies, finding its way into the homes and hands of her subjects in the form of a cheap picture? It simultaneously distances her (by turning her into a reproduction) and brings her closer (by dislodging her former "cult value"). . . . Like the endlessly reproduced *Mona Lisa*, Victoria becomes more, rather than less, revered by [her] subjects but at the price of her own commodification. . . . She becomes image, an imitation of herself, a ghostly ideological construct.[127]

The carte-de-visite images of Victoria and the royal family that began circulating widely at this time thus had conflicting effects, on the one hand disseminating carefully cultivated images meant to "expose" the intimacy of their family life, and on the other subjecting Victoria to the laws of production, ownership, and exchange that governed other commodity texts. Illegal copies of the images got into circulation and provoked prosecutions for copyright infringement.[128] In other instances the dissemination of Victoria's image inserted her into new, often undesirable social relations since the windows of photographic shops might place her near "some louche individual."[129] The cartes of average Victorians, too, are sites of ideological construction, in which aspirants to bourgeois respectability belie their interiority even as they submit to the depressing regularity of the genre. The most nondescript cartes-de-visite, Batchen argues, show people trying to look middle class, "learning how to look like themselves."[130] Such cartes-de-visite do not so much void subjectivity as refigure it to suit capitalist demands, textualizing a truth to which the subject conforms and aspires.

As the examples of copyright, portraiture, and cartes-de-visite all suggest, the ideological pressures that converged in autobiography belonged to a wider cultural field that was creating and authorizing an array of practices for textualizing and commodifying Victorian identity. A cornerstone of these developments was the creation of the General Register Office (GRO) in 1836 to direct a centralized and secularized system of civil registry to replace the longstanding practice of leaving birth, marriage, and death records in the hands of local officers of the Church. By the early nineteenth century, many in Parliament recognized that these local records could be patchy and inaccurate, especially in areas with high numbers of Dissenters who did not undergo religious rites in the Church and thus might never appear in the local registers. In an era defined by a new emphasis on collecting and using numerical data about the population in order to "establish a scientific basis for social policy," inaccurate parish records were obstacles to effective governance.[131] Yet the desire for centralized and complete information about England's subjects was motivated from the start, too, by commercial considerations. In 1834 the competing bills proposing the creation of the GRO both intended it to be only a registry of deeds and wills so that it might deal with problems of inheritance and "the Law of Real Property."[132] These were defeated, and the proposed purpose of the GRO changed by the time Parliament authorized it two years later. But arguments favoring the GRO still stood partly on the grounds that a centralized civil registry would allow the Crown to compile reliable mortality statistics and so enable life assurance societies to create better actuarial tables.[133] The first Registrar-General, Thomas Lister, touted this function in his inaugural annual report in 1839, where he wrote that such statistics were "among the most important materials" the GRO could supply since they allowed one to deduce "the true principles on which should be founded the systems of life annuities and of life assurance."[134] The creation of the GRO this provided a broad legal basis for a key development: British identity came for the first time to be constituted formally in a growing tissue of official texts that reified the subject's entanglement in the economic sphere.

This became especially clear when the GRO assumed command of the decennial census in 1841 and attempted to use it, for the first time, to collect not just aggregate data but also the names of every man, woman, and child in England and Wales. The Crown had conducted the first census in 1801 under the auspices of the 1800 Census Act, which called for local Overseers of the Poor to prepare returns and provide them to the Home Office. Overseers did not have to give names; they needed only to give the total number of people living in the parish, the number of houses occupied and unoccupied, and the number of workers participating in agriculture, trade or manufacture, or some "other" form of employment.[135] In subsequent censuses some questions changed – for instance, in 1821 when the Crown added questions about the age structure of households, again to improve the actuarial tables – but the mechanism for collecting did not.[136] With the GRO in place in 1841, however, responsibility for the census passed to Lister, with his newly defined registration districts and armada of civil servants. Urged along by the London Statistical Society, who advocated a more comprehensive array of questions and, above all, "enumeration *by names*" to provide "security against fallacious returns," Lister revised the procedures and the schedule of questions.[137] For the first time, the census passed literally into the hands of householders, who received a blank schedule during the week before census day, completed it on census day, then returned it to the enumerators who compiled the information the Crown required. That information included the name, age, gender, country of birth, and "profession, trade, [or] employment" of every person in the household.[138]

One result of these innovations, Kathrin Levitan writes, was to shift the focus for the first time "from returns of communities to returns of individuals."[139] Another was to deepen and complicate the link that the census forged between individual identity and economic concerns. The Crown's desire for a census had always been motivated partly by economics, even in the case of the Domesday Book prepared for William the Conqueror in 1086. Historians sometimes describe Domesday as the first rudimentary attempt at a census, but it was less a register of William's subjects than a material reckoning up, a "survey of landholding" in which "[p]eople were only mentioned as appendages to the land, and even then in an incomplete manner."[140] Enthusiasm for a modern census emerged in the 1790s largely due to Malthusian anxieties about population growth and food shortages, which might be understood better, or ameliorated, if the nation could count its subjects.[141] The 1841 census conducted by the GRO particularized these considerations, refiguring each identity as a set of textual and economic negotiations. At mid-century, the GRO's reports on censuses suggested that some parents inflated the ages of children between ten and thirteen to enable them to work despite the restrictions set down by the Factory Acts or, in the case of girls, to qualify them for domestic service, and also that young domestic servants may have exaggerated their age to command higher pay.[142] At the other end of the spectrum, the reports worried that older working-class men might have been tempted to describe themselves as sixty or more to qualify for outdoor relief under the poor law, while middle-class ones may have rounded their age down to "ward off the threat of retirement."[143] In still other cases, the GRO suspected that relatively young women had "depressed their ages" to keep from being regarded as spinsters, thus preserving a kind of sexual currency that kept them relevant in the marriage market.[144]

Though Christopher Kent and Levitan acknowledge the elaboration of the GRO's questions, they downplay the significance of its textualization of individual identities. Kent writes that the detailed information collected by the enumerators "was not used for identity-fixing or individualizing purposes," while Levitan argues that it served principally to make the complexity of Victorian demographics visible to contemporary observers by obliging the Crown to fit individuals into distinct but overlapping groups in order to describe the nation.[145] Though "it asked for specific and intimate details about individual people," she remarks, the census "was abstract, vast, and anonymous."[146] Abstract and vast, yes, but not exactly anonymous, and the implications for individuals were real. Respondents who misrepresented their age obviously understood the potential economic repercussions of their replies despite the GRO's routine assurances that it would not disclose individuals' information. These anxieties make sense when one considers that the GRO typically hired local enumerators to assist with the collection of census schedules – and, often, to help illiterate householders complete them – and that the enumerators tended to come from the literate class of local clergymen, teachers, and government officials. Householders had reason to worry, since completing a return meant disclosing details to employers, magistrates, tax collectors, and others tasked with formalizing the relation between individual identity and economic value. After 1841, it meant doing so longitudinally, providing for the first time for the possibility that an individual would be recorded *by name* across multiple censuses, where she or he appeared textually as a chronological series of residences, occupations, ages, and familial relations. By giving identity a concrete narrative arc, the Crown could subject it to state power. Lies told to secure better work or higher wages might eventually be detected and punished, if not by a magistrate then by an employer, if not now then later. In 1871 census officials even broke their promise of privacy, releasing the names of all children aged three to thirteen to aid enforcement of the 1870 Education Act, and in 1881, police in Louth used the handwriting on a census schedule to identify and prosecute the sender of a threatening letter.[147]

The census thus epitomized the tendency to textualize and economize identity that undergirded other contemporary practices and reforms, from Henry Mayhew's sociological work in *London Labour and the London Poor* (1851) to new regulations involving licensure, divorce, and criminal law. In 1830 Parliament revised laws regarding the sale of alcohol to require that any person running even a simple beer shop appear on the local tax rolls.[148] And in 1849 the Bankrupt Law Consolidation Act introduced a new system for classifying discharged debtors, awarding each a certificate indicating whether his conduct in cleaning up his affairs had been satisfactory and making it a felony to "destroy, alter, mutilate, or falsify any of his Books, Papers, Writings, or Securities."[149] The law illustrates the many texts that constituted subjectivity at mid-century: records and certificates that could testify to legal identity and character, but also bills, receipts, account-books, IOUs, and other financial papers that reified and delineated the subject's relation to the capitalist sphere. The 1857 Matrimonial Causes Act also enacted this relation between subjectivity and textuality by encouraging private detectives to assemble the scraps of evidence necessary to tell excruciatingly private stories – of adultery, illegitimacy, bigamy, and other sexual scandal – in order to "fix" subjectivity as the sum of a diverse textual record that signified in matters of property and patrilineage. Christine Krueger argues that such legal developments were driven by the growing centralization of the courts, which prompted authorities to find "new economic and social practices ... to reinstate the personal engagement that had characterized local justice."[150] Autobiography in the form of testimony and sworn affidavits was crucial in this effort. In this sense, she writes, Victorian autobiography, the Victorian novel, and Victorian legal commentary all converged at interrelated questions of discursive and aesthetic representation.[151]

In "Railway Nightmares," written for *Household Words* in 1858, John Hollingshead captures perfectly the tenor of these textualizing reforms in a description of the absurdities involved in buying a single ticket to travel on "the Great Deadlock line, which has now been taken under the permanent management of the Government":

> The forms of application for tickets are much more elaborate than the old rude method of simply paying your money ... Every man who wishes to go to Burygold, or any intermediate station, must apply for a printed form; such application to be countersigned by at least one respectable house-keeper. The form has then to be filled up according to certain ample printed directions, which occupy about a folio page and a half. The man ... must state his age; must say whether he is a Dissenter or a Church of England man; must state whether he is a housekeeper or a lodger; if the first, how long he has been one; if the second, of what degree; must state whether he has been vaccinated; whether he has had the measles; whether he has any tendency to lunacy, or whether his parents have ever exhibited that tendency; must say whether he has ever been to Burygold, or to any intermediate station, before, and if so, how many times, and upon what dates,

and upon what business; must state what is his present object in going to Burygold, and how long he is likely to stay ... must state the number of his family (if any), and the ages of his wife and children respectively; and must send this return in, accompanied by a letter of application, written upon folio foolscap with a margin, and addressed to the Right Honorable the Duke of Stokers, Governor-General of the Great Royal Deadlock Railway.[152]

The narrator, we learn, has gone bankrupt investing in the railways. But the procedure for railway ticketing, not bankruptcy, is the titular "nightmare." Situated somewhere between the census schedule and a police interrogation, the "cost" of traveling on the Great Deadlock line is an autobiographical record, a textual capitulation to the requirements of the Crown. Hurtling at top speed on the great engine of Victorian capitalism requires that he textualize his subjectivity, transforming it into the great alienable commodity that structures capitalist desire.

But the quintessential illustration of this demand may be the creation of England's Civil Service examination in 1855 in the wake of the Northcote-Trevelyan Report. The purpose of the exam was, in theory, to erode longstanding practices of nepotism and patronage by determining via competition whether those who sought to work for the government were those best qualified to do so. For most positions, candidates were examined in arithmetic, English grammar and composition, history, geography, and penmanship and spelling, while positions in the Treasury required candidates to exhibit additional competencies in Euclid and in Latin, French, German, or Italian.[153] The declared intent was to arrive at an objective measure of intellectual aptitude, though some questions seem rather to explore political leanings. A "Geography" question on the first exam in 1855, for instance, asked exam-takers to name seven of England's colonies – easy enough – and then to "specify wherein their political and commercial importance," a task rife with ideological possibilities and implications.[154] More to the point, the exam served generally to situate the contents of the individual mind within a matrix of economic value. As Jennifer Ruth points out, even an "inferior but successful exam-taker" could at least secure a position exempt from manual labor and mechanical production.[155] Yet the exam-taker entered upon an economic world more fraught than the one he was leaving behind since "[t]he intellectual laborer must be able (at least figuratively) to alienate his personality, or he has nothing to sell."[156] In the form of the civil service examination, the state figured "subject formation ... as an economic process" for the first time and "established a relationship between the subject and the state [that was] mediated by exchange."[157]

These acts of government-sanctioned textualization – rooted, as they were, in the impulses that drove other contemporary textual proliferations – reconstituted the ideological dynamics of Victorian autobiography, transforming identity into a material thing and exposing it to the requirements of ownership and exchange. In his fascinating account of Victorian London's economic transformation, Garrett Ziegler cites a different piece by Hollingshead, "The City of Unlimited Paper," which appeared some months prior to "Railway Nightmares" and imagines Londoners as subjects who have become pure texts under finance capitalism:

> Within a certain circle, of which the Royal Exchange is the centre, lie the ruins of a great paper city. Its rulers – solid and substantial as they appear to the eye – are made of paper. They ride in paper carriages; they marry paper wives, and unto them are born paper children; their food is paper, their thoughts are paper, and all they touch is transformed to paper. They buy paper and they sell paper; they borrow paper, and they lend paper, – a paper that shrinks and withers in the grasp like the leaves of the sensitive plant; and the stately-looking palaces in which they live and trade are built of paper...[158]

Ziegler argues that Hollingshead's essay offers a mode of representation that became common for mid-century journalists and novelists, who wrote often of the modern City as having gone "from a private space of lived experience to a public space of financial labor."[159] Financial writers such as David Morier Evans and novelists such as Dickens portrayed the City as a haunted necropolis even though, as Ziegler points out, its population remained fairly stable through the end of the century. Such narratives were both gross inaccuracies and rhetorical necessities, part of a representational strategy that treated the City as a site of economic labor filled with currencies, shares, account-books, and other paper forms rather than with desiring subjects leading vital biological and emotional lives.

In her recent study of Charlotte Riddell's "City novels," mostly published 1856–1875, Silvana Colella points out that not all Victorian writers treated the City as Hollingshead did and argues further that the popularity of these novels – centered upon the daily realities of middle-class professional life – offer "evidence that in the imagination and perceptions of Victorian observers finance had not yet supplanted the City's more traditional functions."[160] Yet Hollingshead's account of paper men living near the Royal Exchange in 1857 may have less to do with the contemporary realities of City life than with the imaginative force of the period's transformation of identity from an interior, immaterial thing – rooted in intellect, moral fiber, emotion, memory, and so on – into a contingent, contested, and commodified accumulation of texts. Amid the incursions of autobiography, finance capitalism, copyright law, portraiture, photography, the census, and the examination, among other things, Victorian identity had become textual, not spectral or ghostly but all-too-material, indistinguishable from other paper forms, and subject finally to the obligations that capitalism places upon all objects of exchange. In *History and Class Consciousness* (1971), Georg Lukács argues that the "commodity relation ... stamps its imprint upon the whole consciousness of man" such that "his qualities and abilities are no longer an organic part of his personality, they are things which he can 'own' or 'dispose of' like the various objects of the external world."[161] Autobiography and its corollaries reified this commodity relation during the Victorian period by giving subjectivity material form, making it an alienable object of mass production and exchange and exposing it in complicated ways to the operation of the market. The form of identity concretized by autobiography figured the subject as both consciousness and commodity. It eroded the boundary between identity and property, between psychological and economic life. In the process, it created deep cultural anxieties that played out in contemporary commentary on autobiography and – more crucially, and with greater symbolic and ideological force – in the mid-century Victorian novel.

1.3 Autobiography and Anxiety

Not all Victorian reviewers responded to autobiography with the same intense irritation that Lockhart expressed in 1827. But amid the nuances and disagreements that characterized the reviews, one trend stands out: their hostility passed gradually from a general distaste for the practice of "turning a penny" through life writing to specific concerns about the ways in which autobiography disrupted identity by making it into an object of exchange. Even during the 1820s, not all reviewers responded to autobiography so ferociously as Lockhart. On the contrary, some admitted the allure of autobiography and even sanctioned the genre by placing it within the "old Horatian formula from the *Ars Poetica*, pleasure and use," even if they acknowledged that autobiography often turned "pleasure" into "prurience, voyeurism, or gossip" and "use" into "trivial and ephemeral, if not ... actually immoral" knowledge.[162] Implicit was a sense, however dubious, that an autobiography by a respectable person (as distinct from a gallows confession) reflected real identity. As an *Edinburgh Magazine* reviewer put it, "when a man sits down to write his own story, he unavoidably retraces the course of his former thoughts and feelings, and thus puts down a full confession upon paper, without thinking much of the public to whom it is nominally addressed."[163] He continued:

> Indeed, we might cite, more or less, almost every memoir of the modern times, in support of their truth; for the facility which printing gives to publications of all sorts, has let in a torrent of Private Memoirs and Letters, which throw a much clearer and steadier light on individual character, and on the interior of private society, than was ever before enjoyed.[164]

If the great Rousseau appalled readers with his autobiography, it was because he himself was appalling, not because he thought of titillating readers. Perhaps because early autobiographers were mostly great men or religious zealots, early reviewers placed considerable faith in the genre's intention to account honestly for the formation of the author's idiosyncratic self.

But this did little to mollify those who railed against the genre's violation of privacy and the deplorable reading tastes that were making it a commercial force. A March 1828 *London Magazine* review called the insatiable appetite for autobiographies "a disease of our times," sneering at "the countless thousands who derive wit and wisdom from circulating libraries" and pry so relentlessly into the life of the "man of genius" that they become as degradingly familiar with his habits as if they were "his 'valet-de-chambre'."[165] "This," the reviewer continued, "is the secret of the attractive memoir-writing of the present day ... [and] it is equally stimulating, enfeebling, and destructive of the heart and the understanding."[166] Lockhart objected, too, to the sheer number of autobiographical works, most of them uninteresting and badly written and all of them showing the vulgarity of the newly literate class. "There was ... little danger of our having too much autobiography," he writes, "as long as no book had much chance of popularity which was not written with some considerable portion of talent, or at least by a person of some considerable celebrity."[167] But by 1827 autobiographies by the talentless and obscure had already become so numerous that a review of playwright and theater-manager Thomas Dibdin's autobiography lamented, "The malady of memoir-writing continues to rage in the dramatic corps," before adding: "If, however, decayed dramatists find [writing autobiography] a means of obtaining a last benefit from the public ... the public might consider, whether a tax in behalf of their old servants would not be a more commodious and agreeable way of obtaining the same end."[168]

However facetious, the reviewer's comparison of autobiography to a tax implies that autobiography had begun to seem part of a formal set of modern financial relations, a transfer of wealth that would offend less as a state requirement than as a textualized identity made into an object of exchange. For all of these reviewers, the essential problem in autobiography's rise was its commodification in the book market, which meant not only that its invasions of privacy were read more widely but also that its content was increasingly responsive to the wants of a mass readership rather than to the demands of social propriety, literary convention, or psychological need. As some reviewers understood, autobiography enacted specific relationships between identity, textuality, and commodity – relationships that exceeded the obvious logic of self-narrative representation. This was particularly true of courtesan memoirs, which had flourished during the late 1700s and made "[c]ommodification … an explicit theme."[169] Though such works were usually privately printed and thus insulated from the literary market, they underscored the commodification of their authors and advertised them to potential patrons.[170] The most famous, Harriette Wilson's *Memoirs of Herself and Others* (1825), was written only after Wilson offered her lovers the chance to pay her handsomely to avoid mention.[171] The *Literary Chronicle* opined that Wilson had "doubly prostitute[d] herself" by publishing, but the *London Magazine* offered a shrewder assessment, blaming the depravity of "the buying public" for the book but noting, too, the ingenuity of the blackmail scheme, which upset the normal calculus of authorship by allowing Wilson to get "as much by publishing as by suppressing."[172]

Courtesan memoirs were too few in number and too limited in circulation to play much role in the broad commercialization of autobiography. But the narrative, textual, and commercial dynamics that supported them underscore certain relations between texts, identity, and economic exchange. For one thing, because the courtesan memoir casts the narrating I as "the sum of its commercial history," it offers the autobiographical text as a hybrid discourse, as much account ledger as interior narrative meant to describe an idiosyncratic subject.[173] It thus normalized the textual production of subjectivity within a self-narrative – indeed, *as* a self-narrative – of profit and loss, social ambition, and financial rather than spiritual crises and transformations. In this sense, it prefigured the Victorian recasting of the genre as Trollope's self-consciously commercial *An Autobiography* (1883) rather than John Bunyan's *Grace Abounding* (1666). For another, Wilson's memoir in particular illustrated that the danger posed by autobiography went beyond violating privacy or turning a penny, for it demonstrated that *some* autobiographers, at least, sought to maximize financial gain by enacting a tantalizing drama of concealment and revelation – a drama that undercut the notion that they wrote the truth without thinking of their reading public. As one reviewer put it, "a lady who professedly makes the insertion or suppression of disagreeable facts the means of extorting money is hardly a witness to those facts to be relied upon."[174] Wilson's memoir did not fit comfortably within the Horatian matrix of pleasure and use. It sat boldly at the new intersection of commercial gain and narrative power, affirming that self-narration had by the 1820s been pervaded by economic concerns.

Nor was this uncomfortable sense of autobiography's commodification confined to courtesan memoirs. Lockhart complained that many autobiographies by middle-class men read like commercial histories, mocking Brasbridge's *Fruits of Experience* (1824) as a purveyor of trite advice such as, "*Keep your shop, and your shop will keep you*" and "*Advertise frequently, particularly in the St. James's Chronicle.*"[175] He also criticized the *Life and Times of Frederick Reynolds* (1826) for doing little more than summing up "the pecuniary result of his exertions": £19,000 earned from forty years as "'maid-of-all-work' ... universal furbisher, botcher, and grinder, to the great theatre of Covent Garden."[176] Such "results," in Lockhart's view, merely confirmed the artistic bankruptcy of the English stage by showing "that in the present state ... it requires nothing but a beggarly account of empty jokes, and a disgusting familiarity with the green-room ... to be a highly-successful dramatist; [and] that, even on these terms, dramatic success is worthy of the ambition of no man who can attain it."[177] The *London Magazine* said much the same thing, calling Dibdin's autobiography "chiefly *commercial*" and continuing:

> It particularizes the making and selling of every piece he manufactured; and is founded, doubtless, upon the authority of his day-book and ledger. If his example be followed up by dealers and chapmen in other lines of business, what a career may this species of commercial biography run! For why should not Mr. Dibdin's old master, Sir William Rawlins, the upholsterer, write his Recollections, as well as Sir William's old apprentice, Mr. Dibdin, the playwright? His day-book and ledger are of equal authority, and would supply him with materials equally ample and equally interesting.[178]

If such a plan were realized, publishers could soon lay before the public "a series of Mercantile Reminiscences, by the most eminent tradesmen, as long as that of the late dramatical autobiographies."[179]

Such complaints register discomfort with the expansion of the literary market generally, which encouraged authors to adapt their works to popular demands and regard their literary productions as economic rather than artistic endeavors. It is no surprise that Dibdin and Reynolds took early to autobiography: of the various kinds of literary men, playwrights understood best the advantages of writing to suit a wide audience, and they knew the celebrities and *literati* who might buy books or, by appearing in them, help them to sell. Though he disliked the pecuniary details of Dibdin's autobiography, the *London Magazine* reviewer expressed equal distress over the sense of literary commodification that Dibdin's description of his career evoked: "If any edification at all is to be derived from the work ... it can only arise from our observing the mode in which modern plays are concocted. It is apparent, that as much as possible of mercenary, and as little as possible of dramatic spirit enters into their composition."[180] This alone "abundantly account[s] for the degradation of the modern drama" and is the consequence of Dibdin "having let [his muse] out to hire at a weekly stipend."[181] The reviewers who objected most strongly to autobiography's commercial rise were those most likely to view the specter of a literary mass market with dismay, and to feel most acutely the economic entanglements to which literary texts – autobiographical or otherwise – were subject.

By the late 1820s, reviewers thus understood that autobiography comprised what Treadwell calls "a fraught negotiation with the arena of publication and the fact of textuality," in which it was no longer reasonable to "assume that its main interest – overt or covert – [was] producing an interiority which is granted the transcendent status of the work of art."[182] Most Victorian autobiographers simply meant to sell books, even if doing so meant sifting and shaping experience to satisfy publishers and appeal to a wide readership. Before it was written, typeset, printed, bound, subscribed, or displayed in bookshops and railway stalls, autobiography had already begun accommodating identity imaginatively to the literary market. Meanwhile, the democratization and commodification of the genre had made it far more prone to attend explicitly to modes of production and exchange. The rising class of autobiographers understood their relation to and immersion in the market; like so many Pips, they fashioned themselves into narratives of both identity formation and economic progress, unveiling identity's interpenetration by textual and financial concerns. Autobiographies real and fictional began implicitly to ask unanswerable questions. How could the genre preserve, in an age of capitalism and social mobility, the difference between a personal and a financial history, or between an intellectual and a financial transaction? How were both identity and its textual representation being remade by the "conditions of publication," and what were the imaginative and ideological implications of that remaking?[183] The reviews of the 1820s display an incipient awareness of the ways in which these economic contingencies shaped autobiography as it became commercial.

During the next two decades, the energetic hostility to autobiography mostly subsided, perhaps because autobiography proliferated more slowly during those years and thus posed a less immediate threat, or perhaps because even the most incensed reviewers resigned themselves to the genre when they could not staunch its flow. Life writing might also have seemed more legitimate once reputable authors – Scott, Crabbe, Inchbald, Southey – began publishing self-accounts to extend copyright and encourage sales of their earlier works. Still, some reviewers continued to bemoan the mercenary motives of autobiographical production. For instance, the *Monthly Review* asked of Scott's autobiography, "Is it not curious, that one who treated poetry as an occupation in life, as a pursuit of profit . . . should himself have so admirably succeeded as a poet?" then took Scott to task for this success, lamenting the waste of his powers "in the manufacture of mere gew-gaws" instead of finer things:

> With all his invention, with all his elegant fancy, with all that refined sagacity which enables the poet to perform the beautiful task of the painter, what has Sir Walter Scott, regarding him in the former capacity, accomplished for our literature? Taking him, as he himself suggests that he should be estimated, as a poet, Sir Walter, instead of using his intellectual resources to reform the public taste, took advantage of its distempered condition, and consulted more immediately the inclination than the interests of his readers.[184]

Here, in a complaint about poetry, is the same idea of cultural disease that early reviewers had used to describe the appetite for autobiography, the same sense of commodified literature – a "manufacture" – failing to achieve legitimate artistic ends. In John Galt's case, the *Eclectic Review* allowed that his adverse physical and financial circumstances were enough to "disarm" complaints that he had stooped to autobiography, but the *Monthly Review* was less kind, hinting that Galt had arrived at his sorry state by following "youthful passions into devious courses" and arguing that his account of his varied fortunes should be taken as "a beacon of everlasting warning to youth" – a warning, presumably, against the perils of authorship and especially of self-narration.[185]

But beginning in the late 1840s, the resurgence in autobiographical production seems to have provoked a more aggressive response. To be sure, many autobiographies – by Leigh Hunt, Alexandre Dumas, and Cochrane, for example – published at mid-century received qualified or even enthusiastic praise. But many others exasperated reviewers. A review of the *Memoirs of Benvenuto Cellini* (1848) advised, "This is not a crusade against your diaries. Write them, dear reader, as much or as little as you please – but do not *keep* them."[186] The problem, the review continued, was the egoists who had the effrontery to ask "*collaborateurs* (who, for the most part, seek only to turn honest pence or half pence as they can)" to prepare their diaries for presentation to the world.[187] The *Eclectic* called the *Autobiography of William Walford* (1851) an attempt "to immortalize stupid mediocrity" and complained, "The British press, indeed, has teemed with this species of literature, until it has become almost an established custom with us, that so soon as any worthy person has passed away, his likeness ... shall be shown forth, not 'in dull, cold marble,' but by the magic working of the printing-press."[188] And an 1852 *Dublin University Magazine* review of autobiographies by William Jerdan and Mary Mitford invoked the Horatian matrix only to discard it, proclaiming that autobiography was not written for amusement or instruction, nor even for confession since it was addressed "to a public, who ... do not affect any power of absolution."[189] Instead, it aimed at self-fashioning, its author trying to make "from fragmentary recollections a picture which is not altogether inconsistent" while the "credulous Imagination ... [is] occupied with a dream of its own, inventing traditions, and believing what it invents."[190]

Most striking in these reviews is the extent to which they abandon the parameters that had guided commentary on autobiography a quarter century before. Gone, in the main, are shrill complaints about the diseased reading public, the vulgarity of authors, and the violation of privacy. *Chambers's* review of Jerdan, in fact, waives the question of whether autobiography ought to disclose matters "about which living individuals may feel a delicacy," remarking simply, "The time for such questions seems past."[191] In place of these concerns, the reviews offer tacit acceptance of a modern market predicated upon mass readership and commercial exchange – the admission, for instance, that "*collaborateurs*" just want "to turn honest pence" – and a nuanced awareness of the implications of autobiography, in both its relation to other kinds of material representation and its implicit destabilization of a discrete identity distinguishable from its material forms. The *Eclectic*'s analogy between autobiography and sculpture in reviewing Walford is especially striking and might be extended also to the portrait and the photograph. The aim of each form, the review suggests, is the creation of a "likeness" that is partly exterior resemblance, partly the materialization of an essential identity through the "magic" of printing words on the physical page. Autobiography thus constitutes a kind of representational alchemy, a transmutation of intangible essence into material text. But as the *Dublin University Magazine*'s review points out, that alchemy carries its own dangers, giving the handiwork of "Imagination" the status of a definitive text, a privileged account of the self that may offer the factual "[v]eracity ... [of] the tombstones in a country churchyard, but seldom anything which can be called Truth."[192] Mid-century reviews thus portray autobiography as pervaded by economic concerns and also compromised by its status as both likeness and invention.

As autobiographical production neared the end of its remarkable mid-century peak in 1860, reviews reached their angriest pitch, coalescing particularly around three works: the *Autobiography and Correspondence of Mary Granville Delany* (1861), the *Autobiography, Letters, and Literary Remains of Mrs. Piozzi* (1861), and Lady Morgan's *Passages from My Autobiography* (1859). The first two got off easiest, likely because Delany and Piozzi were long dead and had no part in publishing their lives. But critics roundly abused both works even if they took pains to spare their subjects. A slender selection of Delany's letters had been published in 1820 and met with approval from the *Edinburgh Monthly Review* since its aim was "to preserve some interesting accounts of the late king and the royal family" rather than to memorialize Delany.[193] But the 1861 publication of six volumes of Delany's letters sparked considerable critical irritation. The *Saturday Review* protested against such "undue space [being] allotted to the memory of an obscure individual," and the *Westminster Review* called for "a kind of moral censorship which the public only can exercise" to halt the unwarranted publication of such works.[194] The *Christian Remembrancer*, in a review of Delany and Piozzi, called both works "[d]iffuse and often trifling ... full of superfluous and unnecessary matter," and the *Edinburgh Review* added apologetically of Piozzi that it was "almost ignoble work to be disinterring, one by one, the frailties of this poor lady for the idle purpose of a posthumous controversy."[195]

Reviewers were less kind to Morgan, perhaps because she *chose* to write and publish her autobiography, thus asserting her authority to present her controversial career however she liked and profiting by her pen – even if posthumously – one last time. Late in life she composed her autobiography and handed it and other papers over to *Athenaeum* editor Hepworth

Dixon, who collaborated with Geraldine Jewsbury in compiling the work. Neither Dixon nor Jewsbury could save Morgan or her *Memoirs* from violent critical abuse. A savage review in the *Examiner* began, "In these volumes we read how a woman of fourscore, frivolous and vain, bequeathed a monument to the frivolity and vanity of her career. . . . [so that] the catalogue of her empty triumphs should be read to the world over the grave into which she was tottering."[196] *Fraser's* harped, too, on Morgan's "egregious vanities" and opined that "the follies and vanities of such a woman should be held up as a warning to the rising generation, at a time when self-culture and low-priced schooling may cast on the world shoals of women as vain, as volatile, as meddling" as she.[197] Both reviews also abused her other writing, the *Examiner* calling her style "slip-slop" and bemoaning the "often illspelt, or ungrammatical shreds of French that garnish her English," and *Fraser's* pronouncing her works "dead, very dead and forgotten in England" and alive in Ireland only for "a class but two degrees above the very lowest."[198] Only Colburn's crass desire to have a titled author, the reviewer declared, allowed her ever to have a career as a writer.[199]

Attacks like these sound – and probably were – gendered. In their charges of frivolity and vanity, they read as Victorian referenda on the value of female experience; in their regret that works such as Delany's, Piozzi's, and Morgan's should ever have been published, they express a predictable hostility to exposing women's experiences, so often domestic, when these should remain private. Contemporary reviews of Cornelia Knight's autobiography echo these charges, calling it "one of those books of scandal of which it is impossible not to regret the publication" and one of "a class of gossiping productions with which the shelves of our libraries groan."[200] In the cases of Morgan and Piozzi, incidental factors – Morgan's Irishness, Piozzi's public falling out with Samuel Johnson – undoubtedly exacerbated the critical response. But something else was at work, too: resentment regarding the shameless textualization and commodification of the subject in the new era of literary production. In Morgan's case, the *Fraser's* reviewer seems to have been bothered most by her bequest of her papers to Dixon, whom she hardly knew, in an effort to do "a clever stroke in the way of literary business" by "merg[ing] the characters of literary executor, editor, critic, and censor into one entity, that entity being the editor of a widely diffused weekly periodical organ."[201] At mid-century, in fact, no autobiography published in England provoked greater hostility than *The Autobiography of P. T. Barnum* (1855), which *Fraser's* accused of "[courting] the rotten eggs and dead cats of a moral pillory" for the sake of turning a profit.[202] "How far is this state of things to go?" the reviewer asked. "Until all true artists and honest men are driven from a profession where only impudence and charlatanerie shall be able to carry off the prizes – for to this pass things are rapidly verging."[203]

The reviews were also verging, and toward a common complaint: that the identities textualized in and through autobiography were being pressed into new physical and imaginative forms by the material exigencies of the market. In reviewing Knight, for instance, the *Quarterly* remarked provocatively that "Miss Knight" – not her book – "has already reached a third edition," and that such works would be published so long as "money is an object with 'families into whose hands they have got,' and will certainly be read when published."[204] Barnum's offense was not just his power to scatter "moral poison ... far and wide over the Transatlantic soil" but also his unnerving multiplicity, since his celebrity had first caused him to be competed over by American publishers (he had, the reviewer claims, finally received $15,000 for the American copyright of his book), then allowed him to appear suddenly in England in a bewildering array of "library editions, illustrated editions, and people's editions ... [so that] every railway-station and book-stall is overrun with varieties in every form of *The Autobiography of Phineas Taylor Barnum*."[205] The reviewer also saw the parallel between Barnum's shameless self-promotion in the autobiography and the falsehoods and media blitzes by which he had sold Tom Thumb and Jenny Lind to the gullible American and British publics. Through "[p]uffs, posters, transparencies, and woodcuts" – a tissue of textual likenesses that oscillated between the discursive and the pictorial, the real and the imagined, and that made identity into a commodity to be produced, disseminated, displayed, and consumed – Barnum had made a fortune.[206] And he had done so by exploiting the dynamics of identity, textuality, and commodity characteristic of autobiography's commercial rise.

While Knight and Barnum had been multiplied distressingly by their autobiographies, Delany and Piozzi had been attenuated outrageously by theirs, pressed into textual shapes that their subjectivities did not merit. *Fraser's* inveighed "against the unwarrantable extension of [Piozzi's] work to two volumes, whereas one would have amply sufficed to convey all that is worth reading in them," and the *Westminster* wondered "who was Mrs. Delany, that seventy years after her death, her correspondence should be published in six volumes, weighing 224 ounces, and containing 3674 pages?"[207] *Fraser's* protested against Delany's correspondence, too, citing "the unjustifiable space [it] occupied for the moment upon the shelves of the circulating libraries, and upon the tables of their subscribers."[208] The *Christian Remembrancer* declared – shrewdly – that publishers, buyers, and readers were the perpetrators, not the victims, of these assaults on library shelves, the paper supply, and English sense. The reviewer asked, "What circumstances ... can at the same time have brought to light letters and documents which, having slumbered so long, might seem to have passed the period of possible resuscitation?"

> Public libraries generally, and Mr. Mudie in particular, must be the occasion of such publications as those before us; and we recognize something even judicial in the three enormous volumes, two thousand ample pages in all, which embody Mrs. Delany's experience. It must be for Mr. Mudie's sins that a woman's private letters of more than a hundred years old should be given to the world in such unmeasured unexampled profusion.[209]

Driving these complaints is anxiety regarding women physically distended and chronologically displaced, given a misshapen afterlife by the convergence of their own profuse textuality, the economic desires of editors and publishers, and the appetites of readers.

Piozzi's autobiography provoked a different complaint by contradicting other published accounts of her life. Widowed in 1781 by her English husband Henry Thrale, she had suffered a public pillorying during the mid-1780s after marrying her daughter's Italian music master. The move estranged her from Samuel Johnson and Fanny Burney, among others, and her 1786 book *Anecdotes of the Late Dr. Johnson* widened the breach by defending her attachment to Gabriel Piozzi and setting her up, perhaps unintentionally, as a preemptive rival to Boswell, whose *Life of Samuel Johnson* did not appear until 1791. In the end, Piozzi's remarriage and public quarrel with Johnson provoked such a scandal – in literary circles, at least – that Thomas Macauley even discussed it in his *Life of Samuel Johnson* (1856) seventy years later. Edited by the influential Abraham Hayward, Piozzi's *Autobiography* stirred a persistent public debate about her honesty, even regarding the date of her second marriage. The problem, as *Fraser's* described it, was intertextual and proprietary: Piozzi's autobiography was not entirely her own since the great Johnson "claims manorial rights, as it were, over all adjacent lands, and a large royalty is always payable to his memory by those who undertake the biography of any of his cotemporaries [sic] or friends."[210] Hayward designed the new text to remedy old wrongs, disputing Boswell's account of Piozzi's first husband and including letters between her and Johnson that had previously been suppressed. The *Dublin University Magazine* defended her, while *Fraser's* pointed out that her account agreed with two newly available sources, "the diary of the late Miss Williams Wynn" and the recently published diary of Thomas Campbell.[211] The *Edinburgh Review*, conversely, cited the *Gentleman's Magazine*, the *European Magazine*, Macauley's *Life*, and John Wilson Croker's 1831 edition of Boswell in an effort to discredit Piozzi and Hayward alike.[212]

The critical response to Piozzi reflects a view distant from the earlier trust in the truth of autobiography, or even in the later, nuanced sense of autobiography as a coherent narrative created from the unconscious interplay of remembrance and "Imagination." Instead, mid-century reviewers regarded Piozzi's *Autobiography* as part of a network of texts, each offering its own version of her subjectivity. Critics responded this way to Morgan too, rejecting her account of her life out of hand. The *Examiner* quipped, "Lady Morgan, who opens these memoirs with a fragment of insincere autobiography, affects disdain of dates, and seems never in all her life to have told any one the truth about her age."[213] *Fraser's* disputed Morgan's account of her birth, allegedly on Christmas day and "within ear-shot" of the tolling bell of St. Patrick's Cathedral, remarking that "no register of the birth appears . . . in the parish books in which the cathedral is situated, nor in any other parish in the city of Dublin."[214] Citing Frederick Warner's *The History of Ireland* (1763) and Sylvester O'Halloran's *An Introduction to and an History of Ireland* (1803), *Fraser's* also attacks Morgan's account of her christening, her supposed connection with the "Frenches of Galway," the dates of her correspondence, and the identities of her suitors.[215] As the reviewer puts it – in language suited wonderfully to this study – "[w]ithout dates, and accurate dates too, there can be no chronology, no history, personal or general, and assuredly no biography. Dates are as necessary to a biography as to a last will and testament, to a lease, a charter party, a bill of lading or exchange, or an agreement to let or hire a furnished or unfurnished house."[216] Morgan's autobiography, the review implies, belongs to the discursive field of finance, not literature, and must obey the conventions that served generally to situate identity within modern economic relations.

Charted across these critical responses, Victorian autobiography appears at mid-century as a genre capable of provoking specific kinds of anxieties about the implications of having transformed identity into a textual and commodified thing. Made into text, identity appeared as not only the property of a "distempered" reading age but a thing riddled with disorderly and dangerous potential. The marketplace obligations of textual form could attenuate or misshape identity, bloating it so that the bookshelves groaned. Or they could make identity asynchronous and simultaneous all at once by producing the autobiography of a long dead subject, resurrected and then multiplied into thousands of copies gaping at readers from railway stalls and bookshop windows. In its myriad forms, autobiography testified openly to subjectivity's entanglement in the dynamics of production, ownership, and exchange that characterized both the book market and the broad rhythms of Victorian life. And by becoming textual, subjectivity also entered into the curious intertextualities of not just an autobiographical age but also a copyright age, a portrait age, photographic age, a registry age, and a census age, bound to a textual culture intrinsic to the operation of financial, legal, and self-narrative power. Treadwell writes that upon entering the realm of print publication, the autobiography "knows that its position has nothing to do with the thoughts and feelings with which it was written. Its integrity depends on how it is read."[217] The premise may be true, but the phrasing elides the difference between person and book, human "knowing" and inanimate textual form. Compromised alike by the psychological effects of capitalism and the financial requirements of textuality, autobiography embodied by the middle of the nineteenth century the literary market's power to reify and remake the subject.

In his November 1850 review of the *Autobiography of Leigh Hunt*, John Anster wrote:

> At our distance from London there would have been something even of the interest of romance in learning how the struggle for daily bread has been carried on for years by those who depend on the resources of the literary profession. The relations of the author and the bookseller to each other we should wish to know more of than has yet been revealed in any of these autobiographies – more, perhaps, than can with proper delicacy to the feelings of all concerned be ever revealed.[218]

Anster probably did not mean that he wanted deeper knowledge of anything so postmodern as the implications I have traced. Yet at the end of the century, Margaret Oliphant wrote of her conflicted feelings about her own autobiography, which she had begun during the 1850s as a memoir for her sons but did not finish until 1897, after both had died. In December 1894, just two months after the death of her younger son Cecco, she reflected, "How strange it is to me to write all this … now that I am doing it consciously for the public, with the aim (no evil aim) of leaving a little more money … I feel all this to be so vulgar, so common, so unnecessary, as if I were making pennyworths of myself."[219] The reflection captures brilliantly a tension that must have undergirded many Victorian autobiographies, however rarely it was expressed. Writing in their own person and with the aim of turning a penny, most autobiographers were hardly likely to give their misgivings about the genre free play. Nor were the realist conventions of life writing supple enough for run-of-the-mill autobiographers, diarists, and editors of correspondence to use it to express symbolically the imaginative and cultural implications of transforming identity into a commodity.

But those implications appear powerfully, and repeatedly, in the Victorian novel. Kornbluh notes the Victorian novel's ability to depict "'the business of life': the intimate transactions of friendship, kinship, love, and marriage," in language so thoroughly economic that the world becomes "grotesque in . . . its figuring of everything through an economic prism."[220] This may be so precisely because the Victorian novel and Victorian finance capitalism depended upon the same textual culture, in which individual identities and economic value both were understood to inhere in paper forms. During the 1860s, especially, Victorian novelists rooted their fictions in representations of identities made and unmade by their textualization, and by the ways in which that textualization destabilized the cultural sense of identity as a thing apart from materiality and the dynamics of production, consumption, and exchange. Often these fictions ally the fragility of identity to a story of theft or financial fraud, so that the losses they describe are simultaneously economic and psychological, overtly material and intensely psychological. In this sense, novels during the 1860s – sensation novels especially – performed the narrative, cultural, and imaginative work that the remarkable expansion of autobiography had provoked: they revealed amid "the interest of romance" the ideological and imaginative consequences of autobiography's commercial rise.

* * *

The following chapters catch novels of the 1860s in the act of performing this work, expressing the sense of identity under duress, transformed by its position at the nexus of textual production and commodity exchange. Mid-century realist novels often treat identity in this way, most obviously when they center on plots of financial or professional ambition as in Trollope's *The Three Clerks* (1857) and *The Way We Live Now* (1875) and Eliot's *Middlemarch* (1871–1872). But the innovative structures, distemporal plots, and ostentatious symbols of sensation novels especially illustrate the way that identity was compromised by its textual forms – by its simultaneous existence in diaries, wills, portraits, letters, registers, confessions, and signatures, all them able to disrupt both patrilineage and psychology, social and somatic order, gender roles and normative channels of sexual desire. As Alison Case and Harry Shaw argue, escaping "the restraints of social realism ... allowed sensation fiction to channel and exploit more inchoate social anxieties," an engagement with social disruption that provoked much of its popular appeal.[221] The genre "activat[ed] vigorously the nineteenth-century anxiety about people of sudden wealth and power whose background is mysterious," especially by implying that "both personal and class identity in contemporary Britain were fluid and unstable ... subject to manipulation, misrepresentation, and outright theft."[222] Identity was subject to "outright theft" at mid-century precisely because its textuality exposed it to the market, and because the transience of middle-class wealth inhered principally in the textual complications of England's emerging finance capitalism and the related phenomenon of identity's rootedness in textual forms. The sensation novel did not just capitalize on these issues as plot devices or themes. It grew from them as an expression of the cultural anxieties that such problems had engendered.

It also grew from a new relation between textuality and commodity, since it embodied less a set of distinct aesthetic aspirations than a set of economic ones rooted in cheap publication, mass sales, and other features of the modernizing literary market. Sensation's material origins lay mainly in other popular forms – gallows broadsides, Newgate novels, stage melodramas, and penny bloods – that had stoked the public appetite for licentious fare and established cultural dynamics and narrative techniques that permitted sensation to flourish. Gallows broadsides, for instance, turned criminals into "text[s] to be read" but denied them a voice, thus inscribing a "textualised loss of individuality [that] is paralleled in economic terms" as the criminal becomes a profitable text for the authorial other.[223] Many of sensation's thematic commonplaces, such as mystery, suspense, aberrant characters, and sexual irregularities, also originated in these other forms but became the very devices by which sensation novels met the demands of serial publication and turned cultural provocation into mass appeal. Andrew King argues that the development of such commonplaces illustrates "the power of capitalism to adjust its business models" – or, to put it another way, the power of the literary market to catalyze new forms.[224] For many sensation novels, including the genre's presumptive urtext, Collins's *The Woman in White*, one such adjustment was first-person narration, in imitation of both courtroom testimony and popular mid-century works such as William Russell's *Recollections of a Detective Police-Officer* (1856) and Thomas Delf's *Diary of an Ex-Detective* (1859). Patrick Brantlinger argues persuasively in his famous essay on sensation that

Collins and others used first-person narration to escape the "logical limits" of omniscience.[225] But Collins's structural experimentation in *The Woman in White* testifies also to the urgency with which he sought popular appeal, and to the instrumentality of autobiography in provoking the imaginative engagement with identity, textuality, and commodity upon which sensation novels often depend.

The chapters that follow might have begun by addressing *The Woman in White*, with its pervasive sense of identities made and unmade by texts and compromised by economic exchange. Textual/economic dynamics underlie not only Sir Percival Glyde's "Secret" but also the narrative structure, which takes several first-person forms en route to unmasking identity's flimsy basis in church registers, wills, letters, death certificates, and tombstone inscriptions. The machinations surrounding these texts come to light eventually, but not because the novel affirms any faith in nontextual forms of subjectivity; rather, they come to light because the doctor who attends Anne Catherick files her death certificate too promptly, putting a premature textual end to "Lady Glyde" and creating the only "weak place" in Count Fosco's scheme.[226] It matters little to the novel whether Laura recovers her memory and character – her identity, in a conventional sense – but it matters greatly that she be vindicated according to the many texts that affirm her proper relationship to wealth. The novel ends by resolving its money plot, not its love plot, and it does so principally by setting texts to rights. As Walter Hartright puts it, when the statuary's man strikes the false inscription from Anne Catherick's tombstone, "a great heave of relief" passes through the crowd, "as if they felt that the last fetters of the conspiracy had been struck off Laura herself."[227] The novel thus confirms the cultural impulse to conflate Laura with her textual embodiment and paves the way for the Limmeridge estate to pass to the son of a drawing-master, who justifies that transfer by telling its story in a series of autobiographies and whose only notable work is his water-color drawing of Laura. The detective story, Walter Benjamin asserts, appeared in response to commodity culture, which transformed the interior into a space where human subjects leave "traces" in the act of concealing the commodity status of the objects we collect.[228] In *The Woman in White* the crucial traces are the very texts that commodity culture called forth to reify the subject's ineluctable pervasion by the capitalist sphere.

But the chapters that follow do not begin with *The Woman in White*, for it is part of my point that other mid-century novels, too, turned the commodification of identity into a powerful thematic and symbolic refrain. Chapter 2 therefore takes up *Great Expectations*, which uses autobiographical form to illustrate not just the fraught social and psychological position of the individual caught within capitalism but also the ontological status of subjectivity when it is made into a material thing and exposed to capitalist modes of production and exchange. This is a key difference between *Great Expectations* and earlier fictional autobiographies: while novels such as *Jane Eyre* and *David Copperfield* capitalized on the appetite for autobiography during the late 1840s, they did not explore simultaneously the implications of textualizing identity. Kornbluh attributes the novel's mid-century interest in economic matters to finance journalism and its formulation of a "'psychic economy,' the idea that subjectivity is fundamentally economic and that the economy is fundamentally psychological."[229] But it is not just that financial journalism created a discursive field within which subjectivity was understood as economic. It is that, by mid-century, subjectivity and capitalism rested upon indistinguishable textual grounds, that subjectivity had been subsumed imaginatively and ideologically, gradually and thoroughly, into commodity culture. This might be what Winifred Hughes sensed when she observed that, despite the hostilities between realists and sensationalists during the 1860s, both were grappling with "the same overwhelming experience of . . . the newly diminished stature of the individual amid the crowding and the complexities of modern existence."[230]

Hughes's words imply what subsequent chapters argue in detail: that novelists in the 1860s – sensational, realist, and in-between – coincided especially in representing the modern condition of the commodified Victorian subject. *Great Expectations*, *Silas Marner*, and *Our Mutual Friend* illustrate this condition as surely as any sensation novels do. But they give it alternate expression, rooting it within different kinds of plots and narrative structures even while resorting to many of sensation's devices, as if to acknowledge capitalism's power to compass the representation of identity within a certain horizon of discursive possibilities. Beginning with *Great Expectations* helps also to underscore the intergeneric connectedness of Victorian life writing and the Victorian novel, which both rose to commercial prominence within the same expanding, modernizing literary market. They masqueraded as one another, competed for space on Mudie's shelves, and appealed to many of the same readers. Bound alike by their commodity status and their aim of giving human experience discursive form, they played complementary and overlapping roles in the mid-century redefinition of subjectivity as an object of exchange. Kornbluh suggests that the realist Victorian novel "engages economics neither via reference to economic content nor through its production and consumption in the market, but in its narratological, rhetorical, and temporal structures."[231] I argue that novels engaged economics in all of these ways – in their content, plots, themes, their narrative and imaginative structures, and their status as textual commodities – and that they did so by cultivating distinct strategies for representing the cultural anxieties that autobiography had helped to engender.

My analysis of these strategies centers upon moments when identity takes textual form and becomes a commodity, whether in the first-person narration of *Great Expectations* or in textual symbols such as Lady Audley's portrait, Old Harmon's will in *Our Mutual Friend*, or Ezra Jennings's diary in *The Moonstone*. But I am also interested in the ways in which these novels trace identity's commodification to its logical imaginative and ideological conclusions, marking the tenuousness of the boundary between identity and property at a moment when it had become a legal and financial necessity and a broad cultural imperative to make identity into a text. They do so chiefly by treating identity as a thing that can be multiplied, fragmented, and disseminated – like autobiographies and cartes-de-visite – in the bold new age of its textual and mechanical reproduction. Doppelgangers and multiple identities punctuate sensation novels, from Laura Fairlie and Anne Catherick to Lady Audley and Phoebe Marks, and from Collins's two Allan Armadales to Dickens's Landless twins. But the trope recurs also in the new little Pip who appears at the end of *Great Expectations*, John Harmon's murdered double George Radfoot, and Silas Marner mistaking the toddler Eppie for his gold. These novels represent identity by substituting "a plurality of copies for a unique existence," constantly revising and reactivating the meaning of that identity for each beholder.[232] The effect is the linguistic dissociation that Marx finds at the heart of capitalism, the alienation of representation from essence, or as he puts it, of "name" from "nature":

> I know nothing of a man if I merely know his name is Jacob. In the same way, every trace of the money-relation disappears in the money-names pound, thaler, franc, ducat, etc. The confusion caused by attributing a hidden meaning to these cabalistic signs is made even greater by the fact that these money-names express both the values of commodities and, simultaneously ... the weight of the metal which serves as the standard of money.[233]

The common sensational trope of "character splitting" that Brantlinger attributes to the influence of the Gothic might be understood better as originating in the nexus of identity, text, and commodity that helped to provoke the genre.[234]

This reframing of identity as prone to multiplication, fragmentation, and dissemination produced several discursive effects. First, as Benjamin suggests, subjectivity's new potential for plurality remade it as a thing that, though materially finite and "complete," took on multiple idiosyncratic meanings in the hands of the consuming other. Identity appears in these novels as precisely what the commercialization of autobiography had made it: a material thing produced to meet external demands, responding to an extrinsic rather than intrinsic need for expression. Sensation novels especially often depend upon the boundless instability of the identities that characters – particularly bad ones – body forth for public consumption. But they depend, too, like other novels of the time, upon the psychological fragmentation and aberration of characters who bear within them parts of identity from which they are closed off, as with Silas's fits, Captain Dodd's amnesia, and Franklin Blake's unremembered theft. During the 1860s, as if in response to England's first mass-textualization of identity, the novel began to treat subjectivity routinely as a thing alienated from its subject, an example of Lukács's observation that "a man's activity" under capitalism "becomes estranged from himself . . . [and] must go its own way independently of man just like any consumer article."[235] If, as Hughes suggests, sensation novels "insist upon meanings beyond the normally human" by invoking accident and fate, they may do so because identity had become unmoored, appearing more like Marx's dancing table than like Descartes's *cogito ergo sum*.[236] As Victorians developed new techniques for textualizing the subject, novels offered powerful visions of the inadequacy – even impossibility – of imagining an "identity" that might exist apart from textuality and commodity exchange.

Second, identity's potential for not just multiplicity but also dissemination meant that it could be profoundly distemporal, existing simultaneously in many places or living troubling afterlives in the letters, diaries, wills, signatures, and other textual scraps that clutter the spaces of midcentury novels. Writing of the technological reproducibility of art, Benjamin associates this multiplicity with the loss of "aura," "its presence in time and space, its unique existence at the place where it happens to be."[237] While real and fictional autobiographies insisted explicitly on detailed chronologies, then, they eroded the sense of identity's time-boundedness, creating a sense of temporal involution – narratively, via flashbacks, premonitions, dreams, and detective plots, in which the aim is always to reconstruct in the present the criminal event that happened in the past; and materially, via Cochrane's appearance on the bookshelf beside Rousseau, or Bentley's resurrection of Delany. And these unsettling effects coincided with others. The rise of commodity culture provoked generally "the dissolution of the sense of historical time" as Victorians invented anniversaries, ceremonies, and other commemorative acts by which they could project the past onto the present.[238] As these developments collapsed time, the train transfigured it, giving rise to the sense of the "annihilation of space and time" that accompanied the advent of rapid mass-transit.[239] The idea of geographical space was thus supplanted by an obsession with time, just as capitalism and labor theory were also asserting that time is money. Amid these ruptures, novels of the 1860s obsessed over time, in part by over-particularizing it within the machinery of their meticulous plots – Nicholas Daly calls the sensation novel above all "a *punctual* form" – and in part by situating the whir of industrial-capitalist time alongside an imprecise subjective time marked by the gaps and returns of narrative plotting, memory and forgetting, and other figurations.[240] Above all, by acknowledging the transformation of identity into a textual thing bound to the requirements of capitalism, novels of the 1860s illustrate the extent to which Victorian subjectivity collapsed all time into the constant present-tense of economic desire.

Finally, as especially my discussions of *Hard Cash*, *Our Mutual Friend*, and *The Moonstone* show, the decade's fiction suggests repeatedly that the commodification of identity transforms sexual desire into economic desire, as if to underscore the centrality of capitalist transformation to any sense of subjectivity grounded in psychological concerns. Andrew Miller urges this point in *Novels Behind Glass* (1995) when he suggests that Victorian novels resolve inevitably into symbolic expressions of desire for the object of capitalist exchange.[241] Victorian autobiography embodied these expressions by transforming subjectivity quite literally into a commodity that exists solely through and for the desire of the other, and by requiring that this desire be expressed in purely economic terms. In the novels I consider, inheritance plots parallel and impede love plots; detective investigations meant to recover missing wealth resolve instead a disrupted sexual exchange. Through plot and symbol these novels underscore the sexual reality for the commodified Victorian subject: that erotic dynamics under capitalism are always already economic dynamics, so that – in an age of commercial autobiography – the story of desire for material consumption is not just a metonym for the erotic story that Victorian literature, in its obsessive propriety, cannot tell. Rather, the story of desire for material consumption *is* the erotic story. It is the only erotic story possible when the subject has already been remade as a commodity and can express desire only through ownership and exchange.

Bound up in the law, anxious about identity, and obsessed with the transformation of subjectivity into property, novels of the 1860s confront the terrain mapped by autobiography's commercial rise. They do so in *Great Expectations*' play with problems of identity, textuality, and class; in the troubling multiplicity of Lady Audley and equally troubling fragmentation of Silas Marner and Franklin Blake; in the temporal involutions of the detective plot, which demands for its present and future an obsessive digging after the past, binding all tenses into a synchronous desire for an end and resolving them in the subject-made-text, subdued finally by a textual record of the guilty self; and in the hyperbolic erotic dynamics of *Hard Cash*, *Our Mutual Friend*, and *The Moonstone*, which show how capitalist desire confounds the Victorian subject with property, the love plot with the financial plot, as if they cannot tell the difference, or as if the difference is not worth the telling. The following chapters thus explore how Victorian fiction represented the implications of capitalism's incursions against subjectivity, which began with the autobiographers who put subjectivity into the market. "In the mid-nineteenth century," Richards writes, "the commodity became the living letter of the law of supply and demand. It literally came alive."[242] In the case of Victorian autobiography, the commodity was always alive, and trying to live a distinct life of its own. By attending to this proposition, and to autobiography's cultural and ideological position at mid-century, I offer a different way of reading it – not quite from a distance, but certainly in its relation to and provocation of a much wider discursive and imaginative field.

CHAPTER 2

"Portable Property": Commodity and Identity *in* Great Expectations

During Pip's first week in London at the dawn of his expectations, Mr. Wemmick gives him a bit of advice that could serve neatly as an epigraph for the novel.[1] "It don't signify to you with your brilliant lookout," he says, "but as to myself, my guiding-star always is, 'Get hold of portable property.'"[2] The remark comes as they stand in Jaggers's office and Wemmick, like the curator of a seedy menagerie, shows Pip the bizarre relics left by clients who have gone to the gallows: Wemmick's brooch and mourning-rings, the seals hanging from his watch-chain, and "the two odious casts with the twitchy leer upon them" that Wemmick apostrophizes during the scene (156). They are, Wemmick says, "gifts" and "curiosities," less real treasures than synecdochic traces of the criminal subjects who left them behind – materializations of the self that have been made into commodities, and that grant identity an involuntary afterlife or even take on furtive lives of their own (157). At one moment, the casts seem to make "a stupid apoplectic attempt to attend to the conversation"; at others, they appear "to be trying to get their eyelids open" or to be playing "a diabolical game at bo-peep" (218, 252, 290). Wemmick's advice to Pip may be practical, then, but it also reveals the anxiety regarding commodity and identity that structures the novel. By celebrating material accumulation Wemmick endorses what the rest of the novel does not, and, for a moment, he seems to be another Jerry Cruncher, or a precursor to Mr. Venus or Gaffer Hexam: avaricious, potentially violent, and concerned above all with anatomizing and economizing the Victorian subject. Written as Pip's autobiography but named for Magwitch's money, *Great Expectations* centers thematically and symbolically upon the porous boundary between identity and property and the consequences of making identity into a commodity for the market.

It goes almost without saying that *Great Expectations* is concerned with capitalism and dynamics of wealth and class. In 2009 John Plotz seized upon Wemmick's catchphrase in his study of Victorian novels' obsession with "things," arguing that they obsessed over "objects, returned to them repeatedly, and interrogated their significance ... because of the novel's own status as an exemplary portable property."[3] Yet this does not go far enough to explain *Great Expectations*, which embodies in its autobiographical form the very textual and ideological problems that Dickens uses the novel to explore. As Clare Pettitt writes, the novel is largely about "the pathological effects of a capitalist restlessness" and registers these in several ways.[4] Pip's snobbery, his objectification by others, and his investigation of what makes a gentleman all belong to this critique. So, too, does the novel's engagement with the economic dimensions of fairy tale and romance, including its "monstrous parody" of the upward mobility plot, which reveals not only the moral decay caused by unearned wealth but also, through Magwitch, that wealth is invariably "wrung from misery, hard labor, and injustice."[5] Sue Zemka has argued that *Great Expectations* critiques the psychic structures that underlie Victorian commodity culture, which fetishize fascinating appearances and "epiphanic moments" at the expense of quiet necessities such as human empathy and duration through time.[6] The novel thus "encodes an awareness that its own narrated interests are poisoned by the frenetic involutions of time and desire in capitalist society."[7] Capitalism and financial grasping come off rather badly in *Great Expectations*, as they had in Dickens since at least the days of *A Christmas Carol* (1843). But this later novel strikes a new and peculiar chord.

Great Expectations diverges from Dickens's earlier works by indicting capitalism in a text that is itself an identity made into a commodity, an intimate and protracted self-narrative designed for the literary market. The novel is, Peter Ackroyd writes, "a much more frankly autobiographical work than *David Copperfield*," for it takes its shape more entirely from Dickens's pained remembrances and the silent rhythms of his private traumas.[8] But unlike in *Copperfield*, its traumas cannot be undone: Biddy is not Agnes, and Pip cannot go home again, though apparently Biddy and Joe can forge a new Pip to replace the one that has been ravaged by commodity culture. Regret for a life misled is embedded deeply in *Great Expectations*, its confessions welling up as if from a psychic wound and spilling out into self-narration. But if the novel was shaped partly by psychological imperatives, it was shaped also by the economic needs of its author, who was more beset by financial worries in 1860 than he had been for many years. He was maintaining separate residences for himself, his wife, and Ellen Ternan, establishing two unpromising sons in business, and shouldering new responsibilities created by the death of his brother Alfred, who, he wrote, "died worth nothing – and has left a widow and five children – you may suppose to whom."[9] He was also watching the circulation of his fledgling magazine *All the Year Round* fall, fully aware that its financial losses would be his own. *Great Expectations* was forged in the crucible of psychological *and* financial need, and its linguistic and symbolic concerns with narrative self-creation overlap the economic exigencies of its textual production.

Though Pip, like David, eventually writes his autobiography, *Great Expectations* is no portrait of the artist, or at least it does not celebrate the artist's arrival to productivity, celebrity, and economic and emotional fulfillment. It offers instead a deeply ambivalent account of self-narration in which commodity and identity are inextricably tangled and subjected simultaneously to the novel's economic critique. *Great Expectations'* interest in Victorian capitalism, then, is only partly about class and privilege, just as it is only partly about Pip's material and psychic displacements within an emerging Victorian economy. Mostly, it reveals that the instabilities of Pip's self-narrative are bound explicitly and symbolically to its status as a commodified text, on the one hand because no text can express any subjectivity fully, and on the other because commodifying autobiography exposes identity to power relations dictated by ownership and exchange. As the repetitions and recursions of Pip's narrative suggest, the dynamics of capital belong, like Estella, to the "innermost life of [his] life"; they are inseparable from his efforts to express that life in language (182). *Great Expectations* must be read, then, as both an imaginative and a material text, as both an identity made into a commodity and an account of the implications of that self-narrative labor. It opens this study precisely because it articulates so powerfully the nature of the anxiety that had emerged by mid-century regarding the growing tendency to commodify the subject.

* * *

Great Expectations' concern with identity and exchange appears most obviously in its presentation of the extravagant violence of the capitalist market, the center of which is London, which Pip sees for the first time after learning of his expectations. His initial response is to be "scared by the immensity," and nearly the first things he notices in Jaggers's office are the "two dreadful casts" (129–30). Situated, appropriately enough, in Little Britain, Jaggers's office is a diminutive version of the nation, predicated upon a tainting contact with matters of commerce and the law and a grotesque tendency, as the casts imply, to produce and reproduce the self. Nor is Pip impressed more favorably when he finds himself in

Smithfield market, of which he writes, "the shameful place, being all asmear with filth and fat and blood and foam, seemed to stick to me. So I rubbed it off with all possible speed by turning into a street where I saw the great black dome of St. Paul's bulging at me from behind a grim stone building which a bystander said was Newgate Prison" (131). Out of the frying pan into the fire, from the slaughterhouse to the gallows. While Pip complains later that Newgate, too, seems to stick to him when he visits it, he is tainted by the marketplace long before. Along with Little Britain and Newgate, Smithfield compresses the violent images that haunt the novel: death relics, convicts, and grisly kinds of consumption. The casts are especially noteworthy in this regard since Dickens likely based them on ones he saw at Newgate in 1831, of the murderers and body-snatchers Bishop and Williams who sold the corpses of their victims for anatomical study (130). Pip's glimpses of London link the market to the anatomization of the body, the materialization of identity, and the implicit violence of economic exchange.

Writing retrospectively, Pip suggests that his arrival to London marked his entry into the market's horrors. But many of the most disturbing images of production and exchange predate Pip's expectations, hinting that the exigencies of commodity culture pervade even his sense of his psychological origins. The primal scene of his childhood – his encounter with Magwitch on the marshes – makes his first effort at self-narration roughly simultaneous with his entry into relations with property. He names himself, as Magwitch demands, even as he agrees to steal victuals and a file from the forge, and the sites of exchange that the adult Pip recalls are places of childhood terror and alienation. At Uncle Pumblechook's on the eve of his first visit to Satis House, Pip peers into the shop drawers and wonders – aptly, as a "pip" himself – "whether the flower-seeds and bulbs ever wanted of a fine day to break out of those jails, and bloom" (47). He notes also that Pumblechook gets so mixed up with his seeds that they become indistinguishable from his corduroys. In these displacements, Pip suggests that it is in the nature of the commodity to collapse the boundary between self and thing. At Satis House this collapse becomes a Gothic nightmare, the ruined brewery comprising a world of madness and decay complete with a terrifying figure of "wax-work and skeleton" who exists in the liminal space between spectacular commodity and fully-fledged subjectivity (50).

Aaron Landau associates Satis House with Marx's account of the mystifying power of the commodity, for "there is something in the very reality of the house which ... baffles realistic description, since it somehow lies fundamentally beyond the pale of ordinary materiality."[10] Like Marx's table in

Capital, the house appears as "a very strange thing, abounding in metaphysical subtleties" and defying the possibility of stable discourse."[11] Susan Walsh reads Satis House's decay as the hyperbolic result of Miss Havisham's refusal to operate the brewery, "sponsor her male relatives," or otherwise permit capital to circulate "within the proper [masculine] channels of investment and trade."[12] But Satis House remains central as a site of exchange, its physical dilapidation marking the perversion, not the abdication, of its commercial role. Early in her isolation, Miss Havisham acquires Estella, and she eventually establishes some proprietorship in Pip; the brewery decays as Miss Havisham begins to traffic in children instead of beer. In other ways, too, Satis House remains a vital commercial site, for it provides the capital for Pip's final investment in Herbert Pocket and is an object of economic desire for the grasping members of the Pocket clan, who watch uncomfortably as Miss Havisham accuses them of plotting the grossest kind of consumption, rapping the table with her stick and saying, "Now you all know where to take your stations when you come to feast upon me" (72). Satis House terrifies not because its commercial function has ceased but because it collapses the boundary between people and things, binding both to a monstrous cycle of consumption and exchange.

The forge, too, binds Pip uncomfortably to the market by placing him and Joe under the tyranny of a heartless domestic economy. Mrs. Joe butters their bread like a surgeon "making a plaister" and hands it over stuck through with needles and pins, the wounding remnants of her women's work (14). Pip's childish terror at stealing victuals for Magwitch stems partly from knowing "Mrs. Joe's housekeeping to be of the strictest kind," and he returns from the marshes Christmas morning to find her "vigorously reaping the floors of her establishment" (15, 23). She also forces Pip into precocious commercial relations, impressing upon him the debt he owes her for having "brought [him] up by hand" after he "insisted on being born, in opposition to the dictates of reason, religion, and morality" (14, 24). As revenge, she turns Pip into a laboring factotum, making him "odd-boy about the forge" and renting him out for other jobs:

> if any neighbour happened to want an extra boy to frighten birds, or pick up stones, or do any such job, I was favoured with the employment. In order, however, that our superior position might not be compromised thereby, a money-box was kept on the kitchen mantel-shelf, into which it was publicly made known that all my earnings were dropped. I have an impression that they were to be contributed eventually to the liquidation of the National Debt, but I know I had no hope of any personal participation in the treasure. (38)

Pip's relationship to home is decidedly economic, and his "impression" regarding his relation to the National Debt suggests the position of Mrs. Joe's "establishment" within formal networks of exchange. Pip also reminds us that the forge is both domestic and commercial space, since the Christmas dinner – already far from a Pickwickian yule – is interrupted by the demand that Joe conduct his trade, leaving Christmas to unfold around the furnace rather than the hearth. As we learn later, too, Orlick tells Pip "that the Devil lived in a black corner of the forge, and ... it was necessary to make up the fire once in every seven years, with a live boy" (91). The lie offers another image of Gothic horror and bodily consumption and reminds us that the forge, like Satis House, is pervaded by the vaguely supernatural imperatives of the market.

Perhaps this explains why Pip, even in childhood, appears to himself in retrospect as objectified and commodified. Beginning in chapter 3, Pip is "my boy" and "my dear boy" to Magwitch and eventually embodies Magwitch's desire to own a gentleman (21, 239). Likewise, Pumblechook calls Pip "Sixpennorth of halfpence" and "a four-footed Squeaker," metaphors that foreshadow Pip's visit to Smithfield market (25, 27). Especially when money is to be got by it, Pip circulates like a commodity: rented to Miss Havisham and the neighbors, given back to Joe with a "premium," bound apprentice for a fee, and sold finally to Magwitch through Jaggers, though Joe refuses the money (82). As he prepares to leave for London for the first time, Pip affirms his commodification, remarking that Trabb "measured and calculated" him for his new clothes "as if [he] were an estate and [Trabb] the finest species of surveyor" (119). Blurring the distinction between subject and commodity becomes, consequently, Pip's dominant narrative mode, even when he accounts for others. Pip begins calling Magwitch "my convict" almost as soon as Magwitch begins calling him "my boy," and he writes persistently as if Miss Havisham has some proprietorship in Estella – which she does, since she makes Estella "a thing to be bartered in the marriage market," a pure commodity, her behavior dictated by her mother/owner and those who want to buy (32).[13] As Estella tells Pip when she comes to London, "We have no choice, you and I, but to obey our instructions. We are not free to follow our own devices" (202). Later, in his delirious dreams, Pip "confound[s] impossible existences with [his] own identity," at one time believing himself "a brick in the house-wall," and at another "a steel beam of a vast engine, clashing and whirling over a gulf" (343). These nightmares hint that Pip has been made an object rather than a subject, his life so crushing an exercise in Pumblechook's running sums that he becomes, like Bill Barley, emptied out and "totally unequal to the consideration of any subject more psychological than Gout, Rum, and Purser's stores" (281).

The center of these images is the alienating power of capitalism, which forces the self to become productive and transforms it, often violently, into an object of exchange. Pettitt notes that Pip's dreams mimic a "violent effect of market capitalism" by collapsing the "boundaries between people and things" and conflating him with the concrete and steel of the new industrial age.[14] By suggesting that the subject might be absorbed or consumed by the requirements of capital, the novel also makes cannibalism one of its most pervasive concerns.[15] Dread of being devoured is one of Pip's earliest fears, from the time when Magwitch threatens to eat his "fat cheeks" and terrifies him with the story of "the young man" with a knack for "getting at a boy, and at his heart, and at his liver" (10–11). The novel's early chapters center upon eating and consumption: Pip bolting his bread, Magwitch gobbling his food, and Pumblechook calling Pip a "Squeaker" at Christmas dinner – a metaphor that gathers force from the threats of the first chapter and its reinvigoration later in the novel. When Joe first visits Pip in London and sees the unsavory surroundings of Barnard's Inn, Joe remarks, "I wouldn't keep a pig in it myself – not in the case that I wished him to fatten wholesome and to eat with a meller flavor" (171). This idea recurs at Walworth when Pip toasts his old acquaintance, Wemmick's pig, for the Aged P. At the lime kiln Orlick eyes Pip as if his mouth "watered for [him]," and at Satis House Miss Havisham kisses Estella with "ravenous intensity" and eyes her as if she is "devouring the beautiful creature she had reared" (316, 184, 228). Like Miss Havisham's prediction that the Pockets will "feast" upon her, these passages offer a violent refrain linking the commodification of subjectivity to the blood and foam of Smithfield market.

But this refrain also hints at a more complex disintegration, physical and psychological, and for the consumer as well as the consumed. Dickens had a persistent imaginative concern with cannibalism dating back to his interest in Sir John Franklin's arctic expedition, which disappeared in 1845 while looking for a Northwest Passage. Separate discoveries in 1854 and 1859 raised the uncomfortable specter that Franklin's starving crew had turned cannibal, a charge that Dickens refuted vigorously in his journalism and his 1856 Christmas book *The Wreck of the Golden Mary*.[16] He simply refused to believe that the gentlemanly Franklin could have been "brought to the level of the lowest savage in a vain struggle for survival," for if so "the assumed differences between the West and the 'uncivilized world' would be false. . . . identity would disintegrate, and with a sense of identity would go the very meaning of life as the West had attempted to predicate it."[17] *Great Expectations*' hints of cannibalism are not, then, just a requiem for the consumed and disposable bodies of the new industrial age; they are rooted in the dynamics of identity and self-creation at the center of its structural and symbolic plan, and in contemporary anxieties about colonialism and Englishness. They are rooted, too, in *Great Expectations*' narrative form, with cannibalism serving as a figure of the novel's own production and consumption of the self.

No wonder many of the novel's characters respond neurotically or even pathologically to their involvement in capitalist exchange. For Miss Havisham, who was treated as a commodity in the marriage market, the response is to turn consumer, trafficking in children and abandoning legitimate commercial activity. As Pip writes, her conduct coincides with, or perhaps produces, mental illness, for "her mind, brooding solitary, had grown diseased" (297). Jaggers's response is the obsessive hand-washing that belies his sense of his tainting profession, and Wemmick lives divided deliberately between his empathetic self and a commercial identity that must participate in the market. Pip writes that there are "twin Wemmicks," one full of Walworth sentiments and the other "dryer and harder," a self-division that epitomizes the "*cordon sanitaire* Victorians drew around 'Walworth sentiments' to protect them from 'Little Britain'" (290, 163).[18] Grahame Smith argues that in Wemmick's self-division, Dickens captures with "masterly insight the perilous situation of man under the conditions of industrial capitalism."[19] But as we see when Pip exposes Wemmick's home life to Jaggers, such divisions inevitably break down: Walworth is more a castle in the air than an impregnable fortification against commercial relations. This is clear when Pip visits Walworth and sees Wemmick's "portable property": "the pen with which a celebrated forgery had been committed, a distinguished razor or two, some locks of hair, and several manuscript confessions written under condemnation ... 'every one of 'em Lies, sir'" (162). Wemmick has already brought Little Britain into Walworth – has already been, despite his conscious defenses, pervaded and undermined by exchange. Moreover, his collection of "Lies" underscores the novel's concern with identity, its narration, and the consequences of its becoming "portable property."

This concern is embedded deeply in *Great Expectations*, not only as part of the novel's thematic and symbolic operation but also in its imaginative origins and the conditions of its material production. However elaborately wrought artistically and psychologically, *Great Expectations* is the work of an author who wished to sell and did sell books, consistently and in unprecedented numbers during the middle of the nineteenth century. We cannot know whether Dickens wrote *Great Expectations* to capitalize on the mid-century popularity of autobiography, but we do know that, whatever other imperatives also drove him, Dickens planned it carefully and thoroughly for the literary market. He began contemplating the novel no later than summer 1860, when he wrote to the Earl of Carlisle, "I am prowling about, meditating a new book."[20] But as Margaret Cardwell points out, Dickens's short fiction and journalism bear traces of *Great Expectations* as early as 1855, when he was beginning *Little Dorrit*.[21] When he finally began writing in September 1860, he planned to publish in twenty monthly parts, a format he had not used since the June 1857 finale of *Little Dorrit* because he had published *A Tale of Two Cities* in *All the Year Round* to give the new magazine a proper start. By 1860 he was ready for a triumphant return to his old audience, but with a crucial difference: with *Great Expectations*, he planned for the first time to follow serialization with publication in three volumes at the standard price of 31s. 6d.

"Planned" is the key word, for earlier works by Dickens had, at various times, been issued in three volumes after serial publication. In November 1836, he had signed an agreement with Richard Bentley to edit *Bentley's Miscellany* and provide two novels in three volumes. But during the three tumultuous years that followed, Dickens wrenched repeated concessions from Bentley, including that *Oliver Twist*, which he had begun writing as a separately remunerated serial for the *Miscellany*, might be regarded as the first of those triple-deckers. This uncertainty about format characterized much of Dickens's early career, as he oscillated between twenty-number novels like *The Pickwick Papers* and *Nicholas Nickleby*, the magazine serial turned triple-decker *Oliver Twist*, and the weekly periodical *Master Humphrey's Clock*, which included such heterogeneous material as *The Old Curiosity Shop* and *Barnaby Rudge*, and was collected into three volumes by Chapman and Hall in 1841. But none of these was conceived from the first as a triple-decker or structured explicitly to suit the format. Dickens did plan *Great Expectations* this way, and so thoroughly that its volumes appear nearly as the acts in a play, corresponding to both the "stages" of Pip's expectations and the formatting needs of Chapman and Hall.[22] During the 1840s and 1850s, Dickens had settled into a pattern of writing novels in twenty parts and collecting them in two modestly priced volumes, eschewing the circulating libraries' preference for triple-deckers in favor of cheaper formats that promised wide sales. Dickens's decision to plan *Great Expectations* as a triple-decker, therefore, was not "predictable from anything which had gone before in Dickens's life. No other work of his had been issued in that form at that price."[23] The decision to issue *Great Expectations* in three volumes was calculated carefully: not only would a publisher pay Dickens more for his work than he could afford to pay himself if he published in *All the Year Round*, but also the triple-decker format would draw a class of readers he had rarely approached before. Publishing this way would bring his work to the circulating libraries and also to those readers with the greatest ability to pay.

The decision was dictated by Dickens's sense of financial need. By 1860 he could afford to live in relative splendor and had long been beyond any danger of suffering the fate of his impecunious father. Yet he never really outgrew his wrenching childhood experiences at the Marshalsea and Warren's Blacking, nor could he keep the traces of this misery from appearing in his work. Dickens had during the 1850s come to recognize the indelibility of this sadness, and in the years after 1858, when he ended his marriage, he felt it with greater force. As he wrote to Forster, "The never-to-be-forgotten misery of that old time bred a certain shrinking sensitiveness in a certain ill-clad, ill-fed child, that I have found come back in the never-to-be-forgotten misery of this later time."[24] Even in the last year of his life, Dickens baffled his children while playing a memory game, reciting a long series of words when his turn came and then adding "Warren's Blacking, 30, Strand."[25] His son Henry could attach no meaning to the words then, but he understood immediately when Forster published his first volume of *The Life of Charles Dickens* in 1872. Though Dickens had made extraordinary sums of money by the time he wrote *Great Expectations*, he never ceased to be the anxious, unhappy child: too aware of poverty, too ashamed of his secret vulgarity, too worried about sliding into economic and social degradation. He had the economic obligations of a man with a large family and a dispiriting number of financial dependents, and he earned enough to support them all, live well, entertain lavishly, and leave a legacy of £90,000. Yet he could not rest from his lucrative work – could not, like Pip, be content to have "a good name," work hard, and do "very well" (355). Dickens did not need money in 1860. But he *needed* it with a longing that no success could quell.

In this sense, he needed it more than usual when he began planning *Great Expectations*. He separated from Catherine in June 1858, and by year's end he was maintaining homes for her and Ellen Ternan, the old family residence at Tavistock House, and the new one at Gad's Hill.[26] The sale of Tavistock House in August 1860 helped, but by then Dickens's financial worries had compounded. His mother was sliding into dementia, and he needed to arrange for her care, as well as for the care of his brother Alfred's young widow and children. Dickens was increasingly worried too, about the prospects for his sons, the eldest of whom, Charley, had already required a costly setting-up with Baring Brothers. Dickens had purchased a military commission for Walter, the next eldest, but two more sons were nearing their majority. Cardwell and Rosenberg both argue that Dickens wrote his worries for Charley into the novel in Herbert, who appears in the manuscript "not as an Insurer of Ships but as a budding merchant, who will trade, not merely for sugar, tobacco, and rum, to the West Indies ... but to China for teas."[27] In a letter to Charles Lever in January 1861, he commiserated the trouble Lever was having with his own son, writing, "It is a tremendous weight and anxiety to be in our proud and venerable condition. Let me offer you one consolation out of the fulness of my heart – and quiver. You have not seven of them; I have!"[28] Beyond these concerns, Dickens's break with Bradbury and Evans in 1858 – another consequence of his ruined marriage – had caused him to discontinue *Household Words* in favor of *All the Year Round*, which he owned a three-quarters share in and advanced the money to create. Dickens had always written for money: he was a professional who rarely missed a deadline and knew the market value of his work. When he began *Great Expectations*, though, he had specific financial needs, and more pressing ones than he had known in years.

He met them by making himself into "portable property," and not just by writing autobiographically. Besides engaging fully in the textual and economic practices that had turned identity into a commodity in Victorian England, Dickens embarked in the late 1850s on the start of his remarkable second career as a public reader, which had earned him tens of thousands of pounds by the time he died in 1870. To Forster in September 1857 Dickens suggested that he might pay for his purchase of Gad's Hill "by reviving that old idea of some Readings from [his] books."[29] Forster tried to dissuade him, as on past occasions, by urging that a respectable author should not conduct himself like a traveling show.[30] But a year later, as news of his marriage scandal broke, Dickens commenced his first reading tour, to London, the provinces, Ireland, and Scotland, packing houses and earning an average of £200 per show – eighty-eight of them "in a little more than ninety days."[31] As his private life disintegrated, his public identity congealed in a strange oscillation between self-creation and self-erasure: he willfully, even eagerly, *became* his texts for his audiences, performing his characters before the eyes of thousands. He was Scrooge, he was Mrs. Gamp, he was alternately and simultaneously Nicholas Nickleby and Wackford Squeers, and around the margins of these characters he was Dickens himself, or at least Dickens as he wished audiences to see him. He was at once the inventor and embodiment of his writing, the subject and object of his imaginative work. However unconsciously, Dickens used his readings to press to a logical culmination the author-as-text formulation implied by literary copyright. And he capitalized spectacularly on the arrangement.

Though he never quite asked his children to take sides in his domestic strife, he "impressed upon them that 'their father's name was their best possession' – which they knew to be true – and he expected them to act accordingly."[32] He had traded on that name in undertaking the public readings and creating *All the Year Round*. He also did so often to boost the magazine's circulation, writing essays in the guise of an "Uncommercial Traveller" when not supplying the lead serial.[33] Surely this is why Dickens was so incensed when he believed that his marital strife had become the subject of gossip and scandal. Having nearly reached a separation agreement with Catherine in May 1858, he fumed when he learned that her relations were "circulating the story that Ellen Ternan was his mistress."[34] For weeks the settlement languished while he insisted on a written retraction, which he got only after publishing his infamous and ill-advised "Personal" statement in *Household Words*, alluding vaguely to "domestic trouble" that "has been made the occasion of misrepresentations, most grossly false, most monstrous, and most cruel."[35] The outburst indicates how unreasonable he had become. The broken friendships of these years – with Mark Lemon, William Thackeray, and Angela Burdett Coutts, among others – all stemmed from Dickens's overwrought sense that old allies had connived at broadcasting the scandal, or at least failed to help him silence it.[36] More to the point, he understood that the damage done by such connivances and failures was not just emotional but material, a blow to his legacy in more senses than one.

These details suggest that for Dickens the author-as-text model of literary production had become reflexive, an automatic mode that passed seamlessly (and shamelessly) from producing texts to producing the self, and that treated both text and self as commodities designed for the market. In 1861 Dickens's willing embrace of this model even caused a mild quarrel with his friend Edward Bulwer-Lytton just as *Great Expectations* neared its end. Bulwer's *A Strange Story* (1862) was to follow Dickens's novel in *All the Year Round*, but he demurred at being named in the first advertisements.[37] Attempting to smooth matters but keep future notices on the same footing, Dickens wrote gently to Bulwer, "It is so very important to us to avoid any indirect way in any such matter, and to have a name – THE name. I never, for my part, contemplated any other form of announcement, or supposed that you did."[38] Dickens wanted to sell Bulwer as he sold himself: as a subjectivity embedded in, inseparable from, the text he produced. But on the sly – and in defiance, we might say, of the old supposition that autobiography contained or conveyed the truth about identity – Dickens was also using texts to reify and broaden the gap between subjectivity and its textualization, and for the purpose of adapting his identity to the demands of the market.

As Dickens reminded his children and his wife's relations, capitalizing on his name meant hiding his sexual misconduct and ensuring – as in his "Personal" statement and his mother-in-law's retraction – that textual accounts of his affair attest only to its nonexistence. The details of Dickens's sordid private life had to remain hidden: the story of identity had to be the story of an absence. To preserve its market value, his identity had literally to be papered over, constructed and formalized as a textual record that would confirm publicly a palatable, and therefore consumable, version of Dickens the author. Such a textualization belongs generally to the Victorian impulse to separate public from private, and specifically to Dickens's impulse to affirm his identity as a man of high morals and homely sentiments. He wanted to use texts to cement his reputation as a respectable champion of the hearth. But the effect of his maneuvering was to inscribe a kind of purposeful failure on self-narration – to subject the subject, so to speak, to a discursive disfigurement indispensable to the ability of his self-narrative to meet commercial demands. Dickens's entanglement in the author-as-text dynamic thus serves as an allegory of mid-century authorship, in which textual self-creation is also self-loss, precisely because the text is a commodity shaped by capitalist demands. On the eve of writing *Great Expectations*, Dickens enacted this drama of self-creation and self-loss explicitly, making a great bonfire and burning "in the field at Gad's Hill, the accumulated letters and papers of twenty years."[39] The bonfire epitomizes the autobiographical economy that makes self-creation and self-loss simultaneous. Even as Dickens embarked upon the intensely personal self-narration of *Great Expectations* then, he demonstrated a sense of self-narration's limitations and dangers, and a sense of the implications of exposing identity to economic demands.

This did not keep Dickens from shaping *Great Expectations* to meet financial needs even more entirely than he had planned. By October 1860 Charles Lever's *A Day's Ride* was failing in *All the Year Round*, and badly enough that Dickens called "a council of war at the office" over the magazine's falling sales.[40] Two days later he wrote to Forster:

> It was perfectly clear that the one thing to be done was, for me to strike in. I have therefore decided to begin the story as of the length of the *Tale of Two Cities* on the first of December – begin publishing, that is. I must make the most I can out of the book ... The name is GREAT EXPECTATIONS.[41]

"Striking in" meant scuttling the plan to publish in monthly numbers, but it was a sacrifice, he admitted, "really and truly made for myself. The property of *All the Year Round* is far too valuable, in every way, to be much endangered."[42] Pip thus became the commodity within the commodity, a manifestation of not only Dickens himself but also of the sacrifice of identity, through its discursive and textual production, to the exigencies of the market. Though Dickens's letter implies that his decision was made by the "council," he likely arrived having decided his course and had summoned the magazine's staff to inform, not consult. By October 6 he had agreed to a contract "for early proofs of the story to America" where it would appear in *Harper's Weekly* simultaneously with its appearance in England.[43] He had moved rapidly, perhaps preemptively, to arrange that contract, sealing it even before he wrote to Lever to break the news that *Great Expectations* would supplant *A Day's Ride*. There is a suggestive synchronicity to Dickens's artistic and financial work. Even as he imagined Pip's childish labor and contributions to the liquidation of "the National Debt," he pressed Pip into economic service as the means of saving *All the Year Round*.

By any measure, *Great Expectations* became a resounding commercial success.[44] It arrested and then reversed the slide of *All the Year Round* and earned another £1,250 for the early proofs to *Harper's*; in the ten weeks after its serial run, it also passed through four three-volume printings and sold nearly 3,500 copies, mostly to the circulating libraries.[45] In letters Dickens crowed about his triumph, first when the novel was "universally liked" as a serial and subsequently when it sold so briskly as a triple-decker.[46] The novel's serialization had made no difference to Dickens's plan to make it a triple-decker, nor to its popularity or profitability. But the economic anxieties surrounding its writing and publication left indelible marks. For one, the change to weekly serialization almost certainly helped to produce the artistic compression that critics often praise. For another, the novel's consistent concern with commodity and exchange seems to owe as much to its author's subconscious preoccupations as to his deliberate art. Within a week of deciding that *Great Expectations* would be the means of steadying

All the Year Round, Dickens told Forster that it would "be written in the first person throughout."[47] Still, the title suggested what the novel was really about – money – an implication reinforced at the end of each of its three parts, which all close by noting the end of a "Stage of Pip's Expectations." Like Mrs. Joe after she is attacked, Dickens elides the difference between "Pip" and "property," the narrative of identity and the narrative of commodity. Though Elliot Gilbert claims that "[w]e can pretty well dismiss the notion that Dickens acted out of crass commercialism" in revising the novel's ending, this is hardly clear – the less so, as Michael Slater points out, since Dickens told Forster that he believed the story would be "more acceptable," presumably to a popular audience, "through the alteration."[48] It is not even certain, really, whether the novel's "expectations" are Dickens's or Pip's.[49] *Great Expectations* is pervaded thoroughly by its status as a commodity. So while Dickens might have crafted the novel as an intimate account of an identity in the process of self-creation, he did so with an eye to making it pay.

Writing of Dickens's 1848 Christmas book *The Haunted Man*, Rosemarie Bodenheimer suggests that the story is about the "cost" of autobiographical disclosure. It might be read, she argues, "as an allegory of autobiographical anxiety: what uncontrollable damage might result from giving away ineradicable memories? What would happen to Dickens's relationship with his audiences if he revealed his low past, or his personal anger and shame?"[50] The conjecture is the more persuasive because Dickens wrote *The Haunted Man* around the same time that he wrote the autobiographical fragment that Forster eventually published in his *Life*, and that served as the basis for *Copperfield*. But the value of Bodenheimer's reading is in its principle more than its particulars, for it casts Dickens's autobiographical impulse as both commercial and psychological, underscoring the inseparability of these imperatives and allowing us to treat *Great Expectations* as a vehicle for simultaneously meeting intensely private and explicitly material needs. If, as Gail Turley Houston writes, *Great Expectations* is "far more conscious" than *Copperfield* of "how economics infiltrate the construction of the self," it may be because an older Dickens understood how intractable his economic anxiety would remain, how entirely his identity – every identity – is pervaded by economic demands.[51] More, he understood this problem as both psychic and discursive, symbolic and material. *Great Expectations* records this nexus of psychological and economic need in Pip, a textualized and commodified subject working anxiously through the consequences of becoming "portable property."

This work begins in the first chapter as Pip describes his emergence into psychological and linguistic awareness – his "first most vivid and broad impression of the identity of things" (9). Partly the adult Pip's attempt to use language to account for his origins, the first chapter is also the child Pip's attempt to find his origins within language, or, to be precise, within the materiality of texts. Standing in the churchyard staring at the tombstones of his parents, Pip "unreasonably" derives what they were like from "[t]he shape of the letters" and "turn of the inscription"; consequently, he has "an odd idea that [his father] was a square, stout, dark man with curly black hair" and that his "mother was freckled and sickly" (9). Peter Brooks writes that Pip attempts here "to motivate the arbitrary sign, to interpret signs as if they were mimetic and thus naturally tied to the object for which they stand," and he calls the attempt "a metaphorical process unaware of itself, the making of a fiction unaware of its status as fiction making."[52] This may be true of the child, but the narrator's mature recognition that these efforts at interpretation are "unreasonable" suggests that he recognizes and wishes to record the representational limits of language's material form, or what Martine Hennard Dutheil calls its "problematic nature" and "the difficulties of the interpretive act."[53] Pip's account of his childish attempts to "read" the tombstones underscores that the material record of identity never suffices, for it never says all that it would or should about the subject.

Perhaps this explains why Pip's narrative has from the start a peculiar unsaid quality. The dramatic action of the novel's first "stage" illustrates Pip's secrecy regarding his encounter with Magwitch, his theft of victuals and a file from the forge, the real state of things at Satis House, and his growing misery regarding Estella and consequent yearning to be a gentleman. But even as an adult looking back on the churchyard scene, Pip omits something crucial: that the name on his father's tombstone is his own, and that the stone therefore textualizes a potential narrative of his own identity, a death sentence that threatens to preempt or foreclose his autobiography. The "liminary 'primal scene'" in the churchyard thus precedes Magwitch's appearance, for the threat of premature death that Pip faces is a linguistic, not a criminal, matter.[54] But then, Pip is not exactly named for his father, or at least his father's name – his own name – is not the one he claims. Instead, he explains, "My father's family name being Pirrip, and my Christian name Philip, my infant tongue could make of both names nothing longer or more explicit than Pip. So, I called myself Pip, and came to be called Pip" (9). The name he chooses suggests a number of things, but it is no simple mispronunciation; rather, it is an elision, an erasure of nine letters in the middle of "Philip Pirrip," nine letters that appear on the tombstone, nine letters that would name him like his father and permit greater space – by his "infant" logic – to interpret identity from its textualization. Pip's act of self-naming is not a mispronunciation so much as a charm against mis-pronunciation, a rejection of what others might pronounce him and of his death already writ large upon the stone. Dutheil argues that the novel's beginning "celebrates the challenges and the pleasures of [interpretation] while drawing attention to the autonomous creative potential of language."[55] More accurately, *Great Expectations* begins "in mortal terror," not of Magwitch or the young man who may eat Pip's heart and liver, but of the uncontrollable potentialities of texts (18).

Pip's mature narrative reinscribes constantly the lesson of the churchyard, underscoring the instability of written texts and the depth of their economic entanglements. Compeyson, a figure of ghostly terror to Pip, destabilizes the correspondence between text and self because he "writes fifty hands," while he commits forgeries that exploit a capitalist system founded upon paper money (318). More troubling, language in *Great Expectations* often becomes so tied to material goods that it fails even to appear as language. Pip struggles to learn to cipher partly because the "large old English D" that Biddy gives him to copy appears to him "to be a design for a buckle," and the T that Mrs. Joe draws repeatedly after she is attacked turns out to be not a letter but an anvil by which she means to signify Orlick (62). Each such instance plays upon the unstable relation of signifier to signified. But each also suggests the interchangeability of language and property, the sense in which language, even (or especially) when it represents identity, becomes a commodity the moment it takes material form. Mr. Wopsle's great-aunt, "besides keeping [her] Educational Institution, kept – in the same room – a little general shop," so that Pip's lessons from Biddy include not only the inscrutable D but also, fittingly, her "imparting some information from her little catalogue of Prices" (39, 62). As Pip's scarcely decipherable letter to Joe shows, writing is a tenuous business, in large measure because it is prone to misinterpretation and pervaded by commodity exchange.

Not surprisingly, the novel's acts of naming and narration appear often as failed attempts to sanction a particular narrative of identity. It is not only that names in *Great Expectations* are multiple and shifting; it is that textualizations of identity in the novel turn out so often to be false or insufficient.[56] Debrett's *Peerage*, for instance, records Bentley Drummle as a "gentleman" though he is as loutish as Orlick. But Mrs. Pocket anyway reads Debrett's precisely for what it does *not* contain: notice of "the exact date at which her grandpapa would have come into the book, if he ever had come at all" (150). The index to the nineteenth-century aristocracy thus functions in the novel as a doubly flawed text, incredible for what it says and suspect for what it does not. It is a register of identity that registers nothing at all. Magwitch is caught between two accounts of his identity, the official record authorized and produced by the law, which makes him the worst of a very bad lot, and the verbal narrative that he gives to Pip and Herbert, which Pip writes into the novel and which recasts the legal record in ways that make its insufficiency clear. Even Joe, illiterate as he is, is nearly implicated in textualizing identity, as he explains to Pip in recounting his father's death. Joe says, "it were my intentions to have had put upon his tombstone that Whatsume'er the failings on his part, Remember reader he were that good in his hart" (41). At best, the inscription whitewashes his father's drunken abuse; at worst, it cheapens grossly Joe's suffering and his mother's and reifies the gap between identity and its textual representation. The inscription is never cut, though, for, as Joe explains, "poetry costs money, cut it how you will, small or large" (41). It is the novel's second tombstone scene: a seriocomic echo of the first and a palimpsest of the novel's knotty concern with textuality, commodity, and the real and symbolic costs of writing identity.

No character is implicated more thoroughly in this concern than Jaggers, who appears at the Three Jolly Bargemen and immediately "tak[es] possession of Mr. Wopsle" as he gives out the sensational murder described in the newspaper (106). In Pip's memory, Jaggers has from the start "a manner expressive of knowing something secret about every one of us that would effectually do for each individual if he chose to disclose it" (107). He is dangerous because of the stories he might tell – because, as Pip implies, though guilt is private and universal, its narration is an expression of power. As an agent of the law, Jaggers can exert that power to give identity tangible form, as a contract or affidavit, and his legal function ties him so closely to such narrative production that he treats even verbal exchanges as textual ones. Jaggers terrorizes the hapless Mike, making him rephrase his remarks about witnesses and alibis, and he warns Pip after Magwitch's return, "Don't commit yourself ... and don't commit any one. You understand – any one. Don't tell me anything: I don't want to know anything; I am not curious" (251). The warning suggests that everyone, Jaggers included, is susceptible to the law's power to make identity textual, for it is the law that fixes language and meaning. It also reminds us that the very cultural function of the law is to materialize identity, to formalize its existence in certificates, wills, and registers, and to use these material texts to affirm and delineate the subject's relation to property.

Jaggers thus reinforces what we have known since Pip's "unreasonable" reading of his parents' tombstones: that textualizations of identity do not produce complete or stable accounts of the subject. Since prosecutorial logic demands that guilt be fixed formally and certainly upon the narrative of the criminal, Jaggers defends his clients by dispersing their identities across potential narratives, each an alternative to the guilty story the law would tell. The episode with Mike suggests this in its intimation that the business of the defense is to create, not discover, evidence, and to do so by propounding multiple narratives without regard for the truth.[57] And this is so even though Pip treats identity often as an incontrovertible essence that precedes and underlies narration. To his eyes, no disguise can conceal Magwitch after his return, for no matter the alias or dress "there was Convict in the very grain of the man" (252). Though Pip begins later to think of Magwitch as "softened," other characters remain unchanged for him, from Miss Havisham to Compeyson, Joe, and even Estella, who may return at novel's end "bent and broken" but still has her "indescribable majesty and . . . indescribable charm" (282, 358, 357). Here as in his other fiction, this permanence owes partly to Dickens's treatment of psychological trauma as a thing etched indelibly upon the body.[58] But like inscriptions on tombstones, such materializations of identity are both insufficient and excessive, limited indices to subjectivity but also surpluses that open the subject to interpretation and invention.

Jaggers's handling of Molly's case depends entirely upon the body's ambiguity as text, for he uses her slimness, modest dress, and lacerated hands to suggest that she did *not* do exactly what she did, and to argue instead that she might be guilty of murdering her own child. He defends her by rendering her narrative multiple, through what Andrew Miller has described as "the ingenious fabrication of counterfactuals," making her injured hands signify too many things instead of just one.[59] As Jaggers puts it to the Jury:

> We say these are not marks of finger-nails, but marks of brambles, and we show you the brambles. You say they are marks of finger-nails, and you set up the hypothesis that she destroyed her child. . . . For anything we know, she may have destroyed her child, and the child in clinging to her may have scratched her hands. What then? You are not trying her for the murder of her child; why don't you? As to this case, if you *will* have scratches, we say that, for anything we know, you may have accounted for them, assuming for the sake of argument that you have not invented them? (294)

"Mr. Jaggers was," Wemmick boasts, "altogether too many for the Jury" and makes his career because of the shrewd way he works the case (294). That shrewdness inheres in Jaggers's cool exploitation of the body's potential as a material record – at once insufficient and excessive – of the self. Besides Pip, Jaggers is the novel's most prolific producer of narratives of identity, and like Pip he recognizes the limits and perils of textualizing the subject. As the novel's principal financial agent, he also embodies the entanglement of such narratives with material expectations. He handles Miss Havisham's financial affairs and revitalizes her stagnant wealth by restoring it through Pip and Herbert to the masculine world of capitalist circulation, and as Magwitch's legal man, he facilitates the flow of capital from the colonies to the Crown and aids in producing a new model gentleman, founded upon the active generation of wealth rather than the patrilineal interests of an earlier age. Jaggers stands symbolically at the center of *Great Expectations*: an agent for both the narrative production of the self and the regulation of commercial activity – for, we might say, calibrating the ideological relation between texts, identity, and commodity culture.

Situated at this ideological and discursive nexus, he exposes the legal and cultural sanction for trafficking in identity and for using narrative to make it an object of exchange. His "portable property" includes the two hideous casts, whose squalid perch amid the other trinkets at Little Britain reveals how identity can be arrested, suspended, attenuated, and made grotesque by its transformation into a material thing. Indeed, Jaggers treats all textualizations of identity as commodities – that is, fetishistically, ensuring that their valence derives from external demands rather than from the subject's inherent need for self-expression. As Wemmick tells Pip, Jaggers never locks his house, for any theft would be compensated by his "hav[ing] their lives, and the lives of scores of 'em. He'd have all he could get. And it's impossible to say what he couldn't get, if he gave his mind to it" (160). Steeped in language of gluttonous materialism, the remark sounds like Wemmick's philosophy regarding "portable property." But Jaggers trades in people, not things, and in doing so he renders the boundary between identity and property razor-thin. For his Britannia-metal spoons, Jaggers would trade accounts of criminal subjects, which the police would convert into possession of those subjects. This logic is more explicit in Jaggers's dealings with Molly, whom he controls solely through the story he can tell. The price of keeping Molly's story a secret is Estella, the "pound of flesh extracted from her ... as a human fee."[60] More, if, as in

Molly's case, owning the subject's narrative means owning the subject, Estella's fate shows that this relationship is reciprocal. By taking Estella from her mother, Jaggers takes possession of her story, too, alienating her permanently from the narrative of her origins. She originates in a transaction and thus has no churchyard scene. Jaggers thus demystifies the nature of things in *Great Expectations*, revealing the novel's basis in an economics of identity that exposes the subject, through narrative, to the rules of ownership and power that structure exchange.

Magwitch occupies precisely this intersection of identity and property and suffers from the power relations that govern both. He is, of course, vulnerable to the law when he returns to London because of his criminal history. But the longer trajectory of Magwitch's story suggests an older problem, founded upon property, that has always undergirded his identity. Like Pip, he emerged simultaneously into self-awareness and illicit relations with property, "first becom[ing] aware of [him]self, down in Essex, a thieving turnips" (259). Having stolen, Magwitch is seized by the Crown, and his story is taken up by prison officials who tell visitors that he is "a terrible hardened one" who "[m]ay be said to live in jails" (259). What Magwitch calls the "short and handy" version of his story rehearses the extent to which that story has belonged to the Crown ever since. "In jail and out of jail, in jail and out of jail, in jail and out of jail. There, you've got it. That's *my* life pretty much" (258). In his study of *Great Expectations* and social statistics, Michael Klotz calls Magwitch "unassimilable," uncountable and unaccountable, since his transience would exclude him from census records and since we learn so little of his past.[61] But the authorities know *who* he is; they accounted for him long ago as a guilty subject. They do not know *where* he is. What Magwitch must avoid is falling into their hands, letting his identity get into circulation where it might be exchanged for material gain. He is thus in danger from the moment that Compeyson learns of his good fortune in Australia and decides to seek a reward through the forfeiture of Magwitch's money to the Crown. Indeed, Magwitch is truly undone only when his story begins to function as a commodity, taking on, for Compeyson, economic value. As if to reinforce this point, his recapture results in his body, narrative, and money all being taken at once, reminding us of the extent to which Magwitch and his story are inseparable from property – concerned with it, merged in it, and conceived as it. From the first existing as a material record inscribed by the law, he remains subject to the power that governs the commodity.

This equation pervades Pip's account of himself, too, for his narrative reveals profound anxiety regarding his self-narration and the way in which writing entangles the subject in power relations rooted in exchange. Like Magwitch, Pip becomes "portable property" at the moment of his self-naming, for Magwitch literally takes possession of him, grabbing him and demanding that he bring victuals. Pip's narrative underscores the originating power of this moment, as if he senses that in writing his life he makes himself property. The scene in the churchyard functions metonymically to encode the symbolic implications of Pip's attempt at self-narration, which appear most powerfully in Pip's structuring his story around the idea that his life is a debt owed, his subjectivity a deficit that must be made up to repay his sister for bringing him up by hand, or to make amends to Magwitch, Miss Havisham, Joe, and the others who have been his benefactors. The contrast that Pip draws between himself and his five dead brothers in the churchyard is that they died without repaying that debt, lying mendicant "with their hands in their trousers-pockets" after giving up "trying to get a living, exceedingly early in that universal struggle" (9). The language is Darwinian but also Malthusian. Having "insisted on being born," Pip owes a debt embedded in origins, as if biological beginnings, like textual ones, bring subjectivity into economic relations just by making it a material thing.

For Pip as for Magwitch, these relations are embedded deeply. His first self-aware act is to promise to aid a convict by stealing from the forge, but by stealing brandy, too, Pip does more than he has promised, as if his thieving impulse exceeds the requirements of his childish terror. More, just as his crimes are discovered, Pip is snatched at the doorstep by the soldiers who are hunting a criminal on the marshes. Pip's story thus resonates with his symbolic father's, not just here but in his hovering returns to Newgate, his persistent associations with crime, and even his being bound apprentice to Joe, which looks so much like an arrest that a passerby hands him the tract "TO BE READ IN MY CELL" (85). Pip's story, too, is "in jail and out of jail" and begins and ends amid his vexed relation to property and exchange. Through symbol and recurrence, Pip's narrative recreates the sense of objectification that characterized his childhood, which in turn affirms the unsettling reciprocity between owning the subject and owning his story. What Pip records especially about the experience of being owned is the way that it plays havoc with both his self-account and his emergence as a fully realized and psychologically coherent subject. As Pip's "owners," Mrs. Joe, Miss Havisham, Magwitch, and others typically know more than he does about his own story. They produce his identity, not only by impacting his psychological formation but also by making demands and disclosures that fill narrative gaps: that he must go play at Satis House, that

Estella has gone to France, that Magwitch and not Miss Havisham is his benefactor. Such revelations change the course of his life, disrupting Pip in the act of becoming Pip and arriving eventually to self-narration. They also suggest that Mrs. Joe, Magwitch, Miss Havisham, and the rest own Pip precisely because they own his story, or enough of it to dictate how he will circulate through the world of the novel.

Each time Pip changes hands, in fact, his account of himself changes in response to external demands. After meeting Magwitch, Pip returns to the forge filled with lies about his conduct, and after his first visit to Satis House he invents outrageous fictions, wrenched from him by the demand that he describe how he "g[o]t on up town" though he knows that he "should not be understood" (56). Already, through Mrs. Joe and Pumblechook, Pip has lost his childish faith in the power of language to account for himself. The lesson makes Pip sorry – not for his sister and Pumblechook, who regard his story as evidence that Miss Havisham will "do something" for him – but rather for Joe, who retains a child's narrative credulity:

> And then I told Joe that I felt very miserable ... and that there had been a beautiful young lady at Miss Havisham's who was dreadfully proud, and that she had said I was common, and that I knew I was common, and that I wished I was not common, and that the lies had come of it somehow, though I didn't know how. (58–9)

He cannot quite articulate the connection between money and self-narration or understand the psychological effects of shame and economic desire. But the adult Pip dates from this moment his sense that the plot of his life is a "long chain of iron or gold," the stuff of imprisonment or luxury, a polyvalent symbol that binds the narrative of identity to parallel images that constrict and ornament, that make it appear at once too little and a little too much (60). The only question that remains, Brooks notes, is which sort of chain binds Pip, for his narrative suspends his story among overlapping plots: fairy tale, *bildungsroman*, romance, the Newgate novel, and the book of snobs. Each depends upon Pip's economic status, and none can culminate while that status remains unclear. Pip implies repeatedly his powerlessness to close the plot, whether by acknowledging Estella's power over his "boyish life" or wondering at his entanglement in "all this taint of prison and crime" (179, 202). Meanwhile, he drifts between London and the village, often – as when claiming his expectations or asking Miss Havisham to back Herbert – explicitly to conduct or embody exchange.

Murray Baumgarten writes that "Magwitch is [Pip's] author, as Miss Havisham creates Estella. Both ... are new minted unnatural, artificial creatures."[62] This overstates things, for Pip presumably writes his own story, which literally contains Magwitch's rather than the other way around. But it is not Magwitch's or anyone's *physical* proprietorship over Pip that is troubling, any more than it is Miss Havisham's physical ownership of Estella. What troubles, rather, is how deeply the narrative of property is embedded in Pip's self-narrative, how the stories of commodity and identity rise until they converge. Estella must write routinely to Miss Havisham to tell her how she and "the jewels" are getting on, and Pip learns only too late that Miss Havisham has only rented him, that Magwitch has made him a gentleman, and that Joe has paid his debts – too late, though these events have made him, even to the point of requiring him to keep being "Pip" in a constant reiteration of his self-naming (109). Mrs. Joe plays the holy fool when, being told of Pip's expectations, she lapses into a deeper idiocy in which "[s]he laugh[s] and nod[s] her head a great many times, and even repeat[s] after Biddy the words 'Pip' and 'Property'" (113). She conveys the same sense of interchangeability, of identity becoming a commodity, that causes Pip – and Dickens – to call his autobiography *Great Expectations*.

* * *

Brooks argues that *Great Expectations* bears signs of exhaustion, its plot used up and played out long before the novel ends.[63] To the extent that this is so, it is because the financial plot is played out, the expectations lost, the narrative energy expended by Magwitch's recapture and the loss of his fortune. Thereafter, Pip's autobiography dissolves into self-negation as he watches over the dying Magwitch and collapses into a delirium that ends only when Joe pays his creditors and settles his financial and psychological debts. But Zemka takes a different view, arguing that "the secret expectations of Pip's life are completed" by the writing of the narrative and that this is "the compensation [the novel] offers for the ravages perpetrated upon psychic life by the economic belief system of nineteenth-century capitalism."[64] Pip invites us to view his narrative as this sort of culmination, an emotional coalescence, even implying that he writes it because of his near-fatal encounter with Orlick, who makes him fear that he will be "misremembered after death" (317). But Pip's narrative also serves another function: it is the only material expectation that remains to him after Magwitch's death, the last legacy of a life once filled with capital possibilities. The novel itself serves as payment for the debt he owes – literally in the case of Joe, whom Pip repays by writing of his gratitude and painting Joe as the new model gentleman. But the novel also settles old scores, paying back through textual revelation those who have used Pip cruelly. Mrs. Joe, Miss Havisham, Orlick, and Pumblechook all get their comeuppance by the novel's end, either by meeting awful fates or appearing in all of their stupidity, vulgarity, and meanness. Even Estella is punished, first by being portrayed as heartless and cruel, and later by being exposed as the daughter of a murderess and convict, though Pip has promised Jaggers that he will never reveal her story. Of course, Jaggers should have known better, for he has seen at first hand Pip's willingness to expose Wemmick's "Walworth sentiments" in order to squeeze from Jaggers the answers he wants. In writing *Great Expectations*, Pip traffics as freely in identities as Jaggers ever has – to the chagrin, we might imagine, of his family and friends.

In doing so, he reminds us of what he has suggested since the churchyard, that no textual account of identity is definitive or complete because none can escape the rules that govern portable property. Buyers, readers, the other subjects who might tell stories of their own: these always already turn any textualization of identity into contested, commodified ground. However much Pip hates Orlick, the story that he finally tells in *Great Expectations* is exactly the one that Orlick has demanded, for the novel is largely about Pip's smallness and hypocrisy, his implicit guilt for his sister's death, and his deplorable conduct toward Biddy and Joe. And no one is more aware than Pip of the instability of any story he can tell. When he returns for his sister's funeral, he remembers her in tones so "gentle" that they "softened even the edge of Tickler," and he considers that "the day must come when it would be well for [his] memory that others walking in the sunshine should be softened as they thought of [him]" (212).[65] In the very act of writing his story and making his identity into a material thing, Pip notes the impossibility of forcing such a text to mean only what he wants it to say. Written for public consumption, the text will respond to contexts and external demands; it will exist simultaneously as a fixed object and a dynamic, ungovernable thing. Thus Pip writes after his quarrel with Drummle at the Finches of the Grove that he must finally "repudiate, as untenable, the idea that [he] was to be found anywhere" (233). He disappears into the commodity he makes of himself, becomes only an expectation. Having turned himself into "portable property" through self-narrative, Pip ensures that his identity will remain at the mercy of the market.

What *Great Expectations* shows is that Pip's – and Dickens's – plan to write identity might be lucrative, but that textual self-production allows subjectivity to be swallowed up by the demands of capitalist exchange. Gilbert argues that Pip uses narrative as "an instrument for manipulating reality, for imposing one's own vision on others ... To speak or to write, however scrupulously, is of necessity to deceive."[66] The instabilities and discontinuities of Pip's story imply something like this. Yet one wonders whether "deceive" is the right word: can Pip be blamed for deception in a story that warns from the start that textual meanings are multiple and shifting? Can deception exist in a self-narrative that is always already the unstable product of commodity culture? The loss of Magwitch's money means that his self-narrative is the only thing that Pip brings to fruition, the only expectation that he meets. What we "expect" from a novel is completion and resolution, and if we do not necessarily get the latter in *Great Expectations*, we at least get the former: a finished commodity produced by a fictional author who has overcome his capitalist nightmares and become a clerk in the great Victorian capitalist–imperialist machine. Even for Joe at the end of the novel, the new ability to write coincides with his buying up of Pip's debts, as if the price of his textual productivity is his willing participation in the market, if not quite a total abandonment of the older economic mode embodied by the forge. As for Pip, he leaves us at the end of the novel with a vision of his self-alienation, like one of Marx's laborers. He returns to the forge at the novel's end to find "I again!" – a copy of the self he has labored to produce in his writing, and a copy produced by other hands (356). He tells Biddy, "you must give Pip to me, one of these days; or lend him, at all events," to which Biddy replies wisely, "No, no" (356). It is as if he would gladly begin the monstrous cycle over again, denying any integral meaning for identity beyond the reproduction required by the market.

Great Expectations is finally undergirded, Dutheil contends, by "a textual strategy which capitalizes on the impossibility of identifying sign and meaning."[67] For Pip and Dickens both, the novel is very much about capitalizing, in several senses of the word. Dickens's desire to turn his disquieting autobiography to account is analogized in Pip, and both "authors" encode in the novel the potentially devastating implications of their discursive work: narrative insufficiency, multiplicity of identity, unfulfilled sexual desire.[68] There is something fitting in the fact that we only see the adult Pip writing in *Great Expectations* when he and Herbert look into their affairs, an event always preceded by their "produc[ing] a bundle of pens, a copious supply of ink, and a goodly show of writing and blotting paper" (210). The scene echoes *Copperfield*, where Dora holds David's pens as he becomes a famous author. But the precursor to Pip's autobiography is not novel writing, but rather the "Memorandum of Pip's debts," a periodic tallying up that, he says, leaves him feeling "like a Bank of some sort, rather than a private individual," and that might be an alternative title for the novel (210–11). Pip's strategy in this reckoning up is always to "leave a margin," as if in acknowledgement that writing always leaves something to be filled up, some deficit for which it cannot account (211). The strategy tells us what we need to know about the difference between *Copperfield* and *Great Expectations*. The former never acknowledges that the autobiographical text might not suffice; it ignores the practical, psychological, sexual, and ideological implications of turning personal history into a commodity for the market. But *Great Expectations* embodies and explores what it meant in an autobiographical age to turn identity into "portable property."

CHAPTER 3

Lady Audley's Portrait: Textuality, Gender, and Power

The most consequential scene of Braddon's *Lady Audley's Secret* features neither an act of writing nor a disquisition on "the identity of things" but rather an unfinished portrait being studied by two men, Robert Audley and George Talboys, who have squeezed through a secret passage and into Lucy Audley's private rooms to linger over a striking image of the novel's femme fatale. They emerge into "the elegant disorder" of her dressing-room to find a profusion of sights and smells that bespeak her feminine charms: handsome dresses heaped on the floor, the "rich odours of perfumes," and the glittering items of her toilette, all of which George hovers over just long enough to glimpse "his bearded face and tall gaunt figure" in the cheval-glass and realize "how out of place he seem[s] among all these womanly luxuries."[1] The portrait is the "*bonne bouche*," a full view of Lucy Audley in a crimson dress, her golden ringlets falling in masses, her dazzling form depicted against the background of the very room in which the painting hangs (71). Drawing back the green baize cover, each man gazes at the portrait in turn while the narrator muses:

> Yes; the painter must have been a pre-Raphaelite. No one but a pre-Raphaelite would have painted, hair by hair, those feathery masses of ringlets with every glimmer of gold, and every shadow of pale brown. No one but a pre-Raphaelite would have so exaggerated every attribute of that delicate face as to give a lurid lightness to the blonde complexion, and a strange, sinister light to the deep blue eyes. No one but a pre-Raphaelite could have given to that pretty pouting mouth the hard and almost wicked look it had in the portrait.
>
> It was so like and yet so unlike; it was as if you had burned strange-coloured fires before my lady's face, and by their influence brought out new lines and new expressions never seen in it before. The perfection of feature, the brilliancy of colouring, were there; but I suppose the painter had copied quaint mediæval monstrosities until his brain had grown bewildered, for my lady, in his portrait of her, had something of the aspect of a beautiful fiend. (72)

The portrait shocks George by giving him a view of his "dead" wife and so initiates the chain of events that leads to his disappearance, Robert's investigation, and Lucy's confinement and death in a Belgian maison de santé. The portrait eventually disappears, too, ending its days curtained off, hidden even from those visitors to Audley Court who "admire my lady's rooms, and ask many questions about the pretty, fair-haired woman, who died abroad" (436).

The portrait-viewing scene in *Lady Audley's Secret* has a breathtaking symbolic efficiency. In a work defined by fierce interrogations of gender and power, this scene is its palimpsest, bearing many meanings that find fuller expression elsewhere. As Lynette Felber puts it, "the portrait comprises a multivalent critique: it protests the power and authority of the male gaze; it anatomizes fetishistic desire; and it raises questions about the construction of women and their sexuality in Victorian society."[2] Initially, it inscribes Lucy's position in the domestic space of the English country house, affirming her rightful place in an aristocratic order that relies on portraiture to reify familial lines of power. Later, in its capacity to frame and contain, it indicates the "Victorian gender ideology which at once worships women and imprisons them within the domestic sphere," expressed in the novel as a concerted effort to constrain Lucy's unruly femininity, which threatens to wreak "havoc on traditional stabilities and pieties" by challenging male power from a position inside the domestic and social order.[3] At all times it illustrates Lucy's sexualization and commodification, her transformation into a spectacle for the delectation of men and an aesthetic product pictured amid "an excess of the accessories that signify her femininity."[4] As Laurence Talaraich-Vielmas puts it, *Lady Audley's Secret* "explores Victorian representations of femininity and foregrounds woman's commodification."[5] It does so nowhere more forcefully or compactly than in the portrait.

Yet these symbolic evocations come, literally, at a cost. Coaxed early in the novel into speaking to Robert about her time working for the Dawsons, Lucy recalls, as she prepares her easel and palette, how each quarter she used to earn "six dingy old sovereigns, and a little heap of untidy, dirty silver, that came straight from the till in the surgery! And then how glad I was to get it; while *now* – I can't help laughing while I think of it – these colours I am using cost a guinea each at Winsor and Newton's – the carmine and ultramarine thirty shillings" (120–1). To paraphrase Joe Gargery, painting costs money. Whatever else the portrait signifies, it remains an object in a market, a material production and an object of exchange. Just a chapter earlier, Lucy has confided to Phoebe Marks how pleasant it is "to wear sables that cost sixty guineas, and have a thousand pounds spent on the decorations of one's apartments" (110). How much of that money, we might ask, went to pay for the Wouvermans, Poussins, Cuyps, and Tintorettos that hang in the ante-chamber and end up immured with the portrait, awaiting their inevitable defacement by that "blue mould which artists dread" (436)? How much for the skill of the Pre-Raphaelite artist and the quantity of carmine – priced thirty shillings – required to paint "the crimson dress, the sunshine on the face, the red gold gleaming in the yellow hair, [and] the ripe scarlet pouting of the lips" (72)? The very paint that turns Lucy into a multivalent symbol belongs to an economy of raw materials and finished goods, artistic labor and commodity exchange. When Robert and Alicia Audley debate whether the portrait contains some part of her identity, they speculate on a matter at the heart of the novel: whether her identity has been made material and inaugurated into dynamics of ownership and exchange.

This nexus of identity, textuality, and ownership is crucial to *Lady Audley's Secret*, in part because, aside even from the portrait, the novel abounds with texts that materialize Lucy's identity and circulate through the novel. And these texts prove critical to Robert's investigation and, more generally, the operation of male power. Pamela Gilbert has noted the novel's interest in texts and reading, arguing that it underscores "the trope of woman's body as text and text as body."[6] This is certainly true of the portrait and the letters that describe Lucy's appearance. But many of the novel's texts have little to do with her body, though they have much to do with recording the complexities of her identity and bringing her gradually under Robert's power. The evidence he collects consists almost exclusively of texts: he is more interested in old bonnet-box labels and half-burnt telegrams than in her whereabouts on the day George vanished or "the mark upon my lady's wrist" (87). The novel's letters, signatures, inscriptions, labels, telegrams, and other textual relics comprise the chain of circumstantial evidence that, Robert tells Lucy, "is built out of straws collected at every point of the compass, and which is yet strong enough to hang a man" (123). Like the portrait, these textual relics materialize Lucy's identity and implicate her in laws of property. Robert's investigation is less a matter of "discovering" Lucy's secret – which, after all, she confesses before he can detect it – than a contest over textual ownership in which Lucy seeks, like Magwitch, to keep the texts that inscribe her identity from circulating as objects of exchange. This contest reveals partly the extent to which Victorian culture constituted identity textually, but also the extent to which that textuality, by making identity material, rendered it vulnerable to legal, economic, and ultimately masculine forms of power. Despite the portrait's particular symbolic force, *Lady Audley's Secret* expresses a comprehensive interest in the many textual forms that identity might take, and in the implications of exposing it to the market.

Braddon understood these implications in part because, as Gilbert notes, she had constantly to rewrite "her own position in the marketplace and use ... multiple genres to manipulate her placement."[7] *Lady Audley's Secret* does not, like *Great Expectations*, encourage biographical inquiry or engage directly the nexus of autobiography and the market. But Braddon understood how texts affirmed relationships between identity and both literary and economic value.[8] Early in her career, when she needed the money from writing disreputable thrillers for the penny market but also wanted to establish a foothold with middle-class readers, she published *Lady Audley's Secret* and *Aurora Floyd* (1863) under her real name but used the pseudonyms Babington White and Lady Caroline Lascelles for works such as *The Black Band* (1862) and the sensational but plagiarized *Circe* (1867).[9] She also profited by changing the names of the works themselves, revising her scarcely noticed first novel *Three Times Dead* (1860) and reissuing it as *The Trail of the Serpent* (1861), and later bringing her serial potboiler *The Banker's Secret* (1865) to the three-volume market as *Rupert Godwin* (1867).[10] In these (and other) machinations she was aided by her partner and eventual husband, the editor and publisher John Maxwell, who cared so much more for literary commodity than for literary quality that "his usual practice was not to read the manuscripts of his writers but to pay for them by the weight."[11] So far as we know, Braddon did not weigh her manuscripts – though she admitted to Bulwer-Lytton in 1863 that she had already "learned to look at everything in a mercantile sense, & to write solely for the circulating library reader whose palette [sic for palate] requires strong meat, and is not very particular as to the quality" – but she certainly perceived her novels as commodities inseparable from the identity attached to them in the literary market.[12]

Lady Audley's Secret's reflects this perception, treating identity as a textual thing that can be copied, multiplied, fragmented, owned, and otherwise treated as an object of exchange. By locating the cause of Lucy's commodification in a material culture that makes her into many texts, the novel suggests that her "discrete, multiple, and fluid" identities are not only, as Helena Michie argues, dangerous and criminal.[13] They are emblematic of the imaginative and discursive implications of autobiography's anchoring of identity in the textuality of the capitalist sphere. Lucy takes on the discursive effects of her commodification, the multiplication and dispersal of her identity serving as the proximate causes of the chronological ruptures necessary to the detective plot, and her "madness" consisting of neither a cognitive nor moral derangement but rather an intensification of economic longing, a subdual of her erotic potential to capitalist desire. Her eventual defeat thus signifies not only as that of an unruly woman brought to heel by a male detective but also – and perhaps more significantly – as a fantasy of victory over the commodity, which threatens to disrupt male homosociality and the traditions of patrilineage upon which it rests. Yet if the threat to male power in *Lady Audley's Secret* appears most obviously in its femme fatale, it originates in a textual culture that makes men the primary producers, exchangers, and owners of commodities even as, paradoxically, it renders them vulnerable, too, to the exigencies of commodity culture by requiring their textualization as a condition of their entry into and regulation of the market. Ann Cvetkovich writes that *Lady Audley's Secret* protests "the effects of mid-Victorian capitalism on everyday life . . . the feelings and experiences for which capitalist culture provides no other outlet."[14] In an age of portraiture and autobiography, it does so by expressing an anxiety that overlaps, undergirds, and exceeds its interrogation of gender: over the vulnerability of subjectivity – female and male – to the incursions of commodity culture.

* * *

Lucy first appears in the novel as a commodity called into being by Mr. Dawson's advertisement in the *Times*. As would any commodity carried from London to out-of-the-way Audley, she appears from the start as a spectacular object of uncertain origins but magical allure. She delights the village's men and also its women and children, including even the "toothless crone" who "burst[s] out into senile raptures" over her though she leaves the old woman not a penny (11). Sir Michael's marriage proposal tries to negate her commodification, beginning with a solemn prayer "that she would reject him, even though she broke his heart by doing so, than that she should accept his offer if she did not love him" (15). But confronted by the sobering facts that she "*cannot* be disinterested" in considering his proposal and that she does not love him, he retreats quickly into the language of exchange, saying, "I see no reason why we should not make a very happy couple. Is it a bargain, Lucy?" (16–17). For Lucy, it is her second such "bargain," since she married George mostly because her father was a "drunken old hypocrite . . . ready to sell [her] to the highest bidder" (23). As she admits later, while still young she "learnt that which in some indefinite manner or other every schoolgirl learns sooner or later," that her "ultimate fate in life depend[s] upon [her] marriage" (345). In response, she adapts herself to the market, exploiting her beauty's value and making herself, too, into a lovely canvas for other commodities: Russian sables, glittering rings, handsome dresses, and her luxurious apartments at Audley Court. Like *Little Dorrit*'s Mrs. Merdle, she has "a capital bosom to hang jewels upon"; unlike her, she collapses so entirely into the objects around her that the effect is "bewildering" and blurs the "boundary ... between Lucy and the commodity world that she inhabits."[15] Her commodification appears in the novel from the first, inseparable from her sexualization and subjection to male power.

The portrait's introduction in the eighth chapter, then, tells us partly what we already know: that Lucy is an object of male desire amid the novel's sexual and economic exchanges. But it tells us other things, too, not just because carmine paint costs thirty shillings, but because the portrait situates Lucy within both the economic relations particular to portraiture and those activated by depictions of female beauty and Pre-Raphaelite style. In portraiture as in culture, as Pointon notes, beautiful women had "a particular commodity value" since their beauty and its artistic representation signified value within a masculine system of consumption and exchange.[16] Lucy's appearance as the subject of an aristocratic portrait enhances that value, in fact, by contesting implicitly the fact of her pennilessness and placing her within the long visual history of the Audley family and English national identity. Meanwhile, the portrait's heavy-handed Pre-Raphaelism invokes contemporary debates about the relation between painting and the gospel of work – or, as John Ruskin and others framed it, between productive labor and the economic and moral value of works of art.[17] The Pre-Raphaelites painted portraits like Lucy's "hair by hair" in part to show, through meticulous detail, the work that art required. Dante Rossetti, John Everett Millais, and Ford Madox Brown *labored* at their paintings – none so obviously as Brown's aptly named *Work* (1852–1865) – and participated eagerly in the same industrial economy that turned their works into mass-produced prints and led Millais and Brown, at various times, to illustrate for periodicals.[18] Lucy's portrait never changes hands, nor does the novel suggest it is engraved or reproduced. But its existence implies the potential for it – and her – to become a commodity in the same lowbrow market that places Lady Dedlock in the "Galaxy Gallery of British Beauty" in *Bleak House* and exposes her to the vulgar gaping of lower middle-class voyeurs.[19]

Lucy's symbolic existence as an object of male sexual desire coincides, then, with a commodification that is also material, and the novel wonders openly to what extent such a material text can be taken as an embodiment of her subjectivity. After he has viewed the portrait, Robert debates with Alicia its relation to Lucy's subjectivity – whether, like autobiography, it exists in an equivalency with her immaterial self. He complains that there is "something odd" about the portrait's unnerving depiction of Lucy, but Alicia defends it, confessing "a strange fancy on that point. . . . *We* have never seen my lady look as she does in that picture; but I think that she *could* look so" (73). Robert rejects this idea of equivalency, begging Alicia not to "be German" and exclaiming, "The picture is – the picture; and my lady is – my lady" (73). But the picture is not just the picture, as the novel repeatedly suggests. George's agitation at viewing it stems implicitly from the fact that he recognizes his wife for the first time not just as a domestic angel "whose heart is as true as the light of heaven" but as a complex subject, capable equally of virtue and wrenching deceit (22). By the time Lucy sets fire to the Castle Inn, she has practically become the portrait, her hair spreading "into a tangled mass that surrounded her forehead like a yellow flame" so that she "awe[s] [Luke Marks] into silence by the unearthly glitter of her beauty" (316). Lucy is what the narrator calls her, "a beautiful fiend," a woman capable simultaneously of belonging to the domestic order, inspiring rampant sexual desire, and taking violent action as a means of self-preservation. Alicia sees in the portrait, that is, what Robert sees only in his nightmare of Audley Court, uprooted from Essex and presided over by a mermaid "beckoning his uncle to destruction": Lucy "in her 'true' form . . . endowed with all the power and ambiguity that her portrait reveals" (244).[20]

The novel insists on Lucy's existence as woman and painting, subject and text, so that she takes on symbolically and discursively the multiplicity and distemporality of the material commodity. The portrait "plays upon a multiplication of surfaces," Talaraich-Vielmas notes, by featuring in its background the paintings on the walls around it, and her boudoir has "looking-glasses, cunningly placed at angles and opposite corners . . . [that] multiplied my lady's image, and in that image reflected the most beautiful object in the enchanted chamber" (291).[21] These images reinforce Lucy's multiplicity – as Helen Maldon, Helen Talboys, Lucy Graham, Lucy Audley, and finally Madame Taylor – which the novel in turn materializes in a dizzying array of textual forms. Apart even from her deliberate attempts to reinvent herself, Lucy seems to be a copy of the "golden-haired, blue-eyed girlish" mother she visits in the asylum, which may explain why she seems to take her physical multiplicity as a matter of course, using her likeness to Matilda Plowson to fake her own death and treating Phoebe as a faded reproduction (344). As she tells Phoebe, "it is only colour that you want. . . . Why, with a bottle of hair dye, such as we see advertised in the papers, and a pot of rouge, you'd be as good-looking as I any day" – advice that alludes, as Matthew Rubery observes, to the proliferating cosmetic goods that collaborated at mid-century in the unlimited reproduction of a feminine aesthetic ideal (60).[22] Nor is the Pre-Raphaelite painting the only portrait of Lucy. When George races to Ventnor upon learning of his wife's death, he notices his portrait, painted in "the old dragooning days," and also that her portrait no longer hangs alongside it, and wonders aloud "what they have done with it" (43–4). As the investigation discovers, Lucy exists as a profusion of texts: letters, signatures, bonnet-box labels, inscriptions in literary annuals, telegrams, and other texts, each of which constitutes some part of an identity that she has multiplied, fragmented, and dispersed across the novel.

Characterized by this rampant textuality, Lucy unsettles the novel's action and characters by appearing unbound by natural, normative conceptions of time. The portrait contributes to this sense of temporal indeterminacy even as it fixes her image, for it surrounds her with "quaint medieval monstrosities" as well as copies of sixteenth- and seventeenth-century paintings, and it "adumbrates future events" by hinting from the start what she secretly is and will openly become.[23] She carries always this disquieting sense of distemporality; she is both ubiquitous and apart from time, existing certainly only in the present tense of capitalist desire. The narrator remarks that she "owned to twenty years of age, but it was hard to believe her more than seventeen" (55). Yet she must be nearly twenty-two, since she says later that she married George three months after her seventeenth birthday, George left England for "three years and a half," and he did so a week or two after the baby's birth (23). Through much of the novel Robert's investigation seems designed mostly to correct this sense of temporal discontinuity, for he adopts consciously the detective strategy of tracing Lucy back to her chronological vanishing point in Brompton and then "beginning at the other end" by tracing Helen Talboys to Wildernsea (238). He imagines that he is filling chronological gaps, replacing her temporal fragmentariness with narrative continuity, while Lucy disrupts the investigation by destabilizing the sense of natural time. She exploits the rapidity of train travel and the telegraph, and she has a protean ability to adopt new names and histories. She has been Helen Maldon, Helen Talboys, and Lucy Graham, and she will become Madame Taylor when she reaches the asylum. She exists as chronological disruption and semantic shift. But Lucy Audley, that particular article, has no past or future. She is momentary, ephemeral, not just "mad to-day and sane tomorrow" but here today and gone tomorrow, marked by the paradoxical temporariness and perpetuity of the commodity (206).

This distemporality underlies Lucy's disharmony with Audley Court, which harkens to a slow historical past that resists the obsessive punctuality of commodity culture. Greg Howard notes that, as a historical matter, there was no hard divide between the old aristocratic order and the new industrial–capitalist economy, since some landowners turned to the new economy as agricultural revenues declined and thus ended up overseeing "the development of England's infrastructure and the building of docks, harbors, railways, mines, and housing estates."[24] But there is little evidence of such activity at Audley Court, which seems to be, like *Bleak House*'s Chesney Wold, "wrapped up in too much jeweller's cotton and fine wool."[25] The place has "a stupid, bewildering clock, which had only one hand; and which jumped straight from one hour to the next" without marking the precise time of capitalist labor and exchange, and the narrator notes that the house has been built not by industrial workers but rather "that good old builder – Time, who, adding a room one year, and knocking down a room another year, toppling over now a chimney coeval with the Plantagenets, and setting up one in the style of the Tudors . . . [had] run up such a mansion as was not elsewhere to be met with" (7–9). The house is all that Lucy is not: accretive, not seismic; chronological, not discontinuous; unique, not endlessly reproducible. Her infiltration of Audley Court constitutes a threat to not just male power but also precapitalist modes of production, patriarchal succession, and the long-term viability of the country estate.[26] Her marriage to Sir Michael registers doubly the threat she poses to Audley Court's world, for it guarantees the illegitimacy of any child she bears him, then ends anyway without her bearing him a child at all. Made into a material commodity by the portrait and the novel's other texts, Lucy epitomizes a capitalist culture in which "[m]echanical reproduction displaces and replaces unruly biological reproduction."[27]

Indeed, for all of Lady Audley's supposed sexual allure, she is curiously asexual, partly because she is childish, but also because she has no discernible erotic longings of her own. The narrator insists on her childishness, observing that she is as happy in her marriage to Sir Michael "as a child surrounded by new and costly toys," and remarking that "[h]er fragile figure, which she loved to dress in heavy velvets and stuff rustling silks, till she looked like a child tricked out for a masquerade, was as girlish as if she had but just left the nursery" (55). Though she is a mother, she seems in her second marriage to have retreated into prepubescence and abandoned any pretense of sexual desire. Even her bigamy springs from no particular sexual feeling, since she evinces no attraction to Sir Michael, even saying when she confesses that she would have been faithful to him always precisely because she feels no sexual urgency. She tells him, "The common temptations that assail and shipwreck some women had no terror for me. I would have been your true and pure wife to the end of time, though I had been surrounded by a legion of tempters. The mad folly that the world calls love had never had any part in my madness" (348). She desires only other commodities and the wealth that buys them – so much so that, in packing for the maison de santé, she gathers up and takes whatever commodities she can. She stashes Dresden china in the folds of her dresses and puts "jewelled and golden drinking-cups amongst her delicate linen" (376). Like her multiplicity and distemporality, Lucy's erotic subdual belongs to the symbolic and discursive modes that illustrate the implications of her commodification.

The very texts that materialize and commodify Lucy become the mechanism by which Robert subdues her gradually to male power. Rubery suggests that Lucy, like Lydia Gwilt in Collins's *Armadale* (1866), "exploits the abstraction of newsprint by misrepresenting herself as a model citizen in a way unthinkable to Jane Eyre."[28] While this is true, Robert uses texts more effectively in investigating than Lucy does in lying. The "links" in his chain of circumstantial evidence consist almost exclusively of her textual remnants, from the inscription in the literary annual that Helen presented to George in September 1853 to the letter in which George described his pretty young wife to Clara, and from the labels pasted over one another on the old bonnet-box at Crescent Villas to the letters Captain Maldon and his daughter left behind at Wildernsea. Each speaks to the power of texts generally to inscribe identity and expose the subject to modes of social power, and some speak more directly than the portrait to the relation between such texts and economic exchange. This is true of the multiple inscriptions inside the literary annual among George's things, each one indicating a new phase of its commodity status, and also of the "formal epistle" from Harcourt Talboys to Robert denying responsibility – pecuniary or moral – for George's affairs (162). It is especially true at Wildernsea, when Mrs. Barkamb assures Robert that she has "the whole business" of Helen's abandonment of her father and child "in black and white," then excavates the requisite letter from a desk drawer where "[l]etters, receipts, bills, inventories, and tax-papers were mingled in hopeless confusion" (246–7). The document linking Helen Talboys's identity with Lucy's, and hinting at her intensely private "secret," appears as another "business" paper to the world of the novel. Her "madness" belongs discursively and textually, that is, to the world of financial documents and textual transactions, as if her identity must be articulated, like Pip's, in the language of debt and expenditure, of inventories, taxes, and the market.

Robert's investigation seeks to assemble these textualizations of Lucy into a chronologically unbroken account, from the time when George met her until the time when she married his uncle. He is not only, as Simon Petch argues, a novice detective who "must learn the appropriate combination of deductive and inductive logic"; he is an editor and biographer, a producer of subjectivity in textual form.[29] When Robert asks Dawson privately for information about Lucy, he explains that he needs to account for the last six years of her life and that he yet has a "blank of three years to fill up," and later he describes his task as "trac[ing] the histories of Lucy Graham and Helen Talboys to a vanishing point," after which he will investigate "the history of the woman who lies buried in Ventnor churchyard" (221, 249). His activities are not quite designed, in other words, to perform the work of "unmasking" that Lyn Pykett describes, nor is he really interested in proving the "fragments of textual evidence . . . false."[30] And while he carries his work as biographer so far as to invent Lucy's new name, Madame Taylor, when she enters the maison de santé, he does not exactly, as Gilbert asserts, deny her subjectivity.[31] He aims rather to make the textual fragments add up to a subjectivity that includes all of Lucy's aliases, all of her actions, all parts of her discrete, idiosyncratic existence – a subjectivity that has been materialized, commodified, dispersed, and rendered into innumerable texts that she has produced at different times in the hope of turning a penny. Moreover, Robert undertakes this editorial and biographical work with an eye to bringing Lucy under the operation of the law so that, as Cvetkovich argues, "[h]is epistemological power, his capacity to note every detail," appears also as "a juridical power" rooted in the masculine sphere of professional work.[32] As Robert wonders when he first writes down the details of his investigation, "is this paper, with which no attorney has had any hand, to be my first brief?" (157).

The eventual outcomes of Robert's investigation – Lucy defeated, Sir Michael saved from infamy, and Audley Court preserved against an illegitimate heir and "the *esclandre* of a Chancery suit" – make it easy to read the novel's ending as a male victory in "a gendered war for power in which . . . the threat of the femme fatale is doubly contained" by the walls of the maison de santé and her private room of reflective surfaces (369).[33] Yet the novel undercuts this reading in several ways. Most obviously, the investigation does not discover George, who returns on his own at the end of the novel. It does not reveal Lucy's "madness," which she finally confesses. It does not even end by turning over its femme fatale – a bigamist, arsonist, and murderess – to the outraged majesty of England's courts. Robert treats her instead as what she has been all along, and what the novel's texts and her marriages have made her: a commodity to be dealt with according to laws of property. After Lucy confesses, Sir Michael gives her to Robert as a kind of material bequest, telling him, "I leave all in your hands, Robert . . . I leave all to you" (361). He means in part that he leaves "all" of Audley Court in Robert's hands, leaves him to manage the estate. But like the portrait, Lucy comprises a portion of that estate; she is an object subsumed into it and passed from aristocratic landowner to male heir. If *Lady Audley's Secret*'s sensational plot resists closure, it may be because Robert's investigation compounds the original problem by making her textualization more entire. The investigation shows, that is, the extent to which the novel's "gendered war for power" overlaps another contest implied by Lucy's disharmony with Audley Court: between the commodity and the economic forms that preceded autobiography's transformation of identity into an object of exchange.

Ironically, for all that the novel's plot foregrounds Lucy's portrait, the portrait plays no role in Robert's investigation, which relies principally on his ability to *acquire* the texts that bespeak her identity. When he discovers the half-burnt telegram at Ventnor, he folds it carefully and places it "between the leaves of his pocket-book" although it has no date and, if it reveals anything, seems to confirm that George has returned to Australia (98). At Crescent Villas, he takes pains with water and a sponge to loosen the edges of the traveling labels on Lucy's old bonnet-box, peeling them one from the other and depositing them, too, in his pocket-book. Even the letters that Mrs. Barkamb sifts from among her business papers end up in Robert's hands, since "[h]e request[s] permission to retain the two letters" after he has exhausted his questions (249). He also relies on the letters and books that George has left behind at Fig-tree Court, discovering there the literary annual that shows Helen's distinctive hand. And just when he is considering giving up his investigation, he receives the crucial packet of letters from Clara, one of which gives George's account of his new wife, "such a description as a man could only write within three weeks of a love-match" (210). Though Robert does not realize it, his investigation really begins when he receives Alicia's letter saying that Lucy "is too ill" to see Robert and George at Audley Court and thrusts it carelessly "into a pigeon-hole in his office desk marked *Important*" – a space that will also come to hold his "JOURNAL OF FACTS CONNECTED WITH THE DISAPPEARANCE OF GEORGE TALBOYS, INCLUSIVE OF FACTS WHICH HAVE NO APPARENT RELATION TO THAT CIRCUMSTANCE" (54, 103).

Lady Audley is not so much in danger of being detected by Robert as she is in danger of being possessed, and in a way that depends more upon the materiality of her textual existence than upon her obvious sexual commodification. Long before George comes looking for her at Ventnor, she has the good sense to have her first portrait taken down, likely to keep the doctor and other visitors from comparing her painted image to the appearance of the dying Matilda. Likewise, having managed to keep out of Robert and George's way at Audley Court, she takes precautions to cut off access to the ante-chamber and the new portrait "[e]ven in her haste" to get away, "paus[ing] deliberately at the door of this room, double lock[ing] it, and dropp[ing] the key into her pocket" (62). When Robert boasts imprudently to Lucy that he intends to "examine the effects" that George left at his chambers – "letters from his friends, his old school-fellows, his father, his brother-officers. ... [l]etters, too, from his wife" – she takes the extraordinary step of racing to London on the 12.40 express, bribing a blacksmith to help her break into Robert's rooms, and making off with the letters (144). Like Robert, she recognizes the importance of possessing these textualizations of her identity, recognizes that it is the production of such texts in the first place that expose the subject to power. Robert's assumption of authority over Lucy at the novel's end coincides, tellingly, with Sir Michael leaving him in possession of the house and also of the portrait that inscribes her subjectivity. The detail reminds us that her vulnerability to Robert's investigation originates in her textual multiplication and dispersal, the material signs of her commodification.

This is true despite even other physical clues, from the "mark upon my lady's wrist" to the baby shoe and lock of hair that Phoebe discovers in the secret drawer, which may titillate the reader but are superfluous to the investigation. Lucy's bruises pique Robert's curiosity, but they otherwise play no role, nor does he ever seem to learn about the shoe or hair, which become instead partial means by which Phoebe and Luke blackmail her. In this respect, the shoe and hair actually impede the investigation, since Luke admits on his deathbed that only his grievances against Lucy, who has been stingy in responding to their attempts at blackmail, have kept him from disclosing that George is alive. Robert builds his case entirely from texts, acquiring them until he can claim possession of the woman whose identity they record – a detective success aligned implicitly with his affinity for commodities. He is not, like Sir Michael, bound to the English countryside and the economic forms of traditional aristocratic life. He lives in the City, has a middle-class profession (even if he does not pursue it), reads French novels, smokes German pipes, and moves contentedly if indolently through a modern metropolis of brilliant spectacles and exotic goods. Mrs. Plowson even mistakes Robert for the "water-rate" collector when he first comes to Ventnor, a mistake she would not make if the stately but outdated Sir Michael were at the door (165).[34] The older man remains mystified by his pretty wife until she confesses. But Robert knows commodities: initially smitten with his pretty aunt, he recognizes much sooner the danger that she poses to Audley Court.

This view of the investigation deepens *Lady Audley's Secret*'s investment in matters of gender precisely because it elaborates the textual mechanism, rooted in Victorian England's legal and economic cultures, by which women become commodities trafficked in and consumed by men. Grace Wetzel argues that an investigation such as Robert's appears in the novel as "an exclusively male privilege," and Richard Nemesvari contends that Robert "is empowered to expose, punish, and therefore nullify" Lucy because he speaks her "criminal activities ... into existence."[35] Yet Robert speaks mostly what the texts already say; he voices the narrative of a subjectivity that has already appeared in material form. His putatively masculine authority originates in laws of property and depends in the first place upon subjectivity being made into an object of exchange. Dr. Mosgrave tells Robert candidly that his "circumstantial evidence" will not suffice to press a criminal case for George's murder:

> I will not discuss the probabilities of the suspicion that distresses you, Mr. Audley ... but I will tell you this much. I do not advise any *esclandre*. This Mr. George Talboys has disappeared, but you have no evidence of his death. If you could produce evidence of his death, you could produce no evidence against this lady, beyond the one fact that she had a powerful motive for getting rid of him. No jury in the United Kingdom would condemn her upon such evidence as that. (372)

Mosgrave affirms that Lucy's transgressions cannot be dealt with readily by the criminal code. Consequently, Robert claims authority over her by acquiring one final text: Mosgrave's letter to Monsieur Val, presumably attesting to Lucy's suitability as an inmate for his asylum. Having concluded that she is "dangerous" but not mad, Mosgrave fills "three sides of a sheet of note-paper," puts the letter in an envelope, and "deliver[s] it, unsealed, to Robert Audley" (372–3). Robert gets rid of her not via the criminal laws designed to protect property but via the laws of property themselves – via an act of textualization, and textual possession, like the others that have collaborated to make Lucy an object of exchange.

By hinting that its concern with Robert's power over Lucy originates in anxieties regarding the textualization of identity, *Lady Audley's Secret* offers a critique that in some ways exceeds gender since it exposes the implications of a textual culture that renders all subjects, at least potentially, vulnerable to the operation of power. This critique appears as a contest between male authority and female agency in Braddon's novel because men and women did not share equally in the exercise of this power, in fiction or in Victorian England. Men held professional and social positions that made them owners and regulators of texts, as magistrates and barristers, publishers and members of Parliament. While women figured increasingly as consumers of commodities at mid-century – with few things more plainly than with the sensation novel – men owned the capital that drove production and consumption and that gave them proprietary control over the textual forms that entangled identity in the dynamics of exchange. To say that power rested with the owners of texts, then, is to affirm that gender matters to the novel's presentation of social power. Yet if men were more likely than women to possess and control texts, they were also more likely to appear in them as textualized identities, to sign forms and purchase shares, to incur debts, to act in legal proceedings, and generally to be inscribed within the expanding array of discursive practices that served to reify subjectivity's relation to economic concerns. Rachel Heinrichs argues that the various men of *Lady Audley's Secret* articulate "the tensions of [a] transitional moment in the formation of Victorian masculinity."[36] They also articulate the tensions of a moment when masculinity was becoming a greater liability because it appeared so often in textual form, wrenched into materiality by the demands of finance capitalism and an evolving textual culture. If the novel acknowledges in Robert that the control and ownership of texts grants men forms of social power inherent in property law, it also encodes a sense of male vulnerability to the same dynamics of textuality and commodity that threaten Lucy.

This vulnerability appears most clearly in the differences between the novel's men, who parallel Lucy in ways but without quite becoming textual objects of exchange. Like Lucy, Sir Michael marries the first time for pecuniary reasons, having felt none of the longing for Alicia's mother that he feels for his second wife. He recalls his first marriage as "a dull, jog-trot bargain, made to keep some estate in the family," and muses, "What had been his love for his first wife but a poor, pitiful, smouldering spark, too dull to be extinguished, too feeble to burn?" (12). He is Rochester made to marry Bertha Mason, even an earlier version of Lucy herself. Yet he never seems out of sync with Audley Court or exhibits the multiplicity, distemporality, or transfigured desire of his commodity-wife. This may owe partly to the fact that his first marriage belonged less to a marriage market in which the groom goes to the highest bidder than to an older sense of aristocratic obligation requiring the male suitor to marry well to preserve the integrity of the family name and estate. His sexuality, that is, never quite entered the market, and he appears almost nowhere in the novel as an identity made into a text. Once only he writes to Robert, a brief note enclosing blank checks to cover the expense of disposing of Lucy. Otherwise, though his social position undoubtedly means that he appears in legal papers, financial documents, and a host of other material forms, his life is a textual blank, so much so that the novel never mentions the portrait that *must* exist, and that ought to hang alongside the Pre-Raphaelite rendering of his wife. If Sir Michael exists as texts, they remain unavailable for circulation, safeguarded against falling into other hands. Circumstances may have made him a precursor to his second wife, but they have not made him a commodity.

The same cannot be said of George, who eschews the obligations of gender and class and takes the pretty, penniless Helen as his wife. Disowned subsequently by his father, he divests himself of the tokens of his gentility – his military commission, his residence in Italy – moves in with his drunken father-in-law, spends his patrimony, then contemplates how he can enter the modern economy. He tries to find work "as a clerk in a merchant's office, or as accountant, or book-keeper, or something of that kind," but he bears his gentility visibly enough to belie his incapacity for middle-class employment (24). When he decides instead to try Australia, he begins by writing a letter that both textualizes him and indicates the entanglement of his sexual and economic desire, as if to affirm his initiation into commodity culture. "I sat down and wrote a few brief lines," he explains, "which told [my wife] that I never had loved her better than now when I seemed to desert her; that I was going to try my fortune in a new world" (25). Lucy echoes these words in the letter she leaves for her father at Wildernsea, in which she explains that she is leaving him and her child to "go out into the world ... to seek another home and another fortune" (248). George and Lucy both succeed, but Natalie and Ronald Schroeder note that Lucy's eventual punishment implies that only he "may become whoever he wishes. Identity is invention – for men."[37] George's second disappearance, though, suggests that such "invention" is only possible when a man's identity has not already appeared in and as texts. Before dying, Luke gives Robert two letters that reveal George's story: one telling Robert that he is leaving England, and the other to his wife. Only Luke's withholding of these letters keeps Robert from recognizing sooner that George is alive and has taken the name Thomas Brown, who appears in the passenger manifest for the *Victoria Regia* having booked passage late with "his arm ... in a sling," just as Luke describes him to Robert (103). With these texts in hand, Robert would likely have found George – even under his assumed name – just as he found George's wife.

Nor is Robert immune to the power granted by texts. Though Lucy eventually confesses her "madness," for much of the novel he is the one regarded as eccentric and odd, a misfit in his profession, at Audley Court, and amid the conventional forms of sexual desire. He has never sought a brief, prefers French novels to shooting, and arrives to Audley Court for the hunting season with two "miserable curs" very unlike the expensive pointers and setters kept by the other men, who regard him "as an inoffensive species of maniac" (117). Meanwhile, his disinclination to marry Alicia – to say nothing of his homoerotic attachment to George – causes Sir Michael to regard him as a "mystery" and even "half mad" (131, 278). Often Robert wonders himself at his tumultuous feelings, as when he seems to be "falling over head and ears in love with [his] aunt," is surprised "that it is possible to care so much for a fellow" after George disappears, and loses himself in a "mental monologue" that careens from woman-hating, to attraction to Clara, to a disquieting sense that some "hand which is stronger than [his] own" is beckoning him on in his investigation (86, 91, 207, 174). The significance of his eccentricity becomes clear when he confronts Lucy with his circumstantial evidence and she replies, "I would warn you that such fancies have sometimes conducted people, as apparently sane as yourself, to the life-long imprisonment of a private lunatic asylum" (271). Her implied threat plays upon contemporary anxieties regarding lunacy laws that allowed sane people to be certified mad and confined – anxieties that centered mainly, as I explain in Chapter 4, on the ways in which texts defined identity and implicated it simultaneously in economic exchange and state power. Lucy threatens to turn the tables, that is, by making Robert a textualized, economized, disempowered subject rather than a keeper and regulator of texts.

Put plainly, Lucy is no more "mad" than Robert – and she is less so if we take "mad" to mean driven to act upon irrational motives and desires. No invisible hand motivates her actions, nor do eccentricities alienate her from the visitors to Audley Court. As Mosgrave tells Robert after hearing him outline her story:

> there is no evidence of madness in anything that she has done. She ran away from her home, because her home was not a pleasant one, and she left it in the hope of finding a better. There is no madness in that. She committed the crime of bigamy, because by that crime she obtained fortune and position. There is no madness there. (370)

Her actions are criminal, not mad. Yet the novel's denouement centers upon madness, as if to underscore its interest in the dense imbrications of identity, textuality, and commodity that undergirded power relations among genders, among classes, and among the producers and consumers of texts. By threatening each other with the asylum, Robert and Lucy both seek recourse in the forms of cultural authority underwritten by Victorian lunacy laws, which used texts to strip people of agency and make them into property, to transform them into objects rather than subjects of economic exchange. Their contest is over that cultural authority, and it is unequal to the degree that Lucy has no texts that inscribe Robert's eccentricity, no letters or certificates that mark him "mad," while Robert takes possession of the many texts that constitute Lucy, culminating in the letter that Mosgrave writes to Monsieur Val. One wonders whether, if she had the documents secreted in Robert's pocket-book and the "JOURNAL OF FACTS" stuffed in the pigeon-hole, she might build a suitable case regarding Robert's monomania and capitalize on Sir Michael's sense that his nephew is "half mad." As things are, Lucy proclaims finally that she is "a MADWOMAN" even as Robert makes his textualization of her complete (340). The synchronicity of these events reminds us that to be "mad" in *Lady Audley's Secret*, or at least to be "dangerous" and sent off to an asylum, is to be a commodity: to be textualized, and to exhibit the multiplicity, distemporality, and transfigured desire engendered by textual form.

* * *

Lady Audley's Secret ends with more than Robert's victory over the femme fatale, and with more, too, than the preservation of the patriarchy against Lucy's dangerous sexuality and attempt to infiltrate the aristocracy from below. It ends with a fantasy of victory over the commodity, in which the desirable object with a mind of its own is brought to bay and the mysterious operation of the capitalist market is subordinated to the traditional powers of landed wealth, class rigidity, and forms of subjectivity nominally distinct from, and inviolate against, the incursions of commodity culture. Just before Robert's misogynist reverie, in which he describes women as "bold, brazen, abominable creatures," the narrator interposes a rant against the commodity, as if to preface the train of angry thoughts that Robert shapes around Lucy:

> Who has not felt, in the first madness of sorrow, an unreasoning rage against the mute propriety of chairs and tables, the stiff squareness of Turkey carpets, the unbending obstinacy of the outward apparatus of existence? We want to root up gigantic trees in a primeval forest, and to tear their huge branches asunder in our convulsive grasp; and the utmost that we can do for the relief of our passion is to knock over an easy-chair, or smash a few shillings'-worth of Mr. Copeland's manufacture. (208, 206)

Robert's "unreasoning rage" against the commodity takes instead the form of detective work. He recognizes that the commodity he must act against is neither a "mute" inanimate easy-chair nor the commodified woman whom Luce Irigiray describes as an object "of use and transaction" who cannot "claim the right to speak and to participate in exchange in general."[38] He must act against the commodity of Marx's analysis, formidable in its agency and complex in its desires.

It is the commodity par excellence that threatens in *Lady Audley's Secret* to destabilize the old English estate by circulating among different classes and locales, multiplying and dispersing, dragging slow natural time into the persistent immediacy of the capitalist present, and transfiguring erotic desire. As Nicole Reynolds puts it, though she suffers nearly the same fate, Lucy is not quite Robert Browning's "Last Duchess" for she at least "dictates the terms according to which she is killed into art."[39] Driven by market forces that she cannot control, she still acts as a free agent, never quite resisting her commodification but trying over and over to live as she wishes. Gilbert thus describes Lucy's defeat at the end of the novel as an attempt to excise her from the otherwise healthy social body, and Heinrichs argues that Lucy's punishment involves mainly an attempt to remove her from the upper class, with its "value system grounded in birth, money, and leisure" and its interest in preserving the "purity of [the] family name."[40] But Lucy's removal to a Belgian maison de santé is less a social exile than an attempt to banish her from the market. Though she carries away to the asylum as many commodities as she can hide in her things, she reaches Villebrumeuse to find herself in a place where she is not free to circulate and her beauty has no value.[41] The "glimmering something" adorning the walls of her new room turns out not to be "costly mirrors" but "wretched mockeries of burnished tin" (382). Robert disposes of his "dangerous" commodity, in other words, by paying good money to send it abroad, reversing the normal order of capitalist exchange by paying someone to take it off his hands and expel it from England's economy.

But Lucy's institutionalization does not quite end the novel, nor does it solve the problem of capitalism's gradual encroachment on both subjectivity and precapitalist economic and social forms. Robert ends up the presumptive heir to Audley Court and also a rising barrister, an aristocrat who has been subsumed into the new capitalist order even if, in his domestic life, he tries to fend it off. Married to Clara in the novel's final chapter, Robert has realized his "dream of a fairy cottage ... between Teddington Lock and Hampton Bridge, where, amid a little forest of foliage, there is a fantastical dwelling-place of rustic woodwork, whose latticed windows look out upon the river" (435). As Aeron Haynie points out, this new home seems "an even more remote and unrealistic vision of rural, preindustrial England" than Audley Court.[42] Yet the young dandy who never had a brief before George disappeared has become, too, "a rising man upon the home circuit," having distinguished himself in the Pickwickian "breach of promise case of Hobbs *v.* Nobbs, and ... convulsed the court by his deliciously comic rendering of the faithless Nobbs's amatory correspondence" (435). He has, for practical purposes, become a bourgeois professional rather than a member of the landed gentry – has become, despite now being his uncle's presumptive heir, more rather than less unsuited to life at Audley Court. He tries, like Wemmick and Jaggers, to divide himself between the sullying world of business and the outmoded idyll of precapitalist domesticity. But he does so amid a professional life that integrates him into the world of texts: writing briefs, signing papers, and participating fully in a social order that aligns identity with textuality, and textuality with commodity culture and the forms of power that undergird it.

Perhaps this explains why the novel leaves us with a sense of unease, despite its closing reassurance that "a certain Madame Taylor ... expired peacefully at Villebrumeuse, dying after a long ... *maladie de langueur*" (436). Lucy has died the death of all commodities whose time has passed, the death of stagnancy and obsolescence. But the novel's end still strikes "a prevailing tone of nostalgia and loss," as if, Chiara Briganti writes, "Lucy's death brings no relief."[43] This may be because, although the novel affirms both masculine and upper-class power, it concludes with something like acquiescence to the capitalist order that textualizes and commodifies identity and renders it vulnerable to such power. In that acquiescence rests a further capitulation to the cultural and imaginative transformation of identity that first provoked Braddon's anxious response to capitalism, which involves broader vulnerabilities than those etched upon her femme fatale. Though the novel ends by affirming the continued rule of the novel's men, *Lady Audley's Secret* remains, Howard writes, "replete with multiple, and complex, masculine identifications," not all of them affirmed by the logic of the book.[44] Sir Michael has lost his wife and probably his capacity and opportunity for further romantic attachment. The same may be true for George, who appears likely to live out his days in an erotic muddle with Robert and Clara. And Luke simply dies. Of the novel's men, only Robert comes out more or less alright, though even his end is qualified by his absorption into the textual culture that characterizes England's capitalist sphere. At the end of *Lady Audley's Secret*, what remains is a society predicated upon the textualization of the subject, founded imaginatively and ideologically on the role of texts in constituting identity as a material thing. In that society, though Lucy is dead, the threat to the novel's men (and women) remains. Who is to say that George, perfectly sane today, might not be stark raving mad tomorrow? His portrait, so far as we know, still hangs over the mantel at Ventnor.

CHAPTER 4

Amnesia, Madness, and Financial Fraud: Ontologies of Loss in Silas Marner and Hard Cash

Charles Reade was laboring over the early numbers of *Very Hard Cash* in July 1862 when he found the first installment of George Eliot's *Romola* in the *Cornhill*. He reached two immediate conclusions about her new novel: first, that he could "see no trace of George Eliot in the story," though the *Cornhill* had advertised the work as hers; and second, that she must have founded *Romola* upon his own novel of Renaissance Italy, *The Cloister and the Hearth* (1861), which had succeeded critically and commercially the prior year.[1] "Is it egotism," he wrote to his friend Laura Seymour, "or am I right in thinking that this story of the fifteenth century has been called into existence by my success with the same epoch? If it is Georgy Porgy, why then Lewes has been helping her! All the worse for her. The grey mare is the better horse."[2] He could not have known that Eliot's novel had been prompted by her May 1860 trip to Italy with Lewes, who suggested that the "life and times" of Girolamo Savonarola "afford fine material for an historical romance" – an idea that she "at once caught at … with enthusiasm."[3] Nor could he have known that neither Eliot nor Lewes appears ever to have read *Cloister* or its originating story *A Good Fight*, which had run in *Once a Week* from July to October 1859.[4] The combative Reade would probably have been more offended by their total ignorance of his work than by any imitation. Always sensitive to perceived slights and resentful that critics did not regard his work more highly, Reade was tormented by Eliot's success, no less because their artistic sensibilities were so different than because he believed she had not earned her reputation. As Reade's nephew and godson wrote in their memoir of him, he "had no stomach for the fulsome eulogy piled on George Eliot," for he believed fully that it "was the outcome of judicious wire-pulling" by Lewes and others in their literary circle.[5]

It is hard now to imagine any serious rivalry between these writers: Eliot, the careful realist chronicler of slow historical and psychological change, of deep craving after community and sympathy, regarded since at least the publication of *Middlemarch* (1872) as one of the great novelists in English; and Reade, the sensation novelist and provocateur, noisy enemy of scandal and injustice, popular at mid-century but now mostly unread if not quite forgotten. But they vied for publishers and readers in a crowded field that included Dickens, Collins, Braddon, Trollope, and Thackeray. If Reade held Eliot cheap among such company, her publishers did not. While he haggled with Dickens and Wills to secure £800 for *Hard Cash*'s serial run in *All the Year Round*, and worked out for himself complicated arrangements for American sheets, volume editions, and translations, she quietly received £7,000 from George Smith for *Romola*'s twelve monthly installments and a six-year lease on the copyright, and she could have had more.[6] In an effort to wrest her away from Blackwood, Smith first offered her £10,000 for the copyright of her new novel, but she declined "on the ground that her work would not be worth the sum!"[7] Though *Adam Bede* (1859), *The Mill on the Floss* (1860), and *Silas Marner* had each sold wonderfully, one after another, Eliot doubted *Romola*'s suitability for serial publication and suspected that its Italian subject matter would make it less popular than her previous works. Meanwhile, Reade wrenched whatever he could from his publishers, making "no secret of the value he set on his work" and, in the case of *Hard Cash*, even going so far as to purchase the paper for the book himself.[8] In this gap between Eliot's quiet ethical and aesthetic ambitions and Reade's loud demands for justice – for his own labor, and for the victims of social wrongs – we can glimpse many of the differences between their novels.

Silas Marner and *Hard Cash* in many ways epitomize these differences, not least because Eliot's "half fable, half realist" work contrasts so sharply with the sprawl of Reade's sensational triple-decker, which ranges from pirate attacks to banking fraud to the scandalous laws that governed private asylums.[9] Already working on *Romola* in February 1861, Eliot explained to John Blackwood that another story had risen between her and her Italian subject, emerging "quite suddenly, as a sort of legendary tale, suggested by my recollection of having once, in early childhood, seen a linen-weaver with a bag on his back," but giving way upon reflection "to a more realistic treatment."[10] Her words explain *Silas Marner*'s curious hybridity, its mixture of mysticism, psychological portraiture, and historical specificity. Set in the village of Raveloe during and after the Napoleonic Wars, it tells a story of emotional betrayal, miserhood, theft, and a lonely life restored to sympathy and community by the timely appearance of a magical child. For a long while, *Marner* was regarded "as at best a 'minor masterpiece'" among the massive accomplishments of Eliot's longer novels, becoming mainly,

Terence Cave notes, "a 'children's classic', often published in shortened and expurgated editions."[11] *Hard Cash*, on the other hand, grew from Reade's "great system" for writing "matter-of-fact Romance; that is, a fiction built on truths ... gathered by long, severe, systematic labor," and from his crusading desire to win justice for a man named Fletcher, who had been certified insane at the insistence of his father's business partners to prevent him from inheriting £35,000.[12] It also takes up other forms of rapacity and fraud, from the profitable colonial exploits of English ship captain David Dodd, who owns the titular hard cash, to the criminal practices – forgery, embezzlement, and other textual and financial crimes – being described routinely in the Victorian press. If *Silas Marner* is half fairy tale, *Hard Cash* is half sensational reportage, an exposé of contemporary economic life.

Yet these very different novels converge at a crucial point: in associating financial loss with psychological disintegration, not necessarily as cause and effect but rather as a pattern of representation that reveals the growing indistinguishability of property and identity in England's evolving commodity culture. Barbara Weiss has noted of Victorian bankruptcy novels, including Eliot's *The Mill on the Floss*, that they often tell stories in which the "[d]estruction of economic identity" produces "an emotional upheaval in family life ... [and] a crisis in sexual roles" in which "the loss of money, with its dissolution of all sense of personal identity" gives a "foretaste of death."[13] *Silas Marner* and *Hard Cash* hint at a more complex upheaval, rooted in both subjective trauma and a broader ideology. In the former novel, the psychological disruptions occur most obviously in Silas's cataleptic fits, one of which corresponds suggestively with the theft that leads to his expulsion from Lantern Yard. While the novel centers thereafter on the story of his isolation and gradual restoration to community and sympathy, it insists, too, on the ways in which his inauguration into Raveloe's commodity culture disrupts his subjectivity. For Silas, reawakening to sympathy and community means assimilating to capitalist demands and a sense of abstract value that depends upon the forms of community and trust that undergirded the transition to paper money and other objects of textual exchange.[14] *Hard Cash* offers a similar symbolic and imaginative association, following its titular money through a series of thefts, frauds, and other misadventures that provoke psychological trauma and loss: David Dodd's amnesia, Alfred Hardie's "madness," the suicides that follow the Bank of Barkington's failure, and Richard Hardie's eventual mental collapse. In Reade's novel the missing hard cash figures repeatedly as a gap or absence within subjectivity, as if to suggest the inevitability of such a conceptual equivalency in a culture that treats both property and identity as textual objects of exchange.

By converging in this homology between property and identity, *Silas Marner* and *Hard Cash* underscore the extent to which the Victorian tendency to textualize and commodify identity must be understood as a broad cultural imperative rather than, as in *Great Expectations* and *Lady Audley's Secret*, a consequence mainly of the production of autobiography, portraiture, and other particular, and particularly commercial, textual forms. Both novels concern themselves generally with the implications of capitalism's rise, in *Marner* by associating the cultivation of community and sympathy with a broader recalibration of identity's relation to the economic sphere, and in *Hard Cash* by revealing the overlapping discursive practices that undergird finance capitalism and the textualization of identity, and by tracing these to the official practices of the state. Though they differ markedly in other ways, these novels coincide by representing financial loss as a powerful interior crisis – what Colella calls "a form of traumatic or disrupted realism that evokes distress" through its departure from conventional or predictable narrative modes – and by tracing that crisis to its origins in the textualization of identity within the economic sphere.[15] In this way *Silas Marner* and *Hard Cash* describe an ontology of loss that traces crises of memory and desire to the rise of capitalist culture, and particularly to the textual inauguration of subjectivity into the world of textual production and material exchange.

* * *

Eliot did not think of *Silas Marner* as a story about loss. After sharing part of the manuscript with Blackwood, she told him that although she did not wonder at his finding the story "as far as [he had] read it, rather somber," she hoped that he would "not find it at all a sad story, on the whole, since it sets – or is intended to set – in a strong light the remedial influences of pure, natural human relations."[16] Scholars have mostly taken Eliot at her word, treating the novel as a loving fable of sympathy and community and so connecting it to the more ponderous masterpieces that make up Eliot's oeuvre. While admitting that *Marner* has "dark elements," for instance, Nancy Henry argues that its "ultimately uplifting moral" is "that human love and community are greater forces than either religion or money," and Gillian Beer reads the novel as a "healing inversion of the Midas myth" in which "Silas, sustained by Dolly Winthrop's pungent advice, bring[s] up Eppie, and thereby becom[es] again part of the community of humankind."[17] In an especially enthusiastic response, David Sonstroem writes that "[a]ll readers of *Silas Marner* agree with George Eliot's broad statement of purpose" and argues that "human relations" in the novel inevitably "repel raids from the darkness beyond."[18] For these critics and others, the focus has been Silas's emotional and spiritual regeneration, the extent to which his willing acceptance of Eppie as a replacement for his stolen gold restores him to a world of natural – not merely biological or economic – human relations.

Yet human relations in *Silas Marner* cannot be isolated from economic relations, for Eppie's arrival signals not only the end of Silas's miserhood but also his integration into the imaginative and ideological structures of capitalism. Despite its fairy-tale qualities, *Marner* is neither unconscious of history nor immune to the economic upheavals that were reconfiguring nineteenth-century life. The novel depicts the period of change during and after the Napoleonic Wars. It records "the disjunction between the worlds of the country landlords or agriculturalists and manufacturers, the worth of gold and other precious metals deflated by the inflation of paper currency, [and] the transformation of village economies brought by industrialization."[19] The novel's earlier phases in fact return to a past in which commerce was transacted "predominantly in coin," so that Silas's gradual transformation from hoarder of gold to participant in commodity exchange coincides with the transition to paper money that followed the 1797 Restriction Act.[20] To the extent that, as Cave suggests, Eliot's "most serious and far-reaching concerns" in *Silas Marner* are "with history and above all with historical change," those concerns include the emerging structures of Victorian capitalism and the forms of representation to which they gave rise (viii). In a May 1861 response to Blackwood's "pleasant news" that *Silas Marner* was likely to sell out all 7,500 printed copies, Eliot quipped, "There can be no great painting of misers under the present system of paper money – cheques bills scrip and the like: nobody can handle that dull property as men handled the glittering gold."[21] Neither could Eliot handle the subject of human relations without acknowledging that "the present system of paper money," and commodity culture generally, was creating absences and gaps in subjectivity even as – and perhaps because – it transformed identity into a textual, commodified thing.

The novel more or less begins by aligning financial and psychological loss, tracing Silas's isolation in Raveloe back to the fits that catalyze his expulsion from Lantern Yard. His fits stand in metaphorically for losses of several kinds: of money, in the form of the deacon's savings, but also of his community's trust, his psychological coherence, and the erotic potential of his engagement to Sarah. Having once been "highly thought of in [the] little hidden world" of Lantern Yard, Silas finds after his first fit that his best friend William Dane differs from the rest of the community by saying that his trance looks "more like a visitation of Satan than a proof of divine favour," and although Sarah denies wishing to break off their engagement, her manner toward Silas begins "to exhibit a strange fluctuation between an effort at an increased manifestation of regard and involuntary signs of shrinking and dislike" (8, 9, 10). Silas's fits thus lead not only to the theft of the deacon's money but also to ruptures of sympathy that end in self-imposed exile and a thorough alteration of his economic life. He no longer produces linen to save money toward the marriage that will bring him erotic fulfillment but instead sits "unremittingly" at his loom, "seem[ing] to weave, like the spider, from pure impulse, without reflection" (15). Meanwhile, his subjectivity exists in permanent incoherence, his trances constituting gaps that, Linda Shires writes, "erase perspective and point of view" and "annul routine time and space."[22] For Silas, catalepsy consolidates loss into a symbolic trope that is both personal and financial, that insists upon an imaginative homology between property and the self.

This entanglement means that Silas's departure from the world of human relations at Lantern Yard constitutes also the start of a profound economic transformation, a transition from the communal enclave economy of Lantern Yard to the broad capitalist one of Raveloe. As his miserly hoarding shows, Silas does not immediately assimilate to Raveloe's economy when he arrives, even though, "shriveled and distorted to the status of an object, [he] is clearly a fellow of the alienated, commodified worker of Marx's analysis."[23] On the contrary, though he becomes expert at producing linen and accumulating capital, he does not engage fully with the market or enter into Raveloe's broader social relations. His utilitarian aim is "keeping himself strong enough to work sixteen hours a-day on as small an outlay as possible," eschewing commodities and serving as "a mere repository for the coins that mark his labor" (18).[24] He also rejects not only the abstract form of paper money but even the foundational function of gold in embodying economic value since for him the guineas' value "depend[s] not on social standards of exchange" but rather on "his own eye and hand," which measure the coins according only to the sheer erotic pleasure that he takes from fondling their rounded edges and imprinted faces.[25] The paradox of Silas's economic activity is that it draws him further and further from the human agents who are the basis of commodity exchange.[26] He is not initially the commodified subject of *Great Expectations* or *Lady Audley's Secret*, for unlike Pip and Lady Audley he is profoundly atextual, his recorded history belonging to the very type of Dissenting community that prompted the creation of the GRO. Nor, with his singular appearance, does he appear as the reproducible object of a commodified age. During his early years in Raveloe, Silas stands apart, literally and symbolically, from the forces of textualization and commodification.

Yet Silas's move to Raveloe inaugurates him into capitalist structures, however little he notices them at first. For instance, the move improves his material fortunes since formerly "he worked for a wholesale dealer" who paid him at a lower rate, while in Raveloe he earns "five bright guineas" for finishing Mrs. Osgood's table-linen and is the sole proprietor of his work (16). Attuned for the first time to the pleasures of capital accumulation, he begins to associate his labor with the satisfaction of his individual desires rather than the support of communal life – begins to take on the characteristics of the economically desiring subject. And while he still looks distinctive, he begins to exhibit the commodity's deviation from chronological time, partly because he "substitut[es] static repetition for onward development" and partly because he seems to age at a rate incommensurate with the natural course of years.[27] The pleasure he takes in fondling the "bright faces" of his coins suggests, too, the displacement of his erotic desire for Sarah, so that his ritual of touching and counting his guineas becomes, as Jeff Nunokawa puts it, "a condensed catalogue of sexual deviance" (16).[28] Silas's life thus narrows and hardens "into a mere pulsation of desire and satisfaction that had no relation to any other being" and resolves itself steadily into a sense that the gold is "conscious of him" in turn (19, 18). He shrinks and bends "into a constant mechanical relation to the objects of his life, so that he produced the same sort of impression as a handle or a crooked tube, which has no meaning standing apart" (19). He becomes more and more like a material object himself, reinforcing the sense of equivalency between gold and people, the objects and subjects of economic life.

Dunstan Cass's theft of Silas's hoarded gold is not necessarily, then, the unmitigated tragedy that Silas believes it to be, since it serves symbolically as the precondition for Eppie's arrival and promises to arrest Silas's commodification. Cave indeed argues that the robbery, not Eppie, initiates Silas's regeneration, since he cannot "communicate with the villagers in terms other than economic, until the loss of his gold begins to elicit a first groping response" (xvii). Yet it is worth considering precisely what Silas's integration into Raveloe's community entails, whether his return to human sympathy entails a rejection or amplification of the ontology of loss that suffuses the novel. Between Silas's discovery of the robbery and his revelation of it to the Raveloe community, Eliot interposes a chapter depicting that community at the Rainbow and showing the nature of their economic and discursive exchanges. The chapter provides local color and comic relief, from the amiability of the "jolly" butcher to the ill temper of the farrier, and from the landlord's efforts at peacemaking to Mr. Macey's gossip (43). But it offers more than this, too, by identifying the Rainbow as "the place where [Silas] was likely to find the powers and dignities" of the village and the novel's "site of judicial and legal authority ... a community of interpretation and covenant" (42).[29] In both respects, chapter 6 illuminates the nature of life in Raveloe, which is not so "[n]estled in the fertile Midlands" that it is "out of touch with the broader life of England" but rather belongs already to the structures of Victorian capitalism.[30]

The novel's exploration of this problem in the scene at the Rainbow comes in two parts. The first is Mr. Macey's account of the wedding of Nancy Lammeter's parents, which recalls old Mr. Drumlow's error during the wedding ceremony when he asks the bride, "Wilt thou have this woman to thy wedded husband?" and asks the groom, "Wilt thou have this man to thy wedded wife?" (48). Worried that the pair may not therefore be "fast married," Macey wonders whether it's "the meanin' or the words as makes folks fast i' wedlock" and voices his concern to the rector, who replies, "Pooh, pooh, Macey, make yourself easy ... it's neither the meaning nor the words – it's the re*ges*ter does it – that's the glue" (48–9). What holds Raveloe's society together is neither the intent nor the form of language; rather, the "glue" is language's materiality, the ascription of power to the textual forms that accompanied capitalism's rise.[31] The "re*ges*ter" is the authoritative document that transforms the wedding from a mere social, legal, and religious form to an incontrovertible and tangible fact – and it is something more in a culture that uses such registry to determine bloodlines and arrange the transfer of property, to guarantee class immobility and ensure the perpetuation of social power.[32] The plot's hinge is arguably Godfrey Cass's fear that he will be undone by his younger brother's plot "to submit [his] temporary desire for the barmaid Molly to the 'glue' of the marriage register," a maneuver that would imperil his standing with his father.[33] As Squire Cass reminds Godfrey angrily, "my property's got no entail on it; – since my grandfather's time the Casses can do as they like with their land" (68). In these reminders of the economic power of texts, the novel marks Raveloe's modernity compared with Lantern Yard and distinguishes implicitly between Raveloe's modern economy and Silas's obsolete hoarding of gold.

The second part of this exploration comes when Macey's account of "Cliff's Holiday" becomes a quarrel about ghosts that underscores how Raveloe, despite its isolation, is already haunted by capitalist incursions and the psychological disruptions they portend. According to Macey, the reputedly "haunted" stables on the property were built by Mr. Cliff, "a Lunnon tailor, some folks said, as had gone mad wi' cheating" (50). A member of the rising middle class, Cliff builds stables "four times as big as Squire Cass's," then spends countless hours hunting and riding, affecting the country gentleman though "he'd got no more grip o' the hoss than if his legs had been cross sticks" (50). When Cliff's son sickens and dies, the lonely father gets "queerer nor ever, and . . . go[es] out i' the dead o' the night" to the stables "cracking his whip and looking at his hosses" until he finally "die[s] raving" and leaves the land to a London charity (50). The anecdote inverts Silas's story: hoarding becomes excessive expenditure, isolation becomes social ambition, and the end features the death rather than the discovery of a well-loved child. More to the point, Macey's gossip illustrates that commodity culture and the class mobility fostered by capitalism overwrite sympathetic relations with economic ones that provoke psychological disruption, and also that these effects have seeped already from the metropolis to the country, where they disrupt both biological and economic continuance through the loss of the son and his potential for future participation in the market. The story of "Cliff's Holiday" illustrates both Raveloe's susceptibility to capitalist incursions and the imaginative conjunction of psychological disruption and capitalist exchange. Moreover, it does so in a ghost story that activates the Gothicism that suffused mid-century accounts of the commodity.

Eppie's sudden appearance on Silas's hearth on Christmas Eve thus constitutes an equivocal blessing. She is the mechanism of Silas's emotional and spiritual renewal, drawing him into bonds of sympathy at Raveloe and reawakening in him "a consciousness of unity between his past and present" that did not exist during his years of hoarding and isolation (138). This newfound psychological and chronological coherence emerges almost from the moment when Silas finds Eppie on the hearth, touches her "soft warm curls," and wonders, "Could this be his little sister come back to him in a dream – his little sister whom he had carried about in his arms for a year before she died, when he was a small boy without shoes or stockings?" (109). Alexander Welsh calls Eppie's arrival "the chief miracle of *Silas Marner*," an emblem for Silas of the possibility of providence, or at least "continuity and design."[34] Yet if Eppie brings Silas a degree of coherence, it is an exaggeration to say, as Henry Alley does, that he "finds the powers of memory to be completely at his disposal as he reenters society," or that the "past returns with ease and leads directly to a sense of rightness and devotion."[35] Eppie may help Silas bridge the chronological and emotional gaps of his life, but beneath these bridges run the currents of his cataleptic fits, each one a total absence of memory and self. Even after Eppie's arrival, the most significant of these absences – the one that caused his expulsion from Lantern Yard – remains a mystery to Silas, as much as for what happened during the fit as for the metaphysical questions raised by the drawing of lots and the betrayals of his friend, his fiancée, and his religious fellows. Like the novel, which describes three periods of action separated by two gaps of sixteen years, Silas remains stubbornly distemporal, punctuated by psychological disruptions that neither Eppie nor the narrator mends.

Silas's integration into his community also entails psychological transformations of other kinds as he begins to participate in the social and imaginative forms of capitalism. Writing hopefully that Silas "learns to live again" through Eppie, Susan Cohen argues that by "[n]aming Eppie after his dead mother and little sister, he resituates himself not only in the community but also in his own lost family," returning to an idealized state of sympathy and affection.[36] But his naming of Eppie is less a return than an attempt to reconstitute old relations in a new ideological context that locates mother and sister in the commodified form of a golden child. Silas's sense of Eppie is confounded from the first by the sense that she is "Gold! – his own gold – brought back to him as mysteriously as it had been taken away!" and he never quite relinquishes the idea that she is a material equivalent of his hoard (108–9). Instead, throughout the novel he reformulates the equation, finding that he cannot articulate the distinction between his gold and this new form of embodied value, between commodity and living subject. At first he simply tells Godfrey, "My money's gone, I don't know where – and this is come from I don't know where," a point that the narrator amplifies soon after by writing, "he could only have said that the child was come instead of the gold – that the gold had turned into the child" (116, 120). Neither the narrator nor Silas seems able to perceive Eppie as more than a half-symbolic substitution, a living emblem of the homology of property and identity in the modern age.

Together, these details suggest that Silas's adaptation to "the forms of custom and belief which were the mould of Raveloe life" constitute also his assimilation to capitalism, including the alchemy by which subjects become commodities to be owned and exchanged (138). Even late in the novel, when Silas explains to Eppie how he found her, he revives his old formulation, saying that he "had taken her golden curls for his lost guineas brought back to him" (141). Nor can either her adoptive or her biological father speak of Eppie without using proprietary language, Silas saying, "God gave her to me ... He looks upon her as mine," and Godfrey regretting having "left the child unowned" and thinking of her surreptitiously as "my own child" and "my own daughter" (164, 158, 165). Such language reflects generally the position of the Victorian woman, passed from father to husband as an object of economic and sexual exchange. But it also suggests the extent to which, as she saves him from a life of hoarding and isolation, Eppie draws him into new kinds of economic relations. Sixteen years after adopting Eppie, Silas's cottage is "filled with decent furniture, all bright and clean enough to satisfy Dolly Winthrop's eye," Eppie is dressed prettily in a "dark-blue cotton gown," and Silas has taken to the luxury of smoking a pipe (136–7). Eppie has not exactly turned Silas from economic to human relations. But she has bound him to commodity culture by giving his labor a purpose beyond hoarding and opening him to a world of material desires, even if these are met primarily by Godfrey's purse rather than his own. As Courtney Berger puts it, Eppie "draws Silas into the world of human relations while simultaneously clarifying for him the importance of economic relations" and impressing upon him their interdependence.[37]

Eppie might best be understood as a form of currency, an embodiment of the value that once inhered in gold but that capitalism dispersed across textual forms that depend on the structures of sociality and trust that Silas enters at Raveloe. For Silas, Godfrey, Aaron, and the childless Nancy, Eppie is less a desiring subject than the embodiment of others' desire, "while her own inner 'history and metamorphosis' cannot be imagined, much less expressed."[38] She also serves implicitly as a medium of exchange, drawing commodities to Silas that otherwise would not have come, from Dolly's donations of Aaron's baby clothes to the contributions of Godfrey, who, "as every one said in the village, did very kindly by the weaver" (136). She even enters the Raveloe marriage market, making a match with Aaron that may not make her fortune but at least ensures that Silas "needn't work a bit ... only what's for [his] own pleasure" (145). Dolly speaks wisely when she advises Silas to keep baby Eppie busy by giving her "some bits o' red rag and things for her to play wi'; an' she'll sit and chatter to 'em as if they was alive": an economic value in material form, Eppie is the universal commodity, money, and speaks the language of commodities in turn (121). As Ilana Blumberg puts it, "Eppie translates the coins into that more abstract exchange value that waits right around the historical bend of *Silas Marner*" and makes the gold that Silas once hoarded "no longer socially divisive but, in the form of Eppie, cohesive."[39]

The novel's action resolves in two episodes that signal this shift to capitalist forms. The first occurs when Godfrey comes to Silas's cottage to "own" Eppie and is rebuffed, first by Silas, then by Eppie herself. As Beer notes, Godfrey's and Silas's competing claims on Eppie "are set out in terms of class conflict."[40] For Godfrey and Nancy, what is at issue is not only a biological, familial claim but also a sense of how "natural" ties determine economic status. It is not just that Godfrey believes that he has "a natural claim on her that must stand before every other"; it is that allowing Godfrey to "own" her will make Eppie's fortune and project her and her biological line into a comfortable pecuniary future (164). If Silas were to die, Godfrey reminds him, her lot might become "fixed in a way very different from what it would be in her father's home: she may marry some low working-man, and then, whatever I might do for her, I couldn't make her well off" (165). But while Godfrey sounds an economic warning, Eppie emphasizes sympathy. She takes Silas's hand "and grasp[s] it firmly – it was a weaver's hand, with a palm and finger-tips that were sensitive to such pressure" – and she declares that she "can't feel as [she's] got any father but one" (167). She also underscores that her removal to the Red House would be more than an economic dislocation, since it would separate her from "the working-folks, and their victuals, and their ways" (168). If Eppie's determination to stay with Silas emphasizes the role of sympathy in creating human, communal, and even familial, bonds, it also epitomizes the novel's economic transformations: the erosion of agricultural wealth and great country families, and the increasing affinity of capital for an upwardly mobile laboring class.

A variation on this theme appears in Silas's attempt to return to Lantern Yard, which he and Eppie discover has vanished into the dust. Determined after thirty years to make sense of the emotional and spiritual crises that drove Silas away, the pair travels to his birthplace to find that it has become "a great manufacturing town" made bewildering by "the noise, the movement, and the multitude of strange indifferent faces" (171). When they finally twist up Shoe Lane and into Lantern Yard, Silas discovers "with a look of distressed amazement" that there is nothing left of the religious and economic enclave where he was raised.

> "It's gone, child," he said, at last, in strong agitation – "Lantern Yard's gone. It must ha' been here, because here's the house with the o'erhanging

window – I know that – it's just the same; but they've made this new opening; and see that big factory! It's all gone – chapel and all." (173)

Like Elizabeth Barrett Browning's "The Cry of the Children" (1843), *Silas Marner* ends in an image of industrialization swallowing up childhood, nature, memory, and faith. Yet for Silas, the eradication of Lantern Yard means something else, too. Having wanted to talk over the past with Mr. Paston, the minister, and so gain an understanding of the events that led to his exile, Silas returns to Raveloe, confesses his disappointment to Dolly, and says, "Since the time the child was sent to me and I've come to love her as myself, I've had light enough to trusten by; and now she says she'll never leave me, I think I shall trusten till I die" (173). Silas thus abandons the idea of becoming psychologically or temporally whole by filling the gaps left by his fits. Instead, he imagines these gaps as inevitable parts of a subjectivity that he can coalesce around the mysterious figure of the commodity. Through Eppie's sympathy he becomes not uneconomic but thoroughly commodified: the potentially autobiographical subject of Victorian capitalism, inaugurated fully into the imaginative forms of his economic milieu.

If *Silas Marner* celebrates natural human relations, then, it also illustrates how such relations were being shaped by a culture pervaded by capitalist demands. It suggests that there is no choice between sympathetic and economic life, no articulable distinction between the forms of value embodied by bags of gold and a golden-haired child. Nor is Raveloe immune to real historical change, as Efraim Sicher asserts when he calls it "neither a real place nor a literary pastoral, but a reversal of history that undoes the alienating effects of industrialisation and urbanisation."[41] Raveloe and Silas both are prey to the economic forces that transformed England during the first half of the nineteenth century, the country villages no less than the manufacturing towns or the great financial metropolis. As the narrator describes Godfrey's largesse to his "unowned" daughter, she notes that "it was nothing but right a man should be looked on and helped by those who could afford it . . . and when the weaving was going down too – for there was less and less flax spun – and Master Marner was none so young" (136). From the start, Beer notes, Silas is written "*across* the stereotype of the woman weaving," such that he reflects "conditions after the onset of the industrial revolution."[42] By novel's end Godfrey and Nancy are only "Mr and Mrs Godfrey Cass," a reminder that neither the old title nor the old estate has survived "that glorious war-time which was felt to be a peculiar favour of Providence towards the landed interest" (133, 21). Such passages recall the industrial transformation of English textile production, the realities of agricultural decline, and the shift toward a capitalist economy of mechanical production, paper money, and a rising middle class. As in *Great Expectations*, the failed return to an idyllic "Merry Old England" only registers an aching desire for a permanently vanished precapitalist past.

Silas Marner does not, as Blumberg argues, "[trace] a path from gold fetish to human value."[43] Instead, it works to naturalize and even sacralize the transition to capitalism – to represent abstract value and commodified subjectivities as inevitabilities coincidental with the unmitigated goods of community, human sympathy, and spiritual renewal. Silas's bond with Eppie is more "natural" than the biological one she shares with Godfrey, and through Eppie he is reunited with not just humankind but also a natural world with which she too harmonizes: "there was love between the child and the world – from men and women with parental looks and tones, to the red lady-birds and round pebbles" (129). Eppie's fascination with nature even causes Silas to begin "to look for the once familiar herbs again," and she coaxes him later into contriving more space for a garden, partly so that she may plant and preserve the furze bush beneath which her mother died (124). But Silas continues to be baffled by the way she has entered his life – to regard her as a sign of "divine . . . agency" like the sacred but unreadable "I.H.S." that Dolly stamps upon her lard-cakes (79).[44] These indications that Eppie is a natural, even sacred presence in Silas's life coexist with rather than supercede his ineradicable sense that she is a living version of the "bright faces" he once loved. For Silas the implicit cost of human sympathy is a permanent sense of Eppie as both subject and commodity, a permanent inability to articulate a meaningful difference between subjectivity and other objects of exchange. The novel traces an ontology of loss that is financial *and* psychological because it perceives no gap between the workings of property and the emotional and spiritual impulses that sustain "natural" human life.

The novel's happy ending makes it difficult to know whether *Silas Marner* means to express anxiety regarding capitalism's transformation of subjectivity or rather to offer Silas as fulfilled by his assimilation into economic structures that, unlike hoarding, rely upon sympathy and community for their power. But as Jim Reilly argues, the novel's "humanist myth" would hardly be necessary "unless everything it wishes to assert is under threat."[45] Eliot's apparent assertion that England's capitalist transformation aligns well with the natural and spiritual order of things might best be understood, then, as an attempt to ward off a lurking sense of what was being lost through capitalism's rise. Neither Eppie's kind influence nor the recovery of his gold restores Silas to the precapitalist Eden he inhabits before his fits. His inner story remains incomplete, the possibility of filling his mental gaps having been swallowed up along with Lantern Yard by the onward march of industrial production. Thus the novel ends more or less as it began: with Silas unable to resist or interpret the blanks of subjectivity that imply homology between property and identity. Free from any anxiety that his fits are supernatural visitations, "the sages of Raveloe" – gathered, surely, at the Rainbow – urge Silas to prevent them by taking a pipe, advice that Dr. Kimble sanctions "on the ground that it was as well to try what could do no harm" (138). Capitalism thus appears here as the solution to its own problem: consumption, particularly of the exemplary commodity yielded by imperialism, will ward off loss, will prevent rather than cause disruptions of identity. The solution does no good, as is clear from the end of the novel when the narrator remarks that Eppie must always be "on the watch lest one of her father's strange attacks should come on" (173). The novel's end in this figure of pointless consumption should at least give us pause in reading it as an unambiguous celebration of human relations when these cannot help but speak the language of commodity culture.

* * *

Hard Cash traces more definitive relations between financial and psychological loss than *Silas Marner* does, in part because Reade's documentary method immersed him so thoroughly in the textual forms of commodity culture and suggested to him the power of texts to make identity into an object of exchange. The novel is a monument of Reade's documentary practice, involving no fewer than 614 sources from which Reade compiled 37,000 words of notes and 70,000 words of newspaper clippings on topics ranging from joint-stock banking to insanity, and from religious autobiography to contemporary slang.[46] Having succeeded with his "great system" in writing *The Cloister and the Hearth*, Reade sought with *Hard Cash* to produce a "masterpiece" by applying his unusual method to a "subject of [his] own day": financial fraud committed under the auspices of the laws that governed madness and asylums during the middle of the century.[47] The novel centers upon the scheming of ruined banker Richard Hardie, who falsifies accounts to hide his losses in the Railway Bubble, steals the Dodds' life savings, has his son Alfred certified insane and committed when Alfred accuses him of the theft, and goes mad himself by the end of the novel. Amid the tangle of receipts, account-books, railway shares, and medical certifications that litter the novel – to say nothing of the paper

Amnesia, Madness, and Financial Fraud 141

money that gives the novel its title – both financial fraud and madness appear in *Hard Cash* as byproducts of a culture that treats texts as material equivalents of both subjectivity and economic value.

For Reade, preparing to write about a "subject of [his] own day" meant exploring the problem of textuality and commodification that had emerged as a distinctive cultural refrain. In 1858, he became involved in the case of E.P. Fletcher, who had irritated his deceased father's business partners by drinking, having fits, and then claiming a £35,000 inheritance from the firm, whereupon the partners had him "certified insane and committed to a madhouse."[48] A barrister by training, Reade took up Fletcher's cause, hiding him from the asylum's agents and assisting in his legal defense while also placing his case before the public in a series of letters.[49] Before beginning to write *Hard Cash*, Reade supplemented this experience by reading newspaper accounts of asylums and longer works on psychology including Forbes Winslow's influential *The Incubation of Insanity* (1845). He prepared himself to write by studying madness as both a psychological proposition and a set of textual practices that gave it legal form. By the time he retreated to Oxford to begin writing, Reade's researches had overwhelmed him. "I have read and taken notes, but cannot write," he told Seymour. "Don't feel to know enough. But it is always the same story now. And I always end by getting over it."[50] He did "get over it," publishing *Very Hard Cash* in forty installments and 275 pages in *All the Year Round* – eight installments and 115 pages more than Dickens paid him for.[51] It was a "gift," according to legend, that Dickens could have done without.[52] In August 1863, halfway through its serial run, Wills visited Reade to encourage him to wind down the novel since the magazine was "print[ing] 3000 copies less than at the outset."[53] The following month Alfred Hardie entered the asylum.

The few modern scholars who have bothered with *Hard Cash*, as Reade retitled it for volume publication, have tended to focus on its treatment of asylums and Victorian lunacy law. Sheila Smith, Ann Grigsby, and Peter Logan all have assessed the novel's place in contemporary debates over madness and legal reform, while Richard Fantina goes farther, dismissing the parts *not* about Alfred's incarceration as mere "distractions" from the "primary business of exposing corruption and brutality in private lunatic asylums."[54] Deborah Wynne presses this argument, writing that the novel's other subjects – its nautical chapters, love story, and portrayal of financial panic – are not separate strands of a complicated plot but signs of "a serious generic instability" that alienated readers and marred the book.[55] Exposing abuses in asylums was certainly part of Reade's point: the scenes in which

Alfred is drugged, manacled, straitjacketed, and beaten are graphic and sensational, and they elicited pointed contemporary response. In October 1863 Dr. J.S. Bushnan attacked *Very Hard Cash* in a letter to the *Daily News*, provoking an energetic reply from Reade detailing his experiences with Fletcher and describing similar cases that had been reported in the press.[56] Behind the scenes, Sutherland asserts, Dickens faced "urgent pressure ... to interfere" because Forster was a Lunacy Commissioner, and also because he and others in his circle had ties to John Conolly, whom Reade lampoons as Dr. Wycherley.[57] Dickens did finally intervene, printing a disclaimer below the final installment that declared:

> THE STATEMENTS AND OPINIONS OF THIS JOURNAL GENERALLY, ARE, OF COURSE, TO BE RECEIVED AS THE STATEMENTS AND OPINIONS OF ITS CONDUCTOR. BUT THIS IS NOT SO, IN THE CASE OF A WORK OF FICTION FIRST PUBLISHED IN THESE PAGES AS A SERIAL STORY, WITH THE NAME OF AN EMINENT WRITER ATTACHED TO IT. WHEN ONE OF MY LITERARY BROTHERS DOES ME THE HONOUR TO UNDERTAKE SUCH A TASK, I HOLD THAT HE EXECUTES IT ON HIS OWN PERSONAL RESPONSIBILITY, AND FOR THE SUSTAINMENT OF HIS OWN REPUTATION; AND I DO NOT CONSIDER MYSELF AT LIBERTY TO EXERCISE THAT CONTROL OVER HIS TEXT WHICH I CLAIM AS TO OTHER CONTRIBUTIONS.[58]

Whatever he thought of the notice, Reade could not (and did not) reply to Dickens as he had to Bushnan.

These public controversies – especially because they involve Dickens – have probably encouraged the critical preoccupation with *Hard Cash*'s asylums. But Reade believed that his novel was also about other things. In his "Preface" to the second London edition in 1864, Reade lamented, "To hear people talk, one would think that this book is all about private asylums. Yet but one-fifth of the story is so employed."[59] The complaint seems disingenuous: Reade intended to stir, and did stir, debate over lunacy laws and private asylums. But Alfred first enters an asylum in the twenty-sixth installment – nearly two-thirds of the way through the novel – and even then many subsequent chapters center on the Dodds, Richard Hardie's scheming, and Alfred's trial.[60] Reade's notes suggest that he envisioned the novel's parallel engagements with financial fraud and madness as a coherent critique of overlapping spheres of cultural and discursive practice, however clumsily he wedded these in his plot. One card reads, "'Joint Stock Banking,' Limited Liability (see printed article [Madness]).

Amnesia, Madness, and Financial Fraud 143

Also 'Bankruptcy,' (printed article)"; another lists Hollingshead's "City of Unlimited Paper" from *Household Words*.[61] Elsewhere Reade jotted down, "A physician, in Railway Panic, goes mad, & gives the first indication by prescribing shares."[62] For Reade, madness was embedded literally in the related discourses of banking, liability, and bankruptcy; it belonged to a shared ontology of financial and psychological loss. In part this is because, as Susan Walsh writes, *Hard Cash* treats psychic dissolution as an effect of "the ambiguities, hazards, and imperatives of competitive risk" that inhere in Victorian financial markets.[63] But as Christine Krueger has argued in her important work on the Victorian novel and the law, madness in the English courts has for centuries been bound up with questions of agency and the competency to manage wealth and estates.[64] *Hard Cash* portrays madness as both a psychological condition engendered by the uncertainties of Victorian finance and a category constructed in and through texts that make subjectivity a material thing in the act of stripping its agency and entangling it in the market.

Reade thus provides in *Hard Cash* a complex reading of the cultural conditions that encourage the production of both value and subjectivity in textual form, such that property and identity intermingle in the broader discursive field. Explicitly, the novel centers upon Captain Dodd's hard cash, which escapes pirates, a deadly hurricane, French ruffians, and the volatility of foreign markets only to wind up in the hands of the novel's villain, Richard Hardie. In part, the cash's vicissitudes illustrate the vulnerability of texts, which function under capitalism as both contingent signifiers of value and all-too-material objects that can be lost, altered, damaged, or destroyed. But as a matter of both plot and symbol, the vulnerabilities of the hard cash mimic those of Alfred Hardie, whose "value" – intellectually and economically – is indicated and compromised by his existence as financial documents, medical certificates, asylum logs, and correspondence that materialize his identity and expose it to economic liabilities, including his right to inherit his trust, which remains in the hands of the very man who benefits from his incarceration. However much Reade studied *The Incubation of Insanity*, his novel is interested principally not in madness but in the cultural conditions that treat the production of madness, and identity generally, as a textual thing, and also in the way in which identity's materiality situates it within a textual field that is simultaneously legal, financial, and autobiographical, so that identity belongs equally to discourses of the commodity and the subject. Like *Great Expectations*, *Hard Cash* takes its name from the capital that circulates through its pages. It is a story of portable property. But Reade locates the commodification of identity not particularly in autobiography but rather in a textual culture that has thoroughly naturalized the textual production of identity and rendered it indistinguishable from other forms of property.

* * *

The story of David Dodd's eponymous hard cash is largely the story of its imperilment at the hands of racial others, English villains, and the Victorian financial market. *Hard Cash*'s first six chapters describe Oxford boat races and lovers' sighs, tracing the budding romance between Alfred and Julia Dodd. But they do so, as the narrator explains, principally to interest us in the fate of the cash, which becomes relevant to the romantic plot from the moment that Alfred's father refuses him permission to marry Julia and Mrs. Dodd confesses to her heartbroken daughter that the avaricious Hardie once aspired to her hand and is more likely to consider what will "suit the *ledger* best" than to indulge his son (1: 174). She confides to Julia that her father is bringing from Calcutta their life savings of £14,000, a sum large enough to tempt the "mercantile Brutus" into approving the marriage (1: 171). While Julia recoils at being "bought and sold like this" in the marriage market, the narrator explains that Dodd's hard cash is what "connect[s] him with the heart of this story, despite the twelve thousand miles of water between him and the lovers at Barkington" (1: 174, 186). The early chapters thus offer familiar sensational tropes – sexual commodification through marriage, the slipperiness of class standing – as a prelude to recounting Dodd's perilous journey home, during which he is harassed by pirates, nearly robbed by Ramgolam, beset by a hurricane, wrecked in the English Channel by the incompetent Captain Robarts, and attacked on the road by the French ruffians Thibout and Moinard, who try to rob him after spying his bulging pocketbook. Throughout these ordeals, and because of them, the cash's vulnerability provides much of the novel's early tension.

Walsh suggests that this vulnerability – and, more generally, the novel's interest in money and madness – originates in the fact that "cash can never be 'hard,' if by that we mean stable and changeless."[65] The cash's contingency appears in the novel even before Dodd takes it aboard the *Agra*, since the possibility of its being worth anything at all depends on the vagaries of foreign markets and international exchange. Having spent his life "lay[ing] by money for his wife and children," and having always revered great banks "with … childlike confidence," Dodd is alarmed when he lands at Calcutta and learns that "the greatest firm there [has] suspended payments, carrying astonishment and dismay into a hundred families" (1: 186). His bank makes good on his anxious request to withdraw his £14,000, but they give him "half and half," a mix of bank notes and mercantile bills that includes, he realizes, several bills just deposited by an officer who entered the bank while Dodd was waiting (1: 187). The form of the withdrawal reminds us of the variety of texts that signify value under finance capitalism, while its size reinforces cash's contingency by mimicking "on the domestic scale" the £14,000,000 of currency that the 1844 Bank Charter Act allowed the Bank of England to issue without the backing of bullion.[66] For Dodd, the simple fact of having his cash in his hands reassures him against the ambiguities of value and exchange. But as Ramgolam suggests in the oily speech that follows his attempted theft, such paper signs are at best a "sovereign talisman" or "amulet" betokening intangible worth (1: 239–40). The reassuring hardness of the cash cannot really stabilize its contingent significations.

When Dodd reaches England and deposits his cash in the Bank of Barkington, these forms of contingency and peril take center stage, not only because the future value of Dodd's £14,000 depends upon the bank's solvency but because Hardie has himself been the victim of speculation and fluctuation, losing the bank's assets in the Railway Bubble despite his public pronouncements that such investments represent the "Arithmetic of Bedlam!" since the bubble "cannot last a year without collapsing" (1: 206). Driven to extremes by his liabilities, Hardie and his clerk Noah Skinner exploit the contingencies of paper to preserve the appearance of solvency and ward off economic collapse. At first, Hardie borrows money secretly from Alfred's trust to keep the bank afloat. When this salvation fails, he begins "to lay out his arithmetical genius in a subtle process . . . of fabricating and maturing a false balance-sheet" (1: 209). Skinner follows suit, acquainting himself with his master's frauds and hatching his own plan to rescue the bank when Joseph Maxley demands his savings of £904 after hearing rumors of the bank's insolvency. Pressed by Maxley to give over the money though "there were not nine hundred pounds of hard cash in the bank," Skinner issues him Bank of Barkington notes, worthless scrip masquerading as value (2: 41). Dodd's arrival a few hours later with £14,000 thus exposes him to the depredations of two modern-day pirates, a parallel that he draws himself when Hardie refuses to return his deposit: "You want to steal my children's money: I'll have your life first. My money, ye pirate, or I'll strangle you!" (2: 62). As Walsh puts it, he outlives the dangers of his journey home "only to enter the most treacherous zone of all: an English bank parlor."[67]

Yet the novel takes pains to show that Dodd's cash really is hard: an exemplary portable property and a material emblem of the capitalist sphere. The novel revels in its hardness, making the cash a hero through its sheer physical bulk. As Dodd recovers from the pirate attack, and just as Ramgolam is describing the cash disingenuously as a purely metaphysical thing, Dodd notices "something hard – something heavy" lodged in his pocketbook and discovers that "a bullet had passed through [his] coat and waistcoat, etc., and through the oilskin, and the leather pocket-book, and just dented the 'Hard Cash'" (1: 240). Indeed, the cash's hardness more than its contingency imperils it, since its physical presence aboard the *Agra* means that it can be seized, lost, or destroyed, leaving no trace of the value it represents. Dodd's impulse to protect the cash sustains him in his fight against the pirates, and in the face of the subsequent hurricane Dodd "prepare[s] for the worst" by taking precautions to safeguard the cash against destruction:

> He took a bottle, inserted the fatal money in it, with a few words of love to his wife, and of direction to any stranger that should fall in with it; secured the cork with melted sealing-wax, tied oilskin over it and melted wax on that; applied a preparation to the glass to close the pores; and to protect it against other accidents, and attract attention, fastened a black painted bladder to it by a stout tarred twine, and painted "Agra, lost at sea," in white on the bladder. (1: 251–2)

That Dodd should have the time or dexterity to perform such work during a violent hurricane is among the novel's more dubious propositions. Still, the events suggest that Dodd's money would be no less endangered if it were instead a fortune in bullion or part of the *Agra*'s valuable cargo of flexible canes, saltpeter, and "nineteen thousand eight hundred and six chests, sixty half chests, [and] fifty quarter chests of tea" (1: 181).

The cash thus bears a double vulnerability: to the volatility of the abstract economic value it signifies, and also, in its materiality, to the threat of physical annihilation. It occupies a middle ground between the stable, material, but increasingly obsolete wealth embodied in landed estates and the contingent forms of finance capitalism, which created and transferred value in mid-century accounting ledgers even when nothing changed hands. Dodd occupies this middle ground, too, Lucy having married him in defiance of an uncle and aunt who preferred other suitors. While the uncle loves "pedigree" and wants to "graft [her] onto a stick called Talboys, that came in with the Revocation of the Edict of Nantes, known in pedigrees as 'the Norman Conquest'," the aunt prefers Hardie, the parvenu who saved the bank in 1825 but ruins it two decades later "when everything that had a name, and by some immense fortuity could write it, demanded its part in the new and fathomless source of wealth" (2: 55; 1: 204). Asked to choose between these alternatives, Lucy marries Dodd, a middle-class ship captain who serves the new economy by bringing material goods from England's colonies to its commercial center – the very activity, along with industrial production, that stimulated commodity culture, producing men like Hardie and eroding the aristocratic monopoly on wealth and power. Returned from India, Dodd does not lose his cash to abstract contingencies. He loses it to Hardie, who makes it literally disappear, first by placing it behind the locked door of the bank's safe and then by putting it "into his pocket-book; [and] that pocket-book into his breast pocket," where he carries it until he can convert it to gold and then back again to £500 notes (2: 64). The material absence and presence of texts as much as the contingency of their signification undergirds the intrigues at the heart of the novel.

Reade's interest in the materiality of texts shaped even the novel's appearance in *All the Year Round*. Its installments contain several irregularities of layout and form, from common ones such as arranging paragraphs into letters, song lyrics, and diaries to unusual ones that probably alarmed the printer's men. In one spot, Reade arranges the dialogue into two columns to indicate the contemporaneous nature of two conversations, one featuring an exchange between Julia and Jane Hardie and the other an exchange between Sampson and Mrs. Dodd; in another, Reade includes a musical score to the song that the *Agra*'s sailors sing as they load cargo (1: 149, 180). Both examples show Reade's interest in the physical form of representation, in the materiality no less than the significations of texts. This is particularly true in the resolution of the novel's plot, which hinges mainly on recovering the receipt that Hardie gives Dodd for his £14,000. Hardie searches fruitlessly for it after Dodd collapses, even purchasing the enormous dust-heap that contains "the refuse of all Barkington" to ensure that no "farmer's man or farmer's boy" will discover the receipt "strewed on the soil for manure" and cheat him of his stolen money (2: 90). When the receipt reappears at the end of the novel, clutched in Skinner's dead hand, the narrator calls it "the soul of the lost cash," a metaphor that he elaborates when Dodd's lawyer calls with it at Hardie's to claim the £14,000: "O immortal cash! You, like your great inventor, have been a kind of spirit as well as a body; and on this, not on your grosser part, depends your personal identity. So long as that survives, your body may be recalled to its lawful owner from Heaven knows where" (3: 304, 325). The

148 Commodification of Identity in Victorian Narrative

receipt is here a "spirit" and a locus of "personal identity"; it textualizes and even sacralizes a subjectivity bodied forth by the cash, anchoring property and identity alike to discursive form and textual production.

Though volume editions of *Hard Cash* often omit the circumstance, its serial installments show that Reade wished particularly to emphasize the materiality of the receipt, which appeared twice as an illustration in *All the Year Round*. It did so first in the installment for July 11, taking up the bottom 1/3 of the page and appearing as a typical banker's receipt with the date of deposit, the sum "Received of David Dodd Esqr.," and Skinner's signature "For Richard Hardie" (Figure 4.1). The illustration also bears light shading at its top and bottom edges, as if to indicate minor wrinkling of the paper. When the image recurred on December 19 in the installment relating its recovery from Skinner, it bore a very different visual character (Figure 4.2). It is shaded heavily, but for a rectangle that runs from its upper left corner to its center – suggesting the impress of Skinner's finger – and the corner has a creased appearance, so that "Received" reads "R/eived." Considered as a device for organizing wealth by designating who owns it, the receipt fulfills a cardinal function of legal and financial texts, uniting property and identity to the signature, perennial legal symbol of individuality. But the second illustration underscores also the receipt's materiality and vulnerability, the fragility of its power to

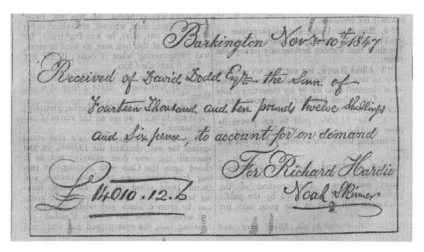

Figure 4.1 Dodd's receipt, from *Very Hard Cash* in *All the Year Round* 9 (July 11, 1863), p. 64. Image courtesy of the Rare & Special Books Collection of the University Libraries, University at Buffalo, The State University of New York.

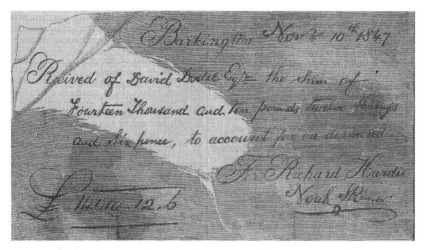

Figure 4.2 The "recovered" receipt, from *Very Hard Cash* in *All the Year Round* 10 (December 19, 1863), p. 395. Image courtesy of the Rare & Special Books Collection of the University Libraries, University at Buffalo, The State University of New York.

transform contingent "personal identity" into a tangible, stable thing. By insisting upon this vulnerability while underscoring the cultural authority that permits texts to function as equivalents of both value and identity, *Hard Cash* coalesces in the receipt its concern with the textualization and commodification of identity in its broader economic culture.

It takes up this concern, too, in the chapters written as Julia's and Jane's diaries, which affirm both the cultural function of the diary in textualizing identity and the extent to which such textualizations adapt identity to the demands of the market. Encouraged by Jane to keep a diary as consolation amid her family's troubles, Julia asks naively whether she can have "a sight of Jane's for a model," but Jane refuses, telling her, "No, dear friend ... a diary should be one's self on paper" (2: 144). This is in some respects just what Julia's diary turns out to be: impetuous, romantic, confiding, and often selfish. Like the receipt, it appears as a repository of "personal identity" that becomes a separately embodied self. In one entry Julia describes singing "Aileen Aroon" to Alfred, and confides, "he whispered things in my ear; oh! such sweet, sweet, idiotic, darling things; I will not part with even the shadow of one of them by putting it on paper" (2: 163). In another she confesses to sitting for a while with her forehead on Alfred's shoulder, then remarks, "I think I should like to grow there. Mem.: to burn this diary, and never let a creature see a syllable" (2: 164). For Julia, the diary is both a confession and divestiture, a deposit of identity onto paper that functions implicitly as self-loss since, she imagines, to write a memory is to "part" with it. The diary thus alienates identity by making it textual. And, as Julia's "Mem." to burn the diary implies, it is a text that remains always vulnerable – to violations of its private disclosures and to the possibility of its annihilation, and in the latter case, to the annihilation of that part of subjectivity it contains.

If Julia's diary reinforces the intimate connection between text and subjectivity, Jane's reinforces the diary's status as a text intended for readership and pervaded by the demands of the market. Though Jane refuses to share her diary with Julia, Alfred steals into her room, reads it ("not to profit by, alas! but to scoff"), and writes in its margins (2: 171). By including Alfred's marginalia, the scene offers the diary as a joint composition, an imitation of the way that self-narrative becomes a hybrid text when it reaches the hands of readers and becomes subject to interpretation. It also underscores the diary's vulnerability to the kinds of public disclosure that Julia fears. Jane recognizes the problems posed by readership and the dynamics of commercial publication, for she explains in one entry that she has finished writing a book on Solomon's Song but "it is *so* difficult nowadays to find a publisher for such a subject. The rage is for sentimental sermons, or else for fiction under a thin disguise of religious biography" (2: 171). She reflects here partly the market savvy of her author, who drew heavily from Adelaide Leaper Newton's *The Heavenly Life* (1856) and Horatio Bonar's *A Stranger Here* (1853) in creating her, and whose notes show that he also consulted dozens of other books, including Margaret Goodman's *Experiences of an English Sister of Mercy* (1862) and Fanny Alford's *Reminiscences of a Clergyman's Wife* (1860).[68] Reade knew the robust mid-century market in religious texts, and he may have designed these chapters of *Hard Cash* to suit their readers. Jane's diary gestures at its immersion in a broad textual culture in which subjectivity takes textual forms that approximate, and become interchangeable with, money and other objects of exchange.

Hard Cash enacts this equivalency of property and identity by adopting a familiar pattern in which economic and psychological loss coincide, so that the financial vacillations that drive the plot appear in the characters as periods of depression, addiction, psychosis, and other kinds of psychic disintegration. By the close of the day on which Hardie suspends business, "the scene at the door was heart-rending": mothers hold their ruined children up to the windows of the bank, men hammer at the doors, and "the house as well as the bank [is] beleaguered by a weeping, wailing, despairing crowd" (2: 95). Alfred soon learns "that he had seen but a small percentage of the distress his father had caused" in this crowd at the bank; the more pitiful cases are the "ruined homes, and broken hearts, and mixed sorrows so unmerited, so complicated, so piteous, and so cruel, that he was ready to tear his hair" (2: 97). Having lost their money, Barkington's people lose their minds. A "steady footman" about to purchase a public-house loses his savings and kills himself; a locksmith turns professional thief. Several middle-class men – a curate, a linen-draper, a shoemaker, and a greengrocer, among others – take "to the national vice, and [go] to the national dogs," while a Sunday-school teacher turns atheist and becomes "an outcast, shunned by all" (2: 100). The most significant example is Maxley, whose wife discovers that he has been duped by Skinner and dies of a heart-attack. Penniless and bereft, he comes to Hardie and begs to be put in an asylum, for "what with losing my money, and what with losing my missus, I think I bain't quite right in the head" (2: 126). He cannot do his gardening work without seeing "snakes and dragons," a psychosis that has fatal consequences when he later attacks Jane (2: 127). Though Maxley is obviously mad, he is not declared so and confined. Hardie, a magistrate, refuses to sign the paperwork to commit him to an asylum.

Dodd, too, spends most of the novel in states of unconsciousness and amnesia that correspond roughly to the tribulations of his £14,000. He spends several days unconscious after pirates attack the *Agra*, awaking only when Vespasian thwarts Ramgolam's attempt to rob him, and he sinks into "a state bordering on insensibility" after fending off Thibout and Moinard (2: 23). Losing his cash also triggers his apoplectic fit at the bank, when Hardie's refusal to return his deposit causes him to turn "black and convulsed with rage" before he falls "headlong on the floor with a concussion so momentous, that the windows rattled and the room shook violently" (2: 63). Though Dodd's collapse allows Reade to use Sampson to ridicule medical practices such as cupping and bleeding, the novel implies that the trouble in Dodd's brain stems from not only failures of medical practice but also the theft of his money. When he regains consciousness briefly, he bellows, "HARDIE! VILLAIN!" waking his family but conveying only "the sound ... not the sense" (2: 77). The next night, the nurse tells Julia that her father has been speaking "hotch-potch," rambling incoherently about "fights ... and wrecks – and villains – and bankers – and sharks" just before he escapes the house to demand his money from Hardie (2: 80). But Dodd's ramblings are not "hotch-potch" to anyone who knows his story: they are the last gasps of a subjectivity that will vanish along with his money and stay gone until the money returns. In the meantime, he believes that he is William Thompson – formerly "a foretopman on board the Agra" – and his memory is recalled only by his near-drowning and the imminent restoration of his cash (3: 311).

Yet if the examples of Dodd and the ruined citizens of Barkington seem mostly to show that financial loss *causes* psychological collapse, the other major strand of the plot suggests the reverse: that the loss of identity, from a legal standpoint, can be a precondition for financial loss. Hardie's plot to incarcerate his son is from the first an attempt to rob Alfred of his property by making him a lunatic – not literally, but textually and legally – and stripping him formally of the agency to inherit his mother's money and settle it on the Dodds. Lured into the asylum on his wedding day, Alfred tries to bribe his way out, offering an attendant "a hundred pounds ... two hundred; three ... I give you my honor I have ten thousand pounds: it was settled on me by grandfather, and I came of age last week" (2: 233). The guard retorts, "Well, you *are* green. Do you think them as sent you here will let you spend your money? No, your money is theirs now," a response that suggests how, as in the Fletcher case, the legal certification of insanity formalizes a loss of agency with economic implications (2: 233). In fact, as trustee, Hardie has for some time treated Alfred's wealth as his own – though he does not know it, Alfred is wrong when he declares that he has "ten thousand pounds" – and his ability to continue to claim it depends entirely upon his using the textual machinery of Victorian lunacy law to return Alfred to the condition of legal nonexistence that he inhabited before coming of age. Alfred's first days in the asylum mark his education regarding this machinery, which originates in written certificates that testify to his mental impairment. When Alfred proclaims that he is being held "illegally" in a madhouse, Mrs. Archbold corrects him, explaining that the legality of his confinement has nothing to do with his sanity and everything to do with texts. "Mr. Baker could be punished for confining a madman in his house without an order and two certificates," she tells him, "but he couldn't for confining a sane person under an order and two certificates" (2: 239).

Alfred's committal obviously figures as the center of Reade's sensational critique of Victorian lunacy law and the dangers of private asylums. But it gestures, too, at a much broader textual culture that invests texts with a dangerous authority to define identity and formalize its relations to wealth and power. Like the fabricated account-books that permit Hardie to embezzle money from the bank – and like the cash – the certificates that commit Alfred to the asylum are material signifiers of abstract value, hard forms that attempt to stabilize the contingency of his subjectivity.

Indeed, the particular force of the certificates is that they inaugurate Alfred into a world that defines his identity not according to his intelligence, beauty, sensitivity, or virtue but rather in and through texts designed to fix his identity and reinforce his economic position. Once in the asylum, Alfred finds himself textualized on all sides, his conduct and demeanor itemized in the visitors' book, case book, and medical journal that the law requires the asylum to keep. Having nearly convinced a visiting justice that he is sane, Alfred loses a chance at liberty when Dr. Bailey "combin[es] the scanty notices in the several books" and creates an account of Alfred as wild and "much excited," alleging that he has "[r]efused food" and even "[a]ttempted suicide" by throwing himself into the water tank in his desperate bid to escape (2: 259). By the time he proceeds to trial against his uncle, the texts associated with his case are so numerous that the narrator simply summarizes them in a "*précis*" that abstracts each document as in a legal brief (3: 86–8). During the trial Alfred learns the danger of having produced his own legal document: the draft settlement that he asks Sampson and Edward Dodd to sign on the eve of his wedding. For his enemies, Alfred's "extraordinary" intention to settle his money on his wife is another sign of madness (3: 320).

Though Hardie intends principally to strip his son of legal agency and render him ineligible to claim his inheritance, the maneuver has complex implications. Turned into a material object by the texts that define his identity, Alfred becomes a literal commodity in the economy of madness that suffuses the novel. Reade addresses the issue of commodified subjects explicitly, and appropriately, in Vespasian, a former slave whom the American adventurer Fullalove has purchased "for eighteen hundred dollars" with the intention of elevating him "morally and intellectually as high as he would go," then cross-breeding him, like livestock, to raise the African race morally and intellectually (2: 241). The plan is obviously problematic on several fronts. But its interest in commodification, exploitation, and inheritance echoes crucial elements of Alfred's experiences in the asylum. Hardie is not the only one who gains from his son's confinement; rather, the novel's asylums form a micro-economy, with proprietors, warders, keepers, and doctors all profiting from keeping – rather than curing – the insane. The proprietor of Silverton Grove House, Mr. Baker, is a "a full-blown pawnbroker of Silverton town, whom the legislature … permitted, and still permits, to speculate in insanity" by keeping lunatics until their grubbing relations redeem them (2: 242). Describing what he calls "THE SUB-LETTING SWINDLE," the narrator relates how

Alfred's fellow inmate Frank Beverley has been "sub-let" by a series of proprietors, each of whom profits by accepting an annual sum for his care then passing him on to someone who will keep him for half the price (3: 107–8). In fact, Baker dismisses instantly any doctor who "rob[s] his employer ... by curing a patient" (2: 242). As Wycherley admits at Alfred's trial, he "received fifteen per cent from the asylum keepers for every patient he wrote insane ... [and has] an income of eight hundred pounds a year from that source alone" (3: 299).

Reade's portrayal of England's private asylums as an industry for the production of insanity draws primarily from his knowledge of Conolly, who earned much deserved praise during the 1840s and 1850s by preaching a system of nonrestraint for lunatics, which endeared him to Dickens and, Sutherland contends, shapes Betsy Trotwood's treatment of Mr. Dick in *David Copperfield*.[69] But by the late 1850s, Conolly was beset by financial problems and "had descended to the condition of a psychiatric harlot," offering paid opinions on cases about which he knew little, accepting unearned payments for consultancy, and even turning his house into "a private asylum for nerve-wracked women."[70] The consequences of Conolly's ugly profiteering came to a head in 1859 when a former patient sued him for false imprisonment and the ensuing trial revealed that he had been paid for "treating" the man despite never having seen him, and that, like Wycherley, he was "paid regularly for referrals" to the asylum "to the tune of £800 per year ... [and] a quarterly fee of 15% on [the patient's] boarding costs."[71] As Sampson quips when Hardie's attorneys produce a medical certificate to excuse a key witness from testifying, "A medical certificut! ... a medical certificut is just an article o' commerce – like an attorney's conscience" (3: 260). For asylum officials with "strong motives to collude against any sane man or woman where property is at stake," Alfred is just another article of commerce, a property in which many persons have a share. His textualization inscribes him within overlapping financial and legal spheres, which collaborate in the big business of commodifying subjects.

And, here as elsewhere, textualization and commodification short-circuit sexual desire, making Alfred, in Walsh's words, "a casualty of modern commercial life before he has even entered it or fully experienced [its] psychosomatic stresses."[72] On what should be his wedding night, he is manacled at the ankles and strapped to the bed, "more helpless than a swaddled infant" (2: 230). He responds in a suggestive frenzy of sexual energy:

"Julia! Julia!" he cried, with a loud heartbroken cry. The half-hour struck. At that he struggled, he writhed, he bounded: he made the very room shake, and lacerated his flesh, but that was all. No answer. No motion. No help. No hope.

The perspiration rolled down his steaming body. The tears burst from his young eyes and ran down his cheeks. He sobbed, and sobbing almost choked, so tight were his linen bands upon his bursting bosom.

He lay still exhausted. (2: 231–2)

The asylum transforms Alfred from desiring subject into feminized object, pursued by the "muscular young virgin" Nurse Hannah and the sexually aggressive Archbold, who creeps into Alfred's locked room and kisses him while he sleeps (2: 262). She pays for her transgression in balked desire that echoes his, "toss[ing] and turn[ing] the livelong night in a high fever of passion" mingled with fear and shame (2: 272). Just before he escapes, she even begs him to run away and keep her as a mistress, threatening that if he does not, she will use her cunning to drive him mad, and then "you shall be my property, my brain-sick, love-sick slave" – a threat that conflates economic with erotic language (3: 122).

Reade's account of Alfred's time in the asylum traces how his commodification overwrites his sexual desire. It becomes the imaginative site of Reade's attempt to work out the implications of textualizing identity and forcing it into the capitalist sphere. The relation between commodification and disrupted desire appears early in the novel, from the time that Sampson first visits the Dodds and examines the lovesick Julia, who, Mrs. Dodd tells him, has already been evaluated by "the ablest men" of his profession (1: 186). An unapologetic critic of social and medical convention, Sampson responds, "Th' ablest? Oh, you mean the money-makingest," and laments their prescribing and fee-taking, giving instead his own more vivifying prescription: tickets to a ball, and directions (in Latin) for Julia to dance with Alfred "and repeat the folly as occasion serves" (1: 86, 118). As he puts it, "let a nice young fellow engage her apart, and, hey presto! she shall be every inch a woman" (1: 103). However tongue-in-cheek, the prescription removes her from the medical economy and nods at her sexual longing, implying that such desire is antithetical to capitalist exchange. Hardie's schemes against his son may be taken as variations on this theme since he begins by refusing Alfred permission to marry for love, then commits him to an asylum when he will not conspire to steal the cash that Dodd has earned through trade and colonial exploitation. Alfred's principled resistance to his father originates partly in his classical education, his adherence to precapitalist modes of thought. While

Hardie looks upon the misery created by the bank's collapse with an eye to his personal enrichment, Alfred opens his copy of Aristotle's *Ethics* and writes on its fly-leaf "a vow to pay every shilling his father owed these poor people – before he died" (2: 96).

But Alfred's resistance to commodification is not permanent; rather, it is a luxury he indulges before he comes of age and becomes subject to the novel's overlapping textual cultures. Though he never quite gives up on a romantic liaison with Julia, one of his first acts at Silverton Grove is to exploit the power of money by attempting to bribe his jailers. Later, he tries to use his money to escape Hannah, convincing a keeper who wants to marry her that helping him to escape will redirect her affections. Alfred asks, "don't you see your game is to get me out of the place? If you do, in forty-eight hours I shall be married to my Julia, and that dumpling-faced girl will be cured" (2: 274). Nor does his escape or restoration to his proper identity come about through this resistance. Alfred escapes Drayton House in a fire – a symbolic acknowledgement of the thwarted desire it contains – and wins his legal suit not because his intelligence or virtue persuades the jury but because other texts appear that contradict the certificates of insanity: the letter from his sister "deny[ing] ... with [her] dying breath and [her] dying hand" that he was ever mad; and the receipt, which proves once and for all that the hard cash is not "a myth, a pure chimera," but a value recalled to life by its material form (3: 294, 285). Ironically, though the receipt arrives in time to vindicate Alfred, its materiality represents a dubious value. By the time the verdict in Alfred's suit is finally handed down, Hardie has again been ruined by his financial speculations, so that the receipt's reassuring materiality seems destined to be betrayed by the contingencies and abstractions of Victorian finance.

For all of Alfred's initial resistance to the logic of capitalism, he ends up integrated into its forms and institutions, first as the heir to his original trust and then, four years later, as the steward and eventual heir of his father's additional fortune of £60,000. He lives at first on half his income, paying the rest to the creditors his father has ruined. But the inheritance allows him "to carry out a deeply cherished design": he "set[s] up the bank again, with Edward as managing partner ... and soon wipe[s] out the last disgraceful episode" (3: 336). These actions suggest that he has finally adopted a conventional disposition toward the workings of capital, and his decision to make Edward the managing partner shows that he recognizes the significance of a man whose skills lay not in the classics but rather in the production, consumption, and regulation of texts. Throughout the novel, Edward has been obsessed with the *Morning Advertiser*, which he scours, clips, and arranges with a diligence that Reade would have admired. Tom Bragg argues that this "practical knowledge-gathering" allows Edward to mimic Reade by "correct[ing] injustice."[73] But it yields really a knowledge of commodity culture, his work with the newspaper mattering little to the plot – besides helping him spot Alfred's cryptic advertisement, "AILEEN AROON. – DISTRUST APPEARANCES" – but allowing him to manage the family after his father falls ill, urging Julia to paint mediocre landscapes and Mrs. Dodd to work as a seamstress (3: 135). When Julia objects, "Oh, dear, my daubs are not good enough for that," Edward retorts, "Stuff! Nothing is too bad to *sell*" (3: 58–9). Julia may know painting, but "*he knows the markets*" (2: 152). Consequently, he is the perfect man to be the bank's managing partner, gauging the relations between texts and value, identity and exchange.

Hard Cash ends much like *Silas Marner*: by naturalizing rather than rejecting a culture that textualizes and commodifies subjects. But it does so more explicitly than Eliot's novel, for while Eliot at least endorses capitalist relations as paths to sympathy and community, Reade warns of profiteering private asylums while implying that one still must, like Alfred, embrace capitalism or be alienated from legal and economic power. *Hard Cash* concludes with competing images of madness, Hardie and Maxley, each of whom spends his days in a condition of altered disposition to wealth. Four years after his marriage to Julia, Alfred discovers Hardie begging in the street and agrees to take him in, upon which Hardie makes him sign an agreement to board and lodge him "and pay him a guinea every Saturday at noon" (3: 333). As Alfred soon learns, his father is actually fabulously wealthy, a monomaniac whose endless grasping has left him unable to see that he has enough. Maxley, conversely, is Julia's charity case, "a *protégé* with equally false views but more cheerful ones" (3: 334). Living under the alias Matthews, Maxley spends his time stamping "leather into round pieces of silver, in his opinion" and so minting his very own hard cash (3: 334). It is a tacit attempt to establish a parallel economy, an echo of Alfred's stay at Drayton House where, as Grigsby notes, "the 'first class' insane dine in formal evening dress and abide by the etiquette of respectable society."[74] Yet neither Hardie nor Maxley ends up in an asylum. What matters, the novel suggests, is that one approximates the forms of capitalism, that one accepts the economic and discursive logic by which people become texts and cash. For those who do not, the narrator remarks, in a chance echo of *Lady Audley's Secret*, "Alfred's turn to-day, it may be yours tomorrow" (2: 232).

* * *

Silas Marner and *Hard Cash* press beyond *Great Expectations* and *Lady Audley's Secret* by suggesting that the problem of textualized and commodified identities inheres not particularly in autobiography and portraiture but rather in the broader textual practices of a capitalist culture that authorizes and requires material forms to fix the "value" of subjectivity. In Eliot's novel, this materialization of the subject appears as a kind of human imperative, an essential part of the commercial activities that cultivate sympathy, community, and familial relations. Eppie, the living commodity, becomes a nexus of economic and sympathetic transactions, a vehicle for not only Silas's emotional and spiritual regeneration but also transactions between social classes, which no longer depend upon the intermittent Christmas festivities at the Red House but rather unfold in continuous time as Godfrey and Nancy try to form genuine human relationships with Silas and Eppie, the novel's visible representatives of the working class. Eppie is not, then, a ward against or alternative to a life founded upon economic desire; she is an invitation to that life, a symbolic means by which the novel justifies its acquiescence to capitalist modes. *Hard Cash*, conversely, cares less for the forms of sympathy and community than for exposing the ways in which the textualization and commodification of identity constitute basic functions of the financial and legal spheres. Reade's novel grants texts remarkable cultural valence, especially when, as in the cases of money and medical certificates, they serve explicitly to concretize and stabilize abstract and contingent values. In such a culture, the novel implies, the *fact* of textuality is what matters, since it seems to demystify identity and economic value by allowing both to circulate as objects of exchange. Though the novel appears for the most part to end in willing submission to this textual logic, it does offer the specter of the truly mad – Hardie and Maxley – expressing their madness precisely by imitating capitalist culture.

The effect of both novels, then, is to present the commodification of identity as fully naturalized by cultural practice, an essential part of sympathetic human relations and of the economic and social order. *Silas Marner* ends with Eppie and Aaron's wedding, which promises both vegetable and human superabundance. Godfrey pays for alterations to Silas's home, so that "Eppie [has] a larger garden than she had ever expected" and the house can accommodate "Silas's larger family" – a nod

Amnesia, Madness, and Financial Fraud 159

to the time when Eppie will have children of her own (176). *Hard Cash* ends in superabundance, too, despite its erotic deferrals. Julia has a son and Albion Villa "show[s] symptoms of bursting"; indeed, it eventually "overflow[s] into the next villa," leaving room for the Dodds to have an unexpected child of their own (3: 328). But neither book leaves behind entirely the disruption and loss engendered by identity's commodification. Silas still has fits, and Dodd's shocking white hair continues to bespeak the temporal disruption caused by the loss of his hard cash, as does the chronological oddity of "the nephew [being] a month or two older than his uncle, a relationship that was early impressed on their young minds" (3: 328). If Julia and Alfred are endlessly happy, as are the Dodds, the novel hardly mentions Edward, who presumably must learn to bear his grief at Jane's death – a death caused largely by the preference for form over value, for the materiality of magistrates' certificates over Maxley's certainty that he ought to be locked up. As we learn at the end of the novel, Alfred has known all along that Julia's "Matthews" is really Maxley, though Alfred tells her, "I could not speak of him, even to you" (3: 335). The novel's happy endings thus remain conditioned by the sexual deferrals and psychological losses of its commodified subjects.

In the end, *Silas Marner* and *Hard Cash* both appear to center upon the loss of money that must be sought and regained, but both turn out to be about the loss and recovery of subjectivity: fits, amnesia, madness, and the eventual restoration of coherent selves. Shortly after the pirates attack the *Agra*, the narrator says, "a good month elapsed without any incident affecting the Hard Cash whose singular adventures I have to record" (1: 241). Despite the suggestive capitalization, which suggests the "Hard Cash" just might be the novel's hero, Reade's novel is never really about the hard cash. Rather, it works through substitution and symbol toward a conclusion that barely registers the cash's return, since Alfred's recovery of his and his father's fortunes makes the original £14,000 inconsequential. The novel's critical stories are of Alfred's escape from the asylum and Dodd's return to his wife and children – of recovered agency, memory, and erotic possibility. *Hard Cash* amplifies *Silas Marner*, which substitutes Eppie for Silas's missing gold in an overt attempt to make the story about human rather than economic relations. Yet both works imply that the story of identity really is the story of property, that identity and property are characterized under capitalism by their fungibility when both become texts and intermingle in the overlapping textual cultures of Victorian finance and law. During the 1860s this fungibility became a dominant symbolic mode, especially in the sensation novel and the detective novel that developed from it, both of which routinely end their investigations by unmasking the identity of the villain rather than recovering the missing property. The ontologies of loss traced by *Silas Marner* and *Hard Cash* are not similar by chance. They are characteristic, even necessary, expressions of the anxieties provoked by England's rising capitalist culture.

CHAPTER 5

"What Money Can Make of Life": Willing Subjects and Commodity Culture in Our Mutual Friend

In September 1863, as he began work on what would be his last finished novel, Dickens's negotiations with Chapman and Hall for *Our Mutual Friend* hit an unexpected snag. They had agreed quickly on a price, a whopping £6,000 for half copyright, but in writing to accept the terms the publishers made a surprise request: would Dickens be willing to provide contractually for the return of some money if he died before finishing the work?[1] It is hard to know for certain what they saw in Dickens that made them ask. He remained hale and energetic – creased and careworn after his domestic troubles, but crackling with energy, running *All the Year Round* with his usual vigor and basking in the relatively recent success of *Great Expectations.* Another year would pass before he began to suffer from the painful swelling of the left foot that would mark the start of his long decline, and Thackeray had not yet shocked the literary world by dying suddenly (as he would three months later) in the middle of *Denis Duval* (1864). Dickens told his solicitor William Farrer that he "did not know what to do about it" and asked, "Would it be well to refer it to them, and ask them if they have any suggestions to offer on that head?"[2] Farrer did so, but Edward Chapman confessed himself equally at a loss, writing that he could not "hit upon any scheme which answers the purpose."[3] In November all parties finally signed a contract that left Forster to arbitrate if Dickens failed to complete the novel.[4] But in the interim Dickens's mother had died after years of pitiable decline, and he had begun writing the novel's early numbers.[5] One wonders whether, coming when it did, the tussle over the contract seemed to Dickens an omen or intimation: of mortality, perhaps, but also of financial entanglement, the implications of authorship, and the postmortem requirements of property and the law. Even he could not have invented a more fitting backdrop for his new novel.

If *Great Expectations* is the autobiography of a reluctant commodity, *Our Mutual Friend* is the story of all commodities, and of the legal and textual processes by which Victorians came to commodify identity so reflexively that such commodification began to appear a natural thing. Like the Dust mounds at its center, Dickens's novel is comprehensive and acquisitive, taking in all manner of people and "all manner of Dust," then heaving forth a literal and symbolic topography that includes the world and everything in it: waste and wealth, matter and spirit, decay and regeneration, quiet individual lives and the noisy excrescences that swallow them up in the great commercial metropolis.[6] "*Our Mutual Friend*," J. Hillis Miller writes, "presents a fully elaborated definition of what it means to be interlaced with the world," particularly if we take "interlaced" to mean entangled hopelessly with inanimate things, and with techniques of power that collapse subjectivity, apparently "naturally," into the commodities that surround it.[7] No single Pip commands our attention here; no particular Miss Havisham or Compeyson is to blame. Nor does the novel suggest that the commodification of subjectivity is individual or idiosyncratic, delimited by private experience or the textual form of autobiography. Instead, it implies that Pip's pinprick perspective is one tiny vantage on a commodifying culture that is endemic, pervasive, and entire — so vast that it appears organic to the world of the novel. Old Harmon throws up an urban "mountain range . . . and its geological formation [is] Dust"; the Thames participates equally in natural cycles of death and regeneration and economic ones of production and exchange (13). As Anna Gibson puts it, "Dickens's city turns acquisitive habits into naturalized affects" so that material grasping "becomes second nature."[8] The textualization and commodification of subjectivity appear in *Our Mutual Friend* to belong to an ecological economics that reduces all things and subjects to the novel's wealth-giving Dust. Where *Great Expectations* is portrait, *Our Mutual Friend* is panorama.

More, it is panorama that Dickens began to imagine even before he started writing the earlier novel. In April 1860 he wrote "Travelling Abroad" for the first "Uncommercial Traveller" series, recounting a trip to Paris during which he is dogged by a corpse he has seen at the Morgue. Every time he goes to Paris, he confesses, he is "dragged by invisible force into the Morgue. I never want to go there, but am always pulled there."[9] On this occasion he views the body of "a large dark man whose disfigurement . . . was in a frightful manner, comic, and whose expression was that of a prize-fighter who had closed his lids under a heavy blow."[10] After staring at this corpse just briefly, he turns ill and lurches out into the street. But he cannot escape what he has seen. Swimming, he is seized by the "idea that the large dark body [is] floating" at him, and in his panic he swallows some water and is sickened by the thought "that the contamination of the creature [is] in it."[11] Dining, he imagines that "some morsel on [his] plate look[s] like a piece of him" and becomes sick again.[12] At the theater, in his hotel, and along the glowing arcades, Paris resolves insistently into this nauseating presence, which he regards darkly as a "possession" that he cannot get "rid of ... until it was worn out."[13] "Travelling Abroad" depicts what Andrew Miller calls the "nocturnal world of show ... [and] presents the commodity fetish in all its glory."[14] And it depicts more, as Paris's glittering plate-glass yields to a primal nightmare of cannibalism and recurrent trauma – to the horror, not of being commodified and consumed, but of being drawn unwillingly and irresistibly to commodify and consume the other. In a capitalist age this "possession," not the bank note, is what must be spent up.

"Travelling Abroad" thus anticipates both *Great Expectations* and *Our Mutual Friend* in articulating capitalism's implications for the Victorian subject. Like *Great Expectations*, it is a first-person narrative that Dickens designed to boost *All the Year Round*, then filled with images of cannibalism and psychological rupture. It even returns to Dickens's childhood, recounting the now-famous exchange he had with his father about someday owning the house at Gad's Hill. On the road near Rochester, the traveler meets "a very small queer boy" who points to the house and explains, "my father ... has often said to me, 'If you were to be very persevering and were to work hard, you might some day come to live in it'," to which the traveler replies inwardly, "that house happens to be *my* house."[15] The scene offers a striking autobiographical tableau: Dickens the man speaking with Dickens the child, the split subject of autobiography made manifest and made to serve distinctly textual and commercial aims. The essay's Paris interlude anticipates *Our Mutual Friend*, not only by centering symbolically on a corpse dredged from the river and made into an object of exchange but also by treating commodification as a psychological compulsion, a cultural condition, a monstrous impulse that may originate in the logic of autobiography but no longer requires the vehicle of a material text. As Peter Gurney puts it, "reification is built into the fundamental structure of [Dickens's] last novel."[16] If "Travelling Abroad" is any indication, by 1860 Dickens had begun to reimagine the link between the individual and the social, the autobiographical and the broadly textual, the increasingly precarious Victorian subject and the commodifying tendencies of the capitalist age.

Our Mutual Friend offers a vision, to borrow a phrase from Bella Wilfer, of "money, money, money, and what money can make of life!" and what it did make of life as capitalism matured during the middle of the century (460). Much has been written, especially recently, about *Our Mutual Friend*'s debt to Darwin's writing about natural selection, competition, and biological networks in *On the Origin of Species* (1859), a line of inquiry that originated in the groundbreaking work of Gillian Beer and George Levine.[17] But as Sally Ledger observes, the significance of Darwin for this novel has less to do with particular biological mechanisms than with the "seismic ontological shift" by which natural selection supplanted political economy as a primary discourse of social relations.[18] Rooted in the gross realities of the Dust mounds and corpse-laden Thames, *Our Mutual Friend* critiques and tries to undo this shift by illustrating that the apparently "natural" operation of mid-Victorian capitalism – with its propensity for turning the living and the dead into objects of exchange – originates in an unnatural legal and textual culture that constitutes the subject as and through texts that inscribe its relation to property. Old Harmon's will sets all things in motion: it establishes relationships, creates mystery, and helps generally to scatter Dust. But as the novel's textual and economic proliferations suggest, the will underwrites a larger culture that textualizes subjectivity and causes it to circulate in an economy of paper money, paper shares, paper mills, and paper waste before it ends up, inevitably, in the mounds. *Our Mutual Friend* illustrates the widespread collapse of the Victorian subject into the realm of property, and it suggests that this collapse is anything but natural, anything but the organic transformation that "Society" would make it. In Bella, Bradley Headstone, John Harmon, and others, *Our Mutual Friend* shows how commodification ruptures subjectivity, divides and multiplies it, drives it to temporal disjunction, and imposes upon it the erotic bankruptcy of a world in which desire is always already economic. This, the novel suggests, is what money makes of life: a commodity that belongs to no natural order, and that has no chance of release from its textualizing, commodifying age.

* * *

Our Mutual Friend's strange beginning on the Thames immerses us from the first in both natural cycles and unnatural dynamics of exchange. The opening paragraphs show us Gaffer and Lizzie Hexam dredging for corpses in their "dirty and disreputable" boat, a description that implies their class position and also an organicism that ties them to the wind, the tide, the river, and the cycles of regeneration and decay in which they participate (1). Gaffer appears "[h]alf savage ... with no covering on his matted head, with his brown arms bare ... [and] with such dress as he wore seeming to be made out of the mud that begrimed his boat," while the boat seems "[a]llied to the bottom of the river rather than the surface, by reason of the slime and ooze with which it was covered" (1–2). Portrayed as a nearly elemental being, Gaffer embraces what we might call a natural law of property, which he voices angrily when his old "pardner" Rogue Riderhood approaches him on the river and tries to renew their association. Telling Rogue, "I am no pardner of yours," Gaffer initiates a telling exchange about property's relation to the subject:

> "Since when was you no pardner of mine, Gaffer Hexam, Esquire?"
> "Since you was accused of robbing a man. Accused of robbing a live man!" said Gaffer, with great indignation.
> "And what if I had been accused of robbing a dead man, Gaffer?"
> "You COULDN'T do it."
> "Couldn't you, Gaffer?"
> "No. Has a dead man any use for money? Is it possible for a dead man to have money? What world does a dead man belong to? T'other world. What world does money belong to? This world. How can money be a corpse's? Can a corpse own it, want it, spend it, claim it, miss it? Don't try to go confounding the rights and wrongs of things in that way."
>
> (4–5)

In his unsophisticated way, Gaffer thus articulates one possible response to a question that dogs the novel: amid the modernizing commodity culture at mid-century, when does a person cease to be a desiring subject and become instead a commodity – literally, in this case, a floating value governed by economic principles of ownership and exchange?

For Gaffer, the answer is simple enough. Only the dead may become commodities, for the corpse is an object that has yielded up its biological vitality and its place, too, in the network of desiring relationships that constitute "life." Working from an intuitive code, Gaffer arrives at the eminently natural conclusion that a corpse cannot possibly own, want, spend, claim, or miss money, distinguishing neatly between the mere human matter that can only be an *object* of desire and the human *subject* who can desire, and for whom money still plays a role in social relations. This code distinguishes him from Rogue, who is perfectly willing to preempt and subvert the natural order, at first by robbing live men or even helping them into early graves, and later by capitalizing on Gaffer, if he can, by accusing him of the Harmon murder and trying to collect a reward. As Michal Peled Ginsburg puts it, "Gaffer defines the difference between life and death as a different relation to money" by asserting tacitly that "the moment of death is the moment in which money becomes free to circulate."[19] A self-taught genius despite his illiteracy, Gaffer reasons out the problem of commodity culture and reaches a conclusion that sounds like natural law: that the living subject must be held sacrosanct from a Victorian economy all too willing to make it an object of exchange.

But even Gaffer understands that matters are not so simple, away from the river at least, for his reasonable expectations about property are not shared by the greater social order. Though he claims to Rogue that he is justified in rifling the corpses he finds, he is careful in talking to the lawyers Mortimer Lightwood and Eugene Wrayburn to blame the empty, inside-out pockets of the Harmon corpse on "the wash of the tide" and to assert that bodies pulled from the river are often found so (22). Likewise – and unlike his fictional forebear, Jerry Cruncher – Gaffer ensures that he economizes corpses under the aegis of the law, turning them over to the police, collecting rewards, and so bringing his traffic in the dead into what Catherine Gallagher calls "a thoroughly civilized network of economic circulation."[20] The effect, she writes, is to tie capitalism to "bioeconomics," by which she means the natural, cyclical functions of death and renewal that characterize the normal functioning of both the individual and the social body. As he moves from disburdening corpses of their possessions to turning the corpses over to the police, then, Gaffer also moves from the intuitive economic order of the river to another order that he senses but does not articulate – from a natural law to the structures of Victorian capitalism, with its very different implications for property, exchange, and the place of the subject in the market.

As the novel moves from the murky Thames to the sparkling show of the Veneerings' dinner-table, it demonstrates that Gaffer's natural sense of things has no place in the broader economy or the society that sanctions it. Instead, as the story of "the man from Somewhere" shows, English property law – particularly as embodied in Harmon's will – refutes explicitly the natural assumption that a dead man has no use for money. Under the law, property is bound by regulations designed to extend the dead subject's relation to it in unnatural, almost magical ways, a message reinforced by Marcus Stone's design for the monthly wrapper, featuring a skeletal Harmon with bell and shovel perched atop the mounds, an undead warden who owns, wants, spends, claims, and misses property long after he is a corpse (Figure 5.1). In life, Harmon treated his daughter as property, seeking to bestow her in marriage, turning her out of doors, and generally making, Mortimer says, "Dust of her heart and Dust of her life ... set[ting] her up, on a very extensive scale, in her father's business" (14). In death, he torments his son, leaving behind a will that attempts to reconstitute John's

"What Money Can Make of Life" 167

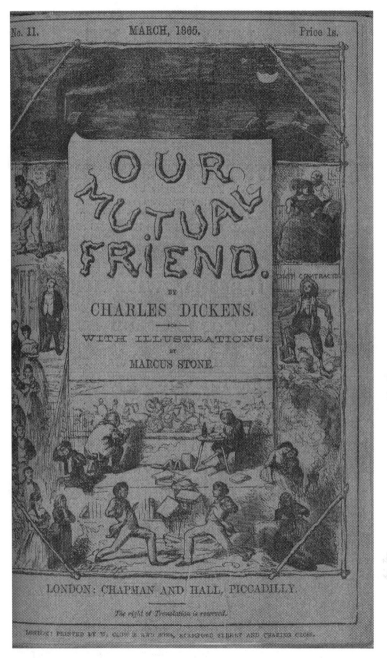

Figure 5.1 Monthly wrapper from *Our Mutual Friend* No. 11, March 1865. Image courtesy of the Henry A. and Albert W. Berg Collection of English and American Literature, the New York Public Library, Astor, Lenox, and Tilden Foundations.

sexual desire as economic desire by making marriage to Bella a condition of his legacy, leaving her to him "like a dozen of spoons" or "a horse, or a dog, or a bird" and robbing the union of erotic potential (37, 377). The will also stipulates that Old Harmon "be buried with certain eccentric ceremonies and precautions against his coming to life" again, a demand that sounds metaphysical but more likely means guarding against being "resurrectioned," Cruncher-style, and inserted into the economy (15). The will inverts Gaffer's natural code by keeping Harmon from becoming a commodity as inanimate matter even as it trades in living subjects and affirms Harmon's continued status – legally and textually – as an owning, desiring subject.

Our Mutual Friend's first two chapters thus position its economic critique between two views of the subject's place within capitalist exchange. One belongs to the marginal community along the squalid banks of the Thames, to Gaffer and his grisly trade, and to something like a natural law or innate ethical code. It situates the human body and its parts within biological and economic cycles of death, decay, reclamation, and production, but it attempts to insulate living subjects against violent or premature transformation into commodities. The other belongs to "Society," the Veneerings and their circle, and the official operation of a commodity culture that stages gaudy dinner parties and traffics in shares, Parliamentary seats, and the tragic story of "the man from Somewhere." It belongs also to the formal workings of a Victorian legal culture that constitutes the subject textually, as an object that embodies in its materiality an attenuated and inevitable entanglement with property of other kinds. While Gaffer's world gives the novel its sinister beginning and persistent Gothic shades, Dickens takes pains to convey that the glittering world of polished mirrors and Podsnappery constitutes the real evil. At the heart of *Our Mutual Friend*'s critique is an emerging finance capitalism premised legally and ideologically on the systematic textualization and commodification of subjectivity, which becomes so automatic and entire that it begins to appear imaginatively and discursively as a natural cultural condition.

For while it is strange that *Our Mutual Friend* begins at twilight on the Thames with a grizzled father and reluctant daughter dredging for corpses, it is stranger still that, having so begun, the novel makes the daughter an incorruptible working-class heroine and rehabilitates the father by showing him to be a hard and skillful worker, a well-intentioned (if misguided) parent, and a relatively honest man. As Deirdre David observes, Gaffer is no "jolly paterfamilias," but he proves to be "very tender with his daughter and content with the meagre comforts afforded by his sinister trade."[21] The novel is not crowded with characters with even this much to recommend them. Rogue, the Veneerings, Silas Wegg, Fascination Fledgeby, Mr. Dolls, the Lammles, the Podsnaps, Bradley Headstone: perhaps no other novel by Dickens features such an unpromising array of greed, envy, indolence, irresponsibility, and violence. Compared with these, and despite his selfishness in trying to deny Charley an education, Gaffer is practically a paragon of industry and virtue. If he is not quite Joe Gargery, he is at least Stephen Blackpool – an example, despite his trade, of Dickens's rough-but-honest poor. And if his trade is distasteful, he at least conducts it according to a less appalling code than that of the Veneering circle, with its sham "work" and idolatrous worship of almighty "Shares" (114). As John Jarndyce says of the "follower" Neckett in *Bleak House*, whose neighbors dislike him for his employment, "He might have done worse . . . He might have undertaken to do it, and not done it."[22]

Despite its somber presentation of Gaffer in the first chapter, in fact, the novel is not much troubled by the pervasive traffic in human matter, allowing Mr. Venus to appear mainly as comic relief, though he owns Wegg's amputated leg and has an unnerving tendency to mix coins with teeth. While Harmon's will blights lives, Venus is Mr. Krook to the Lord High Chancellor, a harmless analog to a gross reality that takes more dangerous forms. His shop might easily be a shop of horrors, but it reads instead as a boisterous menagerie with a semi-articulated Frenchman standing in the corner, playful hands hiding under the counter, frogs dueling in the window, and "a Hindoo baby in a bottle" looking "as though he would instantly throw a summersault if the bottle were large enough" (79). Unlike Cruncher, Venus does not menace. His shop operates within the kinder margins of the law, restoring dead birds to an appearance of animation and supplying skeletons to the medical college. When Wegg challenges Venus over the ownership of his leg – "You can't buy human flesh and blood in this country, sir" – Venus points out that he has bought the leg "in open contract" (297).[23] Besides being darkly funny, the remark shows how Wegg misreads things, as he also does literally when he declines and falls into poetry. As matter severed from its animating force, his leg may circulate freely and comically in the market. Weak-eyed from articulating bones and weak-kneed with desire for Pleasant Riderhood, Venus is no terrifying agent of capitalist reification. He is a late addition to the novel and "a wonderful comi-grotesque satire" on the forms of commodification that trouble it.[24] Venus menaces only insofar as he becomes entangled with Wegg and Harmon's will – only insofar as he tries to speculate in and capitalize on the living rather than the dead.

The novel condemns bitterly this other sort of human traffic: not just in Bella and the miserable children of the niggardly rich but in subjects of all sorts, commodified en masse by the economic structures implied by the Veneering circle. The Veneerings matter thematically partly because their lavish surroundings turn out, in the end, to have been based on nothing at all. But their home is also a kind of alchemical laboratory that puzzles even the narrator in its power to transmute persons into things. It makes Twemlow into "an innocent piece of dinner furniture that went upon easy castors" and the other dinner guests into interchangeable parts, "metonymically reduced from what they subjectively *are* to what they objectively *do*, with the broad implication that they *are* nothing at all."[25] At Georgiana Podsnap's birthday party, too, the narrator identifies the guests as a "Bank Director," a "wealthy Ship-Broker," and "a drifting General Officer," and Podsnap imagines comfortably that his daughter can be "put away like the plate, brought out like the plate, polished like the plate, counted, weighed, and valued like the plate" (134, 143). Alfred Lammle and Fledgeby certainly speculate in her like plate, so much so that Fledgeby finally tells Alfred, "I don't like your coming over me with your Georgianas, as if you was her proprietor and mine too" (271). Likewise, Lady Tippins calls the Veneerings her "exclusive property" and sizes up the finery of the ladies at the Lammles' wedding as if they are "commodities who might just as well have their exchange values tattooed on their foreheads" (250).[26] Even Eugene gets into the act, calling Jenny Wren's father "Mr. Dolls" in reference to her profitable trade (537).

Though the novel salvages Gaffer and Lizzie, it suggests that this impulse to objectify and commodify subjects appears among the lower classes, too. For instance, Jenny "mak[es] a perfect slave of" each wealthy woman who inspires her work, and Rogue complains that he is being "made public property on" when he finds Headstone at Eugene and Mortimer's lodgings after hours (436, 551). Lizzie becomes a working-class version of Georgiana, deployed sexually by her brother "as a commodity to assist his social advancement."[27] Nor is she better off in the hands of Eugene, who invests in her in the hope of leading her into a sexual affair. While Bella chides herself for being "the most mercenary little wretch that ever lived in the world," she also complains of being "degradingly poor, offensively poor, miserably poor, beastly poor" (319, 37). Disappointed in her marriage to the Harmon heir, she tells her father: "I have made up my mind that I must have money, Pa. I feel that I can't beg it, borrow it, or steal it; and so I have resolved that I must marry it" (320). The linguistic displacement that makes money her husband appears metaphorically, and with greater force, when the Boffins try to adopt an orphan only to find that their fortune creates an especially grotesque market:

> it was found impossible to complete the philanthropic transaction without buying the orphan. For the instant it became known that anybody wanted the orphan, up started some affectionate relative of the orphan who put a price upon the orphan's head. The suddenness of an orphan's rise in the market was not to be paralleled by the maddest records of the Stock Exchange. He would be at five thousand per cent. discount out at nurse making a mud pie at nine in the morning, and (being inquired for) would go up to five thousand per cent. premium before noon. The market was "rigged" in various artful ways. Counterfeit stock got into circulation. ... Genuine orphan-stock was surreptitiously withdrawn from the market. ... Likewise, fluctuations of a wild and South-Sea nature were occasioned by orphan-holders keeping back, and then rushing into the market a dozen together. But the uniform principle at the root of all these various operations was bargain and sale. (195–6)

The metaphor of orphans as "Shares" invokes the mystifying emptiness of the stock market, in part by describing "discount" and "premium" while leaving abstract the initial premise of the orphan's financial value, the fetishism that makes it an object of exchange. At the crisis of the novel's marriage plot, Boffin, masquerading as a miser, accuses John of "making Miss Wilfer stand for Pounds, Shillings, and Pence!" as if this transformation of subjectivity into financial value constitutes the grossest of moral and emotional sins (593). As Albert Hutter writes of Wegg's first visit to Venus's shop, "Wegg's question ('Where am I?') has an existential ring to it, until Venus takes him literally" – until, that is, the novel affirms the operation of an economic system that makes living subjects into objects of exchange.[28]

Throughout *Our Mutual Friend*, subjectivity hovers in this contested space between desire and the market, between achieving a meaningful psychological and emotional integrity and needing to collect the material scraps that make one "genteel" (82). The most prominent thematic and symbolic effect is the collapse of the boundary between animacy and inanimacy, life and death. At times, this collapse appears as linguistic confusion, as when the narrator introduces Twemlow as "dinner-furniture" and when John perplexes Boffin by asking to be his "Secretary" (6, 96). Even several chapters later, Boffin remains "puzzled" by the request "because," he tells John, "we have always believed a Secretary to be a piece of furniture, mostly of mahogany, lined with green baize or leather, with a lot of little drawers in it," not unlike the "Secrétaire" that Eugene acquires later, with its "abstruse set of solid mahogany pigeonholes, one for every letter of the alphabet," to help him form the domestic virtues (179, 284). The parallel hints the extent to which the collapse of this boundary has infiltrated cultural values, providing a reflexive basis even for the forms of private morality implied by domesticity. Elsewhere, Jenny uses the term "dolls" equally to describe the children's toys for which she makes clothes and the upper-class women after whom she models them (223–4). As the Inspector notes delicately to Mortimer and Eugene when they inspect Gaffer's corpse, "I still call it *him*, you see," reminding them and the reader that the difference between life and death in *Our Mutual Friend* is more semantic than biological (175).

But semantics mean a great deal in an economy predicated upon the abstract value of the textual sign. At times the collapse becomes violent, even diabolical. The narrator mischievously notes "a number of leathery old registers on shelves, that might be bound in Lady Tippinses," underscoring her likeness to textual commodities and recalling the metaphorical violence done to women life-writers such as Delany, Piozzi, and Morgan when they became distended volumes on Mudie's groaning shelves (119). Tippins, too, is distended, made of enough extraneous matter that, the narrator says, "you might scalp her, and peel her, and scrape her, and make two Lady Tippinses out of her," a violent image that implies the multiplicity of the commodity (119). The novel even suggests that this slippage between categories can genuinely be a matter of life and death. When he falls ill, little Johnny's breathing becomes indistinguishable from the sound of Sloppy's mangle, and several characters suffer literal violence and pass through states of suspended animation. As the narrator points out after Rogue is run down by steamer, "[n]o one has the least regard" for him alive or dead, but he becomes interesting while he is unconscious precisely because he exists in a liminal space, neither a desiring self nor yet a commodity to be articulated and sold in Venus's shop (443). Like Harmon's will, he punctures the distinction between object and subject, the laws of property and laws of nature, the materiality of the commodity and the immaterial promptings of desire.

Petch argues that *Our Mutual Friend*'s simultaneous interest in the law and the dissolution of the Victorian subject originates in the contemporary deterioration of English contract law, which had always been predicated upon people "exchang[ing] 'bits of themselves' with no loss of their individual sovereignty."[29] The novel literalizes this idea, he argues, by showing how "fragmented selves spin out of control and thrash around in the social economy of a post-contractual world . . . in which the contract no longer functions as a principle of social discipline."[30] Petch sheds useful light on the implications of the human matter that circulates through the novel. But the legal text that drives the novel – Harmon's will – transcends this literalization of contract law and the practices of exchange. The will expresses not just property but also familial and domestic relations; as Monika Rydygier Smith writes, it "authorizes: it decides the terms of the social order."[31] It expresses both the law of the Crown and the law of the father, and it does so in the form of the text, the signature, that attempts to codify present and future relations between subjects and property. The will indicates a systematic vastness that hardly appears in *Great Expectations*, but that roots both subjectivity and its representation in the textual practices of England's maturing capitalist sphere. In *Our Mutual Friend* more than any other novel addressed in this study, the commodification of subjectivity is total and crushing, an intrinsic part of a culture that sanctions and seeks to naturalize such commodification and that implicates the subject thoroughly in capitalist exchange.

This sense of commodity culture as a natural formation pervades the novel, appearing as both a discursive pattern and a thematic and symbolic refrain. The Dust mounds – made up of "[c]oal-dust, vegetable-dust, bone-dust, crockery-dust, rough dust, and sifted dust" – aggregate every kind of human, animal, vegetable, and industrial detritus, accumulating into a "geological formation" like the Rocky Mountains that Mortimer recommends to Boffin as an escape from property's obligations (13, 88). The mounds show, Daniel Scoggin argues, "how the demands of mid-Victorian capital have successfully naturalized the most nauseous of economies."[32] The Thames reinforces this sense of a natural economy by carrying corpses to Gaffer, powering the paper mill where Lizzie works, and providing commercial traffic for the Six Jolly Fellowship-Porters, all while flowing, too, with life-giving and life-taking water that brims with biological and sacramental meanings. Like *Bleak House*, *Our Mutual Friend* asks "[w]hat connexion can there be" between divergent people and places.[33] But its mutuality is not forged by illicit sexuality, class intersection, or detective work. It is forged by an economy that is also a Darwinian ecology: competitive and interdependent, made up of Dust mounds that absorb and yield products and raw materials and a river that provides a circulatory connection throughout biological, social, and economic systems. The characters and even the narrator seem to imagine the capitalist economy as thoroughly natural, and thus to naturalize its incessant traffic in the living and the dead.

Yet Harmon's will shows how unnatural this economy is, how thoroughly it depends on the rupture of natural relations and an ideology that binds subjectivity to textual and financial forms. Determined to structure his relations with his children according to his desire for property, the old miser uses his will, and his wealth more generally, to sever those relationships, so that economic matters annihilate natural parental and filial ties. Harmon makes Dust of his daughter's life, driving her and her husband into early graves, and he nearly provokes the unnatural death of his son, who must return to England, where he is attacked almost fatally, to meet the obligations the will imposes on his sexual desire. The will's association with the mounds suggests that these, too, are less natural than they seem, since the will's demands originate in the unnatural activities that Wegg reads about in F. Somner Merryweather's *Lives and Anecdotes of Misers* (1850). The collecting, hoarding, and bequeathing that characterize Harmon's conduct with the Dust mounds impose economic practices on the natural world; they mimic, displace, and disrupt, for economic purposes, ecological cycles of decay, regeneration, and reclamation. The mounds are not heaved up by an "old volcano" as Mortimer would have it (13). They are constructed by an avaricious old man whose ability to raise them depends upon the flotsam of the modern industrial city, the regular paved streets that allow him to collect it, and the contractual right to own the property called Harmony Jail where he can hoard it. The mounds superimpose economic relations on the natural world and even mimic natural effects, but they remain products of mystification and reification, fetishism and commodity culture.

As the legal and textual device that presides over this mystifying property, Harmon's will conjoins what David calls "three important themes of *Our Mutual Friend*: it is written down and is an obvious expression of literacy; it is concerned with the distribution of money and property; and it seeks to determine the social existence of its legatees."[34] Moreover, she argues, since the will lays down "a plot for its beneficiaries," it even "resemble[s] a novel" for it guides and makes necessary all subsequent events.[35] Ordering and authorizing the workings of capital upon which the plot depends, the will becomes a troubling ur-text, its simultaneous power and vulnerability suggested by the anxiety regarding who possesses it and by the several contested forms it takes. Harmon's will also corrupts and truncates the concept of "will" that is central to the very idea of subjectivity, which entails the concept of a free, self-aware, and self-determining agent with the capacity, John Reed writes, "to put himself at one with some transcendent law."[36] "Will" as a basis for human intentionality and subjectivity is one thing, while "the will" as a legal device is something else: a bastardized version of will that reduces intention and desire to the dispensation of the subject in relation to property, thus limiting the fully realized desire of psychology and sexuality to the narrower, grosser, legally constituted desire of capitalist consumption and exchange. More, it does so by rupturing time, "extend[ing] the horizon of death" and "selfishly trying to command the future actions and well-being of the living from beyond the grave" – that is, by projecting into the future an economy of desire that belongs to other subjects, in the very act of affirming the subject's existence in and as a textual form.[37] In a profound corruption, "the will" makes the subject, rather than the reverse. Harmon's will is the vanishing point for the collapse of the boundary between subjectivity and property in *Our Mutual Friend*. That collapse does not, as in *Great Expectations*, require autobiography; it owes instead to the implicit logic of the legal culture that permitted autobiography to rise.

The will thus comprises a legal shorthand for a textual culture that is less literary than economic and that is undergirded and interpenetrated by the law. And, like the Dust mounds, this textual culture is vast and pervasive, seeming to include everything and be everywhere. Early in chapter 12, in which Rogue demands to "take a Alfred David," the narrator remarks:

> That mysterious paper currency which circulates in London when the wind blows, gyrated here and there and everywhere. Whence can it come, whither can it go? It hangs on every bush, flutters in every tree, is caught flying by the electric wires, haunts every enclosure, drinks at every pump, cowers at every grating, shudders upon every plot of grass, seeks rest in vain behind the legions of iron rails. (148, 144)

Drinking, cowering, and shuddering, circulating through both economic and human relations, these "slips of paper," Gregg Hecimovich notes, "begin to take on a special life" characteristic of the subjects they constitute and commodify.[38] The novel's economic totem is not just paper money but "mighty Shares!" which in turn serve as analogs for orphans (114). It teems with wills and letters, account-books and receipts, each one reifying an economic relation as it inscribes subjectivity: Rogue's misnamed and personified "Alfred David"; Betty Higden's letter asserting her financial solvency; Young Blight's Callers' Book filled with invented names, without which "his mind would have been shattered to pieces" (87). For a price, Wegg will even "decline and fall" into poetry and so take us "beyond syntactical declension into misapprehension, loss, the dismemberment of texts and of history."[39] No wonder Wegg infers that Harmon's life, and maybe his own, will conform to the stories he finds in *Lives and Anecdotes of Misers*. In *Our Mutual Friend*'s world, "to be inducted into the written world is to be limited and controlled by it," pressed into a textual form from which there is no escape.[40]

If the novel's texts are often formal records of identity, then, they are also always already financial, always already part of the dynamics of production, ownership, and exchange. Thus Lizzie escapes her sexual commodification in London only to end up working upriver in a paper mill, a "great building, full of lighted windows" and adjoined by a pleasant "plantation of trees" – idyllic, but still part of the system for producing texts, and consequently for producing subjectivity in textual form (511–12). The begging letters that comprise the golden dustman's "Dismal Swamp" may be the best examples of the novel's textual culture, for they epitomize the novel's interest in the intersection of textual self-creation and economic desire. Satires on the requests for aid that Dickens received through most of his life, the letters that John reads for Boffin are of two types: those from "corporate beggars" collecting for causes; and those from "individual beggars" who write autobiographical solicitations, *Great Expectations* peddled to a readership of one (211). As Daniel Hack argues, begging letters parody professional authorship by placing narrative and textual productions on a sliding scale of literary versus nonliterary, scuttling the sharp distinction that Carlyle draws in "Hero as Man of Letters."[41] They economize autobiography by trying explicitly to write the subject into a relationship with capital – with Boffin's capital, in the case of *Our Mutual Friend*, and so with the novel's broader economic and textual concerns.

John begins restoring his real identity in this way when he first begins working for Boffin, auditioning for the job by organizing letters and receipts related to the estate. Asked to "try a letter next" and direct it to himself, John ventriloquizes the golden dustman, essentially hiring himself for the position:

> Mr. Boffin presents his compliments to Mr. John Rokesmith, and begs to say that he has decided on giving Mr. John Rokesmith a trial in the capacity he desires to fill. Mr. Boffin takes Mr. John Rokesmith at his word, in postponing to some indefinite period the consideration of salary. . . . [and] has merely to add, that he relies on Mr. John Rokesmith's assurance that he will be faithful and serviceable. Mr. John Rokesmith will please enter on his duties immediately. (180)

In this letter John initiates his long resurrection, writing himself back into a relationship with the property he ought to have inherited. In a matter of days, he takes full command of the estate, "as zealous as if the affairs had been his own" (193). Though he remains unrecognized by the law – literally, since he "manifestly object[s] to communicate with Mr. Boffin's solicitor" – he embraces the legal logic that treats identity as a thing coincidental with property, confining his writing, as Pip does in his "Memorandum of Debt," to business letters and financial accounts that bind him to economic obligations (194). Such writing is the only autobiography possible in *Our Mutual Friend*, or at least the only one authorized by its legal and textual cultures.

David argues that the novel aligns the "creative power of language and the creative power of money" by showing how these collaborate to subsume "all things . . . under the heading of marketable commodities."[42] But if *Our Mutual Friend*'s legal, educational, and other official textual spheres acknowledge the constitutive power of written language, they usually oppose language's creative potential, attempting anxiously to restrict language to one meaning and make it function as a fixed referent. In Dickens's later novels, especially, this tendency is invariably a problem, emblematic of institutions and ideologies insufficiently flexible to accommodate the complexities of imaginative and subjective experience. It is also, most often, a problem rooted in the law, as with Jaggers's precious use of language in *Great Expectations*. As Patrick O'Donnell writes, the trope of linguistic instability that permeates that novel and *Our Mutual Friend* speaks to Dickens's "sense that identity is a linguistic effect or a figure of speech, a represented form of indeterminacy that reveals its foundations in the 'unrepresentable'."[43] *Our Mutual Friend* lampoons mercilessly the idea that language can be reduced to the single meaning that the law requires, and it celebrates characters who show the greatest creative range. Sloppy "do the Police in different voices," while Lavinia Wilfer demolishes her mother's frosty majesty by continually taking her at her word (198). Dickens also makes comedy generally of the notion that language is material, performing "a kind of verbal amputation on the names of his characters, reducing them to their initials: R.W., MRF, T and P, WMP, and her husband, MP."[44] The problem, the novel suggests, is that language and money each pretend to indicate something definite, but language can no more reduce the subject to a single meaning than money can reduce all things to a common value.

Our Mutual Friend weds this trope directly to economics in its "educational" chapters, which attack the Revised Code and show how literacy "is reduced . . . to a pragmatic, lifeless, money-making activity."[45] This is especially true of Headstone, but even the innocuous Miss Peecher turns linguistic tyrant, badgering her pupil Mary Anne with the niceties of personal pronouns to mask her own balked sexual desire. As Mary Anne explains that Charley and Headstone have gone to visit the boy's sister, Peecher grows increasingly pedantic:

> "They say she's very handsome."
> "Oh, Mary Anne, Mary Anne!" returned Miss Peecher, slightly colouring and shaking her head, a little out of humour; "how often have I told you not to use that vague expression, not to speak in that general way? When you say *they* say, what do you mean? Part of speech They?"
> Mary Anne hooked her right arm behind her in her left hand, as being under examination, and replied:
> "Personal pronoun."
> "Person, They?"
> "Third person."
> "Number, They?"
> "Plural number."
> "Then how many do you mean, Mary Anne? Two? Or more?"
> "I beg your pardon, ma'am," said Mary Anne, disconcerted now she came to think of it; "but I don't know that I mean more than her brother himself." (220)

In this ludicrous attempt to fix the meaning of a "personal pronoun," the personal disappears into a rhetorical exercise that obscures meaning in the very act of trying to inscribe it firmly. As the narrator says, "If Mr. Bradley Headstone had addressed a written proposal of marriage to [Miss Peecher], she would probably have replied in a complete little essay on the theme exactly a slate long, but would certainly have replied yes. For she loved him" (219). There is something awful about compressing love into the fixed boundaries of the schoolhouse slate, where language is made to conform and indicate, not create or express.

In all of Dickens's works, the capacity for linguistic play is a sign of the noneconomic subject who exists outside the stultifying requirements of capitalism and the law. For if textuality attempts to "fix" the subject as a legal and economic entity, then rejecting such fixity constitutes a form of opposition to the textual culture formed by the law and finance capitalism. Though she embodies in several ways the recycling productivity that characterizes the novel's "natural" economics, Jenny thus escapes commodification in part by using language creatively. Like Pip she names herself, preferring "Jenny Wren" to Fanny Cleaver, and she uses "death" to connote retreat from the world and its economic imperatives rather than biological finitude. She also uses language creatively, even subversively, by calling her father her "bad child" and inverting their biological and legal relation, approximating the power of Dickens's narrator who not only metonymizes the guests at the Veneering and Podsnap dinners but also turns the Veneerings' butler into an "Analytical Chemist" with a verbal flourish (240, 10).[46] She is the only character, too, who uses language creatively enough to parry Eugene. Such flights of linguistic fancy are far less insidious than attempts to use language in its formal, legal, objective sense, and this is so precisely because such efforts to fix language rivet the subject to an inevitably insufficient declaration of its meaning while also wedding it seamlessly to property and exchange.

The unnatural consequence of such riveting is Headstone, an appallingly "decent" product of the pedagogical economy that advocated the Revised Code, civil service exams, and other techniques for associating financial and intellectual worth. His brain, the narrator remarks, is a "wholesale warehouse . . . always ready to meet the demands of retail dealers":

> He had acquired mechanically a great store of teacher's knowledge. He could do mental arithmetic mechanically, sing at sight mechanically, blow various wind instruments mechanically, even play the great church organ mechanically. From his early childhood up, his mind had been a place of mechanical stowage. . . . He always seemed to be uneasy lest anything should be missing from his mental warehouse, and taking stock to assure himself. (217)

Were it not so productive of unrestrained violence, Headstone's plight might seem, as Shuman notes, "a comic literalization of the term 'cultural capital'," though "it is quite worthless outside the schoolroom . . . [and] places him, more decisively even than illiteracy would, in a particular, low position in the line of production of labour."[47] Headstone embodies many things: the failures of an increasingly regimented system of education, the resentment of an educated but not truly upwardly mobile pauper class, and the aberrant psychology of the criminal, among them. But most of all he is a subject who thoroughly internalizes his commodification, structuring his economic life, imagination, and desire according to the demands of the market. He is a scarcely less brutish version of Rogue, who responds to his near-death experience with the steamer not with introspection but by declaring that he will "make her pay for it," and who comprehends just enough of his world's economic logic to know that he must be "took down" on paper if he wants to rise up (448).

Subjectivity textualized and structured as property, commodity culture appearing as a natural network of social relations, desire understood not as will but *a* will: the logic of *Our Mutual Friend*'s economy replicates crucial parts of Marx's analysis of mid-century capitalism. And what the novel suggests by mounting this critique of its contemporary legal, economic, and textual cultures is that these ideological formations are not natural, that they mutilate subjectivity and maim desire. Headstone is brutal, rigid, and constrained to the last degree, a would-be killer who "struggles ... towards" his attack on Eugene, "buffet[ing] with opposing waves to gain the bloody shore, not to recede from it" (546). He embodies the monstrous logic that animates Harmon's will and annihilates the distinction between subjectivity and the commodity. Andrew Miller argues that Headstone's attack on Eugene, particularly his neckerchief "saturated with Eugene's blood ... reminds us of the violent, bodily rupture of subject and object, the coloring given by people to things."[48] But it is not only that in the neckerchief, in the Thames, in the Dust, the elements of subject and object mix. It is, the novel suggests, that "subjectivity" no longer exists as a discrete imaginative category or a way of understanding human life and experience, except in its relation to and appearance as property. The Dust mounds thrown up by capitalism masquerade as natural topography, while the Thames – which *is* natural topography – becomes not just gross with the offal of human and industrial waste but thoroughly economized: "meat and drink" to the river rats and an artery for the exchange of commodities from coal to corpses. The river, the mounds, and the schoolmaster are reification writ large, indications of a prevailing social logic that takes its cues from the law, and of a law that constitutes the subject in and through texts as pieces of property.

Despite the discoveries and disclosures that shape its sentimentalized resolution, *Our Mutual Friend*'s most important revelations thus belong to its economic critique, which shows "what money can make of life" by representing subjectivity under capitalism as fragmented, multiplied, and divided, an object of physical and textual violence, a thing vulnerable to the imperatives of ownership, production, and exchange that govern the novel's other commodities. In Bella's case, money has overwritten her sexuality with a rampant economic desire that she must be cured of for the novel to reach a satisfactory erotic conclusion. Singled out by Harmon when she is a little girl with a "little foot ... little voice, and ... little bonnet," Bella's sexual feelings are interrupted and displaced by the will, which forces her to give up her attachment to George Sampson (such as it is) and leave it behind even after John Harmon turns up dead (42). The will makes her, she says, into "a shallow, cold, worldly, Limited little brute," a potential Lady Audley ready to trade on her looks, marry money rather than a man, and help Boffin find books about misers (528). It makes her willing, too, to abjure her biological relations in favor of new ones forged by the will, to become the free-floating value and willing object of exchange the will has made her. So commodified, Bella's subjectivity is distemporal and multiple, divided between economically and erotically desiring selves. At first "a kind of a widow who never was married," she ends up wedding her "dead" husband and dandling a baby that, like Pip, is nominally a posthumous child (45). John Farrell argues that her story ends happily, for she "effects her own release from objectification."[49] But this happy ending reflects still the novel's persistent failure to distinguish between person and property. Even after her rehabilitation, Bella remains, in Mrs. Boffin's words, "the true golden gold," or as John thinks, "a most precious and sweet commodity that was always looking up, and that never was worth less than all the gold in the world" (773, 683). Like paper money, Bella must be valued according to her abstract relation to a precious commodity, her erotic relationship pervaded imaginatively and discursively by the market.

Headstone, too, shows the signs of his commodification, not only because he has made his mind into a "mental warehouse" and eventually turns violent but because, so commodified, he expresses his desire for Lizzie in economic terms. The language of his proposal emphasizes his professional ambition, and he persists in interpreting her rejection in terms of class rivalry with Eugene. Risen from pauperism, Headstone begins at the opposite end of the class spectrum from Eugene; he cannot remain coolly aloof from productive labor and capitalist exchange. As Ginsburg writes, "What maddens Bradley in Eugene is his 'self possession' . . . [for] nothing that [Bradley] owns legitimately belongs to him since, on the one hand, it was acquired . . . and, on the other hand, it has to be given away for him to fulfill the duties of his profession."[50] Indeed, his first disappointment comes from his desire to teach Lizzie, to give her the goods of his mental warehouse. That Eugene foils this plan by purchasing this intellectual work elsewhere figures Headstone as the loser in a capitalist competition. He becomes "murderous not on the grounds of an imprecise emotion," Frances Ferguson writes, but because of the "envy he feels when he and everyone else can instantaneously and accurately assess where he stands in comparison to Eugene Wrayburn."[51] He also becomes fragmented and disembodied, pursuing Eugene through the darkened streets with an expression so "seamed with jealousy and anger" that he goes by "like a haggard head suspended in the air" (544). He sheds figuratively the parts of his body that are not economic, a physical disintegration that the novel reinforces when Rogue appears at his school and offers an impromptu catechism on bodies of water. Recognizing that he is caught in Rogue's trap, Headstone "slowly wipe[s] his name out" from the blackboard and never teaches again (795).[52] Death comes for the schoolmaster shortly thereafter, as if he cannot outlive his existence as a commodity, neither the erasure of his identity as a material text nor the economization of subjectivity implied by his intellectual work.

But the novel's most crucial elaboration of this theme appears in John, who begins, like Bella, as property disposed of by the will, and whose small fortune from selling out his colonial estate makes him such a valuable commodity that he is robbed and nearly killed the moment he reaches England. Thereafter, the novel elaborates the textualization and commodification of his identity, marking his appearance in a wide array of textual forms, from the placard in which he appears as a "BODY FOUND" to the alias he scribbles for Mr. Inspector (22). By the time John finds his way to "his" corpse, Mortimer has already put the story of "the man from Somewhere" into circulation, so that, like the many commodities borne along by the Thames, "the Harmon Murder ... went up and down, and ebbed and flowed, now in the town, now in the country, now among palaces, now among hovels ... until at last, after a long interval of slack water, it got out to sea and drifted away" (31). As Larisa Tokmakoff Castillo observes, too, Mortimer only confers the name "Harmon" on "the man from Somewhere" when he identifies John's "position as inheritor," a reminder of the will's authority to bring identity into existence by tying it to property and exchange.[53] Before John ever appears in the flesh, then, he has already taken on the multiplicity of the commodity, appearing in doubles, aliases, and texts. He has become what Alexandra Neel calls a "corporate identity" – a multiplicity made up, because of his "death," of copies without an original, depthless reflections like those in the Veneering mirror.[54] Though the novel indicates early on that John is really John Harmon, *Our Mutual Friend* remains the story of a copy. It describes life as "John Rokesmith" lives it, as if John and the narrator conspire to undo his commodification by keeping "John Harmon" from appearing either in the novel's texts or in the text of the novel.

The consequences of John's commodification thus appear as a virulent form of self-division that appears in the novel as a problem of narrative representation, as if to acknowledge that textualizing subjectivity – even a fictional one – inevitably requires discursive strategies that affirm its multiplicity and fragmentation, its imaginative collapse into the commodity. This self-division reaches its crescendo in chapter 30, "A Solo and a Duett," which offers John's divided subjectivity as simultaneously a psychological, imaginative, and narrative problem. Wandering by a churchyard and pondering his "death," he considers that he "no more hold[s] a place among the living than these dead do" and thinks, "I lie buried somewhere else, as they lie buried here" (366). He soon dismisses these musings as "the fanciful side of the situation," but his profoundly disjunctive identity is no fancy (366). It is evidence that his attempt to produce memory and narrative coherence from his scattered impressions transforms him into a remarkable instance of capitalist reification. His memories, he considers, "are not pervaded by any idea of time" or any sense of an idiosyncratic self:

> I saw a figure like myself lying dressed in my clothes on a bed. What might have been, for anything I knew, a silence of days, weeks, months, years, was broken by a violent wrestling of men all over the room. The figure like myself was assailed, and my valise was in its hand. I was trodden upon and fallen over. I heard a noise of blows, and thought it was a wood-cutter cutting down a tree. I could not have said that my name was John Harmon – I could not have thought it – I didn't know it – but when I heard the blows, I thought of the wood-cutter and his axe, and had some dead idea that I was lying in a forest.
>
> This is still correct? Still correct, with the exception that I cannot possibly express it to myself without using the word I. But it was not I. There was no such thing as I, within my knowledge. (369)

He is himself, he is Radfoot, he is a figure on the bed. His experience is both immediate and of unfathomable duration. He is finally John Harmon, but he can never be Harmon in the way that Pip is Pip. The impossibility of chronology he describes is the impossibility of his subjectivity as narrative-through-time. That impossibility charts the paradoxical effects of autobiography, which presents subjectivity as temporal order and narrative coherence even as its commodifying effects produce distemporality, psychological rupture, and imaginative collapse.

Though the novel charts these matters most forcefully in Bella, Headstone, and John, they are not its only multiplied, fragmented, and distemporal subjects. Jenny makes "slaves" of upper-class women and uses the death of her "bad child" as a chance to deck out a clergyman for the market. Pleasant "regard[s] seamen, within certain limits, as her prey" (351). Meanwhile, Sloppy disperses himself across many potential subjectivities by "do[ing] the Police in different voices," and the English countryside brims full of little Johnnys in waiting, all available for a price. These matters are ingrained deeply in *Our Mutual Friend*, particularly in Mr. Venus, who may after all be a force for good amid the human matter he commodifies since he probably sells his skeletons to medical colleges. But Venus does not quite "transform death into life," since what he produces are material bodies without real integrity, agglomerations of interchangeable parts – "[o]ne leg Belgian, one leg English, and the pickings of eight other people in it" – that lack the immaterial essence of life and so epitomize the collapse of subjectivity under commodity culture (80).[55] He laments to Wegg that he "can't keep to nature" in assembling such skeletons (79). But he also regards the very quality of Wegg's leg that hints at an individual or idiosyncratic life as evidence of its "Monstrosity" (82). Of all times and places, of no particular integrity, the "warious" pieces from which Venus assembles skeletons mimic the components of the modern commodity, pieces alienated permanently from the agents of their production (81). So natural has the novel's capitalism come to appear to its characters that Wegg's leg, the thing that announces his potential for individuality, is monstrous.

A major consequence of this pervasive commodity culture is temporal disjunction. Simply put, *Our Mutual Friend* cannot tell time. Though it begins with the promising flourish "In these times of ours," the early chapters especially are temporally vague. There is no implacable November weather here, no Gordon Riots, no French Revolution. And this temporal uncertainty afflicts both characters and narrator. When a guest at the Veneering dinner interrupts Mortimer to ask when the "Venerable parent dies," he replies, "The other day. Ten or twelve months ago" (15). For Podsnap, on the other hand, time is meaningless recurrence – "getting up at eight, shaving close at a quarter-past, breakfasting at nine, going to the City at ten, coming home at half-past five, and dining at seven" – a routine that Brian Cheadle describes as "an epitome of the time discipline which increasingly locked the age of industry and capital into the mechanical routines of work" (128).[56] Day and night intermingle when Riah sets out to visit Fledgeby in a fog, leaving the novel temporally muddled while hinting, Gurney suggests, "that the structural immorality of free market capitalism has dissolved both sensory and ethical boundaries."[57] And Riah is himself a temporal riddle, contemporary and ancient, real agent of Pubsey and Co. and timeless Wandering Jew, fairy godmother and big bad wolf. At the plot's center, meanwhile, are the abeyances and regressions demanded by Harmon's will, a carnival of temporal reversions, like Jenny's parenthood over her bad child, and glimpses forward into an imminent future that never quite arrives. "[T]he novel does not close at the Harmon hearth," Scoggin reminds us, "but with next week's 'Books of the Insolvent Fates ... not yet opened'" and the vacuous society "gathered round the still sparkling Veneerings."[58]

As in *Lady Audley's Secret* and *Hard Cash* especially, this absorption of living subjects into commodity culture ends in erotic bankruptcy and sexual depletion – deformations of desire that appear most obviously in the Lammles' empty marriage but also characterize other unions. Fledgeby, whose mother was sold off by the Snigsworths to an unscrupulous moneylender when she could not pay her debts, turns out a moral and physical abortion, vicious in his financial dealings and so stunted sexually that his longed-for whisker never comes.[59] Lizzie's marriage to Eugene, once charged with erotic potential (and little else), ends instead with "Lizzie becom[ing] nurse rather than sexual partner" for him, and the novel closes among the confirmed bachelors Mortimer and Twemlow.[60] Rampant avarice may even figure as the metaphorical cause of the novel's erotic problems since, as Ruth Bernard Yeazell notes, the sexual corollaries to hoarding and selfishness are celibacy, incest, and masturbation.[61] *Our Mutual Friend*'s only overtly sexual image is Wegg's wooden erection as he reads *Lives and Anecdotes of Misers*, which ends with his falling onto Venus in a hilarious "pecuniary swoon" (483). Such reading passes for pornography in a world where the erotic is always already economic, and where love plots become farces like Tippins's "Cupidon" or result in violence, as for Lizzie, who marries Eugene only after he has been shattered and feminized (12). *Our Mutual Friend* may be rife with images of economic productivity, reclamation, and moral and biological renewal, but its end is mostly barren: the Wrayburns have no children, nor do the Lammles, while the Veneerings abscond to the continent with theirs. Only John and Bella's "inexhaustible baby" stands between the novel and total sterility (755). She is the novel's last resource, lone emblem of a natural erotic potential that capitalist ideology seems almost to have spent up.

* * *

Our Mutual Friend does not end happily, then, despite Bella's contrived reclamation from the moral dust-heap, the gradual removal of the mounds, the comeuppances administered to Fledgeby and Wegg, and the birth of the inexhaustible baby. And this is not because John and Bella's love plot is so contrived, because Eugene must be mashed and maimed before he will marry Lizzie, or because Mortimer and Twemlow's quiet alliance seems so unlikely to silence "the Voice of Society." Rather, it is because the novel shows that Victorian commodity culture has collapsed any meaningful distinction between property and the subject. Adrian Poole notes *Our Mutual Friend*'s "urgency for asylum and escape" – an urgency that, Andrew Miller argues, results in the novel "fashion[ing] the home ... and, along with it, the space of writing ... as sanctuaries from the destructive energy of London's social and material environment."[62] But if the novel craves asylum, it does not find it, perhaps because the sheer comprehensiveness of the Dust leaves no escape. Lizzie flees London to find that her sexual commodification follows her upriver, and to find employment at a paper mill replete with economic meanings. Betty's home is a place of business where she keeps "minders" who live in constant danger of having their brains dashed out by a mangle. Even upper-class homes serve as sites of commodification, where living subjects become Boots and Brewer or pieces of furniture, and where snobs perform the vacuous "piece of work" that lands Veneering in Parliament. It is fitting that the novel must be purged of the mounds before it can complete the story of John, Bella, and the baby. Yet even at the end of the novel, John's thoughts of his wife as "golden gold" and a "precious commodity" underscore the imaginative and discursive permeability of the domestic sphere.

Only the determined resistance of individual subjects offers hope: Bella's refusal to be "willed away," and her eventual rehabilitation; Lizzie's flight from her suitors and her selfish brother; Venus's retreat from the friendly move; John's refusal to claim his property even after the Boffins find him out; and the Boffins' equally stubborn determination to give him what he deserves. As Nancy Aycock Metz argues of *Our Mutual Friend*, "no one solution can stand for the reintegration on a larger scale of humanistic values and beliefs. We have instead separate and more or less self-contained victories, significant affirmations though they may be of the power of individuals to come to terms with their pasts, to learn from their errors, to find purpose, and to build lasting relationships."[63] In this sense, even Pleasant offers a model of regeneration, moving from a mercenary proclivity to prey upon seamen to a quieter, less acquisitive life with Venus so long as he confines himself "to the articulation of men, children, and the lower animals" (782). Only on such a condition will the clever Pleasant "give her 'and where she has already given her 'art," a cleverly disambiguating figure of speech to describe matrimony to this articulator of "human warious" (782). She cannot demand that her husband withdraw from the economy, nor can she rewrite the capitalist sphere's appetite for human commodities. What she can do – despite a swivel eye that may keep her from ever becoming an ideal object of erotic desire – is insist at least on *not* becoming an object of economic desire, a commodity, a thing "articulated" within the novel's commodity culture.

It is tempting to read Jenny as a culminating figure in this regard, for Dickens grants her a spiritual potency that few of his characters achieve. She may make a workplace of her home, but she uses it as a space, too, for attempting to undo the temporal perversion of her relation to her "bad child." She also, despite making "slaves" of upper-class women, stops just short of commodifying actual subjects, establishing instead an economy that approximates "Society" but holds in abeyance the world of commodities and thus grants her a peculiar visionary status. She asks Fledgeby and others to "[c]ome up and be dead" – a death, Dominic Rainsford remarks, that "is an ascent into true value and meaning" – and has visions of shining "children" who ease her pain (282, 239).[64] She also penetrates to the mysteries of desire and spirit where Eugene lingers after the attack, and she finds the word that returns him to his redemptive union with Lizzie. Jenny's exhortations to "come up and be dead" reject the world implicitly as too thoroughly corrupted, avoidable but irredeemable. And the novel's ending bears this out, since even the Boffins' remarkable gift of the estate to John comes, tellingly, only after they, John, and Bella have met the requirements of the original will and submitted, however unconsciously, to the forms of commodification it requires. Jean Baudrillard may be right that the lingering obligations of the gift are an antidote to capital's constant reproduction of "surplus domination" against itself.[65] But what are we to make, *Our Mutual Friend* asks, of a gift that seems to require surplus domination as a precondition for giving? Of an act of moral, ethical, and apparently "natural" generosity that is prescribed and foreordered by the legal and textual imperatives of commodity culture?

It is not clear, then, what hope Jenny offers for salvation. As a practical matter, one cannot simply live on a rooftop pretending to be dead to the obligations of the world. Yet there is no real alternative experience available here, no sense that commodification only troubles certain subjects or belongs only to the textual realm of autobiography. Like the narrator of "Travelling Abroad," *Our Mutual Friend*'s characters commodify subjects reflexively, treating capitalism as not just an economic and cultural structure but as an ontology of subjectivity. Unlike the new and improved little Pip at the end of *Great Expectations*, "little Johnny" simply dies. We might read this as reassurance that John Harmon is not infinitely reproducible even in a capitalist age, or more neutrally as an indication that no new John will suffer as the old one has. But we might also remember that, for all we know, little Johnny has died only to wind up in Venus's shop, sealed in a great bottle alongside a Hindu baby. "The novel as a whole speaks," Andrew Sanders writes, "of death neither as a release nor as an escape, but as part of an existence in *this* world."[66] If so, Jenny's injunction to "come and be dead" is not hopeful, for *Our Mutual Friend* teaches us what death means: reentry into a world of circulation and exchange – a dissolution of subjectivity, perhaps, but not a liberation of it from the requirements of the market. As J. Hillis Miller wrote more than half a century ago, "If *Pickwick Papers* was a farewell to the eighteenth century, *Our Mutual Friend* is on the threshold of the twentieth."[67] That threshold bounded a new capitalist age, mature and unapologetic, in which commodity culture would increasingly appear as an inevitability, a necessity, an automatic and "natural" arrangement of people, wealth, resources, and relationships of production, consumption, and exchange. In such an age, the novel suggests, the best that one can hope for is to return to Dust, where one at least becomes insensible to the inexorable operation of the market.

CHAPTER 6

The Moonstone, *Sacred Identity, and the Material Self*

In chapter 6 of Gabriel Betteredge's first narrative in *The Moonstone*, Franklin Blake explains to him the stratagem by which John Herncastle managed for half a century to keep the Moonstone and stay alive despite the persistent menace of the three Indians pledged to recover the stone. Upon returning to England with the diamond, Herncastle left sealed instructions with Franklin's father ordering that, should he die by violence, the Moonstone be sent to Amsterdam and cut into separate stones, which were then to be sold for what they would fetch in the market.

> "Remark," says Mr Franklin, "that the integrity of the Diamond, as a whole stone, is here artfully made dependent on the preservation from violence of the Colonel's life. He is not satisfied with saying to the enemies he dreads, 'Kill me – and you will be no nearer to the Diamond than you are now; it is where you can't get at it – in the guarded strong-room of a bank.' He says instead, 'Kill me – and the Diamond will be the Diamond no longer; its identity will be destroyed.'"[1]

For the Indians, zealous in their Hindu faith, the Moonstone's "identity" depends on its integrity and originates in its fabled connection to Vishnu and the belief that it "feel[s] the influence of the deity whom it adorned . . . growing and lessening in lustre with the waxing and waning of the moon" (1). For Betteredge and Franklin, respectable Englishmen lazing on a beach in Yorkshire, the diamond's identity inheres elsewhere. It is a legal and economic bequest from Herncastle to his niece, a piece of property that they would gladly toss into the Shivering Sand if either of them had "got the value of the stone in [his] pocket" (40). Unlike Betteredge, who surmises that Herncastle's plan means "lowering the value of the stone," Franklin sees that the instructions threaten to transform its imaginative and cultural functions by fragmenting, multiplying, and dispersing it, annihilating its sacred identity in favor of one rooted in economic value and capitalist exchange (38). In the figure of the Moonstone, Collins's novel stages a crucial contest between two ways of imagining identity: as a sacred thing, immaterial and inviolable, bearing a meaning apart from commodity culture; and as a material one, its meaning a function of its physical form, always potentially a commodity for the market.

The Moonstone may well be, as T.S. Eliot proclaimed it a century ago, "the first, the longest, and the best of modern English detective novels."[2] But its study of identity exceeds the detective novel's usual interest in the procedures of investigation, discovery, and disclosure that drive the mystery plot. As Dickens wrote after reading the first three numbers of the manuscript, *The Moonstone* is "wild, and yet domestic," its revelation that Franklin is the thief bound tightly to matters of forensic science and English imperialism, and its central symbol encoding the tropes of psychological fragmentation and integrity that are dramatized by Ezra Jennings's experiment and embodied in the novel's divided narrative structure.[3] The novel is, as Ronald Thomas writes, a forensic reconstruction of crime "performed by a series of individuals who explicitly present their case like witnesses in a trial."[4] But the reconstruction is ambiguous at best, a recovery of Franklin's unconscious that questions the efficacy of forensic techniques and doubles as an act of cultural memory: of the overlapping individual and imperial desires that led to the theft of the Moonstone in the first place, from the treasury of Tippoo Sultan at Seringapatam as well as from the Indian cabinet in Rachel Verinder's boudoir. The recovered story of identity belongs to the longer historical narrative of the East India Company, English complicity in the opium trade, the 1857 Indian Rebellion, and the colonial legacy of *Robinson Crusoe*. As Ian Duncan puts it, the novel "maps the global imperial economy of modernity" by making the diamond into "the vector of a universal history that cuts violently across societies and individuals."[5] The effect, according to Melissa Free, is to transform the valence of the novel's first-person narratives by showing "a private, domestic history as simultaneously imperial, collapsing not only home and away, but also private and public, and family and empire" – and, she might have added, subjectivity and commodity culture.[6]

If scholars have noted often *The Moonstone*'s suggestive entanglement of identity and empire, they have said little about how its first-person form implicates it in Victorian practices of textualization and commodification. For Sutherland as for Thomas, the unusual narrative structure signifies primarily in its mimicry of courtroom testimony, while D.A. Miller has argued famously that, rather than foster uncertainty, *The Moonstone*'s several narrators – who all reach identical conclusions about the crime –

illustrate the social distribution of the policing power reposed nominally in Sergeant Cuff.[7] Yet all of these readings, as Blumberg notes, "tend to look past or 'under' the central material transactions of the novel," though these transactions "indicate truths about enlarged or extrapolated systems of exchange."[8] The novel's unorthodox structure originates partly, to be sure, in Collins's doubts about objectivity, his desire to approximate legal discourse, and his deliberate critique of social power. But it suggests, too, his material interest in self-narration and textual production, reflected obviously in his attempt to recreate the structure and commercial success of *The Woman in White*, and more subtly in *The Moonstone*'s literal and symbolic investments in the conjunction of identity, textuality, and commodity exchange. Like *Our Mutual Friend*, Collins's novel has a questionable will as its first cause, and like *Hard Cash* it worries explicitly over texts and their circulation, within the plot and in the literary market. As Katie Lanning has observed, Betteredge may treat *Robinson Crusoe* with religious veneration, but he also notes its price and page numbers, its illustrations and the color of its cover, reminding us repeatedly that it is a material commodity. "Though he places immense sentimental value on his favorite book," she writes, "he cannot detach that value from the book's value as a physical market object."[9]

Collins began writing *The Moonstone* in May 1867 with matters of value and the market very much in mind, having failed to duplicate *The Woman in White*'s commercial success with *No Name* (1862) or *Armadale*, the latter not even repaying the £5,000 that George Smith had given to lure Collins away from *All the Year Round*.[10] To his mother Collins confessed that Smith had written "lamenting the 'slow sale'" of *Armadale* and declining, albeit gently, to offer for his next novel.[11] "The Smith Elder mess has fired me," he told her, adding, "I have got my name and my brains – and I will make a new start, with a new public!"[12] Really he returned to his old public at *All the Year Round* where he could best capitalize on his name and make himself again "a saleable commodity in the English bookmarket."[13] He acceded quickly to Wills's offer of £300 to write half of the magazine's 1867 Christmas number, but he demurred when pressed to name a price for *The Moonstone*. Formerly, he explained, when he had written novels for the magazine as one of its regular staff, "the literary commodity purchased of [him]" had been his time, whereas now it was "the right of periodically publishing [his] book. . . . I am not quite sure," he continued, "that I can undertake the responsibility of asking terms, because my estimate this time cannot be based on actual facts and figures – and the Virginity of a new book is as difficult a thing to sell – (with or without benefit of Clergy) as the

Virginity of a new girl!"[14] The remark is classic Collins, clever and risqué. But it also reveals the extent to which, by the time he began *The Moonstone*, he regarded professional authorship as a financial and an intimate transaction, textual production as an intensely private form of exchange.

This entanglement of property and identity forms the center of *The Moonstone*, which begins with the theft of the diamond in Seringapatam, sees it stolen again from Rachel's boudoir, and ends with an ambiguous, symbolically overdetermined experiment that fails to recover it but purports to recover Franklin's unconscious actions and motives on the night it disappeared. As in *Silas Marner* and *Hard Cash*, *The Moonstone*'s plot suggests a homology between property and identity, and it reinforces this homology by incorporating a thematic interest in the textual forms that identity takes under commodity culture. The effect is to position Franklin, like the diamond, between the sense of identity as a sacred, immaterial, inviolable thing and the sense of it as a material one, available alike to Cuff's forensic techniques and to discursive practices that reify its relation to property and the law. *The Moonstone* is never really meant, then, as a "private, domestic history," despite its reliance on first-person narrative and the conventions of domestic romance. Rather, it is designed explicitly to serve public and economic functions: literally, to earn money for Collins and make him again "a saleable commodity"; and figuratively, as Franklin says, to save "the characters of innocent people," which can only mean vindicating him, even after he and Rachel marry, against the scandalmongers who have made her "private affairs" the property of the London newspapers (7, 206). Writing of the motifs of gift and theft in *The Moonstone*, Blumberg argues that the novel's interest in material transactions reflects "a historical moment in which writers were professionalizing rather than professionalized," when their works circulated "in a market of prices and bills as well as ideas," and when "the relation between spirit and matter was hardly stable enough merely to be described."[15] By joining first-person form to a thematic and symbolic exploration of forensics, economic value, textuality, and identity, *The Moonstone* points to this instability, and to the uncertain cultural and imaginative status of identity in an autobiographical age.

The Moonstone does not quite deal with the textualization and commodification of identity so explicitly as the other novels included in this study. Though it experiments with and attempts deliberately to capitalize on first-person form, it is not quite, like *Great Expectations*, a fictional autobiography working anxiously through the implications of its form. Though it represents the gender and class tensions provoked by commodity culture, it does not quite, like *Lady Audley's Secret* or *Silas Marner*, sustain its exploration of sexual commodification and male power or posit an alternative to economic life in the salutary effects of sympathetic social relations. Though its plot originates in a ruinous will and complex textual culture, and though it ranges from India to an English country estate and back again, it does not quite provide, like *Hard Cash* or *Our Mutual Friend*, a totalizing vision of Victorian England's textual culture or the individual and social ruptures engendered by capitalism. *The Moonstone* centers symbolically on the diamond and its homolog Franklin, and in this homology it positions identity culturally and imaginatively between the opposing alternatives of sacredness and secularity, the sense of it as an inviolable, immaterial thing and the sense of it as a material object of exchange. The novel ends with an ambiguous "experiment" that leaves Franklin's identity sacrosanct against narration and puts the Moonstone in the Indians' hands, suggesting that preserving subjectivity against the incursions of commodity culture will exorcise both individual and social traumas – will mend Franklin's psychological ruptures, restore the romantic plot, rid the country estate of the police, and banish the imperial menace of the Indians and diamond. Joining the thematic preoccupations of the sensation novel to the ideological and economic valences of first-person form, Collins's novel seems, at least, to undo the anxieties provoked by autobiography by restoring subjectivity to an imaginative position outside of the capitalist market.

* * *

The first, longest, and best of English detective novels ought probably to begin by endorsing a view of identity that coincides closely with policing and the law – for instance, by treating the Moonstone as a valuable commodity rather than a sacred relic, and the investigation as a hermeneutic process involving material evidence and ratiocination. But *The Moonstone* does no such thing. Instead, the "Prologue" foregrounds the competing views of the diamond and undercuts the usefulness of treating Herncastle's identity as material, or at least as knowable principally through its material traces. For centuries, the narrator explains, the Moonstone has been a valuable prize for Muslim conquerors, eventually ending up in the pommel of a dagger that Tippoo Sultan keeps "among the choicest treasures of his armoury" (3). But it never loses its sacred meaning for the Brahmins watching over the stone. This meaning is not lost on Herncastle, who seeks the diamond, the narrator says, not from greed but from his "love of the marvellous," which sounds dubious at first but is supported by the fact that during the next fifty years he never attempts to profit from the stone (3). The other soldiers run riot in the treasury after their victory, but the narrator finds Herncastle across the courtyard with a bloody dagger, two dead Indians nearby, and a third sinking under his wounds. Though he has already described Herncastle as "exasperated to a kind of frenzy" and "very unfit" for his duty, the unnamed narrator stops short of accusing him of murder: "I have no evidence but moral evidence to bring forward. I have not only no proof that he killed the two men at the door; I cannot even declare that he killed the third man inside – for I cannot say that my own eyes saw the deed committed" (4, 6). His disclaimer prioritizes observation over intuition, but his narrative generally suggests the reverse: that Herncastle was maddened enough by the thought of the Moonstone to slaughter its keepers. The "Prologue" undercuts doubly the sense of identity's materiality, first by making the diamond's "marvellous" identity, not its material one, the reason for its theft, and then by hinting that "moral evidence" may be superior to the forensic evidence favored by the law.

This contest over identity pervades the novel and characterizes Herncastle's will, which, like Old Harmon's in *Our Mutual Friend*, embodies the impulse to textualize identity and expose it to relations of ownership and exchange. It asserts his posthumous power over property, in this case by providing for his animals and creating a professorship in experimental chemistry, the latter affirming tacitly the novel's ideological interest in forensic investigation.[16] It also asserts the commodity status of the Moonstone by making it an object of property law rather than letting it revert to its position as a sacred relic in the service of a Hindu god. But if the will reminds us of both the Moonstone's objecthood and the ways that texts materialize identity and bring it under the aegis of the law, it also reinvigorates our sense of the diamond's sacred identity and suggests that motive and desire defeat forensic observation. As Betteredge and Franklin realize, the most urgent question provoked by Herncastle's will is *why* he left the diamond to Rachel – whether as a way of leaving "a legacy of trouble and danger to his sister" or "to prove to his sister that he had died forgiving her . . . by means of a present made to her child" (42).[17] While the latter conjecture reads the diamond as an embodiment of economic value, the former reads it as the mystical talisman that Betteredge fears it to be, "a devilish Indian Diamond – bringing after it a conspiracy of living rogues, set loose on us by the vengeance of a dead man" (33). If Herncastle's will affirms the Moonstone's status as an object of exchange, it also sows anxiety by invoking a sense of the diamond as exotic and mysterious, bearing a meaning that lies beyond conventionally English forms of value and inquiry.

Nearly all of the novel's English characters regard the diamond in this way: they fear it, as Betteredge does, or they revel in its "marvellous" nature. Only the men of business, trusty agents of the rising capitalist class, treat it as a commodity. For the banker Mr. Ablewhite, the Moonstone is an object to be kept in his strong room, while for Septimus Luker it is "a valuable of great price," interchangeable with a receipt, cheque, or bank-notes (199). For Godfrey, "a barrister by profession" and fortune-hunter by inclination, the Moonstone is a lucky windfall, something he can pawn or sell to repay the money he has stolen from his ward (54). Indeed, of all the characters, Godfrey emphasizes most strongly the diamond's materiality, mocking the general admiration of it at the birthday-dinner by ignoring its economic worth while noting its chemical composition: "Carbon, Betteredge! mere carbon, my good friend, after all!" (62). For everyone else, the diamond inspires wonder, its identity cordoned off from commodity exchange. Franklin credits the story of the Indian conspiracy from the first because, he says, he is "an imaginative man; and the butcher, the baker, and the tax-gatherer are not the only credible realities in existence to [*his*] mind" (39). Betteredge remarks, "It seemed unfathomable; this jewel, that you could hold between your finger and thumb, seemed unfathomable as the heavens themselves," and Rachel places it in her Indian cabinet because she fears that it "might take to shining of itself, with its awful moony light in the dark" (61–2, 76). In part, as Jenny Bourne Taylor points out, Rachel's fear owes to the diamond's material properties, as Collins knew from reading about phosphorescence in C.W. King's *The Natural History of Precious Stones* (1865).[18] But Betteredge presents that fear in the language of agency and intentionality, as if the diamond possesses some inscrutable will of its own.

Duncan argues that the Moonstone takes on a new identity as it enters each new culture, passing from being a Hindu fetish to a Mogul trophy to an aristocratic heirloom to a precious commodity.[19] But its sacred identity is never fully expunged, not only because the Brahmins' reappearances constantly reassert the spiritual meaning of the diamond but also because other characters respond to the jewel in ways that suggest that identity's potential to *be* sacred remains embedded in English culture – or at least in the aristocratic families and large country estates that remain mostly segregated from capitalist exchange. This is true even of Bruff, who may be "a barrister by training" like Godfrey but who really bears the character of an old family friend, so much so that he bullies Skipp and Smalley for

Rachel's sake and becomes her guardian for a time after she breaks her engagement. The novel does not overwrite the stone's identity each time it changes hands; rather, it gives the diamond's sacred and material identities an uneasy coexistence, the novel's primary tensions originating in the stone's uncertain position between a material identity that binds it to commodity culture and an immaterial one associated with intangibilities of spirit, motive, and desire. The Moonstone thus epitomizes the novel's deliberate destabilization of the binaries that undergirded Victorian imperialism: the "striking irony" of finding "irrational and 'diabolic' forces" already at work amid the quiet domesticity of upper-class life in Yorkshire, or what Jaya Mehta describes as a mixing of "the rational, the linear, the temporal, the continuous" with "the visionary, the mesmeric, the atemporal, the discontinuous."[20] The Moonstone becomes dangerous and threatening, as Taylor suggests, only because it becomes "a piece of property dislodged from its purely symbolic role" – because its materiality disrupts, but does not erase, its sacred meaning.[21] What is at stake in *The Moonstone* is the erosion of the boundary between materiality and what presumably transcends it, such that once-sacred, inviolable meanings are inaugurated into capitalist exchange.

Initially – and paradoxically – the significance of the Moonstone's sacred identity is heightened by its theft, which at first provokes not a proper police investigation but speculation and innuendo drawn from the diamond's exotic rather than economic meaning. The morning after the theft finds Franklin still "stupefied" by opium, an Eastern influence associated with the Moonstone's mysterious origins. Refreshed by a cup of coffee (another product of empire) he first suggests ensuring that the diamond has not simply "dropped somewhere out of sight – say at the back of the cabinet, or down behind the table on which the cabinet stood" (79). When these searches fail and Lady Verinder recommends the police, he responds immediately, without evidence, "And the first thing for the police to do . . . is to lay hands on the Indian jugglers who performed here last night" (80). His advice reasserts the Moonstone's mysterious identity while expressing also a desire to bring it under the operation of property law, and it does so in the interest of recovering more than the diamond. For the theft has disrupted not only commodity relations but also the course of sexual desire, halting the progress of his burgeoning affair with Rachel and delaying her literal and figurative sexual arrival. As Taylor puts it, the diamond's theft interferes with "social and sexual relationships within the family," so that "[t]he drive of the narrative . . . is to track down the lost object not simply for itself, but to restore what its lack signifies, socially and sexually, within the family."[22] The theft constitutes at once a disruption of property, a psychological crisis, and an erotic deferral, and its story coincides and coterminates with *The Moonstone*'s love story, domestic story, and first-person disclosures. These overlaps suggest the extent of the novel's investment in a symbolic homology between property and identity, and the extent to which Victorian culture imagined the preservation of capitalist order as essential to, or even identical with, the ability to give subjectivity material form.

Cuff's investigation attempts to formalize this homology by constraining the Moonstone to its function as a commodity and attempting also to limit identity generally to a materiality circumscribed by forensics, rational inquiry, and textual practices. For Cuff, discovering the thief depends upon reading material evidence. Deriding Superintendent Seegrave's conclusion that the smudged paint is "a mere trifle," Cuff recounts a case that began with a murder and ended with "a spot of ink on a tablecloth that nobody could account for. In all my experience along the dirtiest ways of this dirty little world," he continues, "I have never met with such a thing as a trifle yet" (99). So he snoops and eavesdrops, sets a watch on Rosanna, and plants a spy in the carriage when Rachel insists on leaving the house to visit Frizinghall. He also praises the excellent forensic properties of sand, calling it "one of the best detective officers I know" because of its power to preserve footprints and so tell the story of Rosanna's suicide (121). Above all, he affirms the sense of identity as observable and traceable, knowable by its material manifestations and effects. His arrival signals a shift in the Verinder household from the anxieties engendered by the diamond's sacred identity to the certainties of a social order safeguarded by the police and predicated upon the values of Enlightenment empiricism and capitalist culture. Betteredge hints at the comfort this shift affords when he describes preparing the pony-chaise that will take Franklin to the train station to summon Cuff, writing, "I saw the pony harnessed myself. In the infernal network of mysteries and uncertainties that now surrounded us, I declare it was a relief to observe how well the buckles and straps understood each other! When you had seen the pony backed into the shafts of the chaise, you had seen something there was no doubt about" (92).

But if Cuff's investigation depends upon the certainties of forensic evidence, his conclusions aim at something more tenuous: a correct reading of motive and desire that will permit him to textualize both, so that identity becomes fully material and fully subject to the operation of the law. From the first, as he declares just hours after he arrives, Cuff believes that "*Nobody has stolen the Diamond*," and his investigation tends more toward reading Rachel's and Rosanna's characters than to recovering the stone (105). As he tells Lady Verinder, his primary role throughout his career has been to muzzle family scandals – to act as "confidential man" in the service of wealthy families, which often means discovering secret debts and heading off clandestine plots and courses of action (163). Putting the case of the Moonstone into this context from the start, Cuff admits that he noted only one thing in Seegrave's initial report: "that Miss Verinder had declined to be questioned by him, and had spoken to him with a perfectly incomprehensible rudeness and contempt" (164). When she treats Cuff the same way, he wants to divine the cause of her "incomprehensible conduct," just as in Rosanna's case he questions Betteredge closely about her motive for lurking in the garden (165). "If there's a sweetheart in the case," Cuff says, "the hiding doesn't much matter. If there isn't . . . the hiding is a highly suspicious circumstance, and it will be my painful duty to act on it accordingly" (112). These speculations bring him no nearer to finding the diamond, which *was* stolen and which he rightly assumes is in London with Luker, but they do annoy the household. More significant, his attempt to decipher Rachel appears finally as a desire to textualize her. As he says in laying his account of the case before Lady Verinder, "If there had been time, my lady . . . I should have preferred writing my report, instead of communicating it by word of mouth" (162).

Critics such as Thomas and Hutter have noted how Cuff's interest in textualizing motive and desire parallels the growing array of contemporary forensic and legal practices that sought to treat criminality, and identity generally, as *embodied*. By the last quarter of the century, these practices included fingerprinting, serology, toxicology, and forensic medicine, all of which sought to locate "the causes and remedies of crime in the biology of the offender rather than in the circumstances of the crime."[23] These measures were meant in part to counteract the growing sense of puzzlement and anonymity engendered by crime as it evolved and organized in response to urbanization and the rise of "the modern corporate state."[24] Charged with protecting the property and person "of the middle-class consumer," Hutter writes, "the police were needed to 'read' a city which had grown far beyond the easy knowledge of its inhabitants."[25] Meanwhile, psychological theory had begun already to define individual character as an "accumulation of sensations and impressions" that were neither reliable nor stable.[26] The collection of material evidence thus became critical in attempts to identify criminals and solve crimes. Detective fingerprinting in England evolved from civil registry in Bengal, where senders had for centuries used fingerprints to seal letters to signal their authenticity; in the aftermath of the 1857 Indian Rebellion, Sir William Herschel coopted the technique into a way of registering and monitoring Indian natives.[27] *The Moonstone*'s Indian content invokes such measures implicitly, associating its investigation with practices that sought to make identity material by treating texts of various kinds as vehicles for reifying and stabilizing motive and desire. In this respect, Thomas writes, "Victorian detective fiction may even be regarded as the principal alternative to the other great novelistic genre of the nineteenth century, the autobiography."[28]

The resistance of *The Moonstone*'s principal characters to Cuff's conclusions about Rachel thus suggests a wider rebellion against a social order that privileges observable evidence and seeks to materialize identity in order to subject it to forensic inquiry. Betteredge hints at this resistance even before Cuff's arrival, when he describes the "awkward rock ahead" in the lives of gentlefolks, who ameliorate their boredom through amateur scientific investigations:

> I have seen them (ladies, I am sorry to say, as well as gentlemen) go out, day after day, for example, with empty pill-boxes, and catch newts, and beetles, and spiders, and frogs, and come home and stick pins through the miserable wretches, or cut them up, without a pang of remorse, into little pieces. You see my young master, or my young mistress, poring over one of their spiders' insides with a magnifying-glass ... and when you wonder what this cruel nastiness means, you are told that it means a taste in my young master or my young mistress for natural history. Sometimes, again, you seem them occupied for hours together in spoiling a pretty flower with pointed instruments, out of a stupid curiosity to know what the flower is made of. Is its colour any prettier, or its scent any sweeter, when you *do* know? (49–50)

The novel thus opposes Betteredge's "knowledge" of the flower's immeasurable qualities – the prettiness of its color, the sweetness of its scent – against the scientific knowledge afforded by dissection and analysis, aesthetic intuition against Herncastle's desire to establish a professorship in experimental chemistry and Godfrey's remark that the diamond is "mere carbon ... after all." As Betteredge suggests, the "cruel nastiness" of scientific inquiry discards both aesthetic and moral values, treating identity as a material thing that may be rendered into a proper object of forensics but that will still resist, in crucial ways, being "known."

Cuff's investigation treats Rachel's identity in this way: as readable through physical traces and available to practices of discovery, narration, and textualization. When he seeks out Lady Verinder to discuss his investigation, she preempts him by declaring, "Now, before you begin, I have to tell you, as Miss Verinder's mother, that she is *absolutely incapable* of doing what you suppose her to have done.... the circumstances have fatally misled you in this case" (163). Betteredge echoes this feeling comically, proclaiming, "I am (thank God!) constitutionally superior to reason," and noting that he retains his faith in Rachel even though "there was no disputing the truth of what [Cuff] said" (166). For mother and servant, D. A. Miller argues, the quarrel with Cuff is "explicitly epistemological," pitting an "'outside' knowledge constituted by an interventionary reconstruction of its object" against an "'inside' knowledge consubstantial with what it comes to know.[29] Moreover, Miller suggests, this disagreement marks a clash of economic ideologies, with Lady Verinder's inside knowledge evoking "the 'old money' her estate represents: so gradually acquired that it becomes a 'natural' possession that never had to be actively possessed," and Cuff's outside knowledge suggesting the acquisitive and constructive forces of capitalism, which not only treat identity as a thing formed by the material traces of the signature, the fingerprint, the "spot of ink," and the smear of paint but even *require* its textual production as part of the financial, legal, and cultural practices inherent to commodity culture.[30] *The Moonstone*'s carefully staged quarrel over epistemology maps, then, a critical contest over the cultural and imaginative status of identity and the implications of its materiality.

The novel invokes these textual practices repeatedly, not only in Herncastle's will and Luker's receipt but also in the debts, shares, checks, and trusts that constitute the broader economy. As Duncan notes, Franklin's romance with Rachel is disrupted even before he gives her the Moonstone when a "strange gentleman, speaking English with a foreign accent," arrives to Yorkshire and charges Franklin with failing to pay his debts abroad, since Franklin has given a restaurateur a "bill" rather than cash and his "name was unfortunately too well known on such documents" for it to be negotiable (56, 334).[31] Cuff suspects Rachel, too, of having debts she cannot acknowledge, and Godfrey racks up secret debts by serving as the "active Trustee" for his ward, using his own signature and forging another to authorize the sale of shares in the Funds (449). Miss Clack also suffers from the textual contingencies of finance capitalism, which drive her to settle in Brittany "from motives of economy" after she suffers losses, presumably in the same Funds that pay for Godfrey's mistress and villa in the suburbs (358). Only those losses, Clack asserts, make her receptive to Franklin's proposal that she "stir up the deplorable scandal of the Moonstone" again by sifting her diary for details about the period after its disappearance (192). His check catalyzes and commodifies her narrative self-production, which she assembles from memory, her diary, and her correspondence with Franklin, compiling her literary remains like one of the religious women writers whom she idolizes and quotes. She declares proudly, "He has purchased my time; but not even *his* wealth can purchase my conscience too," but her narrative embodies the dynamic of textualization and commodification that Collins's novel hoped to exploit and that characterized the Victorian autobiographical trade (192).

So do other parts of *The Moonstone*, from Betteredge's obsessive references to *Robinson Crusoe* to Clack's "precious publications," which themselves parody, as Sue Lonoff notes, the tremendous auto/biographical output of the Religious Tract Society (221).[32] Clack alludes openly to the market for contemporary religious memoirs by remarking that her copy of the *Life, Letters, and Labours of Miss Jane Ann Stamper* is the "forty-fourth edition," and she even attempts to use her pamphlets in lieu of currency in tipping the cabman who drives her to Lady Verinder's door (253).[33] Blumberg argues that texts in *The Moonstone* "always possess two identities: material and symbolic" and that it is "the non-material nature of texts – their identity apart from paper, ink, binding – that bears value."[34] But the novel is acutely aware of the material nature and value of texts, too, and also of their power to materialize the symbolic, making an object of those parts of identity that would otherwise remain unavailable to a modern culture increasingly unable to imagine the immaterial as a locus of value. She may be correct when she argues that Rachel and Rosanna write long letters to Franklin – though Rachel tears up hers when he is "the foremost person in the house in fetching the police" – because they regard letters "as a form that capitalizes upon the difference between a person and her textual self-representation" (348).[35] Yet the novel as a whole rejects this difference by collapsing texts and subjects, or at least suggesting that social institutions do. The financial and social order of *The Moonstone* depend upon the power of texts to drag subjectivity's immaterialities into the world of forensics and commodities. As with the "hocus-pocus" the Indians practice with their English boy, ink becomes the means by which motive and desire are made to signify (19).

The Moonstone embodies this imperative, literally by circulating as a commodity in the book market, and figuratively by treating first-person narration as a device for stabilizing and economizing Franklin's divided identity even as the novel exposes the serious disruptions that commodification engenders. As Franklin implies from the start, he wants to show his innocence by assembling the several narratives of *The Moonstone* into a coherent document that will give "this strange family story" the appearance of "a record of the facts" and so bring the complex, perhaps unanswerable question of his guilt into the realm of material inquiry (7). His true aim is not to account for the loss of the diamond but rather to treat what Duncan calls "a more urgent concern with loss of character," an expression freighted with the useful double meaning of both Franklin's unconsciousness of his "lost" actions on the night of the theft and his potential unsuitability to be Rachel's husband and the new patriarch of the estate.[36] As with Clack, Franklin's editing and writing align the textualization of his identity with economic value and the reification of desire, while the divided narrative materializes his multiplicity and inscribes upon him the disrupted temporality characteristic of both the commodity and the detective plot. As Tzvetan Todorov explains in his famous analysis, the detective story is always "the story of an absence" since it attempts in the present to recover the events of a past crime.[37] Both the investigation and Franklin's editorial and authorial activities retreat chronologically in an effort to produce a sense of completeness that, paradoxically, they achieve only by attesting formally and symbolically to his multiplicity and fragmentation. His multiplicity is at once the cause and result of his textualization, signifies at once the simultaneity and discontinuity of the commodity. As he says of meeting Rachel for the first time after their estrangement, "The past and present rose side by side, at that supreme moment" – a distemporality caused by Rachel's attempt to "read" Franklin as a sum of the evidence that has been afforded by her eyes (338).

The novel thus embodies textually and represents symbolically the way that Franklin's identity may, like the Moonstone's, be fragmented, multiplied, and disseminated as an object of exchange. Though critics have most often associated the diamond with Rachel because of the sexual symbolism of the theft, Franklin may be its more proper analog, hovering as he does between integrity and division, an identity characterized by the immaterialities of unremembered desires and an identity marked by the materiality and multiplicity of the commodity. Betteredge describes Franklin from the first as a divided self, a "universal genius" with English, German, French, and Italian sides formed by his father's resentful determination to give him a foreign education (15). The result, Betteredge suggests, is an "unsettled" character made of parts that tumble out "one on the top of another, like rats out of a bag" after Rachel's sudden departure for Frizinghall (171). Though Franklin says later that Betteredge has taken too seriously Rachel's "many satirical references to [his] foreign education," he does have "sides" to his character (289). When he first arrives to Yorkshire he muses on the "Subjective," "Objective," and "Subjective-Objective" interpretations of Herncastle's will, and on the birthday morning he is in "twenty different minds about the Diamond in as many minutes" (41–2, 59). Most significant in this regard is the "side" of Franklin that stole the diamond under the influence of opium, and that he cannot consciously remember or recreate. Confronted by the plain evidence of the nightgown, Franklin asks Betteredge whether he might have been drunk on the night of the birthday or has ever been known to walk in his sleep. Betteredge dismisses both possibilities, saying, "You're miles away still from getting at the truth" (330). But he is nearer to solving the mystery than he knows. The novel's portrayal of Franklin turns the multiplicity of the narrative structure into a major symbolic trope: he is at once lover and cad, editor and author, detective and thief, inscrutable subject and material object of investigation and narration.

D.A. Miller argues that the novel's seeming polyvocality masks a monologism that "corrects, overrides, subordinates, or sublates all other voices it allows to speak" and forces the several narrators to reach identical conclusions about the crime.[38] But if the narrators agree on the story of the diamond, they do not speak monologically about Franklin, who appears in many guises. To Rosanna he is a cruel romantic ideal, and to Rachel, before he is a lover, he is "the hardest driver of an exhausted little girl in string harness that England could produce" (14). When Betteredge chides Limping Lucy to think of Franklin as "Mr Franklin Blake," she replies, "Murderer Franklin Blake would be a fitter name for him," an opinion that she retains when she last appears in the novel (183). Even Betteredge's congenial testimony makes him out to be "at least a philanderer and a debtor," just as "the unanswerable evidence of the paint-stain" declares him a thief, as does Rachel's shocking revelation that she saw him sneak into her room and make off with the stone (307).[39] Franklin may be the protagonist and romantic hero, but he is morally ambiguous, which may explain why he is so determined to transform the narratives he collects into a full-throated "endorsement of [his] character" despite their disagreements and despite the troubling sexual overtones of the theft.[40] He wants to produce a volume that both explains the crime and brings his identity into the realm of legitimate social and economic relations. Cuff's disappearance from the novel signals that this aim cannot be served by treating the material body as a site of evidence; rather, it requires the reification and textualization of desire. Solving the crime, *The Moonstone* suggests, requires desacralizing the inviolable parts of Franklin's identity so that it may become a proper object of both policing and exchange.

This is the ostensible purpose of Jennings's experiment, which appears symbolically as a manifestation of the East, allied to opium, Jennings's unsettling racial hybridity, and interpretive practices nearer to clairvoyance than to forensics. Franklin is to take laudanum again under conditions that approximate those on the birthday night in hopes that he will repeat his actions, show his innocence, and perhaps even reveal what has become of the diamond. But Jennings's proposed experiment, like his other medical practices, borders on disreputability. As he tells Franklin, the "cloud of a horrible accusation" has pursued him for years, and his unorthodox treatment of Dr. Candy's fever irritates two other medical men into abandoning the case (374). The experiment originates in this treatment and his attempt to vindicate his theory that "the superior faculty of thinking" goes on "more or less connectedly" during delirium, "while the inferior faculty of expression [is] in a state of almost complete incapacity and confusion" (370). Listening at Candy's beside, Jennings treats his disjointed mutterings like a game of Victorian mad-libs, filling in the blanks and arranging punctuation in an effort to textualize his "thinking," and on these flimsy grounds he assures Franklin that Candy gave him laudanum and that he acted under its influence in taking the diamond. As "proof," he recommends passages from Thomas De Quincey's *Confessions of an English Opium-Eater* (1821), John Elliotson's *Human Physiology* (1840), and William Carpenter's *Principles of Human Physiology* (1852), then declares firmly, "Science sanctions my proposal" (385). But only Carpenter's book would have been regarded seriously as "Science"; the others are a drug-addled memoir and the theories of a discredited advocate of mesmerism.[41] As Thomas puts it, "The remarkable achievement of this novel is to convince Blake (and us) to approve of this bold experiment as an acceptable practice and to allow the physician's procedures to declare the protagonist guilty or innocent."[42]

But if Jennings's methods of inquiry are unorthodox or even subversive, his aim is not. He intends to drag identity's immaterialities into the world of forensic observation and textual form – to affirm, like the novel's orthodox structures, identity's status as a material object suited to capitalist exchange. He wants above all to make Franklin's unconscious *visible*, to make his body, as Thomas writes, "into a theatre of scientific observation that tells its own story to the medical expert and to the gathered community."[43] He invites Betteredge, Rachel, and Bruff to watch him prepare the laudanum, and he urges Bruff to return with him to Franklin's room "to see [him] administer the dose" (415). He then asks Bruff to indulge a last request: "One thing more. I must put you to the inconvenience of remaining in Mr Blake's room, and of waiting to see what happens" (415). In the end, all three join Jennings to watch the experiment, tiptoeing after Franklin and waiting breathlessly to see what he will do with the fake diamond. When the action concludes and Franklin settles peacefully on the sofa in Rachel's boudoir, the men gather one last time to ratify what they have seen. Jennings writes, "I put the writing materials before Mr Bruff, and asked him if he had any objection – before we separated for the night – to draw out, and sign, a plain statement of what he had seen. He at once took the pen, and produced the statement with the fluent readiness of a practised hand" (424). The experiment subdues identity to the requirements of materiality twice over: first, as Thomas notes, by reducing Franklin to a body governed by "the biological and chemical conditions of his own physiology"; and second, by affirming that the experiment's cultural function has been to inaugurate subjectivity into the textual forms that uphold the social order.[44]

What the experiment does not do is clear Franklin of the crime. As many critics have pointed out, the effect is rather to "confirm his criminality," to clear him "not of the act of the theft, but of a bad motive for the act."[45] Placed under the influence of opium a second time, Franklin rises and creeps down the hallway, but not before muttering things that – like Candy's delirious ravings – require interpretation, and that might be taken as evidence of a determination to steal rather than save the diamond. When he first throws off the bedclothes, he says, "I wish I had never taken it out of the bank," and, "How do I know? . . . The Indians may be hidden in the house" (420). But other remarks sound more suspicious, as when he observes, "It's not even locked up . . . It's in the drawer of her cabinet. And the drawer doesn't lock. . . . Anybody might take it" (420). Impelled by this ambiguous desire, Franklin wanders to Rachel's rooms, takes the fake diamond out of the cabinet, and slowly loses his senses, letting the crystal drop from his hand before walking to the sofa and falling asleep. Though Jennings hoped that the experiment would shed light on the whereabouts of the diamond, even this purpose fails, an outcome he blames on the impossibility of recreating the original conditions precisely and on the likelihood that he has given Franklin too much laudanum. Franklin neither repeats entirely his actions on the birthday night nor offers an unequivocal view of his motives, yet Bruff and Betteredge affirm "without a moment's hesitation" that the experiment proves his innocence (424). As Taylor puts it, the experiment is "essentially a piece of theatre projected out of a fictional hypothesis which claims the authority of science."[46] Really, it claims the authority of textuality, fitting the story of Franklin's desire to an ideology that requires identity to become a material thing.

Yet the ambiguity of Franklin's exoneration signifies in another way, too, for it suggests that beyond the accumulated texts that account for the crime, some part of his identity ultimately escapes textualization and entanglement in commodity culture. His innocence is foreordained – or at least his guilt is foreclosed – by the several characters who believe in an essential goodness in Franklin that cannot be "proved" by forensic evidence or detected in his actions. He is callous toward Rosanna, dismissive of Lucy, and underhanded in his effort to reconcile with Rachel. Nor is he always kind to Betteredge and Cuff. But no one other than Rachel ever really suspects him of the crime, and she cannot stop loving him though she has seen him take the diamond with her own eyes. Franklin's exoneration is wholly a matter of "faith."[47] It privileges the kind of moral evidence described in the "Prologue" over forensic knowledge, and it does so even as the experiment purports to make desire available to forensic and textual practices. The experiment is an ideologically necessary masquerade, a culturally satisfying means of appearing, at least, to subdue identity's sacredness to the demands of legal and financial culture. That *The Moonstone* as a whole resists these demands is evident in not only the experiment's ambiguity but also Jennings's death, since he insists – verbally, rather than in a written will – that his notes and diary be buried with him. He is the anti-Pip, growing not into self-narration but rather into the recognition that his diary and groundbreaking efforts to textualize the unconscious must be obliterated in his unmarked grave.[48] Mehta calls it "one of the ironies of the novel that it is not the rational but the visionary, not logic and deduction but 'hocus-pocus' that unlocks the mystery."[49] But *The Moonstone* never really gives up its mystery. Like the Shivering Sand, it buries and hides and sucks down, preserving some sacred part of identity against the incursions of forensic work and first-person narration. And "[w]hat the Sand gets, the Sand keeps for ever" (157).

The novel ends happily precisely because of this charade – because it obeys the social imperative to textualize Franklin's identity even as it insists surreptitiously that identity must be preserved against commodification. *The Moonstone* ends with the return of the diamond to India, where it becomes again a Hindu talisman, and the English action of the novel closes amid images of economic plenty, restored domesticity, and fulfilled sexual desire. These results follow not from the solution to the crime in June 1849 but rather from the gradual accumulation of the documents that attest Franklin's innocence and give his identity the textual form that the law and cultural practice require. Cuff submits his report at the end of July, and in late September Candy writes to Franklin of Jennings's death, telling him besides, "The pages of my poor friend's Journal are waiting for you at my house – sealed up, with your name on the wrapper. I was afraid to trust them to the post" (457). Only then does Betteredge's second narrative announce that Rachel and Franklin married on October 9, 1849, more than four months after the experiment but just two weeks after Jennings leaves his papers to Franklin. Franklin's socially necessary textual "completion" is what permits the restoration of domestic and psychological order and the return of erotic possibility, such that the carefully staged transformation of his identity into a material object actually undoes textualization's and commodification's customary imaginative effects. The novel thus ends with the Moonstone restored fully to its sacred identity, and with Franklin's identity bent ostensibly, but not really, into material form. By suggesting in this way that the textualization and commodification of identity always leaves some remainder untouched by commodity culture, *The Moonstone* seems to reassure its readers against the cultural anxieties engendered by its autobiographical age.

* * *

The Moonstone appears then to recuperate the preautobiographical, precapitalist sense of identity, to assert that subjectivity can withstand commodity culture, despite the efforts of copyright laws, bureaucratic expansions, financial and forensic practices, and Victorian literary production to subdue it to the requirements of a social order premised upon textual proliferations. Subjectivity might take textual form and circulate as a commodity – might become entangled with economics and the law, wills and census schedules, and the debts, shares, signatures, and receipts that function so often in Victorian novels to indicate the homology between property and identity upon which capitalism depends. And this commodification might expose subjectivity to the forms of social power epitomized in Cuff's and Robert Audley's investigations, Reade's insane asylums, and Harmon's and Herncastle's wills, and to the powerful psychological disruptions that appear in Pip and Lady Audley, Silas Marner and Richard Hardie, Bradley Headstone and Franklin Blake. But, *The Moonstone* suggests, some essential part of identity cannot be rendered fully material or subsumed fully into the rapacious violence of a capitalist order that produces alienation and colonialism among its primary effects. It cannot be explained fully by scientific inquiry or rendered complete even through the practices of textualization and commodification that entangle identity with the dynamics of production, consumption, and exchange. By suggesting that identity bears within it this fundamental resistance to commodity culture – that it remains immaterial, inviolable, and mysterious – *The Moonstone* appears at least to place identity among those things that defy the social order by demanding a sacred faith in things unseen.

But the diamond's simultaneous associations with Indian mysticism and commodity culture also permit a darker reading, allied to Marx's fundamental analysis of fetishism, which he drew from anthropological theories about the development of savage religions and the primitive willingness to invest nonhuman forms with mystical power. Marx was influenced especially by Charles de Brosses's account in *Du Culte des Dieux fétiches* of the parallels between the fetish religions of the "African Negroes and the ancient Egyptians" and also between these and the religions of "other 'savage' peoples and other ancient peoples."[50] The trick of the fetish, Marx writes, is to cause its worshipper to believe "that an 'inanimate object' will give up its natural character to gratify his desires" – a conceit that causes human agents to invert the proper relation between things and people, between the object of worship and the right functioning of desire.[51] Duncan argues that "the Moonstone signifies the persistence of an archaic ontology despite the displacements of modernity. Where Marx insists on the reality of the commodity, *The Moonstone* insists on that of the fetish."[52] What the novel suggests really is a symbolic parallel between India's fetish worship and an English commodity culture that both materializes identity *and* invests that materialization with mystical meaning, as in Betteredge's fetishistic treatment of *Robinson Crusoe*, and the community's unanimous faith in Franklin on the grounds of an experiment and a text that stabilize identity precisely by treating it as unavailable to discursive representation. India is not "other" to England, nor is its sense of the Moonstone's sacred identity antithetical to a sense of its material value. The novel's ending relocates the Moonstone to India not as a way of cordoning it off from capitalism but as a way of returning it to an earlier phase of capitalism's development, a precapitalist site already swept up in the predations of the East India Company and global capitalist expansion. The very fetishism that sacralizes the diamond marks the continuity of England and the East and foreshadows its inevitable reabsorption into commodity culture.

More so even than *Our Mutual Friend*, then, *The Moonstone* traces the process by which the commodification of identity has become so entire that identity circulates as a material object reinvested with the original mysticism of Marx's commodity. This is evident particularly in the novel's treatment of sexual desire, which ranges from predictable conceits like Godfrey's fortune-hunting and Franklin's dalliances with "unmentionable" women, to Betteredge's cringeworthy decision that it will be "cheaper to marry [Selina Goby] than to keep her" (15, 11). But its real concern is with the emergence of a form of erotic desire that cannot recognize how fully it is conditioned by economics. As Rosanna says in her long confession to Franklin:

> If [Rachel] had been really as pretty as you thought her, I might have borne it better. . . . Suppose you put Miss Rachel into a servant's dress, and took her ornaments off – ? I don't know what is the use of my writing in this way. It can't be denied that she had a bad figure; she was too thin. . . . it does stir one up to hear Miss Rachel called pretty, when one knows all the time that it's her dress does it, and her confidence in herself. (311)

The passage asserts that Rachel's class position, not her appearance, makes her desirable. And Franklin takes no sexual interest in the penniless Rosanna even though, Betteredge says, "there was just a dash of something that wasn't like a house-maid, and that *was* like a lady, about her" (22). Though she puts herself constantly in his way, he takes "about as much notice of her as he took of the cat," and he tosses her letter aside without taking much notice of it, either (57). What divides Rosanna and Franklin, Tamar Heller argues, "is not so much a literal as a metaphorical 'plainness,' her working-class status," just as Rachel and Franklin are divided twice by concerns about property, first when she learns of his debts abroad and again when she thinks he has stolen her diamond.[53] The novel's sexual relationships are, as Betteredge says, matters of "Economy – with a dash of love," and its hero is "a modern consumer who habitually forgets the imperial economic framework that makes his pleasurable acts of consumption possible" (11).[54] *The Moonstone*'s economic critique centers upon this problem of subjectivity forgetting what it once knew: that it once existed apart from the imperatives of commodity culture.

What separates Franklin from Pip is this act of individual and cultural amnesia, this blind faith in the efficacy of commodity culture rather than an urgency to understand its implications. *The Moonstone* naturalizes fully the processes of textualization and commodification in ways that Collins may have recognized but that seem invisible to the novel's characters. Franklin expects to set himself right by making himself into a commodified text – not, that is, by treating autobiography as a form for recording familial, spiritual, or domestic history, but rather by compiling a memoir-prosopography that addresses some vague, broad readership that is neither the Blake-Verinder family nor the spiritual audience imagined by Miss Clack. He writes for those readers who relish the materiality of *Robinson Crusoe*, and who have grown used to seeing personal histories like Rosanna's "told quite often enough in the newspapers" (310). His edited account of the crime, and himself, is designed for mass-circulation. Franklin arrives at sexual, psychological, and economic fulfillment only by transforming himself willingly into a textual commodity – only by imagining his textualization and commodification as unqualified goods and ideological necessities, avenues to shoring up and stabilizing identity, rather than, like Pip, worrying explicitly about the insufficiency of text and language to materialize desire. *The Moonstone* may suggest just how thoroughly Collins perceived the transformation of subjectivity that autobiography had provoked, and that he needed to account for amid the formal innovations and symbolic complexities of his remarkable novel.

CONCLUSION

Money Made of Life: The Tichborne Claimant

In February 1853, the young aristocrat Sir Roger Tichborne left England for South America hoping to soften the disappointment of a failed marriage proposal to his pretty cousin Katherine Doughty. Roger had just turned twenty-four. He was slender, spoiled, and dissolute, prone to heavy drinking and the racy novels of Paul de Kock. His French mother had raised him entirely in her own country over the objections of his English father, so that he "reached the age of sixteen ill-educated, friendless and barely able to speak a word of English."[1] But when his uncle Henry died in 1849, making him third in line to the title, his father acted decisively to send him to England and finish his education so that he would, should occasion arise, make a proper English baronet. He attended Stonyhurst, joined the 6th Dragoon Guards, and fell in love with Kattie, but her parents objected to the match, ostensibly because the two were first cousins but really because they doubted Roger's character. Angry and hurt, Roger sold out and sailed off. By the time he landed at Valparaiso, his uncle Edward had died and his father James had ascended to the title. But Roger pressed on with his travels, to Santiago, Lima, Buenos Aires, and Rio de Janeiro. He shot strange birds and sent their skins home to England, crossed the Andes on horseback, had a daguerreotype taken, and acquired a pet guanaco. By spring 1854 he had exhausted the pleasures of South America and hatched a new plan to visit Jamaica, then Mexico and India, and on April 20 he boarded the *Bella* for Kingston. Neither the ship nor the man was ever seen again.

So began one of the greatest causes célèbres of the nineteenth century and one of the longest, most expensive legal wrangles in English history. Most of Roger's family presumed he was dead since, four days after the *Bella* left Rio, a ship off Brazil's coast discovered wreckage that included one of her overturned longboats. But his mother never lost hope, and when James Tichborne died in 1862, making Roger the baronet if he were alive, the Dowager renewed her efforts to find her son. She had long nursed a belief, gathered from rumor, that Roger had been rescued by an

Australian-bound vessel; now, a clairvoyant in Paris assured her that Roger was safe on an island and that she "would certainly see him within three years."[2] She advertised for him in the *Times* and in other newspapers in English, French, and Spanish, and in June 1865 she applied to Arthur Cubitt of the Missing Friends Agency in Sydney, hinting at a liberal reward.[3] He placed her advertisement in several Australian newspapers and urged her not to lose hope. Six months later, he wrote with incredible news: more than a decade after he vanished, Roger had turned up alive and well, living modestly as a butcher in the remote Australian town of Wagga Wagga. "Your son's circumstances are of such a character," he told her, "that he has not even the means to come to Sydney, much less outfit and passage money for his voyage home."[4] Next came a letter from Roger himself, who asked – quite ungrammatically – for £200 so that he could return to England and claim his estates.[5] Just days earlier, the Dowager's only other child, Roger's younger brother Alfred, had died; in her grief, Roger's miraculous reappearance must have been a divine balm. Cautiously, she sent Roger just £40 rather than £200. But she also enclosed a loving message begging him to come home.[6]

Of course, the man who returned to England on Christmas Day 1866 was not Sir Roger Tichborne. He was Arthur Orton, known in his youth as "The Fat Boy" and in Australia as Tom Castro, the barely educated son of a butcher in Wapping High Street. He had gone off to South America as a captain's apprentice at age fourteen, returned for a time to England, then headed to Australia to try his luck in the gold fields before becoming a drover, butcher, stockkeeper, and minor outlaw. Working as a butcher in Wagga Wagga in 1865, he fell in with an attorney named William Gibbes who had seen the Dowager's advertisement and charged him with being the missing heir – which he did not deny. It had been Gibbes who contacted Cubitt, and who now gave the Claimant preliminary advice about claiming his estates. With Gibbes's help, Castro produced two legal documents before he left Sydney: a statutory declaration describing his life as Roger Tichborne, including events before and after the wreck of the *Bella*, and a will arranging the Tichborne properties in case he met with another accident on the voyage home. But he survived the trip, and backed by his "mother" and dozens of Roger's old friends and military acquaintances, he filed suit against the Doughty-Tichbornes to gain control of the estates. When that suit failed in March 1872, the Crown tried and convicted him for perjury and forgery, sentencing him in February 1874 to fourteen years in prison. Together, the civil and criminal trials featured some 500 witnesses, cost a quarter of a million pounds, and took nearly three years (291 days in the courtroom) to resolve.[7] They preserved what was left of the Tichborne estate, but they also made the Claimant into a popular hero, cheated and shunned, he said, by an aristocratic class that could not abide his unrefined wife and rough colonial manners.

This book concludes with an account of the Tichborne Claimant because the case offers such a stunning parable of modern subjectivity: it shows not just "what money can make of life" but how money had come to be made of life, or at least of identity textualized and commodified by an autobiographical age. The tangled skein of the case is too marvelous to unravel briefly. Whole books have taken up the subject, from Edward Kenealy's *The Trial at Bar of Sir Roger C.D. Tichborne* (1875–1880) to Douglas Woodruff's *The Tichborne Claimant: A Victorian Mystery* (1957) to Rohan McWilliam's recent *The Tichborne Claimant: A Victorian Sensation* (2007). The case provided a moment of powerful cultural inflection, a nexus of class tensions, colonial anxieties, and sensational reportage that unfolded amid the cultural turmoil of the 1867 Reform Act and Matthew Arnold's pronouncements about sweetness and light.[8] The titillating drama of identity and property, McWilliam writes, "mobilised the resources of the media and entertainment industries" to create an unparalleled Victorian spectacle.[9] It inspired extensive newspaper coverage and its own iconography of cartoons, posters, prints, alphabet books, and Staffordshire figurines; it became a touchstone for literary works such as Marcus Clarke's *His Natural Life* (1874) and, possibly, J.R.R. Tolkien's *The Hobbit* (1937).[10] Amid its textual involutions and mass-cultural reifications, it also showed how identity had become a seminal form of value within England's capitalist sphere, in many ways culminating the period's intense anxieties over identity, textuality, and commodity. The Tichborne case was a sensation novel come to life, producing in the real world of Victorian people and things the very ideological and imaginative problem that had provoked the genre.

The Claimant's daring imposture originated in the textual conjunction of identity and property – not just because identity and property were necessarily intertwined in the case of an aristocratic estate, but because he had claimed the identity "Sir Roger Tichborne" from the first by exploiting its textual scraps. Later, after he reached England, the Claimant's "memories" of Roger's early life were probably aided by his conversations with the Dowager and others who believed him. But early on he almost certainly relied on details he had sifted from Australian newspapers, which related more than enough to allow a clever man to find more. The Dowager's advertisement alone explained that Roger had sailed from "Rio Janeiro [sic] on the 20th of April, 1854, in the ship *La Bella,*" was thirty-two, and was "of a delicate constitution, rather tall, with very light brown hair and blue eyes."[11] It also explained that Roger was heir to the Tichborne estates and suggested that readers investigate shipping reports regarding the *Bella* since its survivors had reportedly been carried to Australia.[12] Richard Slate had shown Tom Castro this advertisement in the *Melbourne Argus* or the *Australasian* in 1865, and shopkeeper William Love testified that "Castro had come begging a loan of *The Times* or the *Illustrated London News*" each time the English mail arrived.[13] As Lord Chief Justice Sir Alexander Cockburn noted in his summing up at the criminal trial, the Claimant had never been beyond the reach of the London papers and could have found obituaries for both Edward and James Tichborne in issues of the *Illustrated London News* held by the Wagga Wagga Mechanics' Institute.[14] A pocket-book retrieved from Castro's things in Australia bore out the surmise that the Claimant had cribbed from these sources. His notation "La Bella, R.C.T. arrived Hobart Town July 4, 1854" misnamed Roger's ship (as *La Bella,* not *Bella*) just as the Dowager's advertisement had; another read "Sir James Tichborne, R.C. Tichborne, Bart., Some day I hope."[15]

The civil and criminal trials both made much of such evidence, working principally in and through texts to determine whether the Claimant was Roger, and whether he was – legally speaking – identical with the Tichborne estate. As lawyers for the Doughty-Tichbornes pointed out during the civil trial, the Claimant's Australian statutory declaration was riddled with errors, and he had made strange mistakes, too, in the will he drafted with Gibbes, identifying his mother as "Hannah Frances" when her name was Henriette Felicité (she had signed her early letters to him only "H.F. Tichborne") and bequeathing fictitious Tichborne property in the Isle of Wight.[16] Just before embarking for England, the Claimant had tried impulsively to buy the Metropolitan Hotel, writing a check for £10,000 drawn on a London house where no Tichborne had ever banked.[17] Witnesses for the Claimant insisted that they recognized Roger or were persuaded by his recollections of the past. But the defense counsel seized upon his textual errors to disrupt the supposed correspondence between the Claimant and the property he claimed to own. Experts studied the handwriting in texts known to have been written by Roger and the Claimant, and also in Tom Castro's pocket-book, and the lawyers compared the young Roger's fluent letters to his mother with the lexical monstrosities she had received from the Claimant. During twenty-nine grueling days of cross-examination, the lawyers questioned the Claimant about other textual and linguistic matters, too: his alarming inability to read, write, or speak French; his failure to tell Latin from Greek by sight; a marriage register from Wagga Wagga in which he had given his age as Arthur Orton's, four years younger than Roger's.[18] Both sides sent investigators to Australia, South America, and New York. They returned bearing sheaves of affidavits sworn by people who had known Roger, Orton, or Castro and also copies of shipping registers, passenger manifests, court dockets, and station books that shed light on the movements of all three men. These tended generally to suggest that Roger had vanished utterly in 1854, and that Orton, Castro, and the Claimant were the same man.

The Claimant's body also became an evidentiary text, its material character read by witnesses, jurors, and judges for signs of its identity with Roger's. The young man who had left England in 1854 had been fair, blue-eyed, and slender – so slender that a military tailor had considered sewing belt hooks inside his coat since the weight of his sword invariably pulled his belt to the ground.[19] But the man who arrived to England in 1866 weighed a sturdy 250 pounds, and by the time he appeared at the civil trial in 1871 he had become, Geddes MacGregor writes, "a human hippopotamus," tipping the scale at nearly 400.[20] Jurors were asked to compare the Chilean daguerreotype of Roger to the behemoth seated before them in court and heard extensive testimony regarding scars, birthmarks, the twitch of St. Vitus's dance, and even Roger's alleged genital malformation, of which there was no reliable record. The judges cleared the courtroom so that they and the jurors could examine the Claimant's very real malformation, a buried penis. McWilliam writes that the Claimant "inhabited perhaps the most heavily discussed body of the Victorian age, eclipsing Tom Thumb, the Elephant Man, and other so-called 'freaks'," and Rebecca Stern notes that the trial made his ungentlemanly body "an occasion for popular discourse."[21] Key among this evidence was the testimony of Lord Bellew, who had attended school with Roger and claimed that he had a tattoo – a text inscribed on his body – that he had allowed Bellew to embellish with the initials "R.C.T." to teach him the art. The Claimant had no such mark, a textual absence that sealed his fate.

Inside the courtroom, the agents of the aristocracy and the Crown thus attacked the Claimant in predictable ways. Like Robert Audley and Sergeant Cuff, they treated his identity as a materiality – as a function of his physical body, and as physically embodied in the textual sphere. They invoked explicitly the cultural authority of texts to inscribe identity and its relation to property, and to locate it in material forms rather than nebulous claims about memory or a mother's dubious recognition of her son. Outside the courtroom, the Claimant exploited the textual convergence of identity and property in a remarkable and unprecedented way. In March 1868, well before the civil trial, the Dowager died, costing the Claimant not only his strongest witness but also her £1,000 jointure just as the civil suit began to take shape. His sympathetic Hampshire neighbors collaborated to give him an income of £1,400, but by the end of 1869 he had nevertheless been adjudicated bankrupt, and his legal expenses were mounting.[22] He responded to this financial crisis by printing 1,500 copies of a document he titled "*Tichborne Estate Mortgage Debenture*" – what became known as a "Tichborne Bond" – which promised to pay its holder £100 when he took possession of his estates.[23] Then he sold these to the public for whatever they would fetch. He made himself literally into portable property, an identity and a value, paper currency multiplied and dispersed to the tune of some £40,000.[24] When the failure of his civil suit foreclosed his claim and left him to defend himself against a criminal action, he doubled down, turning showman and touring the nation, charging anything from sixpence to a guinea to hear him speak of his misfortunes. He appeared in Leeds, Birmingham, Bradford, and Bishopsgate, among other places; at Manchester, he performed to a crowd of 20,000.[25] He was *Our Mutual Friend*'s orphans and Dickens the public reader all at once, selling himself as shares and embodying before the public a character whom he had narrated into existence. He was not Roger Tichborne, Arthur Orton, or Tom Castro at such times. He was "Sir Roger Tichborne," a free-floating identity made into a commodity by the overlapping imperatives of the courts, the press, and the Victorian market.

And "Sir Roger Tichborne" stood at the center of a thriving economy, most of it textual, and some of it designed like the Tichborne Bonds and public performances to turn pennies for his legal defense. From the time of his return, he had been constantly in the press, particularly during the many months of his civil and criminal trials. When Cockburn effectively ended the Claimant's profitable speaking tour by ruling that, until the criminal trial ended, inflammatory public comments about the case would constitute contempt of court, the Claimant's allies capitalized on the public appetite for Tichborniana by founding their own penny papers, the *Tichborne Gazette* and the *Tichborne News and Anti-Oppression Journal*, the former of which used its front page to build a subscription list for the Claimant's defense. And these were but a portion of the vast material culture – the "tide of ephemera," McWilliam calls it – that sprung up around the case, some of it sympathetic to the Claimant, but much of it deriding his obesity, Cockney accent, and outrageous claims to gentility.[26] The satirical press especially treated the whole mélange as a preposterous joke. Just days after the civil trial ended, and only months after Lewis Carroll published *Through the Looking Glass* (1872), *Punch* ran a cartoon of a wigged justice slaying the "Waggawock," and soon after *Fun* depicted the Claimant as a mammoth jack-in-the-box.[27] The Tichborne papers were lampooned by a *Tichborne Times* with a "Waggawock Subscription List," and a series of cartoons called "Tichborne Comicalities" began to appear, each one captioned with news of the trial written in the style of a comic alphabet.[28] A poster even announced a facetious "sale of Tichborne relics," including "an 'Egyptian mummy, which it is supposed Lady Tichborne would have recognized as her lost son'."[29] The pressures of mass readership, celebrity culture, the law, and the literary market had given "Sir Roger Tichborne" a bizarre life of his own, rooted in textual production and commodity exchange.

Not long after Lord Bellew testified, the jury preempted the parade of witnesses at the civil trial by hinting that they had heard enough to render a verdict. Anticipating an unfavorable result, the Claimant's lawyers asked that their client be nonsuited, effectively abandoning the case, upon which Chief Justice William Bovill ordered his arrest.[30] The criminal trial unfolded much as the civil one had and ended in a conviction and fourteen-year sentence – though the Claimant served just ten, mostly at Portsea prison. He never stopped insisting that he was "Sir Roger Tichborne," but the machinery of the market he had spawned ceased gradually to whirl. Kenealy, who had represented him at the criminal trial, founded the *Englishman* newspaper, making it an official voice of Tichborne radicalism and publishing in it the serial installments of his account of the trial. Though the Lord Chamberlain excised references to the Claimant from fifteen plays between 1871 and 1876, he also remained for a time a popular subject of ballads and music-hall routines.[31] But by the time the Claimant left prison in October 1884, Kenealy was dead, as was the *Englishman*, and few Tichbornites remained to embrace the cause. He tried unsuccessfully to mount a new speaking tour in England. When he tried in the United States instead, another man came forward also claiming to be Sir Roger Tichborne, upon which the two "confronted each other in an office in Brooklyn and denounced each other as impostors."[32] In 1895, destitute and infirm, the Claimant tried one last time to cash in on his manufactured identity, accepting an offer from the *People* to confess his imposture in a series of articles, then recanting after they appeared.[33] When he died, appropriately enough, on April Fool's Day 1898, his plain casket bore a brass plate inscribed "Sir Roger Charles Doughty Tichborne" and showing Roger's birthdate rather than his own – a textual ambiguity not unlike the one that Pip puzzles over at the start of *Great Expectations*, nor unsuited to a commodified subject of the capitalist age.

Stern reads the outcome of the Tichborne case as an ideological victory for agents of the aristocracy and the Crown against the market's incursions into the domestic sphere. She argues that those agents sentenced him not just to prison but "to the category of popular entertainment," cordoning him off from "actual property, exchange, and relationships" and thus "protect[ing] the family from becoming a site for market-based investment that would potentially allow strangers access to household property."[34] But if the law managed to protect the Tichborne estate, it did so while leaving identity free to circulate as a commodity, sanctioning and codifying a relation between identity and property that held neither identity nor domesticity sacrosanct against the perils of the market. While the Dowager was alive to share her jointure, the identity "Sir Roger Tichborne" was worth £1,000 per year. After she died, "Sir Roger Tichborne" came financially unhinged, rising first to an annual value of £1,400, then really taking off in the form of the Tichborne Bonds. Freed from the yoke of aristocratic roots and precapitalist economics, "Sir Roger Tichborne" entered the market and accumulated value at compound interest before crashing like bubble-era railway shares, all as if it obeyed economic laws of its own. The courts may have foreclosed the possibility that this textualized, commodified identity could be restored to an easy correspondence with either the Tichborne name or the estate it signified. But people of all classes lost by investing in the Claimant. The law did not protect "actual property" unless we construe those words as meaning the property of just one wealthy family and ignore the court's decisive failure to partition the old economy from the new. Of course, by the time of the Tichborne case it was anyway impossible to distinguish cleanly between "actual property" and the phantasmagoria of the Victorian market, with its paper money, commodified texts, and the other fetishized unrealities that Marx had anatomized as the tokens of the capitalist sphere.

The Tichborne case reveals above all how content the law was to treat identity as a textual commodity, and how content it was, too, to allow the Claimant his commodified existence – not cordoned off from the domestic but permeating it thoroughly, disseminated across thousands of textual and material reifications in public thoroughfares, drawing rooms, bookshelves, and curio cabinets all over England. "Sir Roger Tichborne" became a thoroughly modern identity, the kind that can only exist in the presence of both pervasive print culture and capitalist exchange – and, I would argue, the only kind of identity that *can* exist in the presence of both. The story of the Tichborne Claimant reads like a sensation novel because it centers upon the new discursive, imaginative, and ideological form that identity took through autobiography, and also because, by the 1860s, amid the cultural transformations engendered by identity's emergence into the textual and capitalist spheres, Victorian novelists had taken up the task, imaginatively and discursively, of rendering these transformations intelligible through plot, symbol, and form. Scrawled in the pocketbook that Castro left behind in Wagga Wagga, investigators found the observation: "Some men has plenty money and no brains, and some men has plenty brains and no money. Surely men with plenty money and no brains were made for men with plenty brains and no money."[35] It suggested a carefully laid plan to deceive. But here, they discovered, the Claimant was no self-taught genius: he had paraphrased the quote from Braddon's *Aurora Floyd* (1863).[36] During the criminal trial, Braddon sent Justice Cockburn a copy of the novel so that he could check the quotation – after which he admitted to the court that he had stayed up reading the novel instead of focusing on the case. Probably, though, he could have devised no better way to prepare for a trial that rested so entirely upon identity's complex new imaginative and ideological position in an autobiographical and sensational age.

* * *

The Tichborne case was not the first great imposture of its kind. It was preceded by many others, including the famous case of Martin Guerre, and that of the Rajah of Burdwan, whose son died in 1820 but "returned" shortly after the Rajah's death and began collecting rents on family land.[37] What was unique about the Tichborne case, though, was the breadth of its textuality – the way in which the Claimant and the Crown both exploited the textual practices that had entangled identity with property during the first half of the century and that reverberated through the mid-century Victorian novel. The Claimant was both Pip and Magwitch, forging his own new identity as a gentleman by writing himself into relations with property. He was Lucy Audley, hunted by investigators determined to bring his identity to chronological and discursive coherence through its textual traces. He was Eppie and Alfred Hardie, a living subject who became an economic value, economized by the relentless accumulation of texts produced to satisfy the obligations of finance capitalism and the bureaucratic state. He was John Harmon, dead and returned to life, his mysterious story the talk of the town and his body made a consumable object by a totalizing marketplace. He was even Franklin Blake, bearing to the end an inviolable secret subjectivity even as he capitalized on the appetites of a Victorian public hungry alike for confessions and shares. The Claimant forged an identity expressible only as the multiplicity, fragmentation, and distemporality of the commodity. And he did so by exploiting forms of textual production that demystified the imaginative and ideological transformations autobiography had wrought.

It is hard now to imagine a time when identity was not textual – when autobiography was a private rather than a best-selling genre, and when Western culture did not imagine identity as embodied in birth certificates, ID cards, fingerprints, DNA profiles, debt records, and tax returns rather than as an intangible, inviolable character shaped by memory and desire. In the twenty-first century, we are the sums of the interlocking textual records that link us to a materiality that is bureaucratic, biological, and economic, and entangled still, and inextricably, in the imperatives of capitalist culture. There may be no better example of this than the National Archive's decision, a decade ago, to partner with Ancestry.com and UKCensusOnline to digitize Victorian census returns and make them available to the public – for a fee. The bureaucratic state and private enterprise teamed up finally to reify the implicit logic of the Victorian census by turning its textualized subjects explicitly into commodities. Customers can pay Ancestry.com for access to their own (hi)stories, for the chance to bring narrative coherence to their identities and pasts. When I began writing this book, this seemed like closing anecdote enough. But as I revised this conclusion in July 2017, the Wisconsin company Three Square Market announced its intention to begin microchipping employees so that, with a wave of the hand before the proper scanners, they can access buildings, log in to computers, and even pay for a snack from a breakroom vending machine.[38] This, CEO Todd Westby proclaimed, is the future. If so, it is a brilliantly ironic masterstroke: embodying identity – work data, computer logins, even credit card information – in a microchip so that it can be literally re-embodied, all in the name of securing the relation between identity and the capitalist sphere. What remains to be seen is whether this age of digital data will merely revise our old episteme or inaugurate a new one.

Here I have focused on that old episteme in the hope of achieving three aims. I have wanted to trace the commercial rise of autobiography and its textual corollaries in order to show how the convergence of textuality and commodity culture transformed the sense of identity by the middle of the nineteenth century. I have wanted to develop a new sense of the functions that first-person texts serve in mid-century novels, not only by constructing and revealing identity, indicating literacy, and marking out matters of race, class, gender, sexuality, and Englishness, but through their sheer materiality and the way in which that materiality tethers identity to commodity culture. And I have wanted to anatomize how mid-century novels deployed recurrent tropes, symbols, and forms to express the contemporary anxieties about autobiography's transformation of the Victorian subject. In *The Structural Transformation of the Public Sphere* (1962), Jürgen Habermas observes, "Subjectivity, as the innermost core of the private, was always already oriented to an audience."[39] Only during the Victorian period, when autobiography became commercial, did it also orient itself to a market. But if it really is "in the commodity [that] the worker recognises himself and his own relations with capital," then it remains possible to read Victorian autobiography as a hermeneutic genre.[40] The knowledge it produces, though, is not – or at least not only – about the subject. It is about finance capitalism, copyright law, visual culture, the bureaucratic state, police forensics, and the fraught positions of both life writing and the Victorian novel in a richly complex literary market.

Appendix

The information in Chapter 1 regarding autobiography's position in the nineteenth-century literary market draws from two partially overlapping sets of research: (1) searches of the electronic *Nineteenth-century Short Title Catalog* (*NSTC*), mainly to gather quantitative data about the publication of life writing; and (2) the collection of bibliographic and financial details about individual autobiographical titles from the physical and microfilmed archives of Victorian publishers and from relevant secondary sources. Together, these sets of research – described in detail below – yielded the details presented in "1.1 Autobiography in the Literary Market 1820–1860" in Chapter 1. The searches of the *NSTC* allowed me to collect information regarding the proliferation of autobiographical titles published 1820–1860, compare trends in the publication of such titles against trends for the book market as a whole, and discover trends in the publication of sub-genres of life writing such as confessions, diaries, journals, memoirs, correspondence, and conventional autobiographies. My research in Victorian publisher archives permitted me, along with the *NSTC* research, to compile a (still growing) database of 2,482 autobiographical titles published in Britain 1820–1860. Nearly every entry includes at least the full title, author, publisher, and year of publication for the work, and roughly three-quarters of the entries include additional descriptors ranging from information about length and print format to extensive details about the publishing contract, sale price, sales figures, and profits or losses for the title.

Though I have done this work diligently, future scholars will surely improve upon it, particularly given the limitations of both the scope of my research and the capabilities of the *NSTC*, to say nothing of our rapidly expanding access to nineteenth-century titles. They will find more to say about autobiography during the period covered by this study, and they will surely produce an understanding of autobiography's position in the market after 1860, when the mass reading public had mostly been formed and eminent Victorians began publishing their lives. As Simon Eliot writes in his invaluable *Some Patterns and Trends in British Publishing 1800–1919* (1994), any "total enumeration" of titles, "the Holy Grail of enumerative bibliography, is as chimerical for the nineteenth century as it would be for any other period, perhaps more so, in the sense that the Industrial Revolution provided a capacity to produce which far outstripped the administrative and legal capacity to record, at least until the later part of the period."[1] I do not claim to have cracked that code in the present work. But if the data I present in Chapter 1 achieves neither total enumeration nor absolute quantitative certainty, it provides ample evidence for my major claim: that between 1820 and 1860, autobiographies became more numerous, more likely to appear from large commercial houses, more profitable for authors and publishers, and more thoroughly and deliberately commodified.

Nineteenth-century Short Title Catalog (NSTC)

The quantitative data in Chapter 1 originates in keyword searches of the electronic *NSTC* database: for autobiography, memoir, diary, confession, life, letters, journal, and narrative, each one run both with and without the limiting subject designator "Biography" in order to sort, as much as possible, real life writing from fiction. For each decade 1801–1899, I recorded the aggregate number of titles published that decade using each keyword, both with and without the "Biography" designation; for 1840–1860, I recorded this information year by year instead since these decades showed numbers of titles significant enough to warrant more granular counting. For obvious reasons, searches not limited to "Biography" resulted often in unwieldy numbers. Without limiting the results, for instance, the *NSTC* shows just 123 titles using the word "autobiography" during the 1840s. But this same decade shows 6,635 titles using the word "life." I therefore confined my detailed quantitative work to those searches limited to "Biography," using them to build my initial database of autobiographical titles, identify the growing frequency of titles called "autobiography" compared with other forms of life writing (Figure 1.1), produce aggregate annual figures for the publication of all autobiographical titles (Figure 1.2), and evaluate trends in the publication of life writing that I could compare against the market as a whole, at least according to the total titles of all kinds included in the *NSTC* (Figure 1.3).

The results are not perfect. I could have included other keywords: "correspondence" rather than just "letters"; "memoirs" rather than just "memoir"; "travels" to catch travel books not titled as a "journal" or "narrative." Too, even after limiting my results to "Biography," I had to eliminate significant noise from my data, working by hand and often entry by entry, to delete titles published only in the United States and titles that appeared more than once, and noting the phenomenon I describe in Chapter 1, whereby the *NSTC* assigns titles of uncertain date to the first year of their presumed decade of publication, such that 1820, 1830, 1840, 1850, and 1860 show inflated numbers compared to other years. Also, although the *NSTC* assuredly is, as its marketing website boasts, the "Bibliographic spine of the 19th century" and includes 1.2 million titles, it almost certainly misses much that is autobiographical in the century's innumerable periodicals and in subliterary genres like the penny blood. Many first-person narratives, real and fictional, likely passed below the horizon of visibility for Victorian middle-class readers and continue to do so for scholars and databases, though they comprised a significant part of the literary and cultural field.

Compiled Database

My compilation of a database of autobiographical titles began, as I have noted, with my subject-limited searches of the *NSTC* and drew also upon William Matthews's *British Autobiographies: An Annotated Bibliography of British Autobiographies Published or Written before 1951* (1955) and John David, David Vincent, and David Mayall's *The Autobiography of the Working Class: An Annotated, Critical Bibliography* (1984–1989). I also consulted critical and historical studies of nineteenth-century autobiography, including monographs and essay collections by David Amigoni, Carolyn Barros, Trev Lynn Broughton, Oliver Buckton, Regenia Gagnier, George Landow, Clinton Machann, Laura Marcus, James Olney, Linda Peterson, Wayne Shumaker, Sidonie Smith, Eugene Stelzig, and James Treadwell. I added to the database any new title I found in these works. Initially, I wanted to compile these titles and record their basic bibliographic information – author, publisher, year – so that I could determine which Victorian publishers issued the most autobiographical titles, and thus which publisher archives would likely yield the most information about the financial arrangements for individual works. Armed with this initial database, I visited the British Library and handled copies of many of the titles, noting their format, physical characteristics, and other bibliographic details. I tried also to assess whether each work was real or fictional, and whether it was authored by its subject or had been authored or compiled by someone else as a memoir, collection, or heterogeneous mix of autobiography, diary, memoir, correspondence, and other writings. Those titles I could not handle directly I researched using WorldCat, which I used to identify and record as much bibliographic information as I could.

In the second phase of this work, I visited Victorian publisher archives, or viewed them in microfilm, to find contractual, sales, and other financial information about individual autobiographical titles. I consulted in person the records of J.M. Dent and Sons at the Walter Royal Davis Library, University of North Carolina, Chapel Hill; John Murray at the National Library of Scotland; Macmillan and Co. at the British Library; Richard Bentley and Son at the British Library and the Rare Book and Special Collections Library, University of Illinois at Urbana-Champaign; and Smith, Elder and Co. at the National Library of Scotland. I also used the microfilm collection Archives of British and American Publishers (Chadwyck-Healey) to research titles published by Longman and also George Routledge and Co., and I examined the Charles E. Mudie Papers at the Rare Book and Special Collections Library, University of Illinois at Urbana-Champaign. The most useful archives – because the most extensive and complete – were those of John Murray, Richard Bentley and Son, and Smith, Elder and Co., from which I collected financial information on some 450 titles. This information typically included some or all of the following: contractual arrangements between publisher and author; subscription lists; printing costs; publishing information including format, pricing, sales, and profits; and correspondence between author and publisher. In the cases of the Murray, Bentley, and Smith, Elder archives, the material was extensive enough to allow me to find information, too, about the total number of titles they published during certain periods, the profitability of autobiographies relative to titles of other kinds, the frequency and size of payments for copyright to autobiographers and how these compared with those for authors of other kinds of works, and the prevalence of life writing in marketing endeavors such as the Murray Family Library and the Murray Colonial and Home Library. The anecdotes and quantitative data that I give in Chapter 1, part 1 come from these sources.

This book makes selected, critical use of this information since its aim is to illustrate the growing commercialization of autobiography during the first half of the nineteenth century. But I have already begun working to follow up this monograph with a digital project that will convert my database into an online resource that will give scholars access to my raw data and invite them to refine and expand my work. There is much more to do, not only with those titles about which I have found little and the thousands more that were presumably published after 1860, but also – more vitally – with reconceiving and repurposing my data: assessing what else it reveals, where it fails, and how it might be used to advance very different scholarly aims, within and beyond the field of Victorian studies.

Notes

Introduction Life Upon the Exchange: Commodifying the Victorian Subject

1. David Cordingly, *Cochrane the Dauntless: The Life and Adventures of Admiral Thomas Cochrane, 1775–1860* (London: Bloomsbury, 2007), p. 44.
2. Richard Dale, *"Napoleon Is Dead": Lord Cochrane and the Great Stock Exchange Scandal* (Stroud: Sutton, 2006), p. 19.
3. J.K. Laughton, "Cochrane, Thomas, Tenth Earl of Dundonald (1775–1860)," *Dictionary of National Biography*. Vol. 11. Ed. Leslie Stephen (London: Smith, Elder, 1887), p. 174; Cordingly, *Cochrane the Dauntless*, pp. 3–4, 361.
4. Dale, *"Napoleon Is Dead"*, p. 4. Dale gives the most complete account of the Stock Exchange scandal, the ensuing trial, and Cochrane's tireless efforts to clear his name.
5. Dale, *"Napoleon Is Dead"*, p. 9.
6. This last penalty was later revoked on the grounds that it could subject a naval hero to serious indignity at the hands of the mob. See Dale, *"Napoleon Is Dead"*, pp. 77–8.
7. Dale, *"Napoleon Is Dead"*, pp. 78–9.
8. Dale, *"Napoleon Is Dead"*, p. 172.
9. Cordingly, *Cochrane the Dauntless*, p. 360.
10. Dale, *"Napoleon Is Dead"*, pp. 156, 96–7.
11. Dale, *"Napoleon Is Dead"*, p. 19.
12. Dale, *"Napoleon Is Dead"*, p. 101.
13. Brian Vale, *The Audacious Admiral Cochrane: The True Life of a Naval Legend* (London: Conway Maritime Press, 2004), pp. 93, 139, 169.
14. Dale, *"Napoleon Is Dead"*, pp. 166–70.
15. Dale, *"Napoleon Is Dead"*, p. 172.
16. Cordingly, *Cochrane the Dauntless*, p. 343.
17. Vale, *The Audacious Admiral Cochrane*, pp. 204–7.

18. Ian Grimble, *The Sea Wolf: The Life of Admiral Cochrane* (London: Blond and Briggs, 1978), p. 378.
19. Cordingly, *Cochrane the Dauntless*, p. 350.
20. Grimble, *The Sea Wolf*, p. 372.
21. Vale, *The Audacious Admiral Cochrane*, pp. 206–7.
22. Dale, "*Napoleon Is Dead*", p. 175.
23. Publication Lists, Richard Bentley and Son – Papers, 1806–1915 (Rare Book & Manuscript Library. University Library, University of Illinois at Urbana-Champaign), microfilm, reel 18.
24. Agreement and Memorandum Books, Richard Bentley and Son – Papers, 1806–1915, microfilm, reel 29, v. 58, pp. 274–5.
25. Based upon information compiled from the Agreement and Memorandum Books, Richard Bentley and Son – Papers, 1806–1915, microfilm, reels 25–9, vols. 52–8.
26. Grimble, *The Sea Wolf*, p. 381.
27. *The Commodity Culture of Victorian England: Advertising and Spectacle, 1851–1914* (Stanford, CA: Stanford University Press, 1990), p. 1.
28. In George Landow, ed., "Personal Myth: Three Victorian Autobiographers," *Approaches to Victorian Autobiography* (Athens: Ohio University Press, 1979), p. 216.
29. *Autobiographical Writing and British Literature, 1783–1834* (Oxford: Oxford University Press, 2005), pp. 26, 54–5.
30. *Victorian Autobiography: The Tradition of Self-interpretation* (New Haven, CT: Yale University Press, 1986), p. 27.
31. Landow, *Approaches to Victorian Autobiography*, pp. xiii, xviii.
32. Peterson, *Victorian Autobiography*, p. 27.
33. *Fictions of Consciousness: Mill, Newman, and the Reading of Victorian Prose* (New Brunswick, NJ: Rutgers University Press, 1986), pp. 6–7.
34. Eugene Stelzig, ed. *Romantic Autobiography in England* (Farnham: Ashgate, 2009), p. 2.
35. *A Community of One: Masculine Autobiography and Autonomy in Nineteenth-century Britain* (Albany, NY: SUNY Press, 1993), p. 13.
36. David Amigoni, ed. *Life Writing and Victorian Culture* (Aldershot: Ashgate, 2006), p. 2.
37. Treadwell, *Autobiographical Writing*, p. 5.
38. *Men of Letters, Writing Lives: Masculinity and Literary Auto/Biography in the Late Victorian Period* (London: Routledge, 1999), p. 11.
39. "Promoting a Life: Patronage, Masculinity and Philip Meadows Taylor's *The Story of My Life*," in Amigoni, ed., *Life Writing and Victorian Culture*, p. 117.
40. James Boswell, *Life of Samuel Johnson*. Ed. Augustine Birrell. 4 vols. (London: Archibald Constable, 1906), v. 4, p. 29.

41. Karl Marx, *Capital*. 1867. Trans. Ben Fowkes. 3 vols. (London: Penguin, 1976), v. 1, p. 205.

"A Vile Symptom": Autobiography and the Commodification of Identity

1. "Art. VI. Autobiography," *Quarterly Review* 35 (January 1827), pp. 149, 164–5.
2. *Autobiography: Essays Theoretical and Critical* (Princeton, NJ: Princeton University Press, 1980), p. 13.
3. In *Autobiographical Writing*, Treadwell remarks that for William Taylor and Isaac D'Israeli, too, autobiography "now appeared to have grown with remarkable speed from embryo to monstrosity," p. 3.
4. Lockhart, "Art. VI. Autobiography," p. 164.
5. *Romantic Autobiography*, p. 3.
6. The Appendix describes my derivation of the quantitative details contained in this chapter.
7. Thomas Carlyle, *Sartor Resartus*. 1833–1834 (Oxford: Oxford University Press, 1987), p. 73.
8. "Diary, Autobiography and the Practice of Life History," in Amigoni, ed., *Life Writing and Victorian Culture*, pp. 25–6.
9. *Traditions of Victorian Women's Autobiography: The Poetics and Politics of Life Writing* (Charlottesville; London: University Press of Virginia, 1999), p. 25.
10. *Some Patterns and Trends in British Publishing 1800–1919* (London: Bibliographic Society, 1994), p. 20.
11. See "The British Book Trade and the Crash of 1826," *The Library* 9.2 (1987), p. 148.
12. "On the Financial Crisis, 1825–26," *BRANCH: Britain, Representation and Nineteenth-Century History* (2013).
13. Sutherland, "The British Book," p. 148; Dick, "On the Financial Crisis." See also Harold G. Merriam, *Edward Moxon: Publisher of Poets* (New York: Columbia University Press, 1939), p. 23.
14. Dick, "On the Financial Crisis."
15. Sutherland, "The British Book," p. 160.
16. Dick, "On the Financial Crisis."
17. Alexis Weedon, *Victorian Publishing: The Economics of Book Production for a Mass Market, 1836–1916* (Aldershot: Ashgate, 2003), p. 47.
18. Chris Stray, "The Last Eton Grammars," *Paradigm* 8 (July 1992), n.p.; Weedon, *Victorian Publishing*, pp. 111, 128.
19. *On Heroes, Hero-worship, and the Heroic in History*. 1841. Eds. David R. Sorensen and Brent E. Kinser (New Haven, CT; London: Yale University Press, 2013), p. 153.

20. Eliot, *Some Patterns*, p. 8.
21. Eliot, *Some Patterns*, p. 11.
22. *Victorian Novelists and Publishers* (Chicago: University of Chicago Press, 1976), p. 62.
23. Eliot, *Some Patterns*, p. 63. See John Plotz, *"Portable Property": Victorian Culture on the Move* (Princeton, NJ: Princeton University Press, 2009), p. 5, for a discussion of the relation between mass-production and mobility.
24. Sutherland, *Victorian Novelists*, p. 65; Weedon, *Victorian Publishing*, p. 40.
25. While Weedon discounts the impact of the 1843 economic downturn and 1857 depression on the book trade, she writes that "the American Civil War (1861–65) affected both sides of the Atlantic." *Victorian Publishing*, p. 158.
26. [John Wilson Croker,] "Art. XI. – Memoirs of the Life of the Right Honourable Sir James Mackintosh," *Quarterly Review* 54 (July 1835), pp. 250–1. Quoted also in Treadwell, *Autobiographical Writing*, pp. 4, 209.
27. Weedon, *Victorian Publishing*, p. 48.
28. William St. Clair, *The Reading Nation in the Romantic Period* (Cambridge: Cambridge University Press, 2004), p. 118.
29. St. Clair discusses the relation between format, expense, and portability in *The Reading Nation*, p. 205.
30. Details about Lady Morgan and Colburn appear in Lee Erickson, *The Economy of Literary Form: English Literature and the Industrialization of Publishing, 1800–1850* (Baltimore; London: The Johns Hopkins University Press, 1996), p. 156.
31. *Autobiographical Writing*, p. 102.
32. Sutherland, "The British Book," p. 159.
33. Doris Langley Moore, *The Late Lord Byron: Posthumous Dramas* (Philadelphia; New York: J.B. Lippincott, 1961), pp. 29–30.
34. John Knapp to John Murray, November 5, 1827. The John Murray Archive (Manuscript and Archive Collection. National Library of Scotland, Edinburgh), Ms. 40657, f. 13.
35. Account records for *Journal of a Naturalist* appear in The John Murray Archive. See Copies Ledger B of the Publisher John Murray, 1815–1843, Ms. 42725, p. 223; Copies Ledger C of the Publisher John Murray, 1828–1849, Ms. 42727, p. 17; and Copies Ledger D of the Publisher John Murray, 1838–1880, Ms. 42729, p. 47.
36. John Murray to William Harness, November 12, 1834. The John Murray Archive, Ms. 40638, ff. 112–13.
37. John Murray to Fanny Kemble, May 16, 1835. The John Murray Archive, Ms. 40638, ff. 114–16. Kemble's other books included *A Year of Consolation* (1847), *Journal of a Residence on a Georgian Plantation* (1863), *Records of a Girlhood* (1878), *Records of Later Life* (1882), *Far Away and Long Ago* (1889), and *Further Records* (1891).

38. Thomas C. Faulkner, "George Crabbe: Murray's 1834 Edition of the Life and Poems," *Studies in Bibliography* 32 (1979), p. 246.
39. Faulkner, "George Crabbe," p. 247.
40. George Crabbe, Jr. to John Murray, March 2, 1833. The John Murray Archive, Ms. 40287, f. 11.
41. Faulkner, "George Crabbe," pp. 248–50.
42. Faulkner, "George Crabbe," p. 248; Franklin P. Batdorf, "The Murray Reprints of George Crabbe: A Publisher's Record," *Studies in Bibliography* 4 (1951/1952), p. 194.
43. Batdorf, "The Murray Reprints," p. 194.
44. Faulkner, "George Crabbe," p. 252.
45. Information on both the Family Library and the Colonial and Home Library was compiled from Family Library Ledger, The John Murray Archive, Ms. 42769.
46. Titles included Joseph Abbott's *Philip Musgrave, or, Memoirs of a Church of England Missionary in the North American Colonies* (1846), Charles Darwin's *Journal of the Voyage of the H.M.S. Beagle* (1845), Reginald Heber's *Narrative of a Journey through the Upper Provinces of India* (1849), Julia Maitland's *Letters from Madras* (1843), Elizabeth Eastlake's *Letters from the Shores of the Baltic* (1842), and Elizabeth Melville's *A Residence at Sierra Leone* (1849).
47. Information compiled from Profits Ledger of John Murray for 1845–1856, The John Murray Archive, Ms. 42976.
48. Sutherland, *Victorian Novelists*, p. 16.
49. For more on this quarrel, see John Forster, *The Life of Charles Dickens*. Ed. J.W.T. Ley (London: Cecil Palmer, 1928), pp. 93–6; Robert Patten, *Charles Dickens and His Publishers* (Oxford: Oxford University Press, 1978), pp. 75–88; and Michael Slater, *Charles Dickens* (New Haven, CT; London: Yale University Press, 2009), pp. 127–30.
50. Sutherland, *Victorian Novelists*, p. 75.
51. The other two were for Frances Trollope's *Vienna and the Austrians* (1838) and, after much hassling and haggling, *Oliver Twist* (1837–1839).
52. Agreement and memorandum books, Richard Bentley and Son – Papers, 1806–1915, microfilm, reel 29, v. 58.
53. After purchasing the copyright of *Valerie* from Colburn for £50, Routledge pushed the novel through five printings totaling 9,000 copies 1852–1853, then through new editions of 2,000 in 1856 and 1,000 in 1857. He had similar success with Lever's novel, which he revived in 1856: it sold 5,000 copies during its first two years in Routledge's hands and 25,000 more 1859–1873. See *The Archives of George Routledge & Co., 1853–1902* (Cambridge; Teaneck: Chadwyck-Healey, 1973), microfilm, reel 4, v. 1, p. 99; reel 4, v. 2, pp. 165, 271; and reel 4, v. 3, p. 275.

54. Several Newby titles declared themselves "An Autobiography," including Julia Addison's *Evelyn Lascelles* (1855), Annie French Hector's *Agnes Waring* (1856), Bourne Gomerie's *Sybil Grey* (1859), Edward Fitzball's *Thirty-five Years of a Dramatic Author's Life* (1859), Susan Swain Madders's *Mabel Owen* (1859), Selina Bunbury's *Madame Constance* (1861), James MacGrigor Allan's *Last Days of a Bachelor* (1862), and the anonymously written *Dr. Armstrong* (1869).
55. Correspondence 1838–1844, The Layard Papers, Volume XLV (Manuscripts. British Library, London), Add. 38975.
56. Sutherland, *Victorian Novelists*, p. 173.
57. Mary Poovey, *Genres of the Credit Economy: Mediating Value in Eighteenth- and Nineteenth-Century Britain* (Chicago: University of Chicago Press, 2008), p. 145.
58. See James Reynolds's *Confessions of a Pencil Case* (1847), William Paul's *Observations on the Cultivation of Roses in Pots: Including the Autobiography of a Pot-rose* (1853), Margaret Stourton's *The Memoirs of an Arm-chair* (1864), and Julia Attersoll's *The Life and Adventures of a Doll, Told by Herself* (1858).
59. See Richards, *Commodity Culture*, p. 63, and Catherine Waters, *Commodity Culture in Dickens's* Household Words: *The Social Life of Goods* (Aldershot; Burlington: Ashgate, 2008), p. 104. Both discuss the Catalogue's appearance as a narrator.
60. See for instance William Chambers's *Fiddy; an Autobiography, Edited by Her Master* (1851), Elizabeth Grey's *The Autobiography of Frank, the Happiest Little Dog that Ever Lived* (1861), and H.L. Vaucher's *Notes from My Diary, by a Small Dog* (1864), and also the anonymously written *Autobiography of a Cat* (1864), Mrs. E. Burrows's *Tuppy, or the Autobiography of a Donkey* (1860), and Michael Westcott's *Autobiography of a Gossamer Spider* (1857).
61. Westcott, Michael. *Autobiography of a Gossamer Spider* (London: Groombridge and Sons, 1857), p. 1.
62. "Science," *British Quarterly Review* 32 (July 1860), p. 260.
63. Mary Poovey, "Introduction," in Mary Poovey, ed., *The Financial System in Nineteenth-Century Britain* (Oxford: Oxford University Press, 2003), p. 29.
64. P. 11.
65. Poovey, *Genres*, p. 47.
66. Poovey, *Financial System*, p. 9.
67. Poovey, *Genres*, p. 49.
68. Poovey, *Genres*, p. 4.
69. Poovey, *Genres*, p. 36.
70. Barbara Weiss, *The Hell of the English: Bankruptcy and the Victorian Novel* (Lewisburg, PA: Bucknell University Press, 1986), p. 26.
71. Poovey, *Genres*, p. 51.
72. *Money and the Mechanism of Exchange*. 1875 (New York: D. Appleton and Co., 1877), p. 263. Poovey discusses this passage in *Genres*, p. 54.

73. These new laws included the 1826 Country Banks Act, 1844 Joint Stock Companies Act, and 1855 Limited Liability Act. See Weiss, *The Hell of the English*, p. 138.
74. *Realizing Capital: Financial and Psychic Economies in Victorian Form* (New York: Fordham University Press, 2014), pp. 24–6.
75. *Capital*, v. 1, p. 205.
76. *Authors and Owners: The Invention of Copyright* (Cambridge, MA; London: Harvard University Press, 1993), p. 129.
77. Poovey, *The Financial System*, p. 10.
78. Poovey, *Genres*, p. 40.
79. See Kornbluh, *Realizing Capital*, pp. 52, 97–8, and Aeron Hunt, *Personal Business: Character and Commerce in Victorian Literature and Culture* (Charlottesville; London: University of Virginia Press, 2014), p. 12.
80. Hunt, *Personal Business*, p. 23.
81. See "Thoughts on the Improvement of the System of Country Banking," *Edinburgh Review* 63 (July 1836): 419–41.
82. *Forgery in Nineteenth-century Literature and Culture: Fictions of Finance from Dickens to Wilde* (New York: Palgrave, 2009), p. 4.
83. Brian Bailey, *George Hudson: The Rise and Fall of the Railway King* (Phoenix Mill: Allan Sutton, 1995), p. 87. Robert Beaumont gives this same figure in *The Railway King: A Biography of George Hudson* (London: Review, 2002), p. 106.
84. Bailey, *George Hudson*, pp. 105–7.
85. See Rose, *Authors and Owners*, pp. 86–97. Robert Patten also identifies this case as key in *Charles Dickens and "Boz": The Birth of the Industrial-Age Author* (Cambridge: Cambridge University Press, 2012), pp. 11–12.
86. St. Clair, *Reading Nation*, pp. 120–1.
87. Martha Woodmansee makes a similar case in *The Author, Art, and the Market: Rereading the History of Aesthetics* (New York: Columbia University Press, 1994), p. 50. See also Rose, *Authors and Owners*, pp. 114–21.
88. Rose, *Authors and Owners*, pp. 114, 121.
89. Jürgen Habermas, *The Structural Transformation of the Public Sphere: An Inquiry into a Category of Bourgeois Society*. Trans. Thomas Burger with Frederick Lawrence (Cambridge, MA: MIT Press, 1989), pp. 50–1.
90. *A Community of One*, p. 12.
91. *Authors and Owners*, p. 121; *The Genre of Autobiography in Victorian Literature* (Ann Arbor: University of Michigan Press, 1994), p. 9.
92. St. Clair, *Reading Nation*, p. 182.
93. Erickson, *Economy*, p. 39.
94. "Art III. – The Poetical Works of Sir Walter Scott, Bart.," *Monthly Review* 14 (1830), pp. 349, 348.

95. W.A. Speck, *Robert Southey: Entire Man of Letters* (New Haven, CT; London: Yale University Press, 2006), p. 237. See also Jack Simmons, *Southey* (London: Collins, 1945), p. 196.
96. Simmons, *Southey*, p. 196.
97. Stephen Gill, *Wordsworth and the Victorians* (Oxford: Clarendon, 1998), p. 29.
98. Gill, *Wordsworth*, p. 29.
99. Wordsworth had written to notable politicians such as Sir Robert Peel and William Gladstone in 1838 to advocate for passage of the bill to extend the copyright term to 60 years. See Merriam, *Edward Moxon*, pp. 136–7.
100. Merriam, *Edward Moxon*, p. 134.
101. Marcia Pointon, *Hanging the Head: Portraiture and Social Formation in Eighteenth-Century England* (New Haven, CT; London: Yale University Press, 1993), pp. 55–9.
102. Pointon, *Hanging*, pp. 56–62.
103. Pointon, *Hanging*, p. 59.
104. Pointon, *Hanging*, pp. 59, 66.
105. Pointon, *Hanging*, p. 67.
106. Marcia Pointon, "Portrait! Portrait!! Portrait!!!" in David H. Solkin, ed., *Art on the Line: The Royal Academy Exhibitions at Somerset House, 1780–1836* (New Haven, CT; London: Yale University Press, 2001), p. 93 and n. 1; Ann Bermingham, "Landscape-O-Rama: The Exhibition Landscape at Somerset House and the Rise of Popular Landscape Entertainments," in Solkin, ed., *Art on the Line*, p. 127.
107. Sarah Hyde, "Printmakers and the Royal Academy Exhibitions, 1780–1836," in Solkin, ed., *Art on the Line*, p. 222.
108. Pointon, "Portrait!" in Solkin, ed., p. 94.
109. *Art on the Line*, p. 8.
110. *Hanging*, pp. 233, 228.
111. *Hanging*, p. 62.
112. *Hanging*, p. 4.
113. *Signatures of the Visible*. 1992 (New York; London: Routledge, 2007), p. 14.
114. Pointon, "Portrait!" in Solkin, ed., p. 94.
115. "Notes on Some Eighteenth-century Portrait Prices in Britain," *Journal for Eighteenth-Century Studies* 6.2 (1983), p. 187.
116. David H. Solkin, *Painting for Money: The Visual Arts and the Public Sphere in Eighteenth-Century England* (New Haven, CT; London: Yale University Press, 1993), p. 274; See also Iain Pears, *The Discovery of Painting: The Growth of Interest in the Arts in England, 1680–1768* (New Haven, CT; London: Yale University Press, 1988), pp. 139–42.
117. Pointon, *Hanging*, p. 14.

118. Mannings, "Notes," p. 190; Pointon, *Hanging*, p. 48.
119. Pointon, *Hanging*, p. 41.
120. Audrey Linkman, *The Victorians: Photographic Portraits* (London; New York: Tauris Parke, 1993), p. 73.
121. David Lee, "The Victorian Studio: I," *British Journal of Photography* (February 7, 1986), p. 153. Lee further remarks that "even conservative estimates place the figure at 20 million." Steve Edwards cites this figure from Lee in *The Making of English Photography* (University Park: Pennsylvania State University Press, 2006), p. 71.
122. "Dreams of Ordinary Life: Cartes-de-visite and the Bourgeois Imagination," in *Photography: Theoretical Snapshots*. Eds. J.J. Long, Andrea Noble, and Edward Welch (London; New York: Routledge, 2008), p. 89.
123. Edwards, *Making*, p. 74.
124. See Batchen, "Dreams," in Long, et al., eds., *Photography: Theoretical Snapshots*, p. 86, and Edwards, *Making*, p. 100 for elaborations of this point.
125. Lee, "Victorian Studio," p. 152; Edwards, *Making*, p. 74.
126. Quoted in Batchen, "Dreams," in Long, et al., eds., *Photography: Theoretical Snapshots*, p. 82.
127. "Dreams," in Long, et al., eds., p. 90.
128. John Plunkett, "Regicide and Reginamania: G.W.M. Reynolds and *The Mysteries of London*," in Andrew Maunder and Grace Moore, eds., *Victorian Crime, Madness and Sensation* (Aldershot; Burlington: Ashgate, 2004), p. 27.
129. Edwards, *Making*, p. 81.
130. "Dreams," in Long, et al., eds., p. 88.
131. Theodore M. Porter, *The Rise of Statistical Thinking* (Princeton, NJ: Princeton University Press, 1986), p. 30.
132. "London, Wednesday, April 23, 1834," *Times* (April 23, 1834), p. 4.
133. Kathrin Levitan, *A Cultural History of the British Census: Envisioning the Multitude in the Nineteenth Century* (New York: Palgrave, 2011), p. 25.
134. "First Annual Report of the Registrar-General of Births, Deaths, and Marriages in England, 18 May 1839," *Times* (September 6, 1839), p. 7.
135. Edward Higgs, *Making Sense of the Census: The Manuscript Returns for England and Wales, 1801–1901* (London: HMSO, 1989), p. 5.
136. Higgs, *Making*, p. 7.
137. "Report to the Council of the Statistical Society of London, from the Committee Appointed to Consider the Best Mode of Taking the Census of the United Kingdom in 1841," *Journal of the Royal Statistical Society* 3.1 (1840), p. 97.
138. Higgs, *Making*, p. 10.
139. *A Cultural History*, p. 27.
140. Higgs, *Making*, p. 2.
141. Levitan, *A Cultural History*, p. 18. See also Higgs, *Making*, p. 4.

142. Higgs, *Making*, p. 69.
143. Higgs, *Making*, p. 70.
144. Higgs, *Making*, p. 69.
145. "Victorian Self-making, or Self-unmaking? The Tichborne Claimant Revisited," *Victorian Review* 17.1 (1991), p. 26.
146. Levitan, *A Cultural History*, p. 184.
147. Higgs, *Making*, p. 84; Paul Dobraszczyk, "'Give in Your Account': Using and Abusing Victorian Census Forms," *Journal of Victorian Culture* 14.1 (2009), p. 20.
148. Sidney Webb and Beatrice Webb, *The History of Liquor Licensing in England Principally from 1700 to 1830* (London; New York; Bombay: Longmans, Green, and Co., 1903), p. 115.
149. Hunt, *Personal Business*, p. 138. See also Weiss, *The Hell of the English*, pp. 43–5.
150. "Victorian Narrative Jurisprudence," in Michael Freeman and Andrew D. E. Lewis, eds., *Law and Literature: Current Legal Issues 1999* (Oxford: Oxford University Press, 1999), v. 2, p. 448.
151. "Victorian Narrative Jurisprudence," in Freeman and Lewis, eds., p. 441.
152. *Household Words* 18 (November 13, 1858), p. 507.
153. "The Origins of the Modern Civil Service: The 1850s," *CivilService.gov.uk*.
154. "The Origins of the Modern Civil Service."
155. *Novel Professions: Interested Disinterest and the Making of the Professional in the Victorian Novel* (Columbus: Ohio State University Press, 2006), p. 87.
156. Cathy Shuman, *Pedagogical Economies: The Examination and the Victorian Literary Man* (Stanford, CA: Stanford University Press, 2000), pp. 96–7.
157. Shuman, *Pedagogical Economies*, pp. 13, 10.
158. *Household Words* 17 (December 19, 1857), p. 1.
159. "The City of London, Real and Unreal," *Victorian Studies* 49.3 (2007), p. 433.
160. *Charlotte Riddell's City Novels and Victorian Business: Narrating Capitalism* (New York; Oxon: Routledge, 2016), p. 57.
161. *History and Class Consciousness: Studies in Marxist Dialectics*. Trans. Rodney Livingstone (Cambridge, MA: MIT Press, 1971), p. 100.
162. Treadwell, *Autobiographical Writing*, pp. 25, 27.
163. "On Auto-Biography," *Edinburgh Magazine* 10 (June 1822), p. 743.
164. "On Auto-Biography," p. 743.
165. "Scandal of the Court of Napoleon," *London Magazine* 10 (March 1828), p. 410.
166. "Scandal of the Court of Napoleon," p. 410.
167. "Art. VI. Autobiography," p. 164.
168. "Autobiography of Thomas Dibdin," *London Magazine* 18 (June 1827), p. 221.
169. Treadwell, *Autobiographical Writing*, p. 164.

170. Treadwell, *Autobiographical Writing*, p. 164.
171. Her most famous lover was the Duke of Wellington, who replied to her offer – according to legend – "Publish and be damned!" See for instance Rory Muir, *Wellington: The Path to Victory, 1769–1814* (New Haven, CT; London: Yale University Press, 2013), p. 637, n. 19.
172. "Harriette Wilson," *Literary Chronicle and Weekly Review* 6 (March 5, 1825), p. 156; "Loose Thoughts on Harriette Wilson," *London Magazine* 1 (April 1825), pp. 629, 627.
173. Treadwell, *Autobiographical Writing*, p. 165.
174. "Loose Thoughts," p. 627.
175. "Art. VI. Autobiography," p. 158.
176. "Art. VI. Autobiography," pp. 151, 157.
177. "Art. VI. Autobiography," p. 157.
178. "Autobiography of Thomas Dibdin," p. 228.
179. "Autobiography of Thomas Dibdin," p. 229.
180. "Autobiography of Thomas Dibdin," pp. 229–30.
181. "Autobiography of Thomas Dibdin," pp. 230, 233.
182. *Autobiographical Writing*, p. 107.
183. Treadwell, *Autobiographical Writing*, p. 100.
184. "Art III – *The Poetical Works of Sir Walter Scott, Bart.*," p. 359.
185. "Art IV. *The Autobiography of John Galt*," *Eclectic Review* 58 (1833), p. 345; "Art VI. – *The Autobiography of John Galt*," *Monthly Review* 4 (1833), pp. 266–7.
186. [Martha Jones,] "Art. VIII – *Memoirs of Benvenuto Cellini, a Florentine Artist. By himself*," *British Quarterly Review* 8 (1848), p. 492.
187. [Jones,] "Art. VIII," p. 493.
188. "Art. II. – *Autobiography of the Rev. William Walford*," *Eclectic Review* 93 (1851), p. 535.
189. "Autobiography: Jerdan and Miss Mitford," *Dublin University Magazine* 40 (1852), p. 289.
190. "Autobiography: Jerdan and Miss Mitford," p. 289.
191. "Mr Jerdan's Autobiography," *Chambers's Edinburgh Journal* 17 (1852), p. 375.
192. "Autobiography: Jerdan and Miss Mitford," p. 289.
193. "Art. I. – *Letters from Mrs. Delany, Widow of Dr. Patrick Delany, to Mrs. Frances Hamilton, from the Year 1779 to the Year 1788*," *Edinburgh Monthly Review* 4 (October 1820), p. 381.
194. "Autobiography of Mary Granville (Mrs. Delany)," *Saturday Review* 11 (February 16, 1861), pp. 167; "Art. IV. – Mrs. Delany," *Westminster Review* 77 (1862), p. 396.
195. "Art. V. – 1. Autobiography and Correspondence of Mrs. Delany. London: Bentley. 2. Autobiography, Letters, and Literary Remains of Mrs. Piozzi.

London: Longmans," *Christian Remembrancer* 41 (1861), p. 325; [Herman Merivale,] "Art. VII. – *Autobiography, Letters, and Literary Remains of Mrs. Piozzi (Thrale),*" *Edinburgh Review* 113 (1861), p. 519.

196. "Lady Morgan's Memoirs: Autobiography, Diaries, and Correspondence," *Examiner* (January 17, 1863), p. 38.
197. "The Late Lady Morgan and Her Autobiography," *Fraser's Magazine for Town and Country* 67 (February 1863), p. 191.
198. "Lady Morgan's Memoirs," p. 39; "The Late Lady Morgan," p. 189.
199. "The Late Lady Morgan," p. 189.
200. [Herman Merivale,] "Art. II. – *The Autobiography of Miss Cornelia Knight, Lady Companion to the Princess Charlotte of Wales,*" *Quarterly Review* 111 (1862), p. 42; "Art. II. – The Autobiography of Miss Cornelia Knight, Lady Companion to the Princess Charlotte of Wales," *British Quarterly Review* 35 (1862), p. 40.
201. "The Late Lady Morgan," p. 172.
202. "Barnum," *Fraser's Magazine for Town and Country* 51 (February 1855), p. 213.
203. "Barnum," *Fraser's*, p. 222.
204. [Merivale] "Art. II.," p. 42.
205. "Barnum," p. 214.
206. "Barnum," p. 219.
207. "Mrs. Piozzi," *Fraser's Magazine for Town and Country* 63 (March 1861), p. 384; "Art. IV. – Mrs. Delany," p. 374.
208. "Mrs. Delany; Or, a Lady of Quality in the Last Century," *Fraser's Magazine for Town and Country* 65 (April 1862), p. 448.
209. "Art. V. – 1. *Autobiography and Correspondence of Mrs. Delany,*" p. 325. *Fraser's* review of Piozzi also blamed publishers and circulating libraries, writing that the extension of Piozzi's correspondence and memoirs to two volumes was "an offence for which it may be presumed that the editor is not responsible." See "Mrs. Piozzi," p. 384.
210. "Mrs. Piozzi," p. 368.
211. "Mrs. Piozzi," pp. 379, 373.
212. [Merivale,] "Art. VII.," especially pp. 516–20.
213. "Lady Morgan's Memoirs," p. 38.
214. "The Late Lady Morgan," p. 173.
215. "The Late Lady Morgan," pp. 174–81.
216. "The Late Lady Morgan," p. 173.
217. *Autobiographical Writing*, p. 114.
218. "Art. VI. – *The Autobiography of Leigh Hunt, with Reminiscences of His Friends and Contemporaries,*" *North British Review* 14 (1850), pp. 89–90.
219. *The Autobiography of Margaret Oliphant*. 1899. Ed. Elisabeth Jay (Orchard Park, NY: Broadview, 2002), p. 140.

220. *Realizing Capital*, p. 107.
221. *Reading the Nineteenth-century Novel: Austen to Eliot* (Malden, MA: Blackwell, 2008), p. 159.
222. Stephen Knight, "Radical Thrillers," in Ian A. Bell and Graham Daldry, eds., *Watching the Detectives: Essays on Crime Fiction* (New York: St. Martin's, 1990), p. 175; Dallas Liddle, "Anatomy of a 'Nine Days' Wonder': Sensational Journalism in the Decade of the Sensation Novel," in Maunder and Moore, eds., *Victorian Crime, Madness and Sensation*, p. 97.
223. Heather Worthington, *The Rise of the Detective in Early Nineteenth-century Popular Fiction* (Basingstoke: Palgrave, 2005), p. 9.
224. "'Literature of the Kitchen': Cheap Serial Fiction of the 1840s and 1850s," in Pamela Gilbert, ed., *A Companion to Sensation Fiction* (Chichester: Wiley-Blackwell, 2011), p. 51.
225. "What Is 'Sensational' about the 'Sensation Novel'?" *Nineteenth-Century Fiction* 37.1 (1982), p. 14.
226. Wilkie Collins, *The Woman in White*. 1860. Ed. John Sutherland (Oxford: Oxford University Press, 2008), p. 605.
227. Collins, *The Woman in White*, p. 635.
228. "Paris – Capital of the Nineteenth Century," in Peter Demetz, ed., *Reflections: Essays, Aphorisms, and Autobiographical Writings*. Trans. Edmund Jephcott (New York; London: Harcourt Brace Jovanovich, 1978), p. 155.
229. *Realizing Capital*, p. 3.
230. *The Maniac in the Cellar: Sensation Novels of the 1860s* (Princeton, NJ: Princeton University Press, 1980), p. 57.
231. *Realizing Capital*, p. 13.
232. Walter Benjamin, "The Work of Art in an Age of Mechanical Reproduction," in *Illuminations*. Ed. Hannah Arendt. Trans. Harry Zohn (New York: Harcourt, Brace & World, 1955), p. 223.
233. *Capital*, v. 1, p. 195.
234. "What Is 'Sensational'," pp. 23–4.
235. *History and Class Consciousness*, p. 87.
236. *Maniac in the Cellar*, p. 64.
237. "The Work of Art," pp. 223, 222.
238. Richards, *Commodity Culture*, p. 107.
239. Wolfgang Schivelbusch, *The Railway Journey: Trains and Travel in the 19th Century*. Trans. Anselm Hollo (New York: Urizen, 1979), p. 41. See also Michael Freeman, *Railways and the Victorian Imagination* (New Haven, CT; London: Yale University Press, 1999), especially pp. 21–2, 76–8.
240. *Literature, Technology, and Modernity: 1860–2000* (Cambridge; New York: Cambridge University Press, 2004), p. 47.

241. *Novels Behind Glass: Commodity Culture and Victorian Narrative* (Cambridge: Cambridge University Press, 1995), p. 66.
242. *Commodity Culture*, p. 2.

"Portable Property": Commodity and Identity in *Great Expectations*

1. An early version of this chapter was published as "Commodity and Identity in *Great Expectations*," *Victorian Literature and Culture* 40.2 (2012): 617–41. It appears here in revised form courtesy of the editors of that journal and the Cambridge University Press.
2. Charles Dickens, *Great Expectations*. 1860–1861. Ed. Edgar Rosenberg (New York: Norton, 1999), p. 157. Subsequent references are to this edition and appear parenthetically in the text.
3. *"Portable Property,"* p. 1.
4. "Monstrous Displacements: Anxieties of Exchange in *Great Expectations*," *Dickens Studies Annual* 30 (2001), p. 244.
5. Elizabeth Campbell, "*Great Expectations*: Dickens and the Language of Fortune," *Dickens Studies Annual* 24 (1996), p. 158; Bruce Robbins, "How to Be a Benefactor without Any Money: The Chill of Welfare in *Great Expectations*," in Suzy Anger, ed., *Knowing the Past: Victorian Literature and Culture* (Ithaca, NY; London: Cornell University Press, 2001), p. 184.
6. "Chronometrics of Love and Money in *Great Expectations*," *Dickens Studies Annual* 35 (2005), p. 135.
7. Zemka, "Chronometrics," p. 135.
8. *Dickens* (New York: HarperCollins, 1990), p. 900.
9. *The Letters of Charles Dickens*. 12 vols. Eds. Madeline House, Graham Storey, and Kathleen Tillotson (Oxford: Clarendon, 1965–2000), v. 9, p. 287.
10. "*Great Expectations*, Romance, and Capital," *Dickens Studies Annual* 35 (2005), p. 162.
11. *Capital*, v. 1, p. 163.
12. "Bodies of Capital: *Great Expectations* and the Climacteric Economy," *Victorian Studies* 37.1 (1993), p. 90.
13. Gail Turley Houston, "'Pip' and 'Property': The (Re)production of the Self in *Great Expectations*," *Studies in the Novel* 24.1 (1992), p. 15.
14. "Monstrous Displacements," p. 245.
15. Several studies have addressed Dickens's preoccupation with cannibalism in and beyond *Great Expectations*. See for instance James E. Marlow, "English Cannibalism: Dickens after 1859," *Studies in English Literature* 23.4 (1983): 647–66; and Harry Stone, *The Night Side of Dickens:*

Cannibalism, Passion, Necessity (Columbus: Ohio State University Press, 1994), especially "Part I."

16. Dickens published "The Lost Arctic Voyagers" in two parts in *Household Words* on December 2 and 9, 1854, intending to refute the report Dr. John Rae made to the British Admiralty after searching for Franklin's expedition during 1848–1854. Rae related to the Admiralty the findings of his interviews with Inuits who claimed to have seen members of Franklin's crew, and he related also his conclusions that they had likely died from scurvy and starvation, though not before resorting to cannibalism.
17. Marlow, "English Cannibalism," pp. 652–3.
18. Walsh, "Bodies of Capital," p. 96.
19. *Dickens, Money, and Society* (Berkeley; Los Angeles: University of California Press, 1968), p. 208.
20. *Letters*, v. 9, p. 284.
21. "Introduction," *Great Expectations*. Ed. Margaret Cardwell (Oxford: Clarendon, 1993), pp. xiii–xvi.
22. Slater, *Charles Dickens*, pp. 487–8.
23. Patten, *Charles Dickens and His Publishers*, p. 291.
24. *Letters*, v. 10, p. 98.
25. Henry Dickens, "Memories of My Father," in Norman Page, ed., *Charles Dickens: Family History, Volume 1* (London: Routledge 1999), p. 24.
26. Edgar Johnson (*Charles Dickens: His Tragedy and Triumph*. 2 vols. [New York: Simon and Schuster, 1952]) discusses the terms of the separation and notes that Catherine was to receive £600 a year, v. 2, pp. 917–20. Gladys Storey writes in *Dickens and Daughter* (London: Frederick Muller, 1939) that "a settlement was made on Ellen Ternan, who subsequently lived in an establishment of her own at Peckham," p. 97. For the most complete account of Dickens's lifelong arrangements with Nelly, see Claire Tomalin, *The Invisible Woman: The Story of Nelly Ternan and Charles Dickens* (London; New York: Penguin, 1991).
27. Cardwell, "Introduction," *Great Expectations*, p. xxvii. See also Charles Dickens, *Great Expectations*. Ed. Edgar Rosenberg, p. 130, n. 8.
28. *Letters*, v. 9, p. 376.
29. *Letters*, v. 8, p. 435.
30. Forster wrote that it was "a question . . . of respect for himself as a gentleman." *Life*, p. 641.
31. Fred Kaplan, *Dickens: A Biography* (New York: William Morrow, 1988), pp. 412, 406.
32. Storey, *Dickens and Daughter*, p. 95.
33. An ironic title, given Dickens's commercial intent. In *Charles Dickens*, Slater points out that these essays were the first pieces of journalism that

Dickens advertised under his own name, pp. 482–3. The first series of "Uncommercial Traveller" essays began running in *All the Year Round* on January 28, 1860, two months after *A Tale of Two Cities* ended its serial run. Pleased by the success, he commenced a second series in 1863 and a third in 1868, eventually running the total number of essays to thirty-six. For a full account, see Michael Slater's "Introduction" to Charles Dickens, *The Dent Uniform Edition of Dickens' Journalism*. 4 vols. Eds. Michael Slater and John Drew (London: J.M. Dent, 1994–2000), v. 4, pp. xi–xxiii.

34. Johnson, *Charles Dickens*, v. 2, p. 920.
35. The "Personal" statement appeared in the *Times* on June 7, 1858 and in *Household Words* on June 12, 1858. See Charles Dickens, "Personal," *The Dent Uniform Edition of Dickens' Journalism*, v. 3, pp. 488–90.
36. Dickens's splits with his old friends are described in *Letters* v. 8, pp. xiv–xv; Kaplan, *Dickens*, pp. 376–417; Johnson, *Charles Dickens*, v. 2, pp. 929–36; Ackroyd, *Dickens*, pp. 824–8, and Claire Tomalin, *Charles Dickens: A Life* (New York: Penguin, 2011), pp. 316–18.
37. Dickens, *Letters*, v. 9, p. 423. In the footnote to Dickens's letter to Bulwer, the editors point out that Bulwer "clearly feared a recurrence of both personal and literary attacks, if his name appeared."
38. *Letters*, v. 9, p. 423.
39. *Letters*, v. 9, p. 304.
40. *Letters*, v. 9, p. 319. For a thorough account of Lever's failure to satisfy Dickens, see Johnson, *Charles Dickens*, v. 2, pp. 956–66, and Jerome Meckier, "'Dashing in Now': *Great Expectations* and Charles Lever's *A Day's Ride*," *Dickens Studies Annual* 26 (1998): 227–64.
41. *Letters*, v. 9, pp. 319–20.
42. *Letters*, v. 9, p. 320.
43. *Letters*, v. 9, p. 320.
44. Mary Hammond refutes this in *Charles Dickens's* Great Expectations: *A Cultural Life, 1860–2012* (Farnham; Burlington: Ashgate, 2015), pp. 21–3, by focusing on *All the Year Round*'s low profits for the half-years of *Great Expectations*' serial run and by comparing its volume sales to those of *Dombey and Son*. She does not note, however, the extent to which the exceptionally large payment – £1,500 – to Bulwer for *A Strange Story* may have impacted the magazine's profits for these half-years, nor the fact that in volume form *Great Expectations* sold at 31s. 6d., not the 5s. (Cheap edition) or 6s. per volume (Library edition) that had been typical for his earlier novels.
45. Patten, *Charles Dickens and His Publishers*, pp. 289–92.
46. *Letters*, v. 9, p. 354.
47. *Letters*, v. 9, p. 325.

48. "'In Primal Sympathy': *Great Expectations* and the Secret Life," *Dickens Studies Annual* 11 (1983), p. 109; *Charles Dickens*, p. 495. For the letter to Forster, see Dickens, *Letters*, v. 9, p. 433.
49. Jerome Meckier offers an intriguing read of the polyvalence of the novel's title in "Great Expectations: 'A Good Name?'," *Dickens Quarterly* 26.4 (2009): 248–58.
50. *Knowing Dickens* (Ithaca, NY; London: Cornell University Press, 2009), p. 66.
51. "'Pip' and 'Property'," p. 16.
52. *Reading for the Plot: Design and Intention in Narrative* (Cambridge, MA; London: Harvard University Press, 1984), pp. 130–1.
53. "*Great Expectations* as Reading Lesson," *Dickens Quarterly* 13.3 (1996), p. 166.
54. Brooks, *Reading*, p. 122.
55. "*Great Expectations*," p. 172.
56. Pip is called variously Philip, Handel, my boy, dear boy, silly boy, ridiculous boy, and a Squeaker, and Magwitch and Wopsle both adopt multiple aliases. Pip also accuses Orlick of having invented the name "Dolge" as an "affront" to the village, ignoring that he has invented his own name in similar fashion (90). John Jordan points out this last in "Partings Welded Together: Self-fashioning in *Great Expectations* and *Jane Eyre*," *Dickens Quarterly* 13.1 (1996), pp. 28–9.
57. Randall Craig makes a similar point in "Fictional License: The Case of (and in) *Great Expectations*," *Dickens Studies Annual* 35 (2005), p. 112.
58. I discuss this in relation to *The Pickwick Papers* in *The Self in the Cell: Narrating the Victorian Prisoner* (New York; London: Routledge, 2003), pp. 61–4.
59. "'A Case of Metaphysics': Counterfactuals, Realism, *Great Expectations*," *ELH* 79.3 (2012), p. 785.
60. Craig, "Fictional License," p. 120.
61. "Manufacturing Fictional Individuals: Victorian Social Statistics, the Novel, and *Great Expectations*," *NOVEL: A Forum on Fiction* 46.2 (2013), pp. 229, 224–5.
62. "Calligraphy and Code: Writing in *Great Expectations*," *Dickens Studies Annual* 11 (1983), p. 66.
63. *Reading*, p. 138.
64. "Chronometrics," p. 147.
65. James Kincaid discusses this in "Dickens and the Construction of the Child," in Wendy S. Jacobsen, ed., *Dickens and the Children of Empire* (Basingstoke: Palgrave, 2000), pp. 40–1.
66. "'In Primal Sympathy'," pp. 108–9.
67. Dutheil, "*Great Expectations*," p. 166.

Lady Audley's Portrait: Textuality, Gender, and Power

68. Claire Jarvis discusses Pip's sexual disappointment brilliantly in "Pip's Life" (*ELH* 81.4 [2014], pp. 1253–73) where she connects it explicitly to his arrival to middle-class productivity.

1. Mary Elizabeth Braddon, *Lady Audley's Secret*. 1862. Ed. Jenny Bourne Taylor (London; New York: Penguin, 1998), pp. 70–1. Subsequent references are to this edition and appear parenthetically in the text.
2. "The Literary Portrait as Centerfold: Fetishism in Mary Elizabeth Braddon's *Lady Audley's Secret*," *Victorian Literature and Culture* 35.2 (2007), p. 473.
3. Sophia Andres, "Mary Elizabeth Braddon's Ambivalent Pre-Raphaelite Ekphrasis," *Victorian Newsletter* 108 (Fall 2005), p. 3; Jill Matus, "Disclosure as 'Cover-up': The Discourse of Madness in *Lady Audley's Secret*," *University of Toronto Quarterly* 62.3 (1993), p. 336.
4. Ann Cvetkovich, *Mixed Feelings: Feminism, Mass Culture, and Victorian Sensationalism* (New Brunswick, NJ: Rutgers University Press, 1992), p. 49.
5. *Moulding the Female Body in Victorian Fairy Tales and Sensation Novels* (Aldershot; Burlington: Ashgate, 2007), p. 120.
6. *Disease, Desire, and the Body in Victorian Women's Popular Novels* (Cambridge: Cambridge University Press, 1997), p. 93.
7. *Disease*, p. 92.
8. Several scholars have discussed her business savvy. See Gilbert, *Disease*, p. 92; Jennifer Phegley, *Educating the Proper Woman Reader: Victorian Family Literary Magazines and the Cultural Health of the Nation* (Columbus: Ohio State University Press, 2004), pp. 110–26; Robert Lee Wolff, *Sensational Victorian: The Life and Fiction of Mary Elizabeth Braddon* (New York; London: Garland, 1979), pp. 97–126, 134–47; and Jennifer Carnell, *The Literary Lives of Mary Elizabeth Braddon: A Study of Her Life and Work* (Hastings: Sensation, 2000), pp. 142–51.
9. Braddon plagiarized *Circe* from Octave Feuillet's *Dalila* (1857) and was exposed for doing so by the *Pall Mall Gazette*. See Wolff, *Sensational Victorian*, p. 207, and Carnell, *Literary Lives*, p. 220. Carnell gives the title of Feuillet's work incorrectly as *Dahlia*.
10. Wolff, *Sensational Victorian*, pp. 122–5.
11. Carnell, *Literary Lives*, p. 150.
12. Quoted in Wolff, *Sensational Victorian*, p. 155.
13. *Sororophobia: Differences Among Women in Literature and Culture* (Oxford; New York: Oxford University Press, 1992), p. 64.
14. *Mixed Feelings*, pp. 66–7.

15. Charles Dickens, *Little Dorrit*. 1855–1857. Ed. Harvey Peter Sucksmith (Oxford: Clarendon, 1979), p. 241; Tabitha Sparks, "To the Mad-House Born: The Ethics of Exteriority in *Lady Audley's Secret*," in Jessica Cox, ed., *New Perspectives on Mary Elizabeth Braddon* (Amsterdam; New York: Rodopi, 2012), p. 34.
16. *Hanging the Head*, p. 143.
17. Tim Barringer discusses labor, value, and art in *Men at Work: Art and Labour in Victorian Britain* (New Haven, CT; London: Yale University Press, 2005), pp. 76–81, 313–21. Other critics have focused on Pre-Raphaelism and the aesthetics of "photographic realism" in *Lady Audley's Secret*. See Brian Donnelly, "Sensational Bodies: Lady Audley and the Pre-Raphaelite Portrait," *Victorian Newsletter* 112 (Fall 2007), pp. 70, 87; and Talaraich-Vielmas, *Moulding*, p. 121.
18. William R. McKelvy, "*The Woman in White* and Graphic Sex," *Victorian Literature and Culture* 35.1 (2007), pp. 294–6.
19. Charles Dickens, *Bleak House*. 1853. Ed. Nicola Bradbury (London; New York: Penguin, 1996), p. 330.
20. Cvetkovich, *Mixed Feelings*, p. 61.
21. *Moulding*, p. 125.
22. *The Novelty of Newspapers: Victorian Fiction After the Invention of the News* (Oxford: Oxford University Press, 2009), p. 72.
23. Sophia Andres, *The Pre-Raphaelite Art of the Victorian Novel* (Columbus: Ohio State University Press, 2005), p. 2.
24. "Masculinity and Economics in *Lady Audley's Secret*," *VIJ: Victorians Institute Journal* 27 (1999), p. 36.
25. Dickens, *Bleak House*, p. 20.
26. Felber, "The Literary Portrait," p. 477.
27. Talaraich-Vielmas, *Moulding*, p. 116.
28. *The Novelty of Newspapers*, p. 70.
29. "Robert Audley's Profession," *Studies in the Novel* 32.1 (2000), p. 6.
30. *The 'Improper' Feminine: The Women's Sensation Novel and the New Woman Writing* (London; New York: Routledge, 1992), p. 91; Donnelly, "Sensational Bodies," p. 85.
31. *Disease*, p. 105.
32. *Mixed Feelings*, p. 61.
33. Felber, "The Literary Portrait," p. 483.
34. Petch, "Robert Audley's Profession," p. 2.
35. "Homelessness in the Home: Invention, Instability, and Insanity in the Domestic Spaces of M.E. Braddon and L.M. Alcott," in Cox, ed., *New Perspectives on Mary Elizabeth Braddon*, p. 87; "Robert Audley's Secret: Male Homosocial Desire in *Lady Audley's Secret*," *Studies in the Novel* 27.4 (1995), p. 527.
36. "Critical Masculinities in *Lady Audley's Secret*," *Victorian Review* 33.1 (2007), p. 103.

37. *From Sensation to Society: Representations of Marriage in the Fiction of Mary Elizabeth Braddon, 1862–1866* (Newark, DE: University of Delaware Press, 2006), p. 35.
38. *This Sex Which Is Not One*. Trans. Catherine Porter with Carolyn Burke (Ithaca, NY: Cornell University Press, 1985), p. 84.
39. "Boudoir Stories: A Novel History of a Room and Its Occupants," *Literature Interpretation Theory* 15.2 (2004), p. 120.
40. "Critical Masculinities," p. 104. See also Gilbert, *Disease*, p. 95.
41. Felber, "The Literary Portrait," p. 482.
42. "'An Idle Handle that was Never Turned, and a Lazy Rope so Rotten': The Decay of the Country Estate in Lady Audley's Secret," in Marlene Tromp, Pamela K. Gilbert, and Aeron Haynie, eds., *Beyond Sensation: Mary Elizabeth Braddon in Context* (Albany, NY: SUNY Press, 2000), p. 72.
43. Haynie, "'An Idle Handle'," p. 66; "Gothic Maidens and Sensation Women: Lady Audley's Journey from the Ruined Mansion to the Madhouse," *Victorian Literature and Culture* 19 (1991), p. 208.
44. "Masculinity and Economics," p. 41.

Amnesia, Madness, and Financial Fraud: Ontologies of Loss in *Silas Marner* and *Hard Cash*

1. Charles L. Reade and Compton Reade, *Charles Reade: Dramatist, Novelist, Journalist. A Memoir Compiled Chiefly from His Literary Remains*. 2 vols. (London: Chapman and Hall, 1887), v. 2, p. 131.
2. Quoted in Charles L. Reade, *Charles Reade*, v. 2, pp. 131–2.
3. Gordon S. Haight, *George Eliot: A Biography* (Oxford: Oxford University Press, 1968), p. 326.
4. Neither Eliot's letters nor Lewes's journals mention these works by Reade.
5. Charles L. Reade, *Charles Reade*, v. 2, pp. 130–1.
6. John Sutherland, "Dickens, Reade and *Hard Cash*," *Dickensian* 81.1 (1985), p. 7; Haight, p. 356, n. 4.
7. Lewes, quoted in Haight, *George Eliot*, p. 355.
8. Malcolm Elwin, *Charles Reade* (London: Jonathan Cape, 1931), p. 176.
9. Kristen A. Pond, "Bearing Witness in *Silas Marner*: George Eliot's Experiment in Sympathy," *Victorian Literature and Culture* 41.4 (2013), p. 691.
10. George Eliot, *The George Eliot Letters*. 9 vols. Ed. Gordon Haight (New Haven, CT: Yale University Press, 1954–78), v. 3, p. 382.
11. "Introduction," to George Eliot, *Silas Marner: The Weaver of Raveloe*. Ed. Terence Cave. 1861 (Oxford: Oxford University Press, 2008), p. vii. Subsequent references to the "Introduction" and to *Silas Marner* are to this edition and appear parenthetically in the text.

12. Charles Reade, *Hard Cash*. 1863. 3 vols. (Paris: The Grolier Society, 1912), v. 1, p. 3. Subsequent citations to the novel are to this edition and appear parenthetically in the text. See also Elwin, *Charles Reade*, pp. 166–9; Wayne Burns, *Charles Reade: A Study in Victorian Authorship* (New York: Bookman, 1961), pp. 201–4.
13. *The Hell of the English*, pp. 95, 92.
14. Ilana Blumberg makes a version of this argument in "Stealing the 'Parson's Surplice' / the Person's Surplus: Narratives of Abstraction and Exchange in *Silas Marner*," *Nineteenth-Century Literature* 67.4 (2013): 490–519, and Richard Mallen does so in "George Eliot and the Precious Mettle of Trust," *Victorian Studies* 44.1 (2001): 41–75.
15. *Charlotte Riddell's City Novels*, p. 197.
16. Eliot, *Letters*, v. 3, p. 382.
17. *The Life of George Eliot* (Malden, MA; Oxford: Wiley-Blackwell, 2012), p. 125; *George Eliot* (Brighton: Harvester Press, 1986), pp. 126, 132.
18. "The Breaks in *Silas Marner*," *JEGP: The Journal of English and Germanic Philology* 97.4 (1988), pp. 545, 558.
19. Susan Stewart, "Genres of Work: The Folktale and *Silas Marner*," *New Literary History* 34.3 (2003), pp. 527–8.
20. Blumberg, "Stealing," p. 490.
21. *Letters*, v. 3, pp. 410–11.
22. *Perspectives: Modes of Viewing and Knowing in Nineteenth-Century England* (Columbus: Ohio State University Press, 2009), p. 110.
23. Jim Reilly, "'A Report of Unknown Objects': *Silas Marner*," in Nahem Yousaf and Andrew Maunder, eds., The Mill on the Floss *and* Silas Marner (Basingstoke: Palgrave, 2002), p. 192.
24. Courtney Berger, "When Bad Things Happen to Bad People: Liability and Individual Consciousness in *Adam Bede* and *Silas Marner*," *NOVEL: A Forum on Fiction* 33.3 (2000), p. 319.
25. Kate Brown, "Loss, Revelry, and the Temporal Measures of *Silas Marner*: Performance, Regret, Recollection," *NOVEL: A Forum on Fiction* 32.2 (1999), p. 244.
26. Fred Thomson, "The Theme of Alienation in *Silas Marner*," *Nineteenth-Century Fiction* 20.1 (1965), p. 79.
27. Susan Cohen, "'A History and a Metamorphosis': Continuity and Discontinuity in *Silas Marner*," *Texas Studies in Literature and Language* 25.3 (1983), p. 421.
28. "The Miser's Two Bodies: *Silas Marner* and the Sexual Possibilities of the Commodity," *Victorian Studies* 36.3 (1993), p. 274.
29. Efraim Sicher, "George Eliot's 'Glue Test': Language, Law and Legitimacy in *Silas Marner*," in Harold Bloom, ed., *George Eliot's* Silas Marner (Broomall, PA: Chelsea House, 2003), p. 164.
30. Thomson, "The Theme of Alienation," p. 77.

31. Brown makes a similar argument in "Loss," p. 224.
32. Cohen, "'A History and a Metamorphosis'," p. 411.
33. Brown, "Loss," p. 224.
34. *George Eliot and Blackmail* (Cambridge, MA; London: Harvard University Press, 1985), p. 167.
35. "*Silas Marner* and the Anonymous Heroism of Parenthood," in Harold Bloom, ed., *George Eliot's* Silas Marner (Broomall, PA: Chelsea House, 2003), p. 155.
36. "'A History and a Metamorphosis'," p. 414.
37. "When Bad Things Happen," p. 321.
38. Brown, "Loss," p. 245.
39. "Stealing," pp. 509, 498.
40. *George Eliot*, p. 132.
41. "George Eliot's 'Glue Test'," in Bloom, ed., pp. 173–4.
42. *George Eliot*, p. 126.
43. "Stealing," p. 492.
44. Anna Neill, *Primitive Minds: Evolution and Spiritual Experience in the Victorian Novel* (Columbus: Ohio State University Press, 2013), p. 115.
45. "'A Report'," in Yousaf and Maunder, eds., The Mill on the Floss *and* Silas Marner, p. 199.
46. Douglas Bankson, "Charles Reade's Manuscript Notecards for *Hard Cash*" (PhD diss., University of Washington, 1954), p. iii. Emerson Grant Sutcliffe called Reade "the earliest deliberately and thoroughly documentary novelist" in "Charles Reade's Notebooks," *Studies in Philology* 27.1 (1930), p. 64.
47. Burns, *Charles Reade*, pp. 207–8.
48. Elwin, *Charles Reade*, p. 166.
49. These letters were eventually collected and published as "Our Dark Places" in the volume *Readiana* (1882).
50. Charles L. Reade, *Charles Reade*, v. 2, p. 143.
51. *Very Hard Cash* appeared in *All the Year Round* from March 28 to December 26, 1863.
52. John Sutherland, *Victorian Fiction: Writers, Publishers, Readers* (Basingstoke: Macmillan, 1995), p. 60.
53. Charles L. Reade, *Charles Reade*, v. 2, pp. 150–1.
54. *Victorian Sensational Fiction: The Daring Work of Charles Reade* (New York: Palgrave Macmillan, 2010), p. 64. See also Sheila Smith, "Propaganda and Hard Facts in Charles Reade's Didactic Novels: A Study of *It Is Never Too Late to Mend* and *Hard Cash*," *Renaissance and Modern Studies* 4 (1960): 135–49; Ann Grigsby, "Charles Reade's *Hard Cash*: Lunacy Reform through Sensationalism," *Dickens Studies Annual* 25 (1996): 141–58; and Peter Logan, "Imitations of Insanity and Victorian Medical Aesthetics," *Romanticism and Victorianism on the Net* 49 (February 2008).

55. *The Sensation Novel and the Victorian Family Magazine* (Basingstoke: Palgrave, 2001), p. 135.
56. This material later became a "Preface" to volume editions of *Hard Cash*.
57. *Victorian Fiction*, p. 60.
58. "NOTE," *All the Year Round* 10 (December 26, 1863), p. 419.
59. Quoted in Tom Bragg, "Charles Reade," in Pamela Gilbert, ed., *A Companion to Sensation Fiction*, p. 299.
60. Bragg, "Charles Reade," 299.
61. Bankson, "Charles Reade's Manuscript Notecards," pp. 63, 49.
62. Bankson, "Charles Reade's Manuscript Notecards," p. 34.
63. "'Arithmetic of Bedlam!': Markets and Manhood in Charles Reade's *Hard Cash*," *Nineteenth-Century Literature* 63.1 (2008), p. 3.
64. *Reading for the Law: British Literary History and Gender Advocacy* (Charlottesville; London: University of Virginia Press, 2010), pp. 126–7.
65. "Arithmetic of Bedlam!" p. 38.
66. Walsh, "Arithmetic of Bedlam!" p. 13.
67. "Arithmetic of Bedlam!" p. 29.
68. Burns, *Charles Reade*, p. 212; Bankson, "Charles Reade's Manuscript Notecards," p. 17.
69. Sutherland, *Victorian Fiction*, p. 76.
70. Sutherland, *Victorian Fiction*, p. 77.
71. Logan, "Imitations of Insanity," par. 7.
72. "Arithmetic of Bedlam!" p. 33.
73. "Charles Reade," p. 302.
74. "Charles Reade's *Hard Cash*," p. 157.

"What Money Can Make of Life": Willing Subjects and Commodity Culture in *Our Mutual Friend*

1. See Patten, *Charles Dickens and His Publishers*, pp. 301–3.
2. *Letters*, v. 10, pp. 295–6.
3. *Letters*, v. 10, p. 296, n. 1.
4. The contract appears as Appendix E in Dickens, *Letters*, v. 10, pp. 477–8.
5. Dickens wrote to Forster in mid-October announcing that he had begun the novel. See *Letters*, v. 10, p. 300.
6. Charles Dickens, *Our Mutual Friend*. 1865. Ed. Michael Cotsell (Oxford: Oxford University Press, 1989), p. 13. Subsequent references are to this edition and appear parenthetically in the text.
7. *Charles Dickens: The World of His Novels* (Cambridge, MA: Harvard University Press, 1958), p. 280.
8. "*Our Mutual Friend* and Network Form," *NOVEL: A Forum on Fiction* 48.1 (2015), p. 76.

9. "Travelling Abroad," *Dent*, v. 4, p. 88. I discuss these elements of "Travelling Abroad" at length in "Xenophobia to Xenophilia: Dickens's Continental Drift," *Dickens Studies Annual* 48 (2017): 1–19.
10. "Travelling Abroad," *Dent*, v. 4, p. 88.
11. "Travelling Abroad," *Dent*, v. 4, p. 90.
12. "Travelling Abroad," *Dent*, v. 4, p. 90.
13. "Travelling Abroad," *Dent*, v. 4, p. 90.
14. *Novels Behind Glass*, p. 4.
15. "Travelling Abroad," *Dent*, v. 4, p. 86.
16. "'The Age of Veneer': Charles Dickens and the Antinomies of Victorian Consumer Culture," *Dickens Quarterly* 32.3 (2015), p. 232.
17. Beer's *Darwin's Plots: Evolutionary Narrative in Darwin, George Eliot, and Nineteenth-Century Fiction* (London: Routledge and Kegan Paul, 1983) and Levine's *Darwin and the Novelists: Patterns of Science in Victorian Fiction* (Cambridge, MA: Harvard University Press, 1988) initiated this useful critical discussion, which has been reinvigorated many times since. See for instance Howard Fulweiler, "'A Dismal Swamp': Darwin, Design, and Evolution in *Our Mutual Friend*," *Nineteenth-Century Literature* 49.1 (1994): 50–74; Nicola Brown, "What the Alligator Didn't Know: Natural Selection and Love in *Our Mutual Friend*," *19: Interdisciplinary Studies in the Long Nineteenth Century* 10 (2010); Sally Ledger, "Dickens, Natural History, and *Our Mutual Friend*," *Partial Answers: Journal of Literature and the History of Ideas* 9.2 (2011): 363–78.
18. "Dickens, Natural History, and *Our Mutual Friend*," p. 367.
19. "The Case Against Plot in *Bleak House* and *Our Mutual Friend*," *ELH* 59.1 (1992), p. 191.
20. "The Bioeconomics of *Our Mutual Friend*," in David Simpson, ed., *Subject to History: Ideology, Class, Gender* (Ithaca, NY; London: Cornell University Press, 1991), p. 54.
21. *Fictions of Resolution in Three Victorian Novels*: North and South, Our Mutual Friend, Daniel Deronda (New York: Columbia University Press, 1981), p. 64.
22. Dickens, *Bleak House*, p. 243.
23. David makes this same point in *Fictions of Resolution*, p. 90.
24. Michael Cotsell, "Mr Venus Rises from the Counter: Dickens's Taxidermist and His Contribution to *Our Mutual Friend*," *Dickensian* 80.2 (1984), p. 105. See also my discussion of Mr. Venus in *Charles Dickens's* Our Mutual Friend: *A Publishing History* (Farnham; Burlington, VT: Ashgate, 2014), pp. 37–9.
25. J. Fisher Solomon, "Realism, Rhetoric, and Reification: Or the Case of the Missing Detective in *Our Mutual Friend*," *Modern Philology* 86.1 (1988), p. 39.
26. Gurney, "'The Age of Veneer'," p. 233.
27. Michelle Allen, *Cleansing the City: Sanitary Geographies in Victorian London* (Athens: Ohio University Press, 2008), p. 101.

28. "Dismemberment and Articulation in *Our Mutual Friend*," *Dickens Studies Annual* 11 (1983), pp. 152–3.
29. "The Sovereign Self: Identity and Responsibility in Victorian England," in Freeman and Lewis, eds., *Law and Literature: Current Legal Issues 1999*. Vol. 2, p. 406.
30. "The Sovereign Self," in Freeman and Lewis, eds., p. 406.
31. "The W/Hole Remains: Consumerist Politics in *Bleak House*, *Great Expectations*, and *Our Mutual Friend*," *Victorian Review* 19.1 (1993), p. 5.
32. "A Speculative Resurrection: Death, Money, and the Vampiric Economy of *Our Mutual Friend*," *Victorian Literature and Culture* 30.1 (2002), p. 99.
33. Dickens, *Bleak House*, p. 256.
34. *Fictions of Resolution*, p. 73.
35. *Fictions of Resolution*, p. 74.
36. *Victorian Will* (Athens: Ohio University Press, 1989), p. 197.
37. Scoggin, "A Speculative Resurrection," pp. 108, 110.
38. "The Cup and the Lip and the Riddle of *Our Mutual Friend*," *ELH* 62.4 (1995), p. 969.
39. Hutter, "Dismemberment," p. 155.
40. Ruth Tross, "Dickens and the Crime of Literacy," *Dickens Quarterly* 21.4 (2004), pp. 237–8.
41. See his excellent discussion of this in *The Material Interests of the Victorian Novel* (Charlottesville; London: University of Virginia Press, 2005), ch. 4.
42. *Fictions of Resolution*, p. 92.
43. "'A Speeches of Chaff': Ventriloquy and Expression in *Our Mutual Friend*," *Dickens Studies Annual* 19 (1990), p. 248.
44. Andrew Miller, *Novels Behind Glass*, p. 151.
45. Kenneth Sroka, "Dickens' Metafiction: Readers and Writers in *Oliver Twist*, *David Copperfield*, and *Our Mutual Friend*," *Dickens Studies Annual* 22 (1993), p. 51.
46. J. Hillis Miller makes a similar point in *Charles Dickens*, p. 306.
47. *Pedagogical Economies*, p. 153; Eve Kosofsky Sedgwick, "Homophobia, Misogyny, and Capital: The Example of *Our Mutual Friend*," in Steven Connor, ed., *Charles Dickens* (London: Longman, 1996), p. 182.
48. *Novels Behind Glass*, p. 156.
49. "The Partners' Tale: Dickens and *Our Mutual Friend*," *ELH* 66.3 (1999), p. 789.
50. "The Case Against Plot," p. 188.
51. "Envy Rising," in James Chandler and Kevin Gilmartin, eds., *Romantic Metropolis: The Urban Scene of British Culture, 1780–1840* (Cambridge: Cambridge University Press, 2005), p. 144.

52. Brian Cheadle also notes this scene in "Work in *Our Mutual Friend*," *Essays in Criticism* 51.3 (2001), p. 323.
53. "Between 'the Cup and the Lip': Retroactive Constructions of Inheritance in *Our Mutual Friend*," in Barbara Cohen and Dragan Kujundžić, eds., *Provocations to Reading: J. Hillis Miller and the Democracy to Come* (New York: Fordham University Press, 2005), p. 54.
54. "'The Ghost of Slavery' in *Our Mutual Friend*," *Victorian Literature and Culture* 43.3 (2015), p. 528.
55. F.S. Schwarzbach, *Dickens and the City* (London: Athlone Press, 1979), p. 202.
56. "Work," p. 320.
57. "'The Age of Veneer'," p. 242.
58. "A Speculative Resurrection," p. 119.
59. David, *Fictions of Resolution*, p. 101.
60. David, *Fictions of Resolution*, p. 56.
61. "Podsnappery, Sexuality, and the English Novel," *Critical Inquiry* 9.2 (1982), p. 347.
62. "Introduction," *Our Mutual Friend*. 1865. Ed. Adrian Poole (London: Penguin, 1997), p. xiv; *Novels Behind Glass*, p. 11.
63. "The Artistic Reclamation of Waste in Our Mutual Friend," *Nineteenth-Century Fiction* 34.1 (1979), p. 60.
64. "Victorian Moral Philosophy and *Our Mutual Friend*," *Dickens Quarterly* 27.4 (2010), p. 286.
65. Scoggin makes this point in "A Speculative Resurrection," p. 112.
66. "'Come Back and Be Alive': Living and Dying in *Our Mutual Friend*," *Dickensian* 74.3 (1978), pp. 136–7.
67. *Charles Dickens*, pp. 292–3.

The Moonstone, Sacred Identity, and the Material Self

1. Wilkie Collins, *The Moonstone*. Ed. John Sutherland (Oxford: Oxford University Press, 1999), p. 38. Subsequent references are to this edition and appear parenthetically in the text.
2. "Introduction," *The Moonstone* 1868 (London: Oxford University Press, 1928), p. v.
3. Dickens, *Letters*, v. 11, p. 385.
4. "*The Moonstone*, Detective Fiction, and Forensic Science," in Jenny Bourne Taylor, ed., *The Cambridge Companion to Wilkie Collins* (Cambridge: Cambridge University Press, 2006), p. 65.
5. "*The Moonstone*, the Victorian Novel, and Imperialist Panic," *Modern Language Quarterly* 55.3 (1994), p. 310.

6. "'Dirty Linen': Legacies of Empire in Wilkie Collins's *The Moonstone*," *Texas Studies in Literature and Language* 48.4 (2006), p. 340.
7. John Sutherland describes it this way in "Wilkie Collins and the Origins of the Sensation Novel," in Nelson Smith and R.C. Terry, eds., *Wilkie Collins to the Forefront: Some Reassessments* (New York: AMS Press, 1995); D.A. Miller does so in *The Novel and the Police* (Berkeley: University of California Press, 1988), especially pp. 49–50.
8. "Collins's *Moonstone*: The Victorian Novel as Sacrifice, Theft, Gift and Debt," *Studies in the Novel* 37.2 (2005), p. 163.
9. "Tessellating Texts: Reading *The Moonstone* in *All the Year Round*," *Victorian Periodicals Review* 45.1 (2012), p. 2.
10. John Sutherland, "A Note on the Text," in Wilkie Collins, *Armadale*. 1864–1866. Ed. John Sutherland (London; New York: Penguin, 1995), pp. xxxi–xxxii.
11. *The Letters of Wilkie Collins*. 2 vols. Eds. William Baker and William M. Clarke (Basingstoke: Macmillan, 1999), v. 2, p. 282.
12. Collins, *Letters*, v. 2, p. 282.
13. Quoted in Sue Lonoff, *Wilkie Collins and His Victorian Readers: A Study in the Rhetoric of Authorship* (New York: AMS Press, 1982), p. 172.
14. Collins, *Letters*, v. 2, p. 287.
15. "Collins's *Moonstone*," p. 164.
16. Thomas, "*The Moonstone*," in Taylor, ed., p. 72.
17. Mark Hennelly also raises this question of motive in "Detecting Collins' Diamond: From Serpentstone to Moonstone," *Nineteenth-Century Fiction* 39.1 (1984), p. 44.
18. *In the Secret Theatre of Home: Wilkie Collins, Sensation Narrative, and Nineteenth-century Psychology* (London; New York: Routledge, 1988), pp. 195–6.
19. "*The Moonstone*," p. 310.
20. Timothy Carens, *Outlandish English Subjects in the Victorian Domestic Novel* (Basingstoke: Palgrave, 2005), p. 119; "English Romance: Indian Violence," *Centennial Review* 39.3 (1995), p. 632.
21. *In the Secret Theatre*, p. 195.
22. *In the Secret Theatre*, p. 174.
23. Ronald R. Thomas, "Minding the Body Politic: The Romance of Science and the Revision of History in Victorian Detective Fiction," *Victorian Literature and Culture* 19 (1991), p. 236.
24. Albert Hutter, "Dreams, Transformations, and Literature: The Implications of Detective Fiction," *Victorian Studies* 19.2 (1975), p. 194.
25. "Dreams," p. 194.
26. Thomas, "*The Moonstone*," in Taylor, ed., p. 75.

27. Thomas, "*The Moonstone*," in Taylor, ed., pp. 69–70; Thomas, "Minding," p. 249.
28. "Minding," p. 252.
29. *The Novel and the Police*, p. 40.
30. *The Novel and the Police*, pp. 40–1.
31. "*The Moonstone*," p. 307.
32. *Wilkie Collins*, p 184.
33. Blumberg makes this argument in "Collins's *Moonstone*," p. 172.
34. "Collins's *Moonstone*," p. 181.
35. "Collins's *Moonstone*," p. 177.
36. Duncan, "*The Moonstone*," p. 306.
37. *The Poetics of Prose*. Trans. Richard Howard (Ithaca, NY: Cornell University Press, 1977), p. 46.
38. *The Novel and the Police*, p. 54.
39. Elisabeth Rose Gruner, "Family Secrets and the Mysteries of *The Moonstone*," *Victorian Literature and Culture* 21 (1993), p. 138.
40. John Glendening, "War of the Roses: Hybridity in *The Moonstone*," *Dickens Studies Annual* 39 (2008), p. 294.
41. Taylor, *In the Secret Theatre*, p. 183.
42. "Minding," p. 240.
43. "*The Moonstone*," p. 68.
44. Thomas, "*The Moonstone*," in Taylor, ed., p. 74.
45. Janice Allan, "Scenes of Writing: Detection and Psychoanalysis in Wilkie Collins's *The Moonstone*," *Imprimatur* 1.2–3 (1996), p. 191; Tamar Heller, *Dead Secrets: Wilkie Collins and the Female Gothic* (New Haven, CT; London: Yale University Press, 1992), p. 146.
46. *In the Secret Theatre*, p. 175.
47. Ross Murfin, "The Art of Representation: Collins' *The Moonstone* and Dickens' Example," *ELH* 49.3 (1982), p. 666.
48. Heller discusses this at length in *Dead Secrets*, pp. 160–2.
49. "English Romance," p. 630.
50. Alfonso Maurizio Iacono, *The History and Theory of Fetishism*. Trans. Viktoria Tchernichova and Monica Boria, with Elizabeth MacDonald (Basingstoke: Palgrave, 2016), p. 57.
51. "The Leading Article of No. 179 of *Kölnische Zeitung*," in Karl Marx and Friedrich Engels, *Karl Marx and Friedrich Engels: On Religion*. Intro. Reinhold Niebuhr (New York: Schocken, 1964), p. 22.
52. Duncan, "*The Moonstone*," p. 311.
53. *Dead Secrets*, p. 147.
54. Susan Zieger, "Opium, Alcohol, and Tobacco: The Substances of Memory in *The Moonstone*," in Pamela Gilbert, ed., *A Companion to Sensation Fiction*, p. 211.

Conclusion Money Made of Life: The Tichborne Claimant

1. Robyn Annear, *The Man Who Lost Himself: The Unbelievable Story of the Tichborne Claimant* (Melbourne: Text, 2002), p. 13.
2. Douglas Woodruff, *The Tichborne Claimant: A Victorian Mystery* (New York: Farrar, Straus and Cudahy, 1957), p. 33.
3. Kent, "Victorian Self-making," p. 18; Woodruff, *The Tichborne Claimant*, p. 37.
4. Woodruff, *The Tichborne Claimant*, p. 42.
5. Geddes MacGregor, *The Tichborne Impostor* (Philadelphia; New York: J.B. Lippincott, 1957), p. 38.
6. Woodruff, *The Tichborne Claimant*, p. 45.
7. Annear, *The Man Who Lost Himself*, pp. 375, 324. See also Carrie Dawson, "'The Slaughterman of Wagga Wagga': Imposture, National Identity, and the Tichborne Affair," *Australian Literary Studies* 21.4 (2004), especially pp. 2–4.
8. Arnold used this phrase in *Culture and Anarchy* in 1869.
9. *The Tichborne Claimant: A Victorian Sensation* (London; New York: Hambledon Continuum, 2007), p. 189.
10. Rebecca Stern, *Home Economics: Domestic Fraud in Victorian England* (Columbus: Ohio State University Press, 2008), p. 24. For a thorough account of the popular forms that embraced the Tichborne affair, see McWilliam, *The Tichborne Claimant*, chs. 10–13. In "Bilbo's Return and the Tichborne Affair" (*Mallorn: The Journal of the Tolkien Society* 57 [2016]: 23–5), Murray Smith argues that Bilbo's unexpected journey may have been inspired by the Tichborne case.
11. Woodruff, *The Tichborne Claimant*, p. 38.
12. Woodruff, *The Tichborne Claimant*, p. 38.
13. Woodruff, *The Tichborne Claimant*, p. 40; Annear, *The Man Who Lost Himself*, p. 252.
14. Woodruff, *The Tichborne Claimant*, p. 348.
15. Annear, *The Man Who Lost Himself*, p. 297.
16. Woodruff, *The Tichborne Claimant*, pp. 46–7.
17. Woodruff, *The Tichborne Claimant*, p. 49.
18. McWilliam, *The Tichborne Claimant*, pp. 49, 106.
19. MacGregor, *The Tichborne Impostor*, p. 32.
20. MacGregor, *The Tichborne Impostor*, p. 149; McWilliam, *The Tichborne Claimant*, p. 26.
21. *The Tichborne Claimant*, p. 197; *Home Economics*, p. 44.
22. Woodruff, *The Tichborne Claimant*, p. 165.
23. Annear, *The Man Who Lost Himself*, p. 269.
24. Woodruff, *The Tichborne Claimant*, pp. 165–7.
25. Annear, *The Man Who Lost Himself*, pp. 317–19.
26. *The Tichborne Claimant*, p. 56.

27. Annear, *The Man Who Lost Himself*, pp. 311–12; McWilliam, *The Tichborne Claimant*, p. 206.
28. McWilliam, *The Tichborne Claimant*, pp. 207–8.
29. McWilliam, *The Tichborne Claimant*, pp. 204–6.
30. Woodruff, *The Tichborne Claimant*, pp. 215–16.
31. McWilliam, *The Tichborne Claimant*, p. 210.
32. McWilliam, *The Tichborne Claimant*, p. 271.
33. McWilliam, *The Tichborne Claimant*, pp. 271–2.
34. *Home Economics*, pp. 45–6, 48.
35. Quoted in McWilliam, *The Tichborne Claimant*, p. 14.
36. The original passage reads, "I should think fellows with plenty of money and no brains must have been created for the good of fellows with plenty of brains and no money; and that's how we contrive to keep our equilibrium in the universal see-saw." See *Aurora Floyd*. 1863. Ed. P.D. Edwards (Oxford: Oxford University Press, 1996), p. 190.
37. Michael Gilbert, *The Claimant* (London: Constable, 1957), pp. 218–20.
38. Maggie Astor, "Microchip Implants for Employees? One Company Says Yes," *New York Times* (July 25, 2017).
39. Habermas, p. 49.
40. Lukács, *History and Class Consciousness*, p. 168.

Appendix

1. Eliot, p. 4.

Works Cited

Ackroyd, Peter. *Dickens*. New York: HarperCollins, 1990.
Allan, Janice M. "Scenes of Writing: Detection and Psychoanalysis in Wilkie Collins's *The Moonstone*." *Imprimatur* 1.2–3 (1996): 186–93.
Allen, Michelle. *Cleansing the City: Sanitary Geographies in Victorian London*. Athens: Ohio University Press, 2008.
Amigoni, David, ed. *Life Writing and Victorian Culture*. Aldershot: Ashgate, 2006.
Andres, Sophia. "Mary Elizabeth Braddon's Ambivalent Pre-Raphaelite Ekphrasis." *Victorian Newsletter* 108 (Fall 2005): 1–6.
The Pre-Raphaelite Art of the Victorian Novel. Columbus: Ohio State University Press, 2005.
Anger, Suzy, ed. *Knowing the Past: Victorian Literature and Culture*. Ithaca, NY; London: Cornell University Press, 2001.
Annear, Robyn. *The Man Who Lost Himself: The Unbelievable Story of the Tichborne Claimant*. Melbourne: Text, 2002.
[Anster, John.] "Art. VI.—*The Autobiography of Leigh Hunt, with Reminiscences of His Friends and Contemporaries*." *North British Review* 14 (1850): 77–90.
The Archives of George Routledge & Co., 1853–1902. Microfilm. Cambridge; Teaneck: Chadwyck-Healey, 1973.
"Art. I.—*Letters from Mrs. Delany, Widow of Dr. Patrick Delany, to Mrs. Frances Hamilton, from the Year 1779 to the Year 1788*." *Edinburgh Monthly Review* 4 (October 1820): 379–90.
"Art. II.—*The Autobiography of Miss Cornelia Knight, Lady Companion to the Princess Charlotte of Wales*." *British Quarterly Review* 35 (1862): 40–61.
"Art. II.—*Autobiography of the Rev. William Walford*." *Eclectic Review* 93 (1851): 535–42.
"Art. III.—*The Poetical Works of Sir Walter Scott, Bart*." *Monthly Review* 14 (1830): 347–60.
"Art IV. *The Autobiography of John Galt*." *Eclectic Review* 58 (1833): 343–54.
"Art. IV.—Mrs. Delany." *Westminster Review* 77 (1862): 374–99.
"Art. V.—1. *Autobiography and Correspondence of Mrs. Delany*. London: Bentley. 2. *Autobiography, Letters, and Literary Remains of Mrs. Piozzi*. London: Longmans." *Christian Remembrancer* 41 (1861): 325–66.
"Art VI.—*The Autobiography of John Galt*." *Monthly Review* 4 (1833): 249–67.

Astor, Maggie. "Microchip Implants for Employees? One Company Says Yes." *New York Times* (July 25, 2017).
"Autobiography: Jerdan and Miss Mitford." *Dublin University Magazine* 40 (1852): 289–306.
"Autobiography of Mary Granville (Mrs. Delany)." *Saturday Review* 11 (February 16, 1861): 165–7.
"Autobiography of Thomas Dibdin." *London Magazine* 18 (June 1827): 221–40.
Bailey, Brian. *George Hudson: The Rise and Fall of the Railway King*. Phoenix Mill: Alan Sutton, 1995.
Bankson, Douglas. "Charles Reade's Manuscript Notecards for Hard Cash." PhD diss., University of Washington, 1954.
"Barnum." *Fraser's Magazine for Town and Country* 51 (February 1855): 213–23.
Barringer, Tim J. *Men at Work: Art and Labour in Victorian Britain*. New Haven, CT: London: Yale University Press, 2005.
Batdorf, Franklin P. "The Murray Reprints of George Crabbe: A Publisher's Record." *Studies in Bibliography* 4 (1951/1952): 192–9.
Baumgarten, Murray. "Calligraphy and Code: Writing in *Great Expectations*." *Dickens Studies Annual* 11 (1983): 61–72.
Beaumont, Robert. *The Railway King: A Biography of George Hudson*. London: Review, 2002.
Beer, Gillian. *Darwin's Plots: Evolutionary Narrative in Darwin, George Eliot, and Nineteenth-Century Fiction*. London: Routledge and Kegan Paul, 1983.
  George Eliot. Brighton: Harvester Press, 1986.
Bell, Ian A., and Graham Daldry, eds. *Watching the Detectives: Essays on Crime Fiction*. New York: St. Martin's, 1990.
Benjamin, Walter. *Illuminations*. Ed. Hannah Arendt. Trans. Harry Zohn. New York: Harcourt, Brace & World, 1955.
  Reflections: Essays, Aphorisms, Autobiographical Writings. Ed. Peter Demetz. Trans. Edmund Jephcott. New York; London: Harcourt Brace Jovanovich, 1978.
Berger, Courtney. "When Bad Things Happen to Bad People: Liability and Individual Consciousness in *Adam Bede* and *Silas Marner*." *NOVEL: A Forum on Fiction* 33.3 (2000): 307–27.
Bloom, Harold, ed. *George Eliot's Silas Marner*. Broomall, PA: Chelsea House, 2003.
Blumberg, Ilana M. "Collins's *Moonstone*: The Victorian Novel as Sacrifice, Theft, Gift and Debt." *Studies in the Novel* 37.2 (2005): 162–86.
  "Stealing the 'Parson's Surplice' / the Person's Surplus: Narratives of Abstraction and Exchange in *Silas Marner*." *Nineteenth-Century Literature* 67.4 (2013): 490–519.
Bodenheimer, Rosemarie. *Knowing Dickens*. Ithaca, NY; London: Cornell University Press, 2007.
Boswell, James. *Life of Samuel Johnson*. 1791. Ed. Augustine Birrell. 4 vols. London: Archibald Constable, 1906.
Braddon, Mary Elizabeth. *Aurora Floyd*. 1863. Ed. P.D. Edwards. Oxford: Oxford University Press, 1996.

Lady Audley's Secret. 1862. Ed. Jenny Bourne Taylor. London; New York: Penguin, 1998.
Brantlinger, Patrick. "What Is 'Sensational' about the 'Sensation Novel'?" *Nineteenth-Century Fiction* 37.1 (1982): 1–28.
Briganti, Chiara. "Gothic Maidens and Sensation Women: Lady Audley's Journey from the Ruined Mansion to the Madhouse." *Victorian Literature and Culture* 19 (1991): 189–211.
Brooks, Peter. *Reading for the Plot: Design and Intention in Narrative*. Cambridge, MA; London: Harvard University Press, 1984.
Broughton, Trev Lynn. *Men of Letters, Writing Lives: Masculinity and Literary Auto/Biography in the Late Victorian Period*. London; New York: Routledge, 1999.
Brown, Kate E. "Loss, Revelry, and the Temporal Measures of *Silas Marner*: Performance, Regret, Recollection." *NOVEL: A Forum on Fiction* 32.2 (1999): 222–49.
Brown, Nicola. "What the Alligator Didn't Know: Natural Selection and Love in *Our Mutual Friend*." *19: Interdisciplinary Studies in the Long Nineteenth Century* 10 (2010).
Burns, Wayne. *Charles Reade: A Study in Victorian Authorship*. New York: Bookman, 1961.
Campbell, Elizabeth. "*Great Expectations*: Dickens and the Language of Fortune." *Dickens Studies Annual* 24 (1996): 153–65.
Carens, Timothy L. *Outlandish English Subjects in the Victorian Domestic Novel*. Basingstoke: Palgrave, 2005.
Carlyle, Thomas. *On Heroes, Hero-worship, and the Heroic in History*. 1841. Eds. David R. Sorensen and Brent E. Kinser. New Haven, CT; London: Yale University Press, 2013.
Sartor Resartus. 1833–1834. Eds. Kerry McSweeney and Peter Sabor. Oxford: Oxford University Press, 1987.
Carnell, Jennifer. *The Literary Lives of Mary Elizabeth Braddon: A Study of Her Life and Work*. Hastings: Sensation, 2000.
Case, Alison, and Harry E. Shaw. *Reading the Nineteenth-century Novel: Austen to Eliot*. Malden, MA: Blackwell, 2008.
Chandler, James, and Kevin Gilmartin, eds. *Romantic Metropolis: The Urban Scene of British Culture, 1780–1840*. Cambridge: Cambridge University Press, 2005.
Cheadle, Brian. "Work in *Our Mutual Friend*." *Essays in Criticism* 51.3 (2001): 308–29.
Cohen, Barbara, and Dragan Kujundžić, eds. *Provocations to Reading: J. Hillis Miller and the Democracy to Come*. New York: Fordham University Press, 2005.
Cohen, Susan R. "'A History and a Metamorphosis': Continuity and Discontinuity in *Silas Marner*." *Texas Studies in Literature and Language* 25.3 (1983): 410–26.
Colella, Silvana. *Charlotte Riddell's City Novels and Victorian Business: Narrating Capitalism*. New York: Routledge, 2016.

Collins, Wilkie. *Armadale*. 1864–1866. Ed. John Sutherland. London; New York: Penguin, 1995.
The Letters of Wilkie Collins. 2 vols. Eds. William Baker and William M. Clarke. Basingstoke: Macmillan, 1999.
The Moonstone. 1868. Ed. John Sutherland. Oxford: Oxford University Press, 1999.
The Moonstone. 1868. Intro. T. S. Eliot. London: Oxford University Press, 1928.
The Woman in White. 1860. Ed. John Sutherland. Oxford: Oxford University Press, 2008.
Connor, Steven, ed. *Charles Dickens*. London: Longman, 1996.
Cordingly, David. *Cochrane the Dauntless: The Life and Adventures of Admiral Thomas Cochrane, 1775–1860*. London: Bloomsbury, 2007.
Cotsell, Michael. "Mr Venus Rises from the Counter: Dickens's Taxidermist and His Contribution to *Our Mutual Friend*." *Dickensian* 80.2 (1984): 105–13.
Cox, Jessica, ed. *New Perspectives on Mary Elizabeth Braddon*. Amsterdam; New York: Rodopi, 2012.
Craig, Randall. "Fictional License: The Case of (and in) *Great Expectations*." *Dickens Studies Annual* 35 (2005): 109–32.
[Croker, John Wilson.] "Art. XI.—*Memoirs of the Life of the Right Honourable Sir James Mackintosh*." *Quarterly Review* 54 (July 1835): 250–94.
Cvetkovich, Ann. *Mixed Feelings: Feminism, Mass Culture, and Victorian Sensationalism*. New Brunswick, NJ: Rutgers University Press, 1992.
Dale, Richard. *"Napoleon Is Dead": Lord Cochrane and the Great Stock Exchange Scandal*. Stroud: Sutton, 2006.
Daly, Nicholas. *Literature, Technology, and Modernity, 1860–2000*. Cambridge: Cambridge University Press, 2004.
Danahay, Martin. *A Community of One: Masculine Autobiography and Autonomy in Nineteenth-century Britain*. Albany, NY: SUNY Press, 1993.
David, Deirdre. *Fictions of Resolution in Three Victorian Novels:* North and South, Our Mutual Friend, Daniel Deronda. New York: Columbia University Press, 1981.
Dawson, Carrie. "'The Slaughterman of Wagga Wagga': Imposture, National Identity, and the Tichborne Affair." *Australian Literary Studies* 21.4 (2004): 1–13.
Dick, Alexander J. "On the Financial Crisis, 1825–26." *BRANCH: Britain, Representation and Nineteenth-Century History* (2013). Ed. Dino Franco Felluga. Extension of *Romanticism and Victorianism on the Net*.
Dickens, Charles. *Bleak House*. 1853. Ed. Nicola Bradbury: London; New York: Penguin, 1996.
The Dent Uniform Edition of Dickens' Journalism. 4 vols. Eds. Michael Slater and John Drew. London: J. M. Dent, 1994–2000.
Great Expectations. 1860–1861. Ed. Edgar Rosenberg. New York: Norton, 1999.
Great Expectations. 1860–1861. Ed. Margaret Cardwell. Oxford: Clarendon, 1993.

The Letters of Charles Dickens. 12 vols. Eds. Madeline House, Graham Storey, and Kathleen Tillotson. Oxford: Clarendon, 1965–2002.
Little Dorrit. 1855–1857. Ed. Harvey Peter Sucksmith. Oxford: Clarendon, 1979.
"NOTE." *All the Year Round* 10 (December 26, 1863): 419.
Our Mutual Friend. 1865. Ed. Michael Cotsell. Oxford: Oxford University Press, 1989.
Our Mutual Friend. 1865. Ed. Adrian Poole. London: Penguin, 1997.
Dobraszczyk, Paul. "'Give in Your Account': Using and Abusing Victorian Census Forms." *Journal of Victorian Culture* 14.1 (2009): 1–25.
Donnelly, Brian. "Sensational Bodies: Lady Audley and the Pre-Raphaelite Portrait." *Victorian Newsletter* 112 (Fall 2007): 69–90.
Duncan, Ian. "*The Moonstone*, the Victorian Novel, and Imperialist Panic." *Modern Language Quarterly* 55.3 (1994): 297–319.
Dutheil, Martine Hennard. "*Great Expectations* as Reading Lesson." *Dickens Quarterly* 13.3 (1996): 164–74.
Edwards, Steve. *The Making of English Photography.* University Park: Pennsylvania State University Press, 2006.
Eliot, George. *The George Eliot Letters.* 9 vols. Ed. Gordon Haight. New Haven, CT: Yale University Press, 1954–1978.
Silas Marner: The Weaver of Raveloe. 1861. Ed. Terence Cave. Oxford: Oxford University Press, 2008.
Eliot, Simon. *Some Patterns and Trends in British Publishing 1800–1919.* London: Bibliographic Society, 1994.
Elwin, Malcolm. *Charles Reade.* London: Jonathan Cape, 1931.
Erickson, Lee. *The Economy of Literary Form: English Literature and the Industrialization of Publishing, 1800–1850.* Baltimore; London: The Johns Hopkins University Press, 1996.
Fantina, Richard. *Victorian Sensational Fiction: The Daring Work of Charles Reade.* New York: Palgrave Macmillan, 2010.
Farrell, John P. "The Partners' Tale: Dickens and *Our Mutual Friend.*" *ELH* 66.3 (1999): 759–99.
Faulkner, Thomas C. "George Crabbe: Murray's 1834 Edition of the Life and Poems." *Studies in Bibliography* 32 (1979): 246–52.
Felber, Lynette. "The Literary Portrait as Centerfold: Fetishism in Mary Elizabeth Braddon's *Lady Audley's Secret.*" *Victorian Literature and Culture* 35.2 (2007): 471–88.
Forster, John. *The Life of Charles Dickens.* Ed. J.W.T. Ley. London: Cecil Palmer, 1928.
Free, Melissa. "'Dirty Linen': Legacies of Empire in Wilkie Collins's *The Moonstone.*" *Texas Studies in Literature and Language* 48.4 (2006): 340–71.
Freeman, Michael. *Railways and the Victorian Imagination.* New Haven, CT; London: Yale University Press, 1999.
Freeman, Michael, and Andrew D. E. Lewis, eds. *Law and Literature: Current Legal Issues 1999.* Vol. 2. Oxford: Oxford University Press, 1999.

Fulweiler, Howard. "'A Dismal Swamp': Darwin, Design, and Evolution in *Our Mutual Friend*." *Nineteenth-Century Literature* 49.1 (1994): 50–74.
Gibson, Anna. "*Our Mutual Friend* and Network Form." *NOVEL: A Forum on Fiction* 48.1 (2015): 63–84.
Gilbert, Elliot L. "'In Primal Sympathy': *Great Expectations* and the Secret Life." *Dickens Studies Annual* 11 (1983): 89–113.
Gilbert, Michael. *The Claimant*. London: Constable, 1957.
Gilbert, Pamela. *Disease, Desire, and the Body in Victorian Women's Popular Novels.* Cambridge: Cambridge University Press, 1997.
    ed. *A Companion to Sensation Fiction*. Chichester: Wiley-Blackwell, 2011.
Gill, Stephen. *Wordsworth and the Victorians*. Oxford: Clarendon, 1998.
Ginsburg, Michal Peled. "The Case against Plot in *Bleak House* and *Our Mutual Friend*." *ELH* 59.1 (1992): 175–95.
Glendening, John. "War of the Roses: Hybridity in *The Moonstone*." *Dickens Studies Annual* 39 (2008): 281–304.
Grass, Sean. *Charles Dickens's* Our Mutual Friend*: A Publishing History*. Farnham; Burlington, VT: Ashgate, 2014.
    "Commodity and Identity in *Great Expectations*." *Victorian Literature and Culture* 40.2 (2012): 617–41.
    The Self in the Cell: Narrating the Victorian Prisoner. New York; London: Routledge, 2003.
    "Xenophobia to Xenophilia: Dickens's Continental Drift." *Dickens Studies Annual* 48 (2017): 1–19.
Grigsby, Ann. "Charles Reade's *Hard Cash*: Lunacy Reform through Sensationalism." *Dickens Studies Annual* 25 (1996): 141–58.
Grimble, Ian. *The Sea Wolf: The Life of Admiral Cochrane*. London: Blond and Briggs, 1978.
Gruner, Elisabeth Rose. "Family Secrets and the Mysteries of *The Moonstone*." *Victorian Literature and Culture* 21 (1993): 127–45.
Gurney, Peter. "'The Age of Veneer': Charles Dickens and the Antinomies of Victorian Consumer Culture." *Dickens Quarterly* 32.3 (2015): 229–46.
Habermas, Jürgen. *The Structural Transformation of the Public Sphere: An Inquiry into a Category of Bourgeois Society*. Trans. Thomas Burger with Frederick Lawrence. Cambridge, MA: MIT Press, 1989.
Hack, Daniel. *The Material Interests of the Victorian Novel*. Charlottesville; London: University of Virginia Press, 2005.
Haight, Gordon S. *George Eliot: A Biography*. Oxford: Oxford University Press, 1968.
Hammond, Mary. *Charles Dickens's* Great Expectations*: A Cultural Life, 1860–2012*. Farnham; Burlington: Ashgate, 2015.
"Harriette Wilson." *Literary Chronicle and Weekly Review* 6 (March 5, 1825): 155–6.
Hecimovich, Gregg A. "The Cup and the Lip and the Riddle of *Our Mutual Friend*." *ELH* 62.4 (1995): 955–77.
Heinrichs, Rachel. "Critical Masculinities in *Lady Audley's Secret*." *Victorian Review* 33.1 (2007): 103–20.

Heller, Tamar. *Dead Secrets: Wilkie Collins and the Female Gothic*. New Haven, CT; London: Yale University Press, 1992.

Hennelly, Mark M. "Detecting Collins' Diamond: From Serpentstone to Moonstone." *Nineteenth-Century Fiction* 39.1 (1984): 25–47.

Henry, Nancy. *The Life of George Eliot: A Critical Biography*. Malden, MA; Oxford: Wiley-Blackwell, 2012.

Higgs, Edward. *Making Sense of the Census: The Manuscript Returns for England and Wales, 1801–1901*. London: HMSO, 1989.

[Hollingshead, John.] "The City of Unlimited Paper." *Household Words* 17 (December 19, 1857): 1–4.

"Railway Nightmares." *Household Words* 18 (November 13, 1858): 505–8.

Houston, Gail Turley. "'Pip' and 'Property': The (Re)production of the Self in *Great Expectations*." *Studies in the Novel* 24.1 (1992): 13–25.

Howard, Greg. "Masculinity and Economics in *Lady Audley's Secret*." *VIJ: Victorians Institute Journal* 27 (1999): 33–53.

Hughes, Winifred. *The Maniac in the Cellar: Sensation Novels of the 1860s*. Princeton, NJ: Princeton University Press, 1980.

Hunt, Aeron. *Personal Business: Character and Commerce in Victorian Literature and Culture*. Charlottesville; London: University of Virginia Press, 2014.

Hutter, Albert D. "Dismemberment and Articulation in *Our Mutual Friend*." *Dickens Studies Annual* 11 (1983): 135–75.

——. "Dreams, Transformations, and Literature: The Implications of Detective Fiction." *Victorian Studies* 19.2 (December 1975): 181–209.

Iacono, Alfonso Maurizio. *The History and Theory of Fetishism*. Trans. Viktoria Tchernichova and Monica Boria, with Elizabeth MacDonald. Basingstoke: Palgrave, 2016.

Irigaray, Luce. *This Sex Which Is Not One*. Trans. Catherine Porter with Carolyn Burke. Ithaca, NY: Cornell University Press, 1985.

Jacobsen, Wendy S., ed. *Dickens and the Children of Empire*. Basingstoke: Palgrave, 2000.

Jameson, Fredric. *Signatures of the Visible*. 1992. New York; London: Routledge, 2007.

Jarvis, Claire. "Pip's Life." *ELH* 81.4 (2014): 1253–73.

Jevons, William Stanley. *Money and the Mechanism of Exchange*. 1875. New York: D. Appleton and Co., 1877.

The John Murray Archive. Manuscript and Archive Collection. National Library of Scotland, Edinburgh.

Johnson, Edgar. *Charles Dickens: His Tragedy and Triumph*. 2 vols. New York: Simon and Schuster, 1952.

[Jones, Martha.] "Art. VIII.—*Memoirs of Benvenuto Cellini, a Florentine Artist. By himself.*" *British Quarterly Review* 8 (1848): 492–7.

Jordan, John O. "Partings Welded Together: Self-fashioning in *Great Expectations* and *Jane Eyre*." *Dickens Quarterly* 13.1 (1996): 19–33.

Kaplan, Fred. *Dickens: A Biography*. New York: William Morrow, 1988.

Kent, Christopher A. "Victorian Self-making, or Self-unmaking? The Tichborne Claimant Revisited." *Victorian Review* 17.1 (1991): 18–34.
Klotz, Michael. "Manufacturing Fictional Individuals: Victorian Social Statistics, the Novel, and *Great Expectations*." *NOVEL: A Forum on Fiction* 46.2 (2013): 214–33.
Kornbluh, Anna. *Realizing Capital: Financial and Psychic Economies in Victorian Form*. New York: Fordham University Press, 2014.
Krueger, Christine L. *Reading for the Law: British Literary History and Gender Advocacy*. Charlottesville; London: University of Virginia Press, 2010.
"Lady Morgan's Memoirs: Autobiography, Diaries, and Correspondence." *Examiner* (January 17, 1863): 38–9.
Landau, Aaron. "*Great Expectations*, Romance, and Capital." *Dickens Studies Annual* 35 (2005): 157–77.
Landow, George P., ed. *Approaches to Victorian Autobiography*. Athens: Ohio University Press, 1979.
Lanning, Katie. "Tessellating Texts: Reading *The Moonstone* in *All the Year Round*." *Victorian Periodicals Review* 45.1 (2012): 1–22.
"The Late Lady Morgan and Her Autobiography." *Fraser's Magazine for Town and Country* 67 (February 1863): 172–91.
Laughton, J. K. "Cochrane, Thomas, Tenth Earl of Dundonald (1775–1860)." *Dictionary of National Biography*. Vol. 11. Ed. Leslie Stephen. London: Smith, Elder, 1887. 165–75.
The Layard Papers, Volume XLV. Manuscripts. British Library, London.
Ledger, Sally. "Dickens, Natural History, and *Our Mutual Friend*." *Partial Answers: Journal of Literature and the History of Ideas* 9.2 (2011): 363–78.
Lee, David. "The Victorian Studio: I." *British Journal of Photography* (February 7, 1986): 152–6, 165.
Levine, George. *Darwin and the Novelists: Patterns of Science in Victorian Fiction*. Cambridge, MA: Harvard University Press, 1988.
Levitan, Kathrin. *A Cultural History of the British Census: Envisioning the Multitude in the Nineteenth Century*. New York: Palgrave, 2011.
Linkman, Audrey. *The Victorians: Photographic Portraits*. London; New York: Tauris Parke, 1993.
Lister, Thomas. "First Annual Report of the Registrar-General of Births, Deaths, and Marriages in England." *Times* (September 6, 1839): 7.
[Lockhart, John Gibson.] "Art. VI. Autobiography." *Quarterly Review* 35 (January 1827): 148–65.
Loesberg, Jonathan. *Fictions of Consciousness: Mill, Newman, and the Reading of Victorian Prose*. New Brunswick, NJ; London: Rutgers University Press, 1986.
Logan, Peter. "Imitations of Insanity and Victorian Medical Aesthetics." *Romanticism and Victorianism on the Net* 49 (February 2008).
"London, Wednesday, April 23, 1834." *Times* (April 23, 1834): 4.
Long, J.J., Andrea Noble, and Edward Welch, eds. *Photography: Theoretical Snapshots*. London; New York: Routledge, 2008.

Lonoff, Sue. *Wilkie Collins and His Victorian Readers: A Study in the Rhetoric of Authorship*. New York: AMS Press, 1982.
"Loose Thoughts on Harriette Wilson." *London Magazine* 1 (April 1825): 626–31.
Lukács, Georg. *History and Class Consciousness: Studies in Marxist Dialectics*. Trans. Rodney Livingstone. Cambridge, MA: MIT Press, 1971.
MacGregor, Geddes. *The Tichborne Impostor*. Philadelphia; New York: J. B. Lippincott, 1957.
Machann, Clinton. *The Genre of Autobiography in Victorian Literature*. Ann Arbor: University of Michigan Press, 1994.
McKelvy, William R. "*The Woman in White* and Graphic Sex." *Victorian Literature and Culture* 35.1 (2007): 287–308.
McWilliam, Rohan. *The Tichborne Claimant: A Victorian Sensation*. London; New York: Hambledon Continuum, 2007.
Mallen, Richard D. "George Eliot and the Precious Mettle of Trust." *Victorian Studies* 44.1 (2001): 41–75.
Malton, Sara. *Forgery in Nineteenth-century Literature and Culture: Fictions of Finance from Dickens to Wilde*. New York: Palgrave, 2009.
Mannings, David. "Notes on Some Eighteenth-century Portrait Prices in Britain." *Journal for Eighteenth-Century Studies* 6.2 (1983): 185–96.
Marlow, James E. "English Cannibalism: Dickens after 1859." *Studies in English Literature* 23.4 (1983): 647–66.
Marx, Karl. *Capital*. 1867. Trans. Ben Fowkes. 3 vols. London; New York: Penguin, 1976.
Marx, Karl, and Friedrich Engels. *Karl Marx and Friedrich Engels: On Religion*. Intro. Reinhold Niebuhr. New York: Schocken, 1964.
Matus, Jill. "Disclosure as 'Cover-up': The Discourse of Madness in *Lady Audley's Secret*." *University of Toronto Quarterly* 62.3 (1993): 334–55.
Maunder, Andrew, and Grace Moore, eds. *Victorian Crime, Madness and Sensation*. Aldershot; Burlington: Ashgate, 2004.
Meckier, Jerome. "'Dashing in Now': *Great Expectations* and Charles Lever's *A Day's Ride*." *Dickens Studies Annual* 26 (1998): 227–64.
———. "Great Expectations: 'A Good Name?'." *Dickens Quarterly* 26.4 (2009): 248–58.
Mehta, Jaya. "English Romance: Indian Violence." *Centennial Review* 39.3 (1995): 611–57.
[Merivale, Herman.] "Art. II.—*Autobiography of Miss Cornelia Knight, Lady Companion to the Princess Charlotte of Wales*." *Quarterly Review* 111 (1862): 41–72.
———. "Art. VII.—*Autobiography, Letters, and Literary Remains of Mrs. Piozzi (Thrale)*." *Edinburgh Review* 113 (1861): 501–23.
Merriam, Harold G. *Edward Moxon: Publisher of Poets*. New York: Columbia University Press, 1939.
Metz, Nancy Aycock. "The Artistic Reclamation of Waste in *Our Mutual Friend*." *Nineteenth-Century Fiction* 34.1 (1979): 59–72.
Michie, Helena. *Sororophobia: Differences Among Women in Literature and Culture*. Oxford; New York: Oxford University Press, 1992.

Miller, Andrew H. "'A Case of Metaphysics': Counterfactuals, Realism, *Great Expectations*." *ELH* 79.3 (2012): 773–96.
   Novels Behind Glass: Commodity Culture and Victorian Narrative. Cambridge: Cambridge University Press, 1995.
Miller, D. A. *The Novel and the Police*. Berkeley: University of California Press, 1988.
Miller, J. Hillis. *Charles Dickens: The World of His Novels*. Cambridge, MA: Harvard University Press, 1958.
Moore, Doris Langley. *The Late Lord Byron: Posthumous Dramas*. Philadelphia; New York: J. B. Lippincott, 1961.
"Mr Jerdan's Autobiography." *Chambers's Edinburgh Journal* 17 (1852): 375–8.
"Mrs. Delany; Or, a Lady of Quality in the Last Century." *Fraser's Magazine for Town and Country* 65 (April 1862): 448–57.
"Mrs. Piozzi." *Fraser's Magazine for Town and Country* 63 (March 1861): 368–84.
Muir, Rory. *Wellington: The Path to Victory, 1769–1814*. New Haven, CT; London: Yale University Press, 2013.
Murfin, Ross. "The Art of Representation: Collins' *The Moonstone* and Dickens' Example." *ELH* 49.3 (1982): 653–72.
Neel, Alexandra. "'The Ghost of Slavery' in *Our Mutual Friend*." *Victorian Literature and Culture* 43.3 (2015): 511–32.
Neill, Anna. *Primitive Minds: Evolution and Spiritual Experience in the Victorian Novel*. Columbus: Ohio State University Press, 2013.
Nemesvari, Richard. "Robert Audley's Secret: Male Homosocial Desire in *Lady Audley's Secret*." *Studies in the Novel* 27.4 (1995): 515–28.
Nunokawa, Jeff. "The Miser's Two Bodies: *Silas Marner* and the Sexual Possibilities of the Commodity." *Victorian Studies* 36.3 (1993): 273–92.
O'Donnell, Patrick. "'A Speeches of Chaff': Ventriloquy and Expression in *Our Mutual Friend*." *Dickens Studies Annual* 19 (1990): 247–79.
Oliphant, Margaret. *The Autobiography of Margaret Oliphant*. 1899. Ed. Elisabeth Jay. Orchard Park, NY: Broadview, 2002.
Olney, James, ed. *Autobiography: Essays Theoretical and Critical*. Princeton, NJ: Princeton University Press, 1980.
"On Auto-Biography." *Edinburgh Magazine* 10 (June 1822): 742–5.
"The Origins of the Modern Civil Service: The 1850s." *CivilService.gov.uk*.
Page, Norman, ed. *Charles Dickens: Family History, Volume 1*. London: Routledge, 1999.
Patten, Robert. *Charles Dickens and "Boz": The Birth of the Industrial-Age Author*. Cambridge: Cambridge University Press, 2012.
   Charles Dickens and His Publishers. Oxford: Oxford University Press, 1978.
Pears, Iain. *The Discovery of Painting: The Growth of Interest in the Arts in England, 1680–1768*. New Haven, CT; London: Yale University Press, 1988.
Petch, Simon. "Robert Audley's Profession." *Studies in the Novel* 32.1 (2000): 1–13.
Peterson, Linda H. *Traditions of Victorian Women's Autobiography: The Poetics and Politics of Life Writing*. Charlottesville; London: University Press of Virginia, 1999.

Victorian Autobiography: The Tradition of Self-interpretation. New Haven, CT; London: Yale University Press, 1986.

Pettitt, Clare. "Monstrous Displacements: Anxieties of Exchange in *Great Expectations.*" *Dickens Studies Annual* 30 (2001): 243–62.

Phegley, Jennifer. *Educating the Proper Woman Reader: Victorian Family Literary Magazines and the Cultural Health of the Nation.* Columbus: Ohio State University Press, 2004.

Plotz, John. *"Portable Property": Victorian Culture on the Move.* Princeton, NJ: Princeton University Press, 2009.

Pointon, Marcia. *Hanging the Head: Portraiture and Social Formation in Eighteenth-Century England.* New Haven, CT; London: Yale University Press, 1993.

Pond, Kristen A. "Bearing Witness in *Silas Marner*: George Eliot's Experiment in Sympathy." *Victorian Literature and Culture* 41.4 (2013): 691–709.

Poovey, Mary. *Genres of the Credit Economy: Mediating Value in Eighteenth- and Nineteenth-Century Britain.* Chicago; London: University of Chicago Press, 2008.

— ed. *The Financial System in Nineteenth-Century Britain.* Oxford: Oxford University Press, 2003. 1–33.

Porter, Theodore M. *The Rise of Statistical Thinking, 1820–1900.* Princeton, NJ: Princeton University Press, 1986.

Pykett, Lyn. *The "Improper" Feminine: The Women's Sensation Novel and the New Woman Writing.* London; New York: Routledge, 1992.

Rainsford, Dominic. "Victorian Moral Philosophy and *Our Mutual Friend.*" *Dickens Quarterly* 27.4 (2010): 273–91.

Reade, Charles. *Hard Cash.* 1863. 3 vols. Paris: Grolier Society, n.d. [1912].

Reade, Charles L., and the Rev. Compton Reade. *Charles Reade: Dramatist, Novelist, Journalist. A Memoir Compiled Chiefly from His Literary Remains.* 2 vols. London: Chapman and Hall, 1887.

Reed, John R. *Victorian Will.* Athens: Ohio University Press, 1989.

"Report to the Council of the Statistical Society of London, from the Committee Appointed to Consider the Best Mode of Taking the Census of the United Kingdom in 1841." *Journal of the Royal Statistical Society* 3.1 (1840): 72–102.

Reynolds, Nicole. "Boudoir Stories: A Novel History of a Room and Its Occupants." *Literature Interpretation Theory* 15.2 (2004): 103–30.

Richard Bentley and Son—Papers, 1806–1915. Rare Book & Manuscript Library. University Library, University of Illinois at Urbana-Champaign.

Richards, Thomas. *The Commodity Culture of Victorian England: Advertising and Spectacle, 1851–1914.* Stanford, CA: Stanford University Press, 1990.

Rose, Mark. *Authors and Owners: The Invention of Copyright.* Cambridge, MA; London: Harvard University Press, 1993.

Rubery, Matthew. *The Novelty of Newspapers: Victorian Fiction After the Invention of the News.* Oxford: Oxford University Press, 2009.

Ruth, Jennifer. *Novel Professions: Interested Disinterest and the Making of the Professional in the Victorian Novel.* Columbus: Ohio State University Press, 2006.

St. Clair, William. *The Reading Nation in the Romantic Period.* Cambridge: Cambridge University Press, 2004.

Sanders, Andrew. "'Come Back and Be Alive': Living and Dying in *Our Mutual Friend.*" *Dickensian* 74.3 (1978): 131–43.

"Scandal of the Court of Napoleon." *London Magazine* 10 (March 1828): 410–18.

Schivelbusch, Wolfgang. *The Railway Journey: Trains and Travel in the 19th Century.* Trans. Anselm Hollo. New York: Urizen, 1979.

Schroeder, Natalie, and Ronald A. Schroeder. *From Sensation to Society: Representations of Marriage in the Fiction of Mary Elizabeth Braddon, 1862–1866.* Newark, DE: University of Delaware Press, 2006.

Schwarzbach, F. S. *Dickens and the City.* London: Athlone Press, 1979.

"Science." *British Quarterly Review* 32 (July 1860): 258–62.

Scoggin, Daniel. "A Speculative Resurrection: Death, Money, and the Vampiric Economy of *Our Mutual Friend.*" *Victorian Literature and Culture* 30.1 (2002): 99–125.

Shires, Linda M. *Perspectives: Modes of Viewing and Knowing in Nineteenth-Century England.* Columbus: Ohio State University Press, 2009.

Shuman, Cathy. *Pedagogical Economies: The Examination and the Victorian Literary Man.* Stanford, CA: Stanford University Press, 2000.

Simmons, Jack. *Southey.* London: Collins, 1945.

Simpson, David, ed. *Subject to History: Ideology, Class, Gender.* Ithaca, NY; London: Cornell University Press, 1991.

Slater, Michael. *Charles Dickens.* New Haven, CT; London: Yale University Press, 2009.

Smith, Grahame. *Dickens, Money, and Society.* Berkeley; Los Angeles: University of California Press, 1968.

Smith, Monika Rydygier. "The W/Hole Remains: Consumerist Politics in *Bleak House, Great Expectations,* and *Our Mutual Friend.*" *Victorian Review* 19.1 (1993): 1–21.

Smith, Murray. "Bilbo's Return and the Tichborne Affair." *Mallorn: The Journal of the Tolkien Society* 57 (2016): 23–5.

Smith, Nelson, and R. C. Terry, eds. *Wilkie Collins to the Forefront: Some Reassessments.* New York: AMS Press, 1995.

Smith, Sheila M. "Propaganda and Hard Facts in Charles Reade's Didactic Novels: A Study of *It Is Never Too Late to Mend* and *Hard Cash.*" *Renaissance and Modern Studies* 4 (1960): 135–49.

Solkin, David H. *Painting for Money: The Visual Arts and the Public Sphere in Eighteenth-Century England.* New Haven, CT; London: Yale University Press, 1993.

——— ed. *Art on the Line: The Royal Academy Exhibitions at Somerset House, 1780–1836.* New Haven, CT; London: Yale University Press, 2001.

Solomon, J. Fisher. "Realism, Rhetoric, and Reification: Or the Case of the Missing Detective in *Our Mutual Friend*." *Modern Philology* 86.1 (1988): 34–45.
Sonstroem, David. "The Breaks in *Silas Marner*." *JEGP: The Journal of English and Germanic Philology* 97.4 (1998): 545–67.
Speck, W.A. *Robert Southey: Entire Man of Letters*. New Haven, CT; London: Yale University Press, 2006.
Sroka, Kenneth M. "Dickens' Metafiction: Readers and Writers in *Oliver Twist, David Copperfield*, and *Our Mutual Friend*." *Dickens Studies Annual* 22 (1993): 35–66.
Stelzig, Eugene, ed. *Romantic Autobiography in England*. Farnham: Ashgate, 2009.
Stern, Rebecca. *Home Economics: Domestic Fraud in Victorian England*. Columbus: Ohio State University Press, 2008.
Stewart, Susan. "Genres of Work: The Folktale and *Silas Marner*." *New Literary History* 34.3 (2003): 513–33.
Stone, Harry. *The Night Side of Dickens: Cannibalism, Passion, Necessity*. Columbus: Ohio State University Press, 1994.
Storey, Gladys. *Dickens and Daughter*. London: Frederick Muller, 1939.
Stray, Chris. "The Last Eton Grammars." *Paradigm* 8 (July 1992).
Sutcliffe, Emerson Grant. "Charles Reade's Notebooks." *Studies in Philology* 27.1 (1930): 64–109.
Sutherland, John. "The British Book Trade and the Crash of 1826." *The Library* 9.2 (1987): 148–61.
  "Dickens, Reade and *Hard Cash*." *Dickensian* 81.1 (1985): 5–12.
  Victorian Fiction: Writers, Publishers, Readers. Basingstoke: Macmillan, 1995.
  Victorian Novelists and Publishers. Chicago: University of Chicago Press, 1976.
Talaraich-Vielmas, Laurence. *Moulding the Female Body in Victorian Fairy Tales and Sensation Novels*. Aldershot; Burlington: Ashgate, 2007.
Taylor, Jenny Bourne. *In the Secret Theatre of Home: Wilkie Collins, Sensation Narrative, and Nineteenth-century Psychology*. London; New York: Routledge, 1988.
  ed. *The Cambridge Companion to Wilkie Collins*. Cambridge: Cambridge University Press, 2006.
Thomas, Ronald R. "Minding the Body Politic: The Romance of Science and the Revision of History in Victorian Detective Fiction." *Victorian Literature and Culture* 19 (1991): 233–54.
Thomson, Fred C. "The Theme of Alienation in *Silas Marner*." *Nineteenth-Century Fiction* 20.1 (1965): 69–84.
"Thoughts on the Improvement of the System of Country Banking," *Edinburgh Review* 63 (July 1836): 419–41.
Todorov, Tzvetan. *The Poetics of Prose*. Trans. Richard Howard. Ithaca, NY: Cornell University Press, 1977.
Tomalin, Claire. *Charles Dickens: A Life*. New York: Penguin, 2011.
  The Invisible Woman: The Story of Nelly Ternan and Charles Dickens. London; New York: Penguin, 1991.

Treadwell, James. *Autobiographical Writing and British Literature, 1783–1834*. Oxford; New York: Oxford University Press, 2005.
Tromp, Marlene, Pamela K. Gilbert, and Aeron Haynie, eds. *Beyond Sensation: Mary Elizabeth Braddon in Context*. Albany, NY: SUNY Press, 2000.
Tross, Ruth. "Dickens and the Crime of Literacy." *Dickens Quarterly* 21.4 (2004): 235–45.
Vale, Brian. *The Audacious Admiral Cochrane: The True Life of a Naval Legend*. London: Conway Maritime Press, 2004.
Walsh, Susan. "'Arithmetic of Bedlam!': Markets and Manhood in Charles Reade's *Hard Cash*." *Nineteenth-Century Literature* 63.1 (2008): 1–40.
——— "Bodies of Capital: *Great Expectations* and the Climacteric Economy." *Victorian Studies* 37.1 (1993): 73–98.
Waters, Catherine. *Commodity Culture in Dickens's* Household Words: *The Social Life of Goods*. Aldershot; Burlington: Ashgate, 2008.
Webb, Sidney, and Beatrice Webb. *The History of Liquor Licensing in England Principally from 1700 to 1830*. London; New York; Bombay: Longmans, Green and Co., 1903.
Weedon, Alexis. *Victorian Publishing: The Economics of Book Production for a Mass Market, 1836–1916*. Aldershot: Ashgate, 2003.
Weiss, Barbara. *The Hell of the English: Bankruptcy and the Victorian Novel*. Lewisburg, PA: Bucknell University Press, 1986.
Welsh, Alexander. *George Eliot and Blackmail*. Cambridge, MA; London: Harvard University Press, 1985.
Westcott, Michael. *Autobiography of a Gossamer Spider*. London: Groombridge and Sons, 1857.
Wolff, Robert Lee. *Sensational Victorian: The Life and Fiction of Mary Elizabeth Braddon*. New York; London: Garland, 1979.
Woodmansee, Martha. *The Author, Art, and the Market: Rereading the History of Aesthetics*. New York: Columbia University Press, 1994.
Woodruff, Douglas. *The Tichborne Claimant: A Victorian Mystery*. New York: Farrar, Straus and Cudahy, 1957.
Worthington, Heather. *The Rise of the Detective in Early Nineteenth-century Popular Fiction*. Basingstoke: Palgrave, 2005.
Wynne, Deborah. *The Sensation Novel and the Victorian Family Magazine*. Basingstoke: Palgrave, 2001.
Yeazell, Ruth Bernard. "Podsnappery, Sexuality, and the English Novel." *Critical Inquiry* 9.2 (1982): 339–57.
Yousaf, Nahem, and Andrew Maunder, eds. The Mill on the Floss *and* Silas Marner. Basingstoke: Palgrave, 2002.
Zemka, Sue. "Chronometrics of Love and Money in *Great Expectations*." *Dickens Studies Annual* 35 (2005): 133–56.
Ziegler, Garrett. "The City of London, Real and Unreal." *Victorian Studies* 49.3 (2007): 431–55.

Index

Ackroyd, Peter, 79
Addison, Henry, 36
Alexander, Edward, 36
All the Year Round. See Dickens, Charles John Huffam
Alley, Henry, 134
Alton Locke, 19
Ames, Joseph, 46
Amigoni, David, 11, 224
Ancestry.com, 220
Andrews, William, 8
Angelo, Henry, 46
Anster, John, 69
Argentine, an Autobiography, 37
Arnold, Matthew, 213
Athenaeum, 64
Australasian, 214
autobiography, 4–8, 10–15, 17–80, 102–104, 149–150, 200–201, 206, 222–226
   confession, 23
   contemporary reviews of, 17–18, 57–70
   and copyright law, 42–45
   courtesan memoir, 59–60
   cultural anxiety regarding, 6–7, 14, 18–19, 57–70, 78–80
   diary, 23, 29, 149–150, 200–201, 206
      in *Hard Cash*, 149–150
      in *The Moonstone*, 200–201, 206
   domestic memoir, 23
   fictional, 14, 36–37, 73, 79–80, 102–104
      in *Great Expectations*, 14, 79–80, 102–104
   letters and correspondence, 23, 29, 35, 64
   as marketing device, 32–33, 44–45
   method for compiling data, 25, 222–226
   military memoir, 22–23
   by objects (it-narratives), 38–39
   and portraiture, 45–49
   proliferation at mid-century, 21–30
   religious, 6, 11–12, 18, 30, 36, 48, 58, 59, 150
   rise as a commercial genre, 4–7, 10–12, 13–14, 17–39
   and subjectivity, 7–8, 20–21, 37–39, 42–44, 57
   theories of, 10–11, 39
   travel narrative, 11, 22–23, 31, 33–36
   and the Victorian book market, 25–31
   and the Victorian novel, 12–15, 21, 57, 70–77
   and Victorian publishers, 31–37
Autobiography of William Walford, 63
Autobiography: A Collection of the Most Instructive and Amusing Lives Ever Published, Written by the Parties Themselves, 31
autograph, 45–46, *See also* signature
Aycock Metz, Nancy, 186

Babbage, Charles, 36
Bank Charter Act (1844), 40, 145
Bank of England, 38, 40, 145
Bankrupt Law Consolidation Act (1849), 54
Barbauld, Anna Letitia, 44
Baring Brothers, 88
Barnum, P.T. (Phineas Taylor), 30, 66
   Autobiography of P.T. Barnum, The, 30, 36, 65–66
Barrett Browning, Elizabeth
   Aurora Leigh, 19
   "Cry of the Children, The," 138
Barros, Carolyn, 224
Barrow, John, 33, 34
Batchen, Geoffrey, 49–50
Baudrillard, Jean, 187
Baumgarten, Murray, 101
Beer, Gillian, 129, 137, 138, 164
Benjamin, Walter, 72, 75
Bentley, Richard, 5, 28, 34–35, 86, *See also* Richard Bentley and Son
Bentley's Miscellany, 30, 34, 86
Berger, Courtney, 136
Bernard, John, 34
Bewick, Thomas, 36

271

Biographical Magazine, The, 46
Biographical Mirror, The, 46
Blackwood, John, 127, 129, 130, *See also* William Blackwood and Sons
Blake, Robert, General at Sea, 1
Blumberg, Ilana, 136, 139, 191, 192, 201
Bodenheimer, Rosemarie, 92
Bonar, Horatio, 150
Boswell, James, 18, 67–68
Bourne Taylor, Jenny, 195–197, 205
Bovill, William, Chief Justice, 217
Bradbury and Evans, 88
Braddon, Mary Elizabeth, 13, 14–15, 105–125, 127, 219
  Aurora Floyd, 108, 219
  Banker's Secret, The, 108
  Black Band, The, 108
  Circe, 108
  and John Maxwell, 108
  Lady Audley's Secret, 14–15, 21, 74, 77, 105–125, 129, 158, 181, 185, 193, 207, 215
    disruption of sexual desire in, 108–109, 113–114, 121, 123, 125
    Lady Audley as commodity in, 109–110, 111–113, 116, 119–120, 122–124
    multiplicity of identity in, 108–109, 111–112, 114, 117
    portraiture in, 105–108, 110–111
    temporal disjunction in, 111–114
    textualization of identity in, 14–15, 107–109, 110–112, 114–122, 124–125
    and professional authorship, 108
  Rupert Godwin, 108
  Three Times Dead, 108
  Trail of the Serpent, The, 108
Bragg, Tom, 157
Brantlinger, Patrick, 13, 71, 74
Brasbridge, Joseph, 22, 60
Brianti, Chiara, 124
British Cabinet, The, 46
British Institution for Promoting the Fine Arts, 47
British Library, 224, 225
British Quarterly Review, 38
Brontë, Anne, 23, 36
  Agnes Grey, 36
  Tenant of Wildfell Hall, The, 23
Brontë, Charlotte, 37
  Jane Eyre, 19, 73, 114, 120
  Professor, The, 37
  Shirley, 37
  Villette, 37
Brontë, Emily, 36
  Wuthering Heights, 36
Brooks, Peter, 93, 100–101

Broughton, Trev Lynn, 10, 11, 224
Brown, Ford Madox, 110
Browning, Robert, 123
Buckingham, James Silk, 36
Buckton, Oliver, 224
Bulwer-Lytton, Edward, first Baron Lytton, 89–90, 108
  A Strange Story, 89
Bunbury, Selina, 36
Bunyan, John, 59
Buonaparte, Napoleon, 1–2, 22, 33
Burdett Coutts, Angela, 89
Burney, Frances (Fanny, Madame d'Arblay), 67
Bushnan, J.S. (John Stevenson), 142
Byron, George Gordon, sixth Baron Byron, 31, 33, 34

Campbell, Thomas, 68
Cardwell, Margaret, 86
Carlyle, Thomas, 23, 28, 176
  On Heroes, Hero-worship, and the Heroic in History, 176
  Sartor Resartus, 23
Carpenter, William, 204
Carroll, Lewis (Charles Dodgson), 217
cartes-de-visite, 9, 49–50, 74
Cartwright, John, 22
Case, Alison, 71
Castro, Tom. *See* Orton, Arthur
Cathcart, William Schaw, first Earl Cathcart, 2
Cave, Terence, 128, 130, 132
census, 9, 14, 20, 39, 51–53, 55, 57, 98, 207, 220
  collection of data for, 51–52
  digitization of records, 220
  dishonest responses to, 52–53
  in *Great Expectations*, 98
  origins of, 51–52
  textualization of identity through, 52–53
Census Act (1800), 51
Chambers's Edinburgh Journal, 63
Chamier, Frederick, 36
Chapman and Hall, 28, 86, 161
Chapman, Edward, 161, *See also* Chapman and Hall
Cheadle, Brian, 184
Christian Remembrancer, 64, 67
civil service examination, 55–56, 179
Cobbett, William, 40
Cochrane, Thomas, tenth Earl of Dundonald, 1–5, 16, 63, 76
  Autobiography of a Seaman, 1–5, 35
  financial difficulties, 3–4

military career, 4
Narrative of Services in the Liberation of Chili, Peru, and Brazil from Spanish and Portuguese Domination, 4
Stock Exchange scandal, 2–4
Cockburn, Alexander James Edmund, twelfth Baronet Cockburn, 214, 216, 219
Cohen, Susan, 135
Colburn, Henry, 31, 34, 65
Colella, Silvana, 56, 129
Coleridge, Henry, 33
Collins, Wilkie (William Wilkie), 13, 14, 15, 20, 23, 35, 71–73, 74, 114, 127, 189–210
  Armadale, 74, 114, 191
  Basil, 35
  Moonstone, The, 15, 23, 74, 75, 77, 189–210, 215, 220
    commodification of the subject in, 189–190, 191, 193, 200–202, 206–210
    decision to publish in *All the Year Round,* 191–192
    disruption of sexual desire in, 196–197, 206–209
    first-person narration in, 190–193, 201–203, 206
    forensic inquiry in, 190, 192–195, 197–199, 201, 203–207
    Herncastle's will in, 194–195, 199, 200, 202, 207
    Jennings's experiment in, 190, 192, 193, 203–207, 208
    and material identity, 15, 189–190, 192–203, 204–205, 207–208
    multiplicity of identity in, 202–203
    and sacred identity, 15, 189–190, 192–197, 206–208
    textualization of identity in, 190–194, 197–205, 206–208
  No Name, 191
  Rambles Beyond Railways, 35
  Woman in White, The, 14, 35, 71–73, 74, 191
confession. *See* autobiography
Confessions of a Hypochondriac, 36
Confessions of a Too-Generous Young Woman, 36
Confessions of an Etonian, 36
Conolly, John, 142, 154
Constable and Co., 28
Constable, Thomas, 28, *See also* Constable and Co.
copyright law, 9, 12, 14, 39, 42–45, 57, 89, 207, 221
  and autobiography, 42–45
  Donaldson v. Becket, 42–43
  term of copyright, 43
  and textualization of identity, 44
Cordingly, David, 2, 4
Cornhill, 126
correspondence. *See* autobiography
courtesan memoir. *See* autobiography
Cowper, William, 44
Crabbe, George, 32–33, 44, 62
Crabbe, George, Jr., 32
Craddock, Joseph, 22
Crimean War, 1
Croker, John Wilson, 68
Cubitt, Arthur, 212
Cvetkovich, Ann, 109, 115

Daily News, 142
Dale, Richard, 2
Daly, Nicholas, 13, 76
Danahay, Martin, 10, 11, 39, 43
Daniel, John Edgecombe, 22
Darwin, Charles, 6, 19, 34, 164
  Journal of the Voyage of the H.M.S. Beagle, 34
  On the Origin of Species, 34, 164
David, Deirdre, 168, 174, 177
David, John, 224
de Brosses, Charles, 208
de Kock, Paul, 211
De Quincey, Thomas, 204
Defoe, Daniel, 18, 42
  Moll Flanders, 37
  Robinson Crusoe, 30, 37, 190, 191, 201, 208, 210
Delf, Thomas, 71
Denham, Dixon, 33
Descartes, René, 75
diary. *See* autobiography
Dibdin, Thomas, 58, 60–61
Dick, Alexander, 28
Dickens, Alfred Lamert, 79, 88
Dickens, Catherine (Hogarth), 87, 89
Dickens, Charles Culliford Boz, 88
Dickens, Charles John Huffam, 5, 13, 14, 15, 19, 20, 29, 34, 37, 42, 56, 74, 78–104, 127, 141–142, 154, 161–188, 190, 216
  All the Year Round, 14, 37, 80, 86–92, 127, 141, 142, 147–149, 161, 163, 191
  Barnaby Rudge, 86
  Bleak House, 110, 113, 169, 173
  Christmas Carol, A, 79, 88
  David Copperfield, 19, 37, 73, 79, 80, 92, 104, 154
  financial worries, 79–80, 87–92
  Gad's Hill Place, 87, 88, 90, 163

Dickens, Charles John Huffam (cont.)
  Great Expectations, 14, 21, 48, 61, 73–74, 77,
      78–104, 106, 107, 108, 115, 124, 129, 131,
      139, 143, 158, 161–163, 169, 173, 175, 176,
      177, 178, 181, 183, 187, 192, 206, 207,
      209–210, 218, 219
    as capitalist critique, 80–85
    as critique of autobiographical form, 14,
      79–80, 102–104
    cannibalism in, 82, 84–85
    commodification of the subject in, 73–74,
      78, 83–84, 101–102
    plans for publication, 85–91
    textualization of identity in, 21, 74, 93–104
    violence in, 80–85
  Hard Times, 169
  Haunted Man, The, 92
  Household Words, 54, 88, 89, 143
  Little Dorrit, 5, 42, 86, 110
  Marshalsea Prison, 87
  Martin Chuzzlewit, 88
  Master Humphrey's Clock, 86
  Nicholas Nickleby, 86, 89
  Old Curiosity Shop, The, 86
  Oliver Twist, 34, 86
  Our Mutual Friend, 15, 21, 73–74, 76–77, 78,
      161–188, 191, 193, 194, 207, 208, 216, 219
    commodification of the subject in, 161–164,
      168–173, 175–176, 178–184, 186–188
    contract negotiations with Chapman and
      Hall for, 161
    disruption of sexual desire in, 164, 166–168,
      174, 177–178, 180–182, 185
    Dust mounds in, 162, 164, 173, 174, 175, 180
    Harmon's will in, 74, 164, 166–170, 172–175,
      180, 184
    monthly wrapper, 166–168
    multiplicity of identity in, 164, 172, 180–184
    natural law in, 165–168
    naturalization of commodification in, 15,
      161–168, 173–174, 180, 188
    temporal disjunction in, 164, 181–185
    textualization of identity in, 162, 164, 168,
      173–178, 180, 182–183
  "Personal," 89–90
  Pickwick Papers, The, 5, 28, 83, 86, 124, 188
  public readings, 88–89
  relationship with Ellen Ternan, 79, 87, 89
  separation from Catherine, 87, 89
  Tale of Two Cities, A, 78, 86, 91, 166, 168, 169
  Tavistock House, 87
  "Travelling Abroad," 162–163, 187
  Uncommercial Traveller, The, 89, 162
  Warren's Blacking, 87
  Wreck of the Golden Mary, The, 84

Dickens, Henry Fielding, 87
Dickens, Walter Landor, 88
Dictionary of National Biography, 1
Disdéri, André Adolphe-Eugéne, 49–50
Dixon, Hepworth, 64–65
domestic memoir. *See* autobiography
Donaldson v. Becket, 42–44
Donaldson, Alexander, 42, *See also* Donaldson
    v. Becket
Donaldson, Joseph, 22
Doughty, Katherine (Kattie), 211
Dublin University Magazine, 63, 64, 67
Dumas, Alexandre, 63
Duncan, Ian, 190
Duodecimo: or, the Scribbler's Progress, 38
Dutheil, Martine Hennard, 93, 94, 103

Earp, George Butler, 1, 4–5
Eastlake, Elizabeth (Rigby), 34
Eclectic Review, 62, 63
economic crash of 1826, 28
Edinburgh Magazine, 58
Edinburgh Monthly Review, 64
Edinburgh Review, 41, 64, 68
Eliot, George (Mary Ann Evans), 13, 15, 20, 70,
    126–140
  Adam Bede, 127
  Middlemarch, 70, 127
  Mill on the Floss, The, 127, 128
  Romola, 126–127
  Silas Marner, 15, 21, 73–74, 75,
      77, 126–140, 157–160, 192–193,
      207, 219
    commodification of the subject in, 77,
      130–132, 135–137, 158–160
    disruption of sexual desire in, 130–132,
      158–159
    Eppie as commodity in, 134–137
    financial loss as psychological loss in, 15,
      130–132, 134–135, 137–138
    multiplicity of identity in, 74
    naturalization of capitalism in, 139–140,
      158–160
    relation to capitalism, 130–133, 135–140
    temporal disjunction in, 132, 134–135,
      137–138
    textualization of identity in, 131–133, 158–160
    writing of, 127–130
Eliot, Simon, 12, 25, 222
Eliot, T.S. (Thomas Stearns), 190
Elliotson, John, 204
Englishman, 217
European Magazine, 68
Evans, David Morier, 56
Examiner, 65, 68

Index

Fantina, Richard, 141
Farrell, John, 181
Farrer, William, 161
Felber, Lynette, 106
Ferguson, Frances, 181
Fergusson, Robert, 44
fictional autobiography. *See* autobiography
finance capitalism, 7, 9, 12, 14, 15–16, 38, 39–42, 56–57, 70–71, 119, 129, 145, 146, 168, 178, 200, 219, 221
    paper currency under, 39–40
    textual basis of, 39–42, 56–57, 70–71
    textualization of identity under, 41–42
Fleishman, Avrom, 7
Fletcher, E.P., 128, 141–142, 152
Forbes, William, 38
Forester, C.S. (Cecil Louis Troughton Smith), 1
Forster, John, 87, 88, 91, 92, 142, 161
Fortune, Robert, 34
Franklin, John, 84–85
Fraser's Magazine for Town and Country, 65, 66, 67, 68
Free, Melissa, 190
Fun, 217

Gagnier, Regenia, 10, 224
Gallagher, Catherine, 166
Galt, John, 62
Gambier, James, first Baron Gambier, 1
Gardiner, Marguerite, Countess of Blessington, 35
    Marmaduke Herbert, 35
    Memoirs of a Femme de Chambre, 35
General Register Office, 50–53
    census-taking, 51–53
    civil registry, 50–51
    creation of, 51
Gentleman's Magazine, 68
George Bell and Sons, 28
George Routledge and Co., 28, 35, 225
Gibbes, William, 212, 214
Gibbon, Edward, 18
Gibson, Anna, 162
Gilbert, Elliot, 92, 103
Gilbert, Pamela, 13, 107–108, 115, 123
Gladstone, William Ewart, 19
Goodman, Margaret, 150
Goyder, David George, 30
Granger, James, 46
grangerization. *See* Granger, James
Granville Delany, Mary, 76, 172
    Autobiography and Correspondence of Mary Granville Delany, 35, 64–67
Great Exhibition of 1851, 29, 38

Grigsby, Ann, 141, 157
Grimble, Ian, 5
Guizot, Francois, 35
Gurney, Peter, 163

Habermas, Jürgen, 221
Hack, Daniel, 176
Haggart, David ("the Switcher"), 23
Hale, James, 22, 36
Harper's Weekly, 91
Harris, James, first Earl of Malmesbury, 35
Hawke, Edward, first Baron Hawke, 1
Haydon, Benjamin Robert, 36
Haynie, Aeron, 124
Hayward, Abraham, 67–68
Hecimovich, Gregg, 175
Heinrichs, Rachel, 119, 123
Heller, Tamar, 209
Henrietta Marie, Queen Consort of England, Scotland, and Ireland, 35
Henry, Nancy, 129
Herschel, William James, second Baronet Herschel, 199
Hewitt, Martin, 23
Hollingshead, John, 54–57, 143
    "City of Unlimited Paper, The," 56–57, 143
    "Railway Nightmares," 54–55
Hook, Theodore, 30
Horace (Quintus Horatius Flaccus), 57, 60, 63
Horrid Confession of John Kean, 19
Household Words. See Dickens, Charles John Huffam
Howard, George William Frederick, seventh Earl of Carlisle, 86
Howard, Greg, 113, 125
Hudson, George ("The Railway King"), 42
Hudson, Thomas, 48
Hughes, Winifred, 13, 73, 75
Hunt and Clarke, 28, 31
Hunt, Aeron, 13, 41
Hunt, Leigh, 19, 63
    Autobiography of Leigh Hunt, 69
Hurst and Blackett, 35
Hurst and Robinson, 28
Hutter, Albert, 171, 198

identity. *See* subjectivity
Illustrated London News, 214
In Memoriam, A.H.H., 19
Inchbald, Elizabeth, 44, 62
Indian Rebellion (1857), 190, 199

J.M. Dent and Sons, 225
Jackson, William, 4
Jameson, Frederic, 48

Index

Jerdan, William, 63
Jervis, John, first Earl of Vincent, 3
Jevons, William, 40
Jewsbury, Geraldine, 65
John Murray (publisher), 28, 30, 31–34, 225,
    See also Murray II, John
  Colonial and Home Library, 33, 225
  Family Library, 33, 225
Johnson, Samuel, 12, 65, 67
Joint Stock Companies Act (1856), 40
Journal of James Hale, 36

Kemble, Frances Anne (Fanny), 31–32
Kenealy, Edward, 213, 217
Kent, Christopher, 53
Keppel, George Thomas, 34
Klotz, Michael, 98
Knapp, John, 31–32
Knight, Cornelia, 65–66
Kornbluh, Anna, 13, 41, 70, 73
Krueger, Christine, 54, 143

Landau, Aaron, 81
Landow, George, 10, 23, 224
Lanning, Katie, 191
Leaper Newton, Adelaide, 150
Ledger, Sally, 164
Leigh, W.G., 36
Lemon, Mark, 89
letters. *See* autobiography
Letters and Works of Lady Mary Wortley Montagu, The, 35
Letters of Lord Chesterfield, 35
Lever, Charles, 36, 88, 90–91
  Confessions of Con Cregan, 36
  Day's Ride, A, 90–91
Levine, George, 164
Levitan, Kathrin, 52, 53
Lewes, George Henry, 126
Life and Times of Frederick Reynolds, 60
Life of an Architect, 30
life writing. *See* autobiography
Life-book of a Labourer, The, 37
Lind, Jenny, 66
Lister, Thomas, 51–52
Literary Chronicle, 59
Lockhart, John Gibson, 17–18, 20, 22–23, 31, 32, 57, 58, 60
Loesberg, Jonathan, 10
Logan, Peter, 141
London Magazine, 58, 59, 60, 61
London Statistical Society, 52
Longman, 28, 36, 44
Lonoff, Sue, 201
Lukács, Georg, 57, 75

Lupton, Mary Ann, 36
Lyell, Charles, 34

Macauley, Thomas, 67
Machann, Clinton, 43, 224
Malton, Sara, 42
Mannings, David, 48
Marcus, Laura, 224
Marryat, Frederick, 36
Martineau, Harriet, 6, 19
Marx, Karl, 6, 16, 41, 74–75, 81–82, 103, 123, 131, 180, 208, 218
Matrimonial Causes Act (1857), 54
Matthews, William, 224
Maxwell, John, 108
Mayall, David, 224
Mayhew, Henry, 53
McWilliam, Rohan, 213, 215, 216
Mehta, Jaya, 196, 206
Melbourne Argus, 214
Memoir of the Rev. Henry Martyn, 19
Memoirs of Benvenuto Cellini, 63
Memoirs of George Selwyn and His Contemporaries, 35
Memoirs of the Life and Religious Experience of William Lewis, 22
Merryweather, F. Somner, 174
Michie, Helena, 108
military memoir. *See* autobiography
Mill, John Stuart, 6, 19
Millais, John Everett, 110
Miller, Andrew, 76, 96, 163, 180, 186
Miller, D.A., 190, 200, 203
Miller, J. Hillis, 162, 188
Milton, John, 42
Missing Friends Agency (Sydney), 212
Mitford, Mary, 63
Moffat, James, 22
Monthly Review, 62
Morgan, Sydney (Owenson), 31, 64–65, 68, 172
  France, 31
  O'Donnel, 31
  Passages from My Autobiography, 64–65, 68
Morning Advertiser, 157
Moxon, Edward, 45
Mudie, Charles, 5, 67, *See also* Mudie's Lending Library
Mudie's Lending Library, 29, 73, 172, *See also* Mudie, Charles
Murray II, John, 31–33, 44
Murray, Lindley, 22

Napoleonic Wars, 1–2, 22, 127, 130
Narrative of the Life and Travels of Serjeant B—, 19

Index

National Library of Scotland, 225
National Portrait Gallery, 46, 47
Nelson, Horatio, first Viscount Nelson, 1, 33
Nemesvari, Richard, 118
Newby, Thomas Cautley, 36, *See also* Thomas Cautley Newby (publisher)
Newman, John Henry, 19, 29
Newton, Isaac, 33
Nicol, John, 22
Nineteenth-century Short Title Catalog, 22, 23–25, 29–30, 37, 222–224
Northcote-Trevelyan Report, 55
Nunokawa, Jeff, 132

O'Brian, Patrick, 1
O'Donnell, Patrick, 177
O'Halloran, Sylvester, 68
Oliphant, Margaret, 19, 36, 37, 69
  Autobiography of Margaret Oliphant, The, 69
  Days of My Life: An Autobiography, The, 36
  Margaret Maitland, 19, 37
Oliver and Boyd, 28
Olney, James, 18, 224
Once a Week, 126
Orton, Arthur, 15–16, 212–220
  and *Aurora Floyd*, 219
  body as text, 215
  civil suit to claim Tichborne estates, 212, 214–216, 217
  criminal prosecution, 212–213, 217
  death, 217
  early life, and life in Australia, 212, 219
  imposture as Sir Roger Tichborne, 212–214
  as popular sensation, 213, 215–217
  speaking tours, 216–217
  and Tichborne Bonds, 16, 216, 218

Peled Ginsburg, Michael, 165, 181
Pepys, Samuel, 18
Petch, Simon, 115, 172–173
Peter I, Tsar of Russia (Peter the Great), 33
Peterson, Linda, 8, 10, 23, 39, 224
Pettitt, Clare, 79, 84
photography, 14, 20, 49–50, 57, 64, 69, *See also* cartes-de-visite
Pickersgill, Henry, 45
Piozzi, Gabriel, 67
Piozzi, Hester Lynch, 36, 64–68, 172
  Autobiography, Letters, and Literary Remains of Mrs. Piozzi, 64–68
Plotz, John, 78
Pointon, Marcia, 45, 47, 110
Poole, Adrian, 186
Poovey, Mary, 12, 39–40
Pope, Alexander, 42

portraiture, 14, 20, 45–50, 57, 105–108, 110–111, 129, 158
  and books, 45–46
  and coins, 45–46
  and commodity culture, 48–49, 106–107, 110
  in *Lady Audley's Secret*, 105–108, 110–111
  and photography, 49–50
  and subjectivity, 47–48
Punch, 217
Pykett, Lyn, 115

Quarterly Review, 17–18, 22, 29–30, 31, 33, 66

Railway Bubble, 140, 143, 145
Rainsford, Dominic, 187
Ramsey, Allan, 48
Rare Book and Special Collections Library, University of Illinois at Urbana-Champaign, 225
Reade, Charles, 13, 15, 126–129, 140–160, 207
  Cloister and the Hearth, The, 126, 140
  Good Fight, A, 126
  "great system" for writing, 128, 140
  Hard Cash, 15, 75, 126–129, 140–160, 207, 219
    and autobiographical form, 150
    commodification of the subject in, 129, 141, 143–144, 149–150, 153–156, 157–160
    critique of Victorian lunacy law in, 128, 152–154
    disruption of sexual desire in, 154–156, 159
    financial loss as psychological loss in, 15, 128–129, 150–152, 157–160
    public controversy provoked by, 141–142
    textualization of identity in, 128–129, 141, 142–144, 149–150, 152–154, 157–159
  involvement with Fletcher case, 128, 141–142
  opinion of George Eliot, 126
Reed, John, 174
Reform Act (1832), 28
Reform Act (1867), 213
Reilly, Jim, 139
religious autobiography. *See* autobiography
Religious Tract Society, 201
Restriction Act (1797), 40, 130
Reynolds, Frederick, 22, 61
Reynolds, Joshua, 47, 48
Reynolds, Nicole, 123
Richard Bentley and Son, 5, 34–35, 37, 76, 225, *See also* Bentley, Richard
Richards, Thomas, 6, 12, 77
Richardson, Samuel, 18
Riddell, Charlotte, 56
Ridgway, James, 5
Rodney, George Brydges, first Baron Rodney, 1

Index

Rose, Mark, 41, 42, 43
Rosenberg, Edgar, 88
Rossetti, Dante (Gabriel Charles Dante), 110
Roswell, Edward, 38
Rousseau, Jean-Jacques, 18, 58, 76
Rowe, Eliza, 36
Royal Academy of Arts, 46–49
Rubery, Matthew, 112, 114
Rundell, Maria, 34
Ruskin, John, 19, 110
Russell, William, 71
Ruth, Jennifer, 55
Rydygier Smith, Monika, 173

Sanders, Andrew, 188
Saunders and Otley, 36
Savonarola, Girolamo, 126
Schroeder, Natalie, 120
Schroeder, Ronald, 120
Scoggin, Daniel, 173, 185
Scott and Ballantyne, 28
Scott, Walter, first Baronet, 28, 44, 62
Sennett, Richard, 12
sensation fiction, 5, 7, 13–15, 21, 70–77, 119, 144, 159–160, 193, 213, 219
  origins of, 13, 70–72
  relation to autobiography, 13–15, 21, 70–77
  representation of the commodified subject in, 21, 74–77
Seymour, Laura, 126, 141
Shakespeare, William, 42
Shaw, Harry, 71
Shee, Martin Archer, 47
Shires, Linda, 131
Shumaker, Wayne, 224
Shuman, Cathy, 179
Sicher, Efraim, 138
signature, 41–42, 46, 70, 75, 107, 112, 148, 173, 200, 207, *See also* autograph
  in financial transactions, 41–42
  in *Hard Cash*, 148
  in *Lady Audley's Secret*, 107, 112
  as marker of identity, 42, 46
Simpkin, Marshall and Co., 30, 35, 36
Slater, Michael, 92
slavery. *See* United States
Smith, Andrew, 36
Smith, Charles John, 46
Smith, Elder and Co., 28, 36–37, 191, 225, *See also* Smith, George
Smith, George, 127, 191
Smith, Grahame, 85
Smith, Sheila, 141
Smith, Sidonie, 10, 224
Smith, W.H. (William Henry), 29

Smollett, Tobias, 18
Society of Antiquaries, 46
Solkin, David, 47
Sonstroem, David, 129
Southey, Robert, 19, 44, 62
St. Clair, Richard, 12
Stanhope, Philip Dormer, fourth Earl of Chesterfield, 35
Stationers' Company, 42
Stelzig, Eugene, 10, 20, 224
Stern, Rebecca, 215, 218
Sterne, Laurence, 18
  Tristram Shandy, 37
Stock Exchange, 2, 4, 5, 16, 38
subjectivity, 7–9, 12–16, 20–21, 37–39, 42–57, 59–60, 65–77, 218–221
  relation to autobiography, 7–8, 20–21, 37–39, 42–44
  relation to identity, 7
  representation in the Victorian novel, 12–13, 21, 70–77
  as textual commodity, 14–16, 39, 43–57, 59–60, 65–70, 219–221
Sutherland, John, 12, 28, 29, 34, 37, 142, 154, 190
Swift, Jonathan, 42

Talaraich-Vielmas, Laurence, 106, 111
Ternan, Ellen Lawless, 79, 87, 89
Thackeray, William Makepeace, 20, 37, 89, 127, 161
  Denis Duval, 161
  Henry Esmond, 37
Thomas Cautley Newby (publisher), 35, 37, *See also* Newby, Thomas Cautley
Thomas, Ronald, 190, 198, 199, 204–205
Thrale, Henry, 67
Three Square Market, 220
Thumb, Tom (Charles Sherwood Stratton), 66, 215
Tichborne Claimant. *See* Orton, Arthur
Tichborne Gazette, 216
Tichborne News and Anti-Oppression Journal, 216
Tichborne Times, 217
Tichborne, Alfred (Henry Alfred), eleventh Baronet Tichborne, 212
Tichborne, Henriette Felicité, Dowager, 211–214, 216, 217, 218
Tichborne, Henry, eighth Baronet Tichborne, 211
Tichborne, James, tenth Baronet Tichborne, 211
Tichborne, Roger Charles Doughty, 16, 211–215, 216, 217, 218
  falls in love with cousin, 211
  physical traits, 213–214, 215

travels in South America, 211
Tichborne-Doughty, Edward, ninth Baronet Tichborne, 211
Todorov, Tzvetan, 202
Tokmakoff Castillo, Larisa, 182
Tolkien, J.R.R. (John Ronald Reuel), 213
travel narrative. *See* autobiography
Treadwell, James, 8, 11, 31, 61, 69, 224
Trollope, Anthony, 6, 19, 20, 35, 37, 42, 59, 70, 127
  Autobiography, An, 59
  Three Clerks, The, 70
  Way We Live Now, The, 6, 42, 70
Trollope, Frances, 36

United States, 8–9, 29, 66, 91, 217
  Civil War, 29
  slavery in, 8–9

Victoria, Queen of England, 50
Vincent, David, 224

Wagga Wagga, 212, 215, 219
Wagga Wagga Mechanics' Institute, 214
Walpole, Horace, 35
Walsh, Susan, 143, 144, 145, 154
Walter Royal Davis Library, 225
Ward and Lock, 30, 35, 36
Warner, Frederick, 68

Weedon, Alexis, 12
Weiss, Barbara, 128
Wellesley, Arthur, first Duke of Wellington, 1, 29
Westby, Todd, 220
Westcott, Michael, 38
Westminster Review, 64, 66
Wetzel, Grace, 118
Whyte-Melville, George, 36
William Blackwood and Sons, 28, 127, *See also* Blackwood, John
Wills, W.H. (William Henry), 127, 141, 191
Wilson, Harriette, 59–60
Winslow, Forbes, 141
Wood, Ellen (Mrs. Henry), 35
  Channings, The, 35
  East Lynne, 35
Woodruff, Douglas, 213
Wordsworth, William, 44–45
  additive publication, 44–45
  Excursion, The, 45
  Prelude, The, 19, 45
  Recluse, The, 45
Wynne, Deborah, 141

Yeazell, Ruth Bernard, 185

Zemka, Sue, 79, 101
Ziegler, Garrett, 56

CAMBRIDGE STUDIES IN NINETEENTH-CENTURY
LITERATURE AND CULTURE

GENERAL EDITOR: Gillian Beer, *University of Cambridge*

Titles published

1. *The Sickroom in Victorian Fiction: The Art of Being Ill*
   MIRIAM BAILIN, *Washington University*
2. *Muscular Christianity: Embodying the Victorian Age*
   edited by DONALD E. HALL, *California State University, Northridge*
3. *Victorian Masculinities: Manhood and Masculine Poetics in Early Victorian Literature and Art*
   HERBERT SUSSMAN, *Northeastern University, Boston*
4. *Byron and the Victorians*
   ANDREW ELFENBEIN, *University of Minnesota*
5. *Literature in the Marketplace: Nineteenth-Century British Publishing and the Circulation of Books*
   edited by JOHN O. JORDAN, *University of California, Santa Cruz*
   and ROBERT L. PATTEN, *Rice University, Houston*
6. *Victorian Photography, Painting and Poetry*
   LINDSAY SMITH, *University of Sussex*
7. *Charlotte Brontë and Victorian Psychology*
   SALLY SHUTTLEWORTH, *University of Sheffield*
8. *The Gothic Body: Sexuality, Materialism and Degeneration at the Fin de Siècle*
   KELLY HURLEY, *University of Colorado at Boulder*
9. *Rereading Walter Pater*
   WILLIAM F. SHUTER, *Eastern Michigan University*
10. *Remaking Queen Victoria*
    edited by MARGARET HOMANS, *Yale University* and
    ADRIENNE MUNICH, *State University of New York, Stony Brook*
11. *Disease, Desire, and the Body in Victorian Women's Popular Novels*
    PAMELA K. GILBERT, *University of Florida*
12. *Realism, Representation, and the Arts in Nineteenth-Century Literature*
    ALISON BYERLY, *Middlebury College, Vermont*
13. *Literary Culture and the Pacific*
    VANESSA SMITH, *University of Sydney*
14. *Professional Domesticity in the Victorian Novel: Women, Work and Home*
    MONICA F. COHEN
15. *Victorian Renovations of the Novel: Narrative Annexes and the Boundaries of Representation*
    SUZANNE KEEN, *Washington and Lee University, Virginia*
16. *Actresses on the Victorian Stage: Feminine Performance and the Galatea Myth*
    GAIL MARSHALL, *University of Leeds*

17. *Death and the Mother from Dickens to Freud: Victorian Fiction and the Anxiety of Origin*
    CAROLYN DEVER, *Vanderbilt University, Tennessee*
18. *Ancestry and Narrative in Nineteenth-Century British Literature: Blood Relations from Edgeworth to Hardy*
    SOPHIE GILMARTIN, *Royal Holloway, University of London*
19. *Dickens, Novel Reading, and the Victorian Popular Theatre*
    DEBORAH VLOCK
20. *After Dickens: Reading, Adaptation and Performance*
    JOHN GLAVIN, *Georgetown University, Washington DC*
21. *Victorian Women Writers and the Woman Question*
    edited by NICOLA DIANE THOMPSON, *Kingston University, London*
22. *Rhythm and Will in Victorian Poetry*
    MATTHEW CAMPBELL, *University of Sheffield*
23. *Gender, Race, and the Writing of Empire: Public Discourse and the Boer War*
    PAULA M. KREBS, *Wheaton College, Massachusetts*
24. *Ruskin's God*
    MICHAEL WHEELER, *University of Southampton*
25. *Dickens and the Daughter of the House*
    HILARY M. SCHOR, *University of Southern California*
26. *Detective Fiction and the Rise of Forensic Science*
    RONALD R. THOMAS, *Trinity College, Hartford, Connecticut*
27. *Testimony and Advocacy in Victorian Law, Literature, and Theology*
    JAN-MELISSA SCHRAMM, *Trinity Hall, Cambridge*
28. *Victorian Writing about Risk: Imagining a Safe England in a Dangerous World*
    ELAINE FREEDGOOD, *University of Pennsylvania*
29. *Physiognomy and the Meaning of Expression in Nineteenth-Century Culture*
    LUCY HARTLEY, *University of Southampton*
30. *The Victorian Parlour: A Cultural Study*
    THAD LOGAN, *Rice University, Houston*
31. *Aestheticism and Sexual Parody 1840–1940*
    DENNIS DENISOFF, *Ryerson University, Toronto*
32. *Literature, Technology and Magical Thinking, 1880–1920*
    PAMELA THURSCHWELL, *University College London*
33. *Fairies in Nineteenth-Century Art and Literature*
    NICOLA BOWN, *Birkbeck, University of London*
34. *George Eliot and the British Empire*
    NANCY HENRY, *The State University of New York, Binghamton*
35. *Women's Poetry and Religion in Victorian England: Jewish Identity and Christian Culture*
    CYNTHIA SCHEINBERG, *Mills College, California*
36. *Victorian Literature and the Anorexic Body*
    ANNA KRUGOVOY SILVER, *Mercer University, Georgia*
37. *Eavesdropping in the Novel from Austen to Proust*
    ANN GAYLIN, *Yale University*

38. *Missionary Writing and Empire, 1800–1860*
    ANNA JOHNSTON, *University of Tasmania*
39. *London and the Culture of Homosexuality, 1885–1914*
    MATT COOK, *Keele University*
40. *Fiction, Famine, and the Rise of Economics in Victorian Britain and Ireland*
    GORDON BIGELOW, *Rhodes College, Tennessee*
41. *Gender and the Victorian Periodical*
    HILARY FRASER, *Birkbeck, University of London*
    JUDITH JOHNSTON and STEPHANIE GREEN, *University of Western Australia*
42. *The Victorian Supernatural*
    edited by NICOLA BOWN, *Birkbeck College, London*
    CAROLYN BURDETT, *London Metropolitan University* and
    PAMELA THURSCHWELL, *University College London*
43. *The Indian Mutiny and the British Imagination*
    GAUTAM CHAKRAVARTY, *University of Delhi*
44. *The Revolution in Popular Literature: Print, Politics and the People*
    IAN HAYWOOD, *Roehampton University of Surrey*
45. *Science in the Nineteenth-Century Periodical: Reading the Magazine of Nature*
    GEOFFREY CANTOR, *University of Leeds*
    GOWAN DAWSON, *University of Leicester*
    GRAEME GOODAY, *University of Leeds*
    RICHARD NOAKES, *University of Cambridge*
    SALLY SHUTTLEWORTH, *University of Sheffield* and
    JONATHAN R. TOPHAM, *University of Leeds*
46. *Literature and Medicine in Nineteenth-Century Britain from Mary Shelley to George Eliot*
    JANIS MCLARREN CALDWELL, *Wake Forest University*
47. *The Child Writer from Austen to Woolf*
    edited by CHRISTINE ALEXANDER, *University of New South Wales* and
    JULIET MCMASTER, *University of Alberta*
48. *From Dickens to Dracula: Gothic, Economics, and Victorian Fiction*
    GAIL TURLEY HOUSTON, *University of New Mexico*
49. *Voice and the Victorian Storyteller*
    IVAN KREILKAMP, *University of Indiana*
50. *Charles Darwin and Victorian Visual Culture*
    JONATHAN SMITH, *University of Michigan-Dearborn*
51. *Catholicism, Sexual Deviance, and Victorian Gothic Culture*
    PATRICK R. O'MALLEY, *Georgetown University*
52. *Epic and Empire in Nineteenth-Century Britain*
    SIMON DENTITH, *University of Gloucestershire*
53. *Victorian Honeymoons: Journeys to the Conjugal*
    HELENA MICHIE, *Rice University*
54. *The Jewess in Nineteenth-Century British Literary Culture*
    NADIA VALMAN, *University of Southampton*

55. *Ireland, India and Nationalism in Nineteenth-Century Literature*
    JULIA WRIGHT, *Dalhousie University*
56. *Dickens and the Popular Radical Imagination*
    SALLY LEDGER, *Birkbeck, University of London*
57. *Darwin, Literature and Victorian Respectability*
    GOWAN DAWSON, *University of Leicester*
58. *'Michael Field': Poetry, Aestheticism and the Fin de Siècle*
    MARION THAIN, *University of Birmingham*
59. *Colonies, Cults and Evolution: Literature, Science and Culture in Nineteenth-Century Writing*
    DAVID AMIGONI, *Keele University*
60. *Realism, Photography and Nineteenth-Century Fiction*
    DANIEL A. NOVAK, *Louisiana State University*
61. *Caribbean Culture and British Fiction in the Atlantic World, 1780–1870*
    TIM WATSON, *University of Miami*
62. *The Poetry of Chartism: Aesthetics, Politics, History*
    MICHAEL SANDERS, *University of Manchester*
63. *Literature and Dance in Nineteenth-Century Britain: Jane Austen to the New Woman*
    CHERYL WILSON, *Indiana University*
64. *Shakespeare and Victorian Women*
    GAIL MARSHALL, *Oxford Brookes University*
65. *The Tragi-Comedy of Victorian Fatherhood*
    VALERIE SANDERS, *University of Hull*
66. *Darwin and the Memory of the Human: Evolution, Savages, and South America*
    CANNON SCHMITT, *University of Toronto*
67. *From Sketch to Novel: The Development of Victorian Fiction*
    AMANPAL GARCHA, *Ohio State University*
68. *The Crimean War and the British Imagination*
    STEFANIE MARKOVITS, *Yale University*
69. *Shock, Memory and the Unconscious in Victorian Fiction*
    JILL L. MATUS, *University of Toronto*
70. *Sensation and Modernity in the 1860s*
    NICHOLAS DALY, *University College Dublin*
71. *Ghost-Seers, Detectives, and Spiritualists: Theories of Vision in Victorian Literature and Science*
    SRDJAN SMAJIĆ, *Furman University*
72. *Satire in an Age of Realism*
    AARON MATZ, *Scripps College, California*
73. *Thinking About Other People in Nineteenth-Century British Writing*
    ADELA PINCH, *University of Michigan*
74. *Tuberculosis and the Victorian Literary Imagination*
    KATHERINE BYRNE, *University of Ulster, Coleraine*

75. *Urban Realism and the Cosmopolitan Imagination in the Nineteenth Century: Visible City, Invisible World*
    TANYA AGATHOCLEOUS, *Hunter College, City University of New York*
76. *Women, Literature, and the Domesticated Landscape: England's Disciples of Flora, 1780–1870*
    JUDITH W. PAGE, *University of Florida* and
    ELISE L. SMITH, *Millsaps College, Mississippi*
77. *Time and the Moment in Victorian Literature and Society*
    SUE ZEMKA, *University of Colorado*
78. *Popular Fiction and Brain Science in the Late Nineteenth Century*
    ANNE STILES, *Washington State University*
79. *Picturing Reform in Victorian Britain*
    JANICE CARLISLE, *Yale University*
80. *Atonement and Self-Sacrifice in Nineteenth-Century Narrative*
    JAN-MELISSA SCHRAMM, *University of Cambridge*
81. *The Silver Fork Novel: Fashionable Fiction in the Age of Reform*
    EDWARD COPELAND, *Pomona College, California*
82. *Oscar Wilde and Ancient Greece*
    IAIN ROSS, *Colchester Royal Grammar School*
83. *The Poetry of Victorian Scientists: Style, Science and Nonsense*
    DANIEL BROWN, *University of Southampton*
84. *Moral Authority, Men of Science, and the Victorian Novel*
    ANNE DEWITT, *Princeton Writing Program*
85. *China and the Victorian Imagination: Empires Entwined*
    ROSS G. FORMAN, *University of Warwick*
86. *Dickens's Style*
    DANIEL TYLER, *University of Oxford*
87. *The Formation of the Victorian Literary Profession*
    RICHARD SALMON, *University of Leeds*
88. *Before George Eliot: Marian Evans and the Periodical Press*
    FIONNUALA DILLANE, *University College Dublin*
89. *The Victorian Novel and the Space of Art: Fictional Form on Display*
    DEHN GILMORE, *California Institute of Technology*
90. *George Eliot and Money: Economics, Ethics and Literature*
    DERMOT COLEMAN, *Independent Scholar*
91. *Masculinity and the New Imperialism: Rewriting Manhood in British Popular Literature, 1870–1914*
    BRADLEY DEANE, *University of Minnesota*
92. *Evolution and Victorian Culture*
    edited by BERNARD LIGHTMAN, *York University, Toronto* and
    BENNETT ZON, *University of Durham*
93. *Victorian Literature, Energy, and the Ecological Imagination*
    ALLEN MACDUFFIE, *University of Texas, Austin*
94. *Popular Literature, Authorship and the Occult in Late Victorian Britain*
    ANDREW MCCANN, *Dartmouth College, New Hampshire*

95. *Women Writing Art History in the Nineteenth Century: Looking Like a Woman*
    HILARY FRASER *Birkbeck, University of London*
96. *Relics of Death in Victorian Literature and Culture*
    DEBORAH LUTZ, *Long Island University, C. W. Post Campus*
97. *The Demographic Imagination and the Nineteenth-Century City: Paris, London, New York*
    NICHOLAS DALY, *University College Dublin*
98. *Dickens and the Business of Death*
    CLAIRE WOOD, *University of York*
99. *Translation as Transformation in Victorian Poetry*
    ANNMARIE DRURY, *Queens College, City University of New York*
100. *The Bigamy Plot: Sensation and Convention in the Victorian Novel*
     MAIA MCALEAVEY, *Boston College, Massachusetts*
101. *English Fiction and the Evolution of Language, 1850–1914*
     WILL ABBERLEY, *University of Oxford*
102. *The Racial Hand in the Victorian Imagination*
     AVIVA BRIEFEL, *Bowdoin College, Maine*
103. *Evolution and Imagination in Victorian Children's Literature*
     JESSICA STRALEY, *University of Utah*
104. *Writing Arctic Disaster: Authorship and Exploration*
     ADRIANA CRACIUN, *University of California, Riverside*
105. *Science, Fiction, and the Fin-de-Siècle Periodical Press*
     WILL TATTERSDILL, *University of Birmingham*
106. *Democratising Beauty in Nineteenth-Century Britain: Art and the Politics of Public Life*
     LUCY HARTLEY, *University of Michigan*
107. *Everyday Words and the Character of Prose in Nineteenth-Century Britain*
     JONATHAN FARINA, *Seton Hall University, New Jersey*
108. *Gerard Manley Hopkins and the Poetry of Religious Experience*
     MARTIN DUBOIS, *University of Newcastle upon Tyne*
109. *Blindness and Writing: From Wordsworth to Gissing*
     HEATHER TILLEY, *Birkbeck College, University of London*
110. *An Underground History of Early Victorian Fiction: Chartism, Radical Print Culture, and the Social Problem Novel*
     GREGORY VARGO, *New York University*
111. *Automatism and Creative Acts in the Age of New Psychology*
     LINDA M. AUSTIN, *Oklahoma State University*
112. *Idleness and Aesthetic Consciousness, 1815–1900*
     RICHARD ADELMAN, *University of Sussex*
113. *Poetry, Media, and the Material Body: Autopoetics in Nineteenth-Century Britain*
     ASHELY MILLER, *Albion College, Michigan*
114. *Malaria and Victorian Fictions of Empire*
     JESSICA HOWELL, *Texas A&M University*

115. *The Brontës and the Idea of the Human*
    ALEXANDRA LEWIS, *University of Aberdeen*
116. *The Political Lives of Victorian Animals*
    ANNA FEUERSTEIN, *University of Hawai'i-Manoa*
117. *The Divine in the Commonplace*
    AMY KING, *St John's University, New York*
118. *Plagiarizing the Victorian Novel: Imitation, Parody, Aftertext*
    ADAM ABRAHAM, *Virginia Commonwealth University*
119. *Literature, Print Culture, and Media Technologies, 1880–1900: Many Inventions*
    RICHARD MENKE, *University of Georgia*
120. *Aging, Duration, and the English Novel: Growing Old from Dickens to Woolf*
    JACOB JEWUSIAK, *Newcastle University*

Printed in the United States
by Baker & Taylor Publisher Services